TRADE AND ENVIRONMENT
A Theoretical Enquiry

Studies in Environmental Science

Volume 1 **Atmospheric Pollution 1978**
Proceedings of the 13th International Colloquium, held in Paris, April 25–28, 1978
edited by M.M. Benarie

Volume 2 **Air Pollution Reference Measurement Methods and Systems**
Proceedings of the International Workshop, held in Bilthoven, December 12–16, 1977
edited by T. Schneider, H.W. de Koning and L.J. Brasser

Volume 3 **Biogeochemical Cycling of Mineral-Forming Elements**
edited by P.A. Trudinger and D.J. Swaine

Volume 4 **Potential Industrial Carcinogens and Mutagens**
by L. Fishbein

Volume 5 **Industrial Waste Water Management**
by S.E. Jørgensen

Volume 6 **Trade and Environment: A Theoretical Enquiry**
by H. Siebert, J. Eichberger, R. Gronych and R. Pethig

Volume 7 **Field Worker Exposure during Pesticide Application**
Proceedings of the Fifth International Workshop of the Scientific Committee on Pesticides of the International Association on Occupational Health held in The Hague, The Netherlands, October 9–11, 1979
edited by W.F. Tordoir and E.A.H. van Heemstra-Lequin

Volume 8 **Atmospheric Pollution 1980**
Proceedings of the 14th International Colloquium, held in Paris, May 5–8, 1980
edited by M.M. Benarie

Studies in Environmental Science 6

TRADE AND ENVIRONMENT

A Theoretical Enquiry

H. Siebert, J. Eichberger, R. Gronych and R. Pethig

Lehrstuhl für Volkswirtschaftslehre und Ausenwirtschaft, Universität Mannheim (WH), D-6800 Mannheim, F.R.G.

ELSEVIER SCIENTIFIC PUBLISHING COMPANY
Amsterdam – Oxford – New York 1980

ELSEVIER SCIENTIFIC PUBLISHING COMPANY
335 Jan van Galenstraat
P.O. Box 211, 1000 AE Amsterdam, The Netherlands

Distributors for the United States and Canada:

ELSEVIER/NORTH-HOLLAND INC.
52, Vanderbilt Avenue
New York, N.Y. 10017

Library of Congress Cataloging in Publication Data
Main entry under title:

Trade and environment.

(Studies in environmental science ; v. 6)
Bibliography: p.
Includes indexes.
1. Environmental policy. 2. Commerce--Environmental aspects. I. Siebert, Horst, 1938-
II. Series.
HC79.E5T73 333.7'007 80-12941
ISBN 0-444-41875-X

ISBN 0-444-41875-X (Vol. 6)
ISBN 0-444-41696-X (Series)

Printed in The Netherlands

Preface

Environmental quality has become a major issue of economic policy. Whereas in the past the environment was treated as a free good with a zero price being attached to it the 1970's have taught us that a variety of different economic uses compete for the environment and that a positive price has to be set for environmental services. In this book we analyze the relationship of environmental quality, environmental policy and international trade. Environmental quality management will redefine comparative advantage of pollution-intensively producing sectors and will affect trade flows, the balance of payments and sectoral structure in industrialized nations as well as in developing countries. Since pollution-intensively producing sectors are also energy-intensive and belong to the so-called basic industries, we can expect that the issue will be of political interest in the next decades.

This book has developed out of our common work at the University of Mannheim and can be interpreted as the result of a process of interaction and discussion. Besides interaction there was a division of labour. Chapters 1,3 - 6 and section 2.1 were written by H. Siebert, chapters 7,3,12 and section 2.2 and 2.3 by R. Pethig, now at the University of Oldenburg, chapters 9 and 10 by R. Gronych and chapter 11 by J. Eichberger.

We would like to acknowledge inspirations and encouragement from Blair T. Bower, Ron Cummings, Ralph d'Arge, I. Krutilla, Talbot Page, Cliff Russel, Walter Spofford and especially Allen Kneese and Ingo Walter. Also we are endebted to Wolfgang Vogt and our other colleagues at the University of Mannheim and the stimulating atmosphere there. We also acknowledge support from the Deutsche Forschungsgemeinschaft.

The manuscript was typed by M. Börresen, M. Schnepf and W.

Schreyer. The diagrams were prepared by H. Gebauer. She also was helpful in some of the editorial problems. We are grateful to all of them. Of course, all the errors are ours, but since we are multiple authors we are in the fortunate position to point to the other guy who is responsible for all the mistakes.[1)]

Mannheim 1979

H.S.

J.E.

R.G.

R.P.

1) For an interesting variation of this final-preface-sentence compare R. Dorfman, P.A. Samuelson and R. Solow, (1958, p. viii).

Contents

Part I

Basic Analytical Concepts

In the first part of the book we present the problem and lay down the theoretical foundations of the analysis. In chapter 1 we discuss the international aspects of environmental disruptions and of environmental quality management. Environmental endowment represents an important factor influencing comparative advantage, trade flows, the balance of payments, sector structure, the allocation of resources and the location of industry. Also environmental quality is one aspect of social welfare and should be considered when the gains from trade are evaluated.

In chapter 2 important assumptions and basic concepts used throughout the book are developed. Environmental quality is treated as a public good being negatively affected by pollutants emitted from production. Pollutants are a joint product, and the production and emission functions are specified. Also abatement is introduced explicitly and the properties of the transformation space are derived. An alternative production theoretical approach is developed in which net emissions are treated as an input to a production process. The two different approaches are finally compared to each other.

1. The Problem

Environmental disruption and environmental quality management have important international aspects. Since the environment is defined over space we may distinguish different spatial extensions of environmental media such as international, transfrontier and national environmental systems (section 1.1). In this book we are interested in the problem to what extent endowment with environmental services or environmental policy will affect comparative price advantage, trade flows and related variables (sections 1.2 and 1.3). We can expect that environmental policy will have a marked impact on sector structure.

Environmental quality affects overall welfare, since the gains from trade may be reduced if the increased specialization towards a pollution-intensively produced commodity will cause a loss of environmental quality (section 1.4). The effects of environmental policy will depend on the policy instruments used. Consequently we have to discuss the possible policy approaches (section 1.5). In section 1.6 we briefly survey the literature of the field. Finally, section 1.7 gives an outline of the book.

International Aspects of Environmental Protection

1. The environment has three functions for the economic system. It serves as a public consumption good (i.e. air, amenities of the landscape), it provides basic inputs for production processes (i.e. oxygen for combustion, raw materials) and it is used as a receptor of wastes. Wastes or pollutants arise as a joint output of consumption and production activities.

The three different uses of the environment compete with each other, if the demand for environmental use is not met by environmental endowment. Historically, the environment has been used at a zero price, and using it as a receptor of wastes has negatively affected environmental quality as a consumption good. The environment has been heavily overused, and sectoral allocation has been biased in favour of pollution-intensively producing sectors.[1] From an efficiency point of view, the pollution-intensively producing sectors obtain a hidden protection. Economists have long recognized the distorting effects of negative externalities [Pigou (1920), Kapp (1958), Mishan (1971)]and have asked for an internalization of all social costs. Potential solutions have been discussed in the literature such as institutional arrangements [Kneese (1964), Klevorick and Cramer (1973b)], bargaining and property right assignment [Coase (1960), Dales (1968)], optimizing procedures [Tietenberg (1973), Mäler (1974)] and fixed target policy [Baumol-Oates (1975)].

2. We are here interested in the international aspects of environmental protection [Baumol (1971), d'Arge and Kneese (1972), Siebert (1974a,b), Walter (1974a,b)].In order to approach this problem it is worthwhile to note that environmental systems are defined over space. Due to the spatial dimension of environmental media we can distinguish the following environmental problems with an international aspect

i) Global or international environmental problems relating to the world as a whole such as the increasing carbon dioxide concentration in the atmosphere, or referring to spatially

1) A pollution-intensively producing sector produces a large quantity of pollutants per unit of output (or per unit of resources used) relatively to another sector.

limited international environmental systems such as the Baltic Sea or the Mediterranean. In this case, many polluters discharge effluents into an international common property resource and damage arises to many countries, though not necessarily to the same extent.

ii) One-way or two-way transfrontier pollution where two countries are linked to each other via some environmental system and where the home country influences environmental quality in the foreign country by discharging effluents into the environment that diffuses pollutants to the foreign country. Examples are upstream-downstream relations in river systems such as in the Rhine-valley or the Colorado and interactions via atmospheric systems such as in the case of acid rains in Sweden.

iii) National pollution where pollutants are emitted into a national environmental system and not diffused to another country.

In this book we are only interested in national environmental systems or in national environmental policy and its impact.

1.2 The Environment as a Determinant for Trade

Whereas international and transfrontier environmental problems have international repercussions it is often felt that national environmental policy does not have international ramifications. This, however, is not true.

The environment as a reception medium of pollutants is a production factor and thereby a determining factor of comparative price advantages. Is a country richly endowed with environmental services by nature, this will have a different effect on its foreign trade position than if the country was only scarcely equipped with environmental services. The distinction must be drawn between the following two cases:

i) A country is richly endowed with certain public consumption goods. To the extent that these public environmental goods are nationally restricted (e.g. amenity of the landscape), the foreign trade position of a country in the service sector (such as tourism) can be influenced. We will not pursue this type of case here.

ii) A country has a relatively high assimilative capacity. The abundancy or the scarcity of the assimilative capacity is influenced by the following four factors:

- The natural assimilative capacity, i.e. the capacity of the environmental systems to reduce pollutants by natural processes;

- The value accorded to the public consumption good environment. Instead of an assessment of environmental quality, the tolerable level of emissions can be used in the sense of the standard price approach, in other words, in the amount of emissions which exceed the natural assimilative capacity and which the society is willing to accept. This tolerable emission level is dependent on preferences, income level, population density etc. of the society in question;

- The demand for assimilative services of the environment, measured by the quantity of emissions released into the environment, dependent on the consumption, production and emission technology (and the level of development) of an economy;

- The public or private investments in order to increase the assimilative capacity or to decrease the demand for assimilative services.

1.3 Effects of Environmental Policy on Trade

1. Besides differences in endowment with labour, capital, technical knowledge, tastes or government policies, environmental scarcity influences comparative advantage. Consequently, we can expect that environmental policy will affect comparative advantage. Comparative advantage, however, determines which country will export which commodity. It also determines location. Consequently environmental policy will affect sector structure. Most of the pollution-intensively producing sectors tend to belong to the so-called industrial base (steel, chemistry, oil, raw material production, pulp and paper). These industries also are energy- and raw material-inten-

sive and will be affected by the energy problem. We can expect that environmental policy will influence the industrial base and will have a considerable impact on industrialized nations.

2. Also, environmental policy may have international ramifications on the North-South problem. It can be argued that developing countries have a comparative advantage with respect to environmental endowment.

The comparative price advantage is not only an indicator of the competitive position with regard to the international commodity exchange, but also permits a statement about the international location advantage of a nation. If environmental policy is pursued in environmentally poor economies, then the production conditions of the pollution-intensive producing sector will be affected. Its production costs will rise. At the same time the location favour of an environmentally rich country betters. If capital is internationally mobile, one can expect that ceteris paribus capital of the environmentally poor country (industrialized nation) migrates to the environmentally rich country, i.e. the less developed country.

Without considering regional agglomeration some developing countries appear to have a high assimilative capacity in relation to their population density. Since wastes are a joint product of economic activities and since developing nations have not yet achieved a higher level of industrialization, also the demand for assimilative services of the environment is not yet as high as in the industrial countries. In addition, environmental quality can be accorded different values in developing and industrialized countries if the value of the environmental quality increases with the income or with the quantity of private goods available.

Another factor contributing to the comparative price advantage of developing countries is that cost and price differences do not vary proportionally with environmental policy measures. Assume that an industrial country pursues environmental policy. Empirical studies show that the abatement costs rise progressively with the quantity of abated pollutants. Therefore the comparative price advantage of the developed countries deteriorates progressively. Since a comparative price advantage also represents a comparative location advantage, developing nations will attract pollution intensive industries away from the industrialized countries and so expand their export base.

This type of specialization for the developing countries, however, can in the long run lead to serious problems. An ideal form of diversification of exports for an urgent problematic situation might represent the wrong export specialization in the long run. An increase in population raises the social damage of a given level of pollution, industrial growth multiplies the wastes produced, and thereby also the level of pollution; and, finally, increases in per capity income trigger changes in the value accorded to environmental quality by the population. For these cases, the specialization must possibly be altered in long-term. Then adjustment costs will arise, and one should ask to what extent future frictions and sectoral adjustments should be considered in present decisions about the export diversification.

3. Analyzing the effects of environmental policy on comparative advantage, we get an answer to the question how environmental policy will affect trade flows. Since trade flows determine the balance of payments, we also get preliminary information on changes in the balance of payments and, since deficits and surpluses correspond to depreciation and appreciation of the home currency, we also have information on the exchange rates. These monetary aspects of foreign trade will, however, not be considered explicitly.

4. An interesting problem exists if besides trade flows capital movements are regarded so that the economic system of

a country can adjust to environmental policy measures not by changing its export-import-structure alone, but by a reallocation of its capital endowment. The question whether a country needs more capital as a result of severe environmental protection to substitute for pollutants or whether this policy will push industries to transfer capital to other countries is of utmost importance for a reasonable evaluation of the costs of environmental protection.

5. In one way or another national environmental regulation always aims at reducing the flows of emission. This can be done with the help of waste abatement devices, with waste avoidance technologies, but also with the device of recycling, i.e. the recovery and re-use of basic material from waste products. Recycling clearly expands when the emission tax is raised to achieve an improvement in environmental quality since the emission tax essentially is a negative price on waste products which in turn is an input for the recycling industry. Thus the stimulation of recycling appears to be an attractive policy instrument because it promises to fight simultaneously and successfully the battle against both pollution and natural resource depletion. An immediate international dimension of recycling lies in its resource conservation effect, because resource depletion is a worldwide issue. But there is another major international aspect of recycling that has not yet received due attention in the literature. Since national environmental policies affect national recycling patterns as well as trade flows there is clearly an interdependency between recycling, environmental management and trade.

1.4 Trade, Welfare and Environmental Quality

1. It is a well established theorem that countries benefit from trade. Does this statement also hold if we take environmental disruption into account? Assume, for instance, a country has a comparative advantage in the pollution-intensively produced commodity and that the country exports the pollution-intensively produced commodity. Then the country specializes in the production of that commodity. Consequently more pollutants are emitted, and environmental quality declines. There is a trade-off between welfare gains from trade and environmental quality. Trade only pays for an economy when the welfare rises per balance, i.e. when the traditional "gains from trade" overcompensate the deterioration of the environmental quality (or when the home country exports the environment-favourably produced commodity). From this consideration also follows that in an open economy the reduction of the gains from trade can be ascribed to the target losses of the environmental policy.

If environmental policy is undertaken, the correct social costs of production are shown; in the example given above the comparative advantage of the pollution-intensively producing sector is reduced. Consequently the correct benefits from trade are shown.

2. Environmental policy in one country affects environmental quality in the other country in the following way. Assume the home country undertakes environmental policy and it reduces production of the pollution-intensively produced commodity. The foreign country will become more competitive with respect to the pollution-intensively produced commodity. It will specialize in the production of that commodity, pollutants will increase and environmental quality will decline.

Does this pollute-thy-neighbour-via-trade thesis mean that the home country can force a degraded environmental quality on the foreign country, that for instance the industrialized nations can export their pollutants to the developing countries through trade? Is this a new type of imperialism, a "pollution or environment imperialism"? The answer to all these questions is no, for the following reasons:

i) Environmental policy involves costs for the nations concerned, namely in terms of resource use as well as losses in other goals (unemployment, the loss of the comparative price advantage). A country is only to some extent willing to put up with these costs in favour of a better environmental quality.

ii) The costs of a better environment (the pollution abatement) increase progressively so that environmental policy is quite restricted here.

iii) The environmentally rich foreign country can with regard to its foreign trade situation put itself by its own environmental policy in a position in which it had been before the introduction of environmental policy in the environmentally poor country.

3. It can be expected that in the political debate environmental policy may not be understood as an allocation policy. Especially it is realistic to assume that specific groups of society will be negatively affected by environmental policy, such as the export- and import-substitute sector and workers (or trade unions) in these sectors. These political forces will ask for compensations or countervailing measures to make up for the loss of their relative economic position. If these political groups are successful, environmental policy may give rise to new trade distortions.

Against these political demands for "restoring" a given competitive position the economist has to point out that without environmental policy comparative advantage is distorted and the pollution-intensively producing sector receives a hidden subsidy. The allocation of resources is biased in its favour. Environmental policy is an attempt to express the correct social costs. Similarly as it would be absurd to compensate international disadvantage in endowments with labour, skills, capital and land by policy measures, we have to let environmental advantages rule in the long run.

Trade distortions also may arise if product norms are used as a policy instrument. For example there are product norms with regard to the tolerable content of chemicals (DDT) or even emission norms for technical processes (capital goods). In this case the export opportunities of a nation, especially of developing countries, can be impaired. It is known that the export capacity presupposes the existence of an export base, i.e. the production for the native market can be regarded as a starting point for the expansion of the market into exports. Product standards, however, destroy the connection between the production for the home and the export market because product requirements on the national and international market are different.

This barrier to trade through product standards is aggrevated if one discriminates between product standards for domestic and foreign goods. GATT regulations do not permit a discrimination and product standards should be applied on import goods as well as on import substitutes. In reality, however, product standards can be formulated in such a way as to permit national industries to meet the standards more easily than foreign competitors.

1.5 Approaches of Environmental Policy

1. A variety of environmental policy instruments have been proposed and are used in practice. Moral suasion attempts to change the preference function of consumers and managers in firms so that the environmental repercussions are taken into account in private decisions. Subsidies appear in different forms, for instance as governmental contributions to capital outlays in abatement activities. Also in federal states the central government transfers funds to federal states or local communities in order to stimulate purification activities. France uses environmental policy to modernize capital in industry in general and to modernize industrial structure in order to built up comparative advantages in new fields. Governments have used emission norms for firms or individual plants specifying the allowable quantity of pollu-

tants. Another device is a permit system where firms are only allowed to produce (or locate) if they use a given production (and purification) technology with the government defining the state of the art. Emission taxes have been proposed and are used, especially in water management. Finally, pollution licences in combination with a price per pollutant have been proposed.

2. It is apparent that the effects of environmental policy vary with the type of instrument used. In this book we only consider two types of approaches.

i) Emission taxes. The government levies an emission tax per unit of pollutant. We do not analyze the political process of setting the tax and adjusting it to new situations. From the economists point of view the tax should be calculated in a benefit-cost analysis or should emerge as a shadow price in an optimization model. The information required for setting the tax would include purification costs, evaluation of damages and monitoring the emissions. It need not be mentioned that the tax is influenced by groups active in the political arena. We here assume that the tax is given exogenously.

ii) Fixed target policy. Alternatively we sometimes assume the government sets a target with respect to environmental quality, i.e. it limits the quantity of tolerable emissions. In this case we do not consider the political processes of fixing the target. We also do not analyze the mechanism that transforms the target into prices.

3. Both approaches are very similar. Note, however, one important difference. If emission taxes are used and are introduced exogenously into our models, the private sector will determine net emissions and the resulting environmental quality. If the fixed target approach is used, environmental quality is determined by a political decision, and the system adjusts via prices. Some of the conclusions of the book vary with this interpretation.

Other environmental policy instruments could partly be interpreted in terms of emission taxes. For instance, a specific emission norm for a firm may be transformed into a cost factor for not violating the restriction.

1.6 Survey of the Literature

1. The international aspects of environmental pollution were first discussed in the early 1970's. International environmental systems such as international and transfrontier pollution were studied by the OECD (1972). The interrelationship of trade and environmental policy was analyzed by Baumol (1971), GATT (1971), Kneese (1971), d'Arge and Kneese (1972), Majocchi (1972), Magee and Ford (1972), Walter (1973), Koo (1974), Siebert (1974a, b, c), Walter (1974a, b, 1975), Pethig (1975) and Walter (1976).

2. Five different approaches to the problem of environmental quality and international trade may be distinguished.

i) The verbal-analytical approach, sometimes supported by graphical illustrations and the shifting-curve technique, attempts to outline the scope of the problem, to analyze the important aspects of it, and to integrate environmental quality (policy) into trade theory [Walter (1975), Grubel (1976)].

ii) The more rigorous theoretical approach integrates the environment as a public good into production, allocation and pure trade theory. This approach uses neoclassical models [Siebert (1974a, b, c, 1975, 1979); Pethig (1975)], with Koo (1974) starting from a Leontief-approach.

iii) Empirical studies attempt to estimate the pollution content of foreign trade [Walter (1973)], to evaluate the price effects of environmental policy [Leontief (1973), Walter (1974a, b), Mutti and Richardson (1976)]. Also balance of payments effects are estimated empirically [d'Arge and Kneese (1972)].

iv) Trade policy oriented research attacks the problem from the policy point of view, especially with respect to distortions and trade barriers [GATT (1971)]. Problems such as the effects of environmental policy instruments (e.g. product norms) on free trade and the possible use of trade policy measures in environmental policy are analyzed. Also the problem of harmonization of environmental policy in a common market is an important topic.

v) Development theory looks into the problem from the point-of-view of the North-South dialogue and the negative or positive effects of environmental policy on growth processes in developing countries.

1.7 Outline of the Book

1. In the following chapter of part I we present some of the basic assumptions and develop the theoretical foundations that are relevant for the analysis. Specifically, pollutants are integrated into production theory. One approach treats pollutants as joint outputs of production activities (gross emissions approach). Abatement activities are explicitly introduced and resources are used for production as well as abatement. The alternative approach is more compact in integrating production and abatement into one activity and treating environmental services (wastes reception) as an input to the production function (net emissions approach). Some of the properties of the economy considered such as the transformation space are developed.

2. In part II we follow the gross emissions approach and consider abatement activities explicitly. We develop the model for a closed economy and discuss the properties of a two-sector, one-factor economy with production and abatement. The effects of environmental policy on comparative advantage, allocation of resources, national income and other variables are analyzed. The model is extended to the small-country case and the two-country case. The implications of environmental policy in open economies are discussed. Also we study the interrelation of environmental quality and the gains from trade.

3. In part III the net emissions approach is used, i.e. abatement is implicitly taken into consideration. In chapters 7

and 8 we consider one traditional factor of production and environmental services and discuss the properties of a closed economy and some results with respect to trade theory. In chapters 9 and 10 two traditional factors of production are introduced with environmental services being the third factor. Abatement is taken into account implicitly. The properties of the closed economy and possible outcomes of trade specialization are discussed. Also the implications in the two-country case especially with respect to the terms of trade are studied.

4. Part IV represents two extensions of the analysis. In chapter 11 we introduce capital mobility. This is an important feature since capital is at least partially mobile between countries and empirical evidence suggests that firms relocate due to environmental policy if comparative advantage changes. In chapter 12 we introduce recycling as another important aspect of environmental quality management. If emissions are taxed this represents an incentive to save material so that environmental policy has some interesting impacts on the resource problem in an international context.

2. Production, Emission, and Abatement Technology

Environmental quality can be considered as a public good being influenced by emissions from consumption and production. In the following we treat the environment as a national public good and ignore international and transfrontier environmental systems. The frame of reference is a two-sector model in which production generates pollutants as a joint product. This chapter presents the basic assumptions used throughout the book. Elementary concepts such as the emission-intensity of sectors are defined and some basic properties of the allocation model such as the transformation space are analyzed.

In order to incorporate emissions into production functions two different approaches may be followed:
i) Gross emissions can be interpreted as joint output; there exists an abatement technology so that we have a production, an emission and an abatement function. This gross-emissions approach is developed in section 2.1.
ii) Net emissions may be regarded as a specific factor of production so that a net production function incorporates the regular production function, emission and abatement technology. This net-emissions approach is described in section 2.2. Section 2.3 compares the two approaches.

2.1 The Gross-Emissions Approach

2.1.1 Assumptions

A 2.1 Production function. In order to keep the model as simple as possible we assume two sectors i = 1,2, only one type of resource R,and a production function with decreasing marginal returns

$$Q_i = F^i(R_i) \qquad \text{with } F^i_R > 0,\ F^i_{RR} < 0 \qquad (2.1)$$

where Q_i denotes quantities produced.

A 2.2 Emission function. The production of commodities Q_i generates pollutants S^p_i as a joint product. For simplifying purposes there is only one type of pollutants. Emissions may be linked either to the quantities produced or to the inputs used. It is here assumed that pollutants emitted rise proportionally or progressively with resources used, i.e.

$$S^p_i = H^i(Q_i) = H^i(F^i(R_i)) = Z^i(R_i) \text{ with } Z^i_R>0,\ Z^i_{RR}\geq 0;\ H^i_Q>0 \quad (2.2)$$

The convex emission function Z^i is suggested intuitively by engineering production functions[1]. With the activity level of an engine reaching or exceeding capacity, it is realistic to assume that inputs have to be increased progressively for an additional unit of output. This suggests that emissions rise progressively. A more precise explanation for the convexity of the emission function follows from the application of the mass balance concept to production functions. In terms of weight a mass balance exists between input and output. Since mass cannot be lost in a production process, regular output and emissions must be identical to inputs, in weight terms. Let α and β

---

1) E. Gutenberg (1972, p. 326)

be the resource content of the commodity and the emission in weight terms[1]. Then we have for sector i

$$\alpha Q_i + \beta S_i^p = R_i$$

so that

$$S_i^p = \frac{1}{\beta}(R_i - \alpha Q_i) = \frac{1}{\beta}(R_i - \alpha F^i(R_i)) = Z^i(R_i)$$

Since F^i is concave, the emission function Z^i must be convex (compare diagram 2.1a).

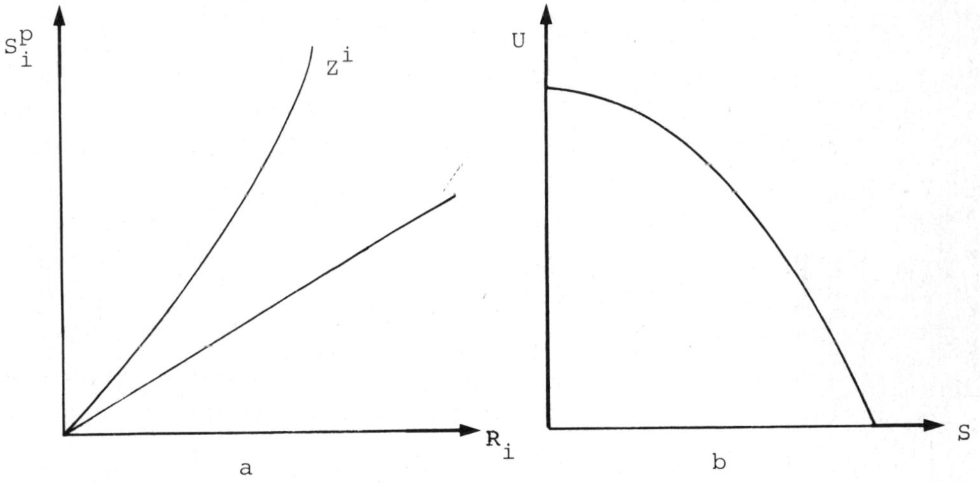

Diagram 2.1

1) Compare K. Sontheimer (1975).

A 2.3 Abatement function. Resources R_i^r may also be used for abatement purposes. Let S_i^r indicate the quantity of pollutants reduced in sector i. The abatement function is given by

$$S_i^r = F^{ri}(R_i^r) \qquad \text{with } F_R^{ri} > 0,\ F_{RR}^{ri} < 0 \qquad (2.3)$$

Pollution abatement is here used in a broad sense. It includes the prevention of emissions by filter processes and the reduction of emissions that have occurred in a firm before the emissions are discharged to the environment. The abatement function 2.3 is specific to the sector i. In contrast to this assumption we could allow for pollution abatement processes that reduce pollutants ambient in the environment (water treatment).

A 2.4 Diffusion function. This function explains the interrelationsship between emissions and pollutants ambient in the environment. The diffusion function takes into account how emissions are spatially distributed in different environmental media, to what extent they are assimilated or degraded, how they interact with other pollutants (smog) and which factors influence the spatial distribution of pollutants. The Streeter-Phelps equation[1)] for water systems is such an example. In the following this interrelationship is only taken into consideration in a rudimentary form, namely as the definition of net emissions S_i of sector i

$$S_i = S_i^p - S_i^r \qquad (2.4)$$

and of pollutants S ambient in the environment

$$S = \Sigma S_i \qquad (2.5)$$

1) A. V. Kneese and B. T. Bower (1972, p. 30).

Equation 2.4 can explicitly account for the assimilative capacity of the environment S^a by subtracting S^a on the right side. The assimilative capacity of the environment may be defined as the quantity of pollutants that can be absorbed by environmental systems in a given period without a negative effect on environmental quality. We here do not take into consideration that the assimilative capacity may be increased by environmental policy (i.e. in-stream aeration). Also we neglect that diffusion processes may be affected by environmental policy (i.e. stack height).

A 2.5 Damage function. Pollutants ambient in the environment S determine environmental quality U.

$$U = G(S) \qquad \text{with } G_S > 0,\ G_{SS} < 0 \qquad (2.6)$$

The damage function (diagram 2.1b) encloses environmental services that are inputs to consumption or production (water, oxygen) in a physical sense; it is also representative for qualitative services such as amenities of the landscape or ecological stability. In reality the damage functions are much more complex. Pollutants ambient in the environment may also affect the quality of inputs in production processes, the production procedures, produced commodities, capital goods (wealth damages) etc.

A 2.6. Resource restraint. A resource restraint limits the production and abatement possibilities of the economy

$$\Sigma R_i + \Sigma R_i^r \leq R \qquad (2.7)$$

If equation 2.7 is treated as an equation (and not as an inequality) it implies that the resource is fully employed.

2.1.2 The Emission-Intensity of Sectors

The two sectors of the economy have to be distinguished with respect to their emission intensity. In the gross-emission-type model we define a sector i as relatively more emission-intensive compared to sector j if $Z_R^i > Z_R^j$. $Z_R^i = H_Q^i F_R^i$ is the first derivative of the emission function and indicates the quantity of emissions arising with one unit of a resource being additionally used in a sector. It can be interpreted as the marginal tendency to pollute. The additional quantity of emissions per unit of resource used in a sector seems to be a good indicator of pollution intensity. This measure denotes the change in gross emissions from a reallocation of resources and it also denotes to what extent a sector is affected by environmental policy "at the margin". Similarly as in foreign trade models we must assume that the ranking of the two sectors does not change with other variables.

A 2.7 Non-reversal of emission-intensities. The emission intensity of sectors does not change with the variables of the system. We assume here that sector 1 is the relatively pollution-intensive sector, i.e. $Z_R^1 > Z_R^2$.

The condition $Z_R^1 > Z_R^2$ can be stated in terms of $S_1^p/R_1 >$ $> S_2^p/R_2$ if i) $Z^1(R_1) > Z^2(R_2)$ for $R_1 = R_2$, ii) $Z_R^1 > Z_R^2$ for $R_1 = R_2$ and iii) if the pollution-intensively producing sector 1 is not too small compared to sector 2. The iii-condition reflects the fact that "small is beautiful" and that - under the assumptions made - the sector that may be potentially damaging has a low propensity to pollute below a certain size. In diagram 2.2a $Z^1(R_1) > Z^2(R_2)$ has been assumed for all R_i. Consider an allocation with sector 1 being in $A(R_A)$ and sector 2 being in $B(R_B)$. Then, given sector 2 is in B, $Z_R^1 > Z_R^2$ will be fulfilled for all $R_1 > R_A$. If, however, sector 1 is relatively small, $R_1 > R_A$, sector 2 becomes the pollution-intensively producing sector due to its relative size. Diagram 2.2b illustrates a situation where $Z_R^1 > Z_R^2$ is violated.

Assume pollutants ambient in the environment have a negative effect on output, so that the production function is

$$Q_i = F^i(R_i, S) \qquad \text{with } F^i_S < 0 \qquad (2.1')$$

Alternatively the quality π of the input may be affected by S, so that efficiency inputs $R(S) = \pi(S)R$ are dependent on S. In these cases the transformation curve may bend back from a certain level of pollutants and the transformation space may not be concave[1].

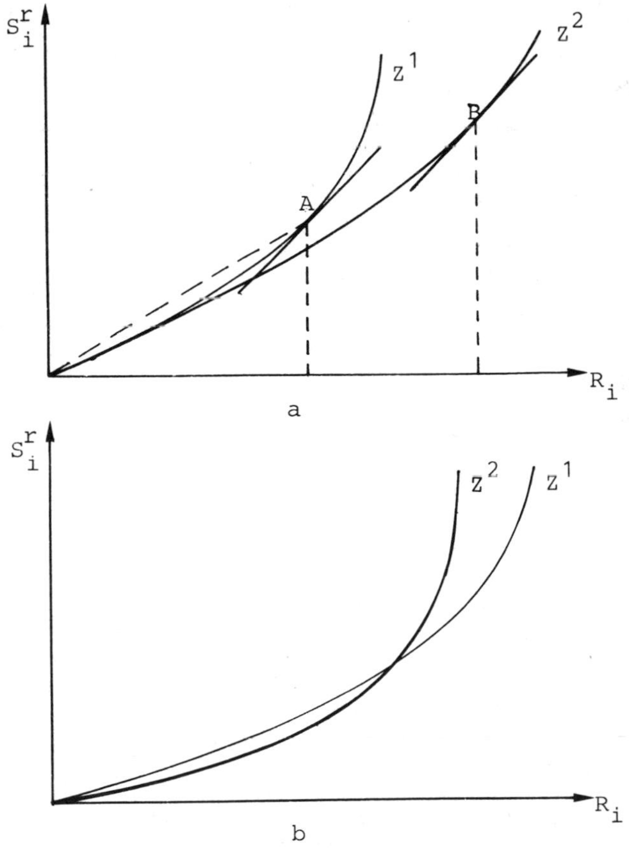

Diagram 2.2

1) R. Pethig (1977a, p. 322-342).

2.1.3 Transformation Space

Equations 2.1 - 2.7 describe the restrictions relevant for environmental use. If we want to produce more goods, emissions will increase for a given technology, and environmental quality will decline. Improving environmental quality is only possible if resources are shifted to abatement and/or if the production of commodities is reduced (assuming given technology and full employment of resources). The basic dilemma consists in competing uses of the environment: either as a public good for consumption or as a receptor of wastes.

Diagram 2.3 illustrates the transformation space $U = \Phi(Q_1, Q_2)$ of production and environmental quality. If nothing is produced in both sectors, we reach maximal environmental quality, so to say "nature at its best" (OA). Assume there continues to be no production of commodity 2 and we increase output of commodity 1. Then we can imagine a resource allocation (R_1, R_1^r) with all emissions being abated (line AG). At point G resources are fully employed. Similarly AH indicates the quantities of output of commodity 2 for maximum environmental quality and for $Q_1 = 0$. The horizontal roof AGH denotes maximum environmental quality; line GH indicates full employment of resource R with maximum environmental quality.

Consider point G with full employment and $Q_2 = 0$. Assume production of commodity 1 is increased by one unit with $Q_2 = 0$. Then emissions rise progressively. Since environmental quality deteriorates progressively with emissions, environmental quality must be reduced progressively. Also with increased resource use in production, the quantity of emissions abated will be reduced. Due to the law of decreasing marginal returns, each additional resource unit withdrawn from abatement would have had a higher marginal productivity in abatement, so emissions abated will decline progressively (and consequently environ-

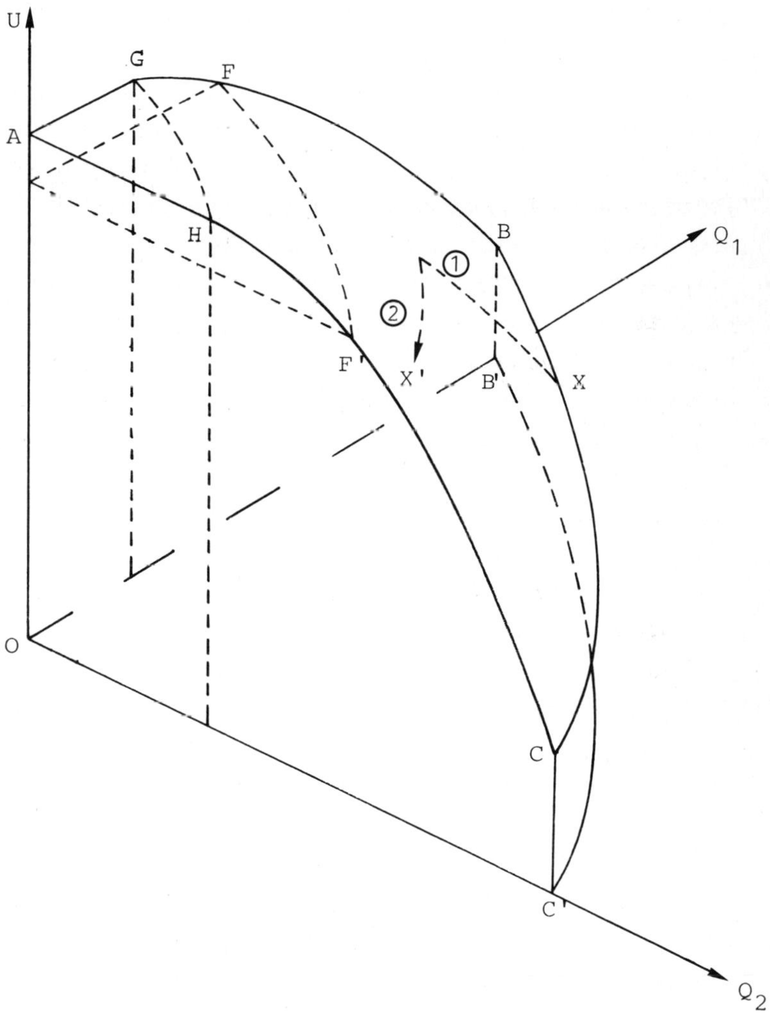

Diagram 2.3

mental quality will deteriorate progressively). The curve GB is concave. Similarly, the curve HC is concave[1].

Define a relation $\alpha = Q_1/Q_2$ and keep α constant. Consider a point on the curve GH. Withdraw one resource unit out of abatement and switch it to production with α constant. In both production activities emissions will rise progressively with emissions of sector 1 rising more than in sector 2 if $Z_R^1 > Z_R^2$. Also progressively less pollutants are abated due to declining marginal productivity in abatement. We can expect that the transformation space is concave for α constant. It can be formally shown that the transformation space is concave. (Appendix 2.1).

Line BB'denotes the environmental quality associated with a complete specialization of the economy in producing commodity 1 (and no abatement). Line CC' denotes environmental quality in the case of a complete specialization of commodity 2. CC' > BB' suggests that sector 1 is the emission-intensively producing sector.

Curve BC illustrates the transformation problem for the case that no resources are used in abatement. The projection of the curve BC into the Q_1-Q_2-plane, i.e. the curve B'C', is the traditional transformation curve.

Diagram 2.3 assumes a given resource supply and given technology. With an increase in resources, the transformation space is shifted outward. If technical progress occurs in the production of sector 2, the production space will be stretched outward with a bias for that commodity 2 and with AGB remaining fixed. Improved abatement technology and less emission-intensive production technology in sector 2 will shift the transformation space in the same way. Note that technical progress may affect the ranking of sectors according to their emission intensity.

---

1) Compare H. Siebert (1978a, p.36).

An alternative definition of emission intensity defines sector i as emission-intensive relative to sector j if $S_i/\tilde{R}_i > S_j/\tilde{R}_j$ where S_i, S_j denote net emissions, and $\tilde{R}_i$, $\tilde{R}_j$ indicate resource used in production and abatement of sector i or j, i.e. $\tilde{R}_i = R_1 + R_1^r$. From

$$\frac{S_i}{\tilde{R}_i} = \frac{S_i^p - S_i^r}{R_i + R_i^r} > \frac{S_j^p - S_j^r}{R_j + R_j^r} = \frac{S_j}{\tilde{R}_j}$$

we see that rankings according to gross and net emissions are consistent if $S_i^r(R_i^r) \leq S_j^r(R_j^r)$ for $R_i^r = R_j^r$, i.e. sector i has at least as productive an abatement technology as sector j. Note that the classification according to net emissions presupposes that environmental policy is undertaken and that firms use resources efficiently in allocation. Then sector 2 will use more resources in abatement than sector 1 and S_i^p/R_i implies $S_i/\tilde{R}_i$.

2.2. The Net-Emissions Approach

2.2.1 Assumptions

A 2.8 Net-production function.[1] For sector i = 1,2 we consider the function $F^i : D_{Fi} \rightarrow \mathbb{R}_+^1$. $D_{Fi} \subset \mathbb{R}^2$ and $\mathbb{R}_+^1$ are the domain and the range of F^i, respectively[2], and

$$Q_i = F^i(\tilde{R}_i, S_i) \qquad (i = 1,2) \tag{2.8}$$

is the quantity of commodity i that is produced by the amount $\tilde{R}_i$ of the resource when simultaneously S_i units of a by-product are generated ($S_i > 0$) or used as input ($S_i < 0$). Irrespective of its sign, we call S_i the net emissions of sector i. Note that if $S_i > 0$, then part or all of the by-product generated in sector i could be used as an input in sector $j \neq i$. Production wastes are only emitted into the environment by the amount $S := S_1 + S_2$, the economy's net emission. S must be non-negative in feasible allocations.

1) See the similar assumption in A.K. Klevorick and G.H. Kramer (1973, p. 107).

2) By $\mathbb{R}^n$ we denote the n-dimensional Euclidean space, and by $\mathbb{R}_+^n$ its non-negative orthant.

The definitions of S_i and S coincide with those in equations 2.4 and 2.5.
It is important to emphasize that in F^i the variable S_i is only formally treated as an input. We are mainly interested in situations, where S_i is an output ($S_i > 0$), but the case of an input ($S_i < 0$) is not ruled out. In the sequel we specify the net-production function F^i by four assumptions.

The production technology is essentially one of producing two outputs (Q_i, S_i) out of one input $\tilde{R}_i$. Let us fix $\tilde{R}_i$ at an arbitrary positive level and consider the associated production possibility set. If this set consists of a single element (Q_i, S_i), then we would have "strict" joint production as described, for example, by the equations 2.1 and 2.2. We are, however, interested in "flexible" joint production in which case - as a necessary condition - the production possibility set must contain more than one element. Moreover, we define production wastes to be a by-product of the consumption good i in the production vector (Q_i, S_i, $\tilde{R}_i$) with strictly positive components, if in the production possibility set assigned to $\tilde{R}_i$ there is no output vector ($\hat{Q}_i$, $\hat{S}_i$) such that $\hat{Q}_i \geq Q_i$ and $\hat{S}_i < S_i$. For differentiable functions F^i, this by-product property of the waste product can be stated as follows:

A 2.8i By-product property:

There is $(\tilde{R}_i, S_i) \in D_{Fi}$ with $S_i > 0$,

such that[1] $F^i_S \Big|_{(\tilde{R}_i,\, S_i)} > 0$.

A 2.8ii No free production:

$\tilde{R}_i = 0$ implies $F(\tilde{R}_i, S_i) = 0$ and $S_i = 0$.

This straightforward assumption needs no comment. Note, however, that A 2.8ii does not exclude that $F(\tilde{R}_i, S_i) > 0$ for $\tilde{R}_i > 0$ and $S_i \leq 0$.

---

1) $F^i_S \Big|_{(\tilde{R}_i,\, S_i)}$ is the partial derivative of F^i with respect to S_i, evaluated at $(\tilde{R}_i, S_i)$.

A 2.8iii Bounded waste production with given resource input. It is an elementary material balance requirement that with limited inputs one can only produce limited amounts of outputs. In other words, the production possibility set associated to given resource inputs must be bounded from above. With respect to the generation of wastes this requirement implies the following constraint on the domain D_{Fi} of F^i:

There is a strictly monotone increasing function $Z^i : \mathbb{R}_+ \rightarrow \mathbb{R}_+$ with $Z^i(0) = 0$,

such that $(\tilde{R}_i, S_i) \notin D_{Fi}$, if $S_i > Z^i(\tilde{R}_i)$.

A 2.8iv Non-increasing returns to scale. For most standard results of general equilibrium theory, in particular, when combined with the concept of perfect competition the assumption of convex production sets cannot be disposed of. This restriction is mainly motivated by "technical" or analytical convenience. It is satisfied in our technology, by the assumption A 2.8iv:

D_{Fi} is convex and F^i is a concave function.

The assumptions A 2.8i, ii and iv imply that F^i_R, the marginal resource productivity, is positive. Further, by A 2.8iii and iv the production possibility set is bounded from below for every $\tilde{R}_i > 0$ and we can conclude from the convexity of D_{Fi} (A 2.8iv) that the function Z^i defined in A 2.8iii has to be concave. A diagrammatic representation of the net production function is given by the diagrams 2.4 and 2.5. The line OB is the graph of the function Z^i so that the domain D_{Fi} of F^i is given by the area between the lines OB and OA in both diagrams. An "isoquant" like GHKL in diagram 2.5 is the locus of all tuples $(\tilde{R}_i, S_i) \in D_{Fi}$ yielding the same commodity output via F^i. By A 2.8iv these isoquants are convex functions and by A 2.8i and A 2.8iv they are downward sloping from some line OKD to the left in diagram 2.5. Moving from point K on the isoquant AHKL towards point H means that the net emissions S_i can be reduced at the cost of some extra resource input. Such a reduction of S_i can be

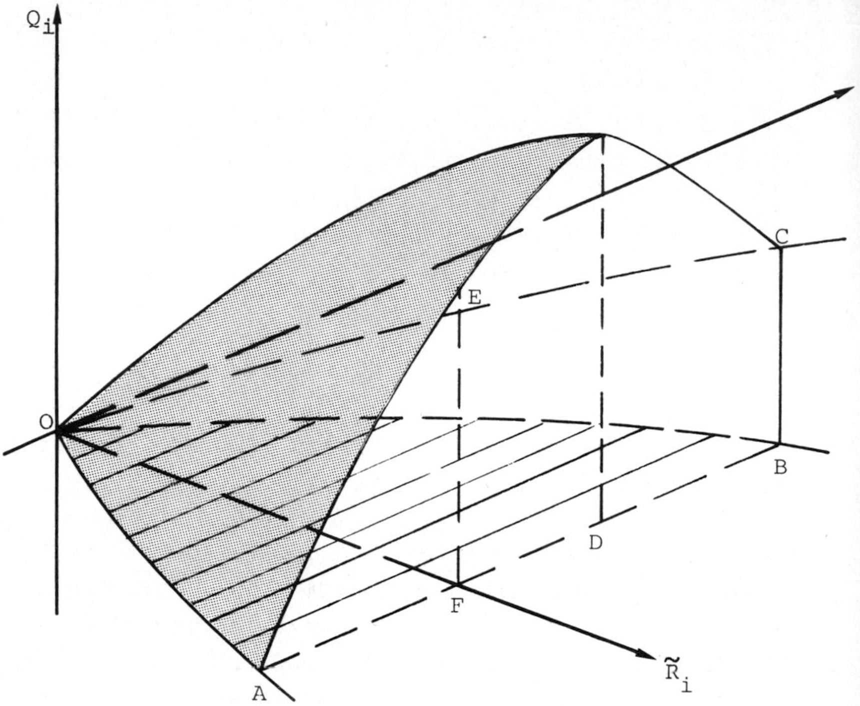

Diagram 2.4

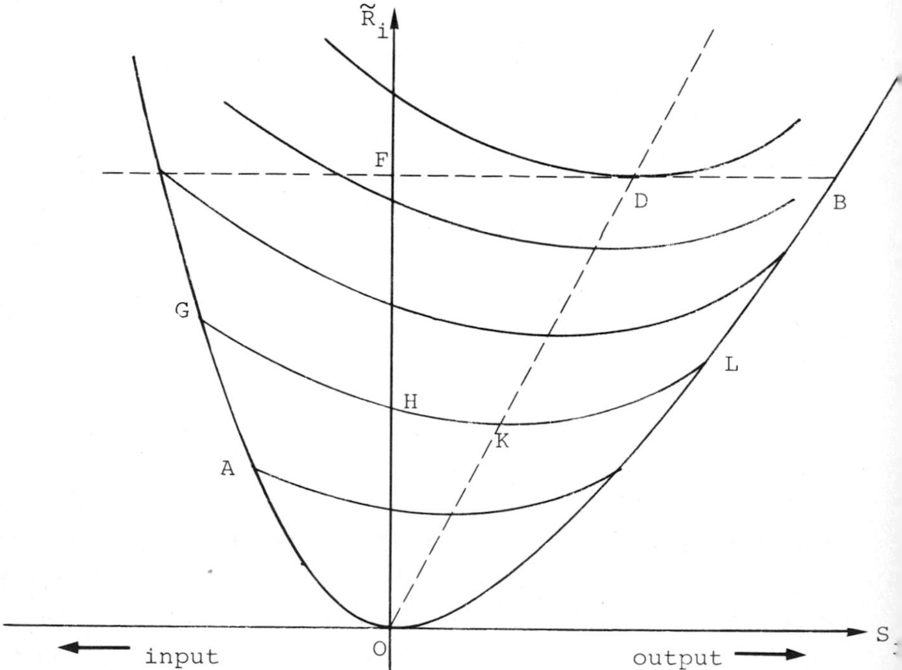

Diagram 2.5

interpreted as the operation of waste abatement (treatment) or waste avoidance facilities within the sector i which require resource inputs[1]. The isoquants may also but need not have an upward sloping segment like KL of the isoquant GHKL in diagram 2.5. Production activities on KL are by no means technologically inefficient. Whether profit maximizing producers will select such an activity or not is an entirely different question[2]. Note also that D_{Fi} may but need not have a subset where $S_i < 0$, i.e. where the waste product is used as an input. The boundary OAG of D_{Fi} in diagram 2.5 may, for example, coincide with the $\tilde{R}_i$-axis.

2.2.2 The Transformation Space in the Net-Emissions Approach

At a first glance the net-emissions approach appears to be highly different from the gross-emissions approach introduced in section 2.1. As a first step to show their similarity we want to compare their implications with respect to the transformation space of a two-sector economy.
We therefore define the economy's transformation space T as the set of all triples (Q_1, Q_2, U) such that the resource constraints

$$\tilde{R}_1 + \tilde{R}_2 \leq R, \qquad (2.7')$$

$$S_1 + S_2 = S \qquad (2.5')$$

the net production functions 2.8 and the damage function 2.6 are satisfied.
For analytical reasons, it is convenient to study the properties of the set

$$\overline{T} := \{y | y \leq \overline{y} \text{ and } \overline{y} \in T\}$$

instead of those of T. This substitution will not affect our results, since as in standard models (with suitable assumptions on preferences) equilibrium allocations will always be represented by points on the transformation frontier, i.e. on the upper boundary of the transformation space.

1) For more details see section 2.3.
2) The subset of D_{Fi} where the isoquants are upward sloping will turn out to be irrelevant for the solutions discussed in the subsequent parts of this book except in the case of recycling (chapter 12).

Lemma 2.1: Under A 2.5 and A 2.8iv $\overline{T}$ is convex.

Proof: We define $y := (Q_1, Q_2, U)$ and $y' := (Q_1', Q_2', U')$. Let $y, y' \in \overline{T}$ and associate to y and y' the 6-tuples $v := (\tilde{R}_1, \tilde{R}_2, S_1, S_2, S, U)$, $v' := (\tilde{R}_1', \tilde{R}_2', S_1', S_2', S', U')$, respectively, such that they satisfy 2.5, 2.6, 2.7' and 2.8. $\overline{T}$ is convex if $y^\lambda := (\lambda y + (1 - \lambda) y')$ can be shown to be an element of $\overline{T}$ for $\lambda \in [0,1]$. The vector $v^\lambda :=$ $\lambda v + (1 - \lambda) v' = (\tilde{R}_1^\lambda, \tilde{R}_2^\lambda, S_1^\lambda, S_2^\lambda, S^\lambda, U^\lambda)$ satisfies the resource constraint 2.7'. Hence $y'' := [F^1(\tilde{R}_1^\lambda, S_1^\lambda), F^2(\tilde{R}_1^\lambda, S_2^\lambda), U(S_1^\lambda + S_2^\lambda)] \in \overline{T}$. By the concavity of F^i (A 2.8iv) we obtain $Q_i^\lambda := \lambda F^i(\tilde{R}_i, S_i) + (1 - \lambda) F^i(\tilde{R}_i', S_i') \leq F^i(\tilde{R}_i^\lambda, S_i^\lambda)$ and by the concavity of G (A 2.5)
$U^\lambda := \lambda U(S) + (1 - \lambda) U(S') \leq U(S_1^\lambda + S_2^\lambda)$.

Therefore $y'' \in \overline{T}$ is component-wise not less than y^λ, and $y^\lambda \in \overline{T}$ follows from the definition of $\overline{T}$. Thus $\overline{T}$ is convex.

q.e.d.

From lemma 2.1 we conclude that in the net-emissions approach the transformation frontier of the two-sector economy is qualitatively the same as described in section 2.1.3 and in diagram 2.3 for the gross-emissions approach. The two approaches will be compared in more detail in the subsequent section.

2.2.3 Production Possibilities with Limited Emissions

In diagram 2.3 one can see that the production possibilities of the two consumption goods crucially depend on the environmental quality. For the purpose of environmental management it is important, therefore, to ask the following question: What are an economy's options between the production of two consumption goods, if, for fixed total resources R, the environmental quality must not be less than some value U^s and how do these production possibilites vary with U^s?

Let OK in diagram 2.3 be equal to the predetermined environmental quality index U^s and let KFF' be a plane through U^s and parallel to the Q_1-Q_2-plane. The requirement $U \geq U^s$

implies that all points (Q_1, Q_2, U) of the transformation space such that $U < U^s$ are no longer admitted. So we are left with the "truncated" transformation space consisting of the area on and between KF'F and AHG. Consider now the projection of this area into the Q_1-Q_2-plane, whose upper boundary is denoted by LL' in diagram 2.3. LL' is the economy's transformation curve with respect to the consumption goods subject to the constraint $U \geq U^s$.

Since by equation 2.6 G is a strictly monotone decreasing function of S the constraint $U \geq U^s$ can equivalently be expressed by the inequality $S \leq S^s$, where $S^s := G^{-1}(U^s)$. In the remainder of this section we want to specify and study some properties of the commodities transformation function

$$Q_1 = T^1(Q_2, S_o), \tag{2.9}$$

that is the locus of all efficient production points (Q_1, Q_2) relative to a given emission level S^s.

<u>Definition D 2.1:</u> An allocation $a := (Q_i^d, Q_i, \tilde{R}_i, S_i, U)_{i=1,2}$ (and the associated production point (Q_1, Q_2)) is said to be efficient relative to S^s,

(i) if it is feasible relative to S^s, i.e., if it satisfies the conditions $Q_i = F^i(\tilde{R}_i, S_i)$ for $i = 1,2$, $\tilde{R}_1 + \tilde{R}_2 \leq R$ and $S_1 + S_2 \leq S^s$;

(ii) if there is no production (Q_1', Q_2') that is feasible relative to S^s and that, in addition, satisfies $Q_i' \geq Q_i$ for $i = 1,2$ and $Q_j' > Q_j$ for $j = 1$ or $j = 2$.

In order to investigate the properties of T^1, it is convenient to introduce a few additional assumptions on the net production functions F^i:

A 2.9 Well-behaved net production functions.

A 2.9i Non-negative domain: $D_{Fi} \subset \mathbb{R}_+^2$

A 2.9ii Linear-homogeneity:

$$\lambda F^i(\tilde{R}_i, S_i) = F^i(\lambda\tilde{R}_i, \lambda S_i) \text{ for } \lambda > 0$$

A 2.9iii Strict quasi-concavity:

For every $Q_i^o > 0$ the upper contour set

$\{(\tilde{R}_i, S_i) \in D_{Fi} \mid F^i(\tilde{R}_i, S_i) \geq Q_i^o\}$ is strictly convex

A 2.9iv Non-reversal of emission intensities:

$$B^2\left(\frac{F_S^2}{F_R^2}\right) > B^1\left(\frac{F_S^1}{F_R^1}\right) \text{ for all } \frac{F_S^1}{F_R^1} = \frac{F_S^2}{F_R^2},$$

where $B^i\left(\frac{F_S^i}{F_R^i}\right) = b_i := \frac{\tilde{R}_i}{S_i}$ is the labour intensity in the production of good i, when the marginal rate of substitution is F_S^i/F_R^i.

By standard arguments it follows from A 2.9ii and iii that the function B^i exists and is strictly monotone increasing in (F_S^i/F_R^i).

These assumptions A 2.9 require some comment. By A 2.9i we exclude the waste product as an input. We already mentioned that our main interest is not focussed on this input aspect. Note, however, that the gross emissions approach logically implies $D_{Fi} \not\subset \mathbb{R}_+^2$. The assumptions A 2.9ii and iii help very much to simplify our analysis. They enable us in particular, to use many tools being familiar from and powerful in the standard pure theory of international trade. In our view they should be accepted or critisized (or even rejected) for the same reasons as the analogue assumptions in the pure trade theory.

One of the "technical" advantages of the assumptions A 2.9ii and iii has immediately been utilized in A 2.9iv, namely the fact that (for all homothetic functions) marginal rates of factor substitution are constant as long as the "factor intensity" does not change. As in the last paragraph of section 2.1.2 we define the emission intensity of sector i as

$$\frac{S_i}{\tilde{R}_i} = \frac{1}{b_i}$$

and assume throughout that for every alternatively given marginal rate of substitution, sector 1 is more emission intensive than sector 2. From A 2.9ii it follows that the function Z^i from assumption A 2.8ii is linear, i.e. has a constant first derivative. But A 2.9iv does not imply A 2.7. Nor is A 2.9iv implied by A 2.7, that is, A 2.9iv is independent of any sign of the difference between Z_R^1 and Z_R^2.

When A 2.9 is combined with A 2.8i we know that $F_S^i(\tilde{R}_i, S_i) > 0$ for some $(\tilde{R}_i, S_i) \in D_{Fi}$. But we did not and need not exclude $F_S^i < 0$. More generally, either there exists $\bar{b}_i \in (0, Z_R^i)$, such that

$$F_S^i(\tilde{R}_i, S_i) \gtreqless 0 \text{ for } (\tilde{R}_i/S_i) \gtreqless \bar{b}_i \qquad (2.10)$$

or, alternatively

$$F_S^i(\tilde{R}_i, S_i) > 0 \text{ for every } (\tilde{R}_i, S_i) \in D_{Fi} \qquad (2.11)$$

Considering these two cases, efficient production points can be characterized as follows:

<u>Lemma 2.2:</u> (i) Let 2.10 hold and let $S^S \geq R/\bar{b}_1$. Under the assumptions A 2.8 and A 2.9 a production point $[F^1(\tilde{R}_1, S_1), F^2(\tilde{R}_2, S_2)]$ is efficient relative to S^S if and only if $\tilde{R}_1 + \tilde{R}_2 = R$ and $S_i = \tilde{R}_i/\bar{b}_i$ for i = 1,2.

(ii) Let 2.11 hold and let $S^S \geq R/\bar{b}_1$. Then the second sentence of lemma 2.2i holds when $\bar{b}_i$ is substituted everywhere by Z_R^i.

Proof: Ad (i): (Sufficiency). We consider an allocation $A := (Q_1, Q_2, \tilde{R}_1, \tilde{R}_2, S_1, S_2)$ such that $Q_i = F^i(\tilde{R}_i, S_i)$, $S_i = \tilde{R}_i/\bar{b}_i$ for i = 1,2, and $\tilde{R}_1 + \tilde{R}_2 = R$. A 2.9iv and $S^S \geq R/\bar{b}_1$ yield $S_1 + S_2 \leq S^S$. Hence A is feasible relative to S^S. Suppose without loss of generality that the resource is redistributed so that $\tilde{R}_1' < \tilde{R}_1$, $\tilde{R}_2' > \tilde{R}_2$ and $\tilde{R}_1' + \tilde{R}_2' = R$. Then it follows from A 2.9ii and iii that $Q_1' = F^1(\tilde{R}_1', S_1) < Q_1$ and $Q_2' = F^2(\tilde{R}_2', S_2) > Q_2$. Hence (Q_1', Q_2') does not dominate (Q_1, Q_2). Now suppose that the allocation A is changed into an allocation A'' such that $\tilde{R}_i'' = \tilde{R}_i$, but $S_i'' \neq \tilde{R}_i/\bar{b}_i$ (and $S_1'' + S_2'' \leq S^s$). If $S_i'' < \tilde{R}_i/\bar{b}_i$, then $F_S^i > 0$ by 2.10 and hence $Q_i'' = F^i(\tilde{R}_i, S_i'') < Q^i$. But the same is true if $S_i'' > \tilde{R}_i/\bar{b}_i$ since, by 2.10, $F_S^i < 0$ in this case. Hence (Q_1, Q_2) dominates every commodity bundle (Q_1'', Q_2'') resultin[g] from a change in the allocation of S_i. This proves the efficiency of (Q_1, Q_2) relative to S^s.

(Necessity). Let $[Q_1 = F^1(\tilde{R}_1, S_1), Q_2 = F^2(\tilde{R}_2, S_2)]$ be efficient relative to S^s. But we assume now contrary to this presupposition that $\tilde{R}_1 + \tilde{R}_2 < R$ and $S_i = \tilde{R}_i/\bar{b}_i$ for i = 1,2. From $F_a^i > 0$ a contradiction obviously follows. It is also easy to show that (Q_1, Q_2) cannot be efficient as long as $\tilde{R}_1 + \tilde{R}_2 = R$ and $S_1 \neq \tilde{R}_1/\bar{b}_1$ or $S_2 \neq \tilde{R}_2/\bar{b}_2$.

Ad (ii): The proof of lemma 2.2ii follows from the proof of lemma 2.2i with minor qualifications.

q.e.d.

By now we have completed our rather "technical" preparations to inquire into the properties of the commodities transformation function $Q_1 = T^1(Q_2, S_o)$ from 2.9 for alternative values of S^s.

<u>Lemma 2.3:</u> Let the assumption A 2.8 and A 2.9 hold and let

$f^i : \mathbb{R}_+ \to \mathbb{R}_+$ be defined by $\frac{Q_i}{S_i} = f^i(\frac{\tilde{R}_i}{S_i}) := F^i(\frac{\tilde{R}_i}{S_i}, 1)$.

(i) If 2.10 holds and $S^s \geq R/\bar{b}_1$, 2.9 is given by the affine function

$$Q_1 = \frac{Rf^1(\bar{b}_1)}{\bar{b}_1} - \frac{\bar{b}_2 f^1(\bar{b}_1)}{\bar{b}_1 f^2(\bar{b}_2)} Q_2. \qquad (2.12$$

(ii) If 2.10 holds and $S^s < R/\bar{b}_2$, we have[1)] for all Q_2 in

1) Lemma 2.3ii also holds for $S^s = R/\bar{b}_2$. In this case, the inequality in lemma 2.3iib becomes an equality for $Q_2 = Rf^2(\bar{b}_2)/\bar{b}_2$.

domain of T^1

a) $T^1_{QQ} < 0$ (strict concavity)

b) $T^1(Q_2, S^S) < \frac{Rf^1(\bar{b}_1)}{\bar{b}_1} - \frac{\bar{b}_2 f^1(\bar{b}_1)}{\bar{b}_1 f^2(\bar{b}_2)} Q_2.$

(iii) If 2.10 holds and $\frac{R}{\bar{b}_2} < S^S < \frac{R}{\bar{b}_1}$, then T^1 is continuous

and given by

$$Q_1 = \frac{\hat{R}_1 f^1(\bar{b}_1)}{\bar{b}_1} - \frac{\bar{b}_2 f^1(\bar{b}_1)}{\bar{b}_1 f^2(\bar{b}_2)} Q_2 \qquad (2.13)$$

for $Q_2 \in [\hat{Q}_2(S_o), Rf^2(\bar{b}_2)/\bar{b}_2]$ and by a strictly concave function for $Q_2 \in [0, \hat{Q}_2(S_o)]$, where for i = 1,2 $\hat{Q}_2(S_o) := F^i(\hat{R}_i, \hat{S}_i)$ and where the vector $(\hat{R}_1, \hat{R}_2, \hat{S}_1, \hat{S}_2)$ is such that $\hat{R}_1 + \hat{R}_2 = R$, $\hat{S}_1 + \hat{S}_2 = S^S$ and $\hat{R}_i = \bar{b}_i \hat{S}_i$ for i = 1,2.

(iv) If 2.11 holds, then lemmata 2.3i to iii apply with Z^i_R substituted everywhere for $\bar{b}_i$.

Proof: Ad (i): Equation 2.12 from lemma 2.3i is obtained with the help of the equations $\tilde{Q}_i = S_i f^i(\bar{b}_i)$, $S_i \bar{b}_i = \tilde{R}_i$ for i = 1,2 and $\tilde{R}_1 + \tilde{R}_2 = R$.

Ad (ii, a): The proof of lemma 2.3iia can be found in the literature[1].

Ad (ii, b): If an allocation is efficient, the ratio of sectorial marginal productivities must be the same. Hence from $S^S < R/\bar{b}_2$ and 2.11 it follows that $F^i_S > 0$ and $S_i < \tilde{R}_i/\bar{b}_1$ for i = 1,2. Therefore with given resource input the production of both commodities could be increased by relaxing the constraint $S \leq S^S$. This proves that the graph of the transformation function 2.12 lies above that of function 2.9 for $S^S < R/\bar{b}_2$.

1) See H. Herberg (1969, p. 204, Lemma 2).

Ad (iii): The commodity bundle $[\hat{Q}_1(S^S), \hat{Q}_2(S^S)]$ defined in lemma 2.3iii is efficient relative to $S^S \in [R/\bar{b}_2, R/\bar{b}_1]$. It remains to show that in this case the transformation function 2.9 is composed of two parts as indicated in lemma 2.2iii. In the first step we determine two transformation functions $Q_1 = T^{1\alpha}(Q_2, S^\alpha = \hat{S}_1)$ and $Q_1 = T^{1\beta}(Q_2, S^\beta = \hat{S}_2)$ that may be interpreted to belong to two distinct economies (α and β) with the resource endowments $R^\alpha = \hat{R}_1$ and $R^\beta = \hat{R}_2$, respectivel Then by lemma 2.3i the function $T^{1\alpha}$ is given by the linear function from 2.12, whereas $T^{1\beta}$ is strictly concave according to lemma 2.3ii, a. If all resources R^α $[R^\beta]$ are employed in sector 1 [2], the (auxiliary) economy α $[\beta]$ produces the bundle $(\hat{Q}_1(S^S), 0)$ $[0, \hat{Q}_2(S^S)]$. Hence the joint production possibilities of the economies α and β - and therefore those of the original economy with the resource endowment $R = R^\alpha + R^\beta$ - are described

(1) by the function $Q_1 = \hat{Q}_1(S^S) + T^{1\beta}(Q_2, \hat{S}_2)$
for all $Q_2 \in [0, \hat{Q}_2(S^S)]$ and

(2) by the function 2.13 from lemma 2.3iii
for all $Q_2 \in [\hat{Q}_2(S^S), Rf^2(\bar{b}_2)/\bar{b}_2]$.

Ad (iv): Obvious.

q.e.d.

Lemma 2.3 helps to clarify the important influence of the environment on the production possibilities of the consumptic goods. S^S can be interpreted as an indicator of the abundance of the environment as a waste receptor. If the environmental waste recepting services are abundant in the sense that $S^S \geq R/\bar{b}_1$ (or $S^S \geq R/Z^1_R$) then the production possibilities are left unaffected by the environment, even though there may be severe environmental disruption. In this case the producti possibilities are exactly like those that would have been obtained if the waste product would have been neglected in th analysis from the beginning. In diagram 2.3 this transformati curve is given by the dotted line B'C'. The less abundant the environment becomes in the sense of an increasing positive difference $(R/\bar{b}_1 - S^S)$, the more the transformation curve T^1

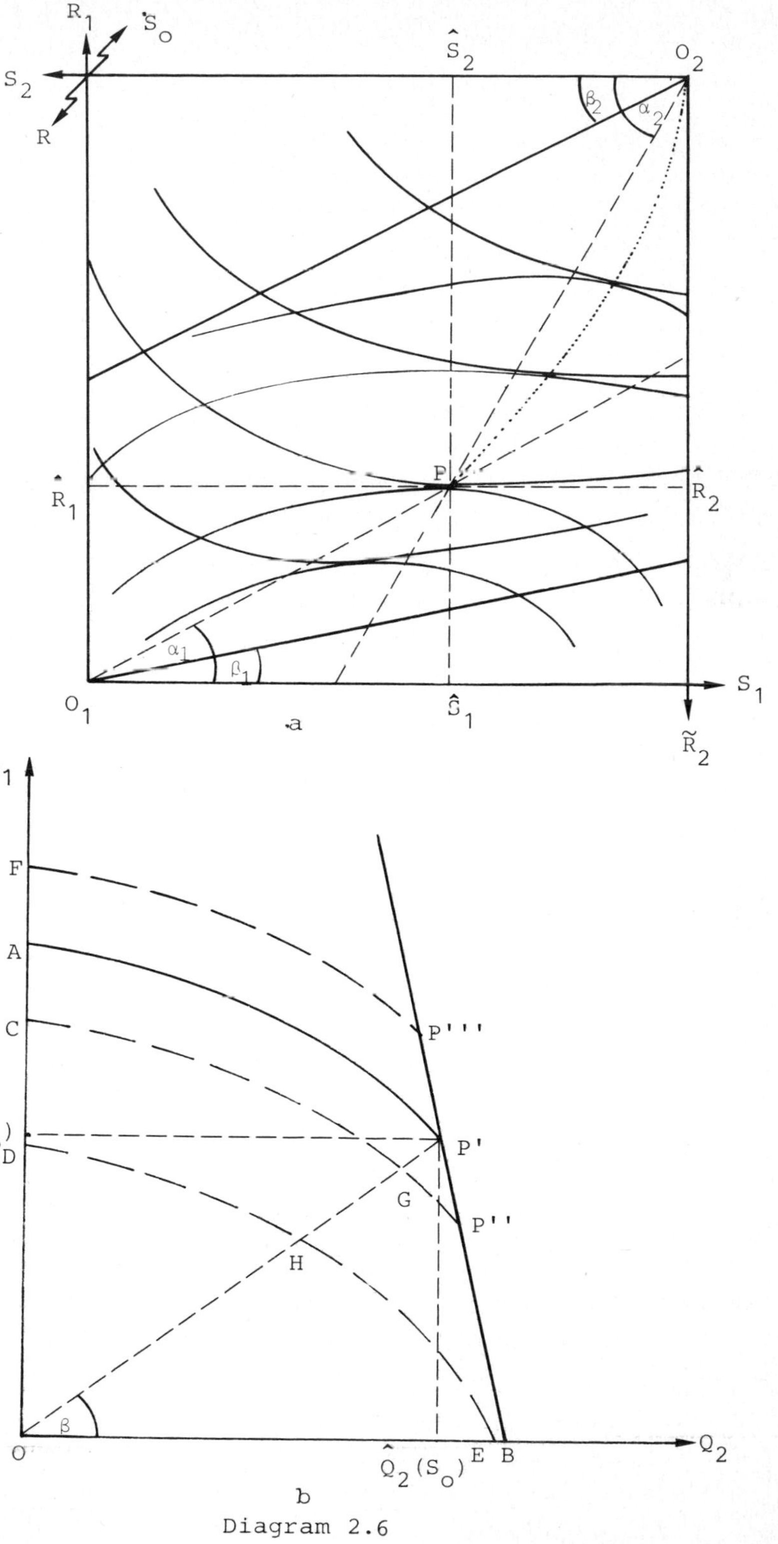
R̃1
So
Ŝ2
O2
S2
R
β2
α2
P
R̂1
R̂2
α1
β1
O1
a
Ŝ1
S1
R̃2
Q1
F
A
C
P'''
Q̂1(So)
D
P'
G
P''
H
β
O
Q̂2(So)
E
B
Q2
b

Diagram 2.6

shrinks towards the origin.

The diagrams 2.6a and b illustrate for the case of lemma 2.3iii, how the transformation function T^1 is diagrammatically derived from the "factor box". The box of diagram 2.6a is of size RXS^s and we have for i = 1,2 $\tan \alpha_i = \bar{b}_i$ and $\tan \beta_i = Z_R^i$. The commodities transformation curve associated to this box is AP'B in diagram 2.6b. Suppose now, that S^s is successively (parametrically) reduced. As a consequence, O_2 in diagram 2.6a moves to the left so that the box gets smaller. Simultaneously the transformation curve in diagram 2.6b shrinks towards the origin, as indicated by the lines CP''B and DE in diagram 2.6b. One may also choose a greater value of S^s than shown in diagram 2.6a. Then the factor box has to be extended to the right hand side, yielding a transformation curve such as FP'''B in diagram 2.6b. In fact, S^s may be increased until the associated transformation curve is equal to the straight line given in diagram 2.6b by BP''P'P''' up to the vertical axis.

Diagram 2.7 illustrates the situation of lemma 2.3iv for $S^s < R/Z_R^2$ with $\tan \beta_i = Z_R^i$ (i = 1,2). The dotted line between O_1 and O_2 is the efficiency curve as in the standard neo-classical factor box with two substitutable productive factors. The commodities transformation curve being uniquely assigned to this efficiency curve is strictly concave (like the curve ED in diagram 2.6b).

2.3 Comparison Between the Gross and Net-Emissions Approaches

It has already become clear from the preceding sections that the phenomenon of joint production is at the core of environmental economics. In order to further improve its understanding and to better evaluate and compare the assumptions underlying the gross and net emissions approaches we now analyze the gross emissions approach from a slightly different perspective than in section 2.1 and then we compare it with the net emissions approach. For this purpose we consider only one sector, and, for convenience, suppress the index i (= 1,2).

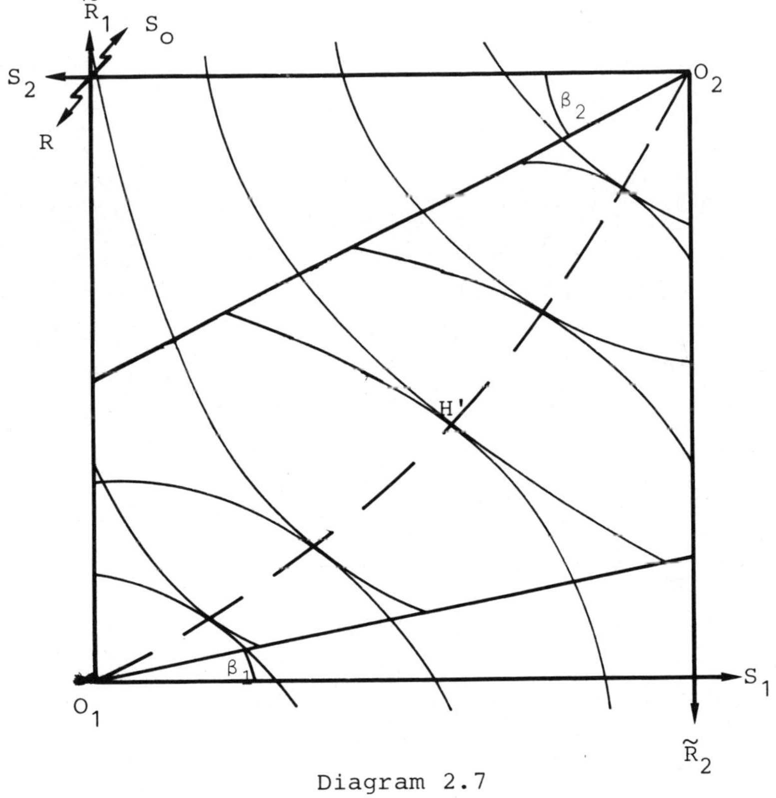

Diagram 2.7

We first define the production set

$$Y^{\alpha} := \{y_{\alpha} := (-R_{\alpha}, Q_{\alpha}, S^{p}_{\alpha}, V_{\alpha}) \in \mathbb{R}^4 \,|\, R_{\alpha}, Q_{\alpha} \text{ and } S^{p}_{\alpha} \text{ satisfy 2.1' and 2.2'; } V_{\alpha} := 0 \text{ and } R_{\alpha}, Q_{\alpha}, S^{p}_{\alpha} \geq 0\},$$

where

$$Q_{\alpha} = F(R_{\alpha}) \quad \text{and} \tag{2.1'}$$

$$S^{p}_{\alpha} = Z(R_{\alpha}) \tag{2.2'}$$

with $F(0) = Z(0) = 0$.

Let us, for the moment, disregard the fourth and empty dimension in Y^{α}. Then it is easily seen that Y^{α} captures a strict joint production technology[1] between the consumption good and the waste product whose quantities are here denoted by Q_{α} and S^{p}_{α}, respectively. This technology forms the first part of the gross approach of section 2.1. If we again omit the fourth dimension of Y^{α} this set can be represented by all points on the dotted line OA (and beyond A) in diagram 2.4. The projection of this line OA into the (S_{α}, R_{α})-plane is the line OB in diagram 2.4. The line OB, in turn, is the graph of the function Z from 2.2 or from A 2.8iii[2].

If in the real world strict joint production between useful goods and (useless) waste products would be predominant, then improvements of environmental quality could only be achieved by reducing the scale of the rigidly given joint production process. Fortunately (from the environmental economist's point of view) there is, however, ample empirical evidence for some flexibility in the joint production technology. One way, to make this flexibility analytically explicit and precise is to model a net production function satisfying the assumption A 2.8. It may be interpreted as an approximation of many different fixed joint production processes of the type Y^{α}.

---

1) Compare, for example, C.S. Shoup (1965, p. 254 - 264) and D.K. Whitcomb (1972, p. 19). Observe also, that we follow the usual convention that in $y_{\alpha} \in Y^{\alpha}$ negative components denote inputs and positive components denote outputs.

2) Note, that the function Z is assumed to be convex, whereas by A 2.8iii and iv Z is assumed to be concave. This discrepancy requires some comment, which we will postpone, however, until lemma 2.4 is discussed below.

But there is also another interesting way to establish analytically a technology with flexible joint production: by introducing a waste abatement or waste treatment technology. Essentially, a waste treatment activity uses some resource input, say R^r, and some waste product, S^r, being generated in a strict joint production activity, and transforms these two inputs into an output that is itself a waste product[1]. Hence we have to distinguish between primary and secondary waste. We use the symbol S for the quantity of primary waste whereas V denotes the quantity of secondary waste. The abatement technology is formalized by the production set

$$Y^{\beta} := \{y_{\beta} := (R^r_{\beta}, Q_{\beta}, -S^r_{\beta}, V_{\beta}) \subset \mathbb{R}^4 \mid R^r_{\beta}, S^r_{\beta} \text{ and } V_{\beta} \text{ satisfy } 2.14 \text{ and } 2.15;\ Q_{\beta} := 0 \text{ and } R^r_{\beta}, S^r_{\beta}, V_{\beta} \geq 0\},$$

where

$$V_{\beta} = G^{\beta}(R^r_{\beta}, S^r_{\beta}) \quad \text{and} \tag{2.14}$$

$$S^r_{\beta} \leq F^r(R^r_{\beta}) \tag{2.15}$$

with $G^{\beta}(0,0) = F^r(0) = 0$.

The function F^r in 2.15 serves to restrict the domain of the waste treatment function G in 2.14. $F^r(R^r_{\beta})$ is the maximum amount of primary waste that can be transformed into secondary waste with the help of the resource input R^r_{β}. Note, that the function F^r from 2.15 is intended to be identical to the "abatement function" F^r_i in 2.3. Such an assertion demands some explanation of the interrelationship between Y^{β} and 2.3. In particular, the question arises, why we should expand the analytical framework to Y^{β} with 2.14 and 2.15 when all we need is 2.3.

Let us first observe what follows from the relevance of material balance considerations in the context of environ-

1) If the waste treatment output were useful for some consumption or production purposes, we would have introduced a recycling technology instead of a waste abatement technology. For more details on the recycling issue see chapter 12.

mental economics[1]: It is impossible to produce "nothing" from positive amounts of inputs whenever these inputs involve mass, i.e. are no pure services. This basic fact requires to introduce the abatement technology Y^{β} in favour of F_i^r from 2.3. But there is an elegant (and not implausible) way to avoid all the additional analytical complications from replacing 2.3 by Y^{β}. We simply assume that the discharge of secondary waste into the environment neither deteriorates nor improves environmental quality. This assumption implies that (1) we can neglect the secondary waste from our further considerations and (2) that abatement activities chosen from Y^{β} will be always such that 2.15 is satisfied with the equality sign. Under these conditions the approaches 2.3 and Y^{β} to the abatement problem coincide.

In the next step we want to integrate the strict joint production technology Y^{α} and the abatement technology Y^{β}. Due to our sign convention with respect to outputs and inputs we obtain the integrated technology $Y^{\alpha+\beta}$ by simply adding the two production sets:

$$Y^{\alpha+\beta} := Y^{\alpha} + Y^{\beta} := \{y \in \mathbb{R}^4 \mid y = y_{\alpha} + y_{\beta},\ y_{\alpha} \in Y^{\alpha},\ y_{\beta} \in Y^{\beta}\}$$

Under the assumption discussed above that the emission of secondary waste does not affect the environmental quality, we can drop from $Y^{\alpha+\beta}$ the dimension reserved for the secondary waste. We further focus our attention on the "upper boundary" reduced production set

$$\hat{Y}^{\alpha+\beta} := \{(R + R^r, Q, S^p - S^r) \mid (R + R^r, Q, S^p - S^r, V) \in Y^{\alpha+\beta} \text{ and } (R + R^r, \bar{Q}, S^p - S^r, V) \notin Y^{\alpha+\beta}, \text{ if } \bar{Q} > Q\}.$$

Clearly, this set $\hat{Y}^{\alpha+\beta}$ can be shown to be the graph of some function[2] $\hat{F} : D_{\hat{F}} \longrightarrow \mathbb{R}_+$ with $D_{\hat{F}} \subset \mathbb{R}^2$. Hence it is natural to ask under which conditions $\hat{F}$ satisfies the assumptions A 2.8i to iv.

1) Compare A.V. Kneese, R.U. Ayres and R. d'Arge (1970).
2) For the general problem, how to define and derive a production function on a given production set, see also W. Hildenbrand (1966, p. 65 - 80).

Lemma 2.4: If F, Z and F^r from 2.1', 2.2' and 2.15, respectively are strictly monotone increasing, if F and F^r are concave functions and if Z is a linear function, then the set $\hat{Y}^{\alpha+\beta}$ is the graph of a function $\hat{F} : D_{\hat{F}} \longrightarrow \mathbb{R}_+$, satisfying the properties A 2.8i to iv.

Proof: (1) Let $\bar{R} > 0$, $R_\alpha + R^r_\beta = \bar{R}$ and let 2.15 be satisfied as an equality. Then it follows from 2.1', 2.2' and 2.15 that $S := S^p_\alpha - S^r_\beta = Z[F^{-1}(Q_\alpha)] - F^r[\bar{R} - F^{-1}(Q_\alpha)]$. Since F, Z and F^r are strictly monotone increasing by assumption, we obtain $\frac{dS}{dQ_\alpha} = (Z_R + F^r_S)\ F_Q^{-1} > 0$. Therefore $\hat{F}$ fulfils assumption A 2.8i.

(2) A 2.8ii follows for $\hat{F}$ immediately from $F(0) = Z(0) = F^r(0) = 0$.

(3) The function Z in 2.2' plays the role of the function Z^i in A 2.8iii. Let $\bar{R} > 0$ and $R_\alpha + R^r_\beta = \bar{R}$. It is to show that $(\bar{R}, Q, S^p - S^r) \notin \hat{Y}^{\alpha+\beta}$, if $S^p - S^r > Z(\bar{R})$. $S^p = Z(R_\alpha)$, $S^r \leq F^r(R^r_\beta)$ and $R_\alpha + R^r_\beta = \bar{R}$ yield the unequality $Z(R_\alpha) \geq S^p - S^r \geq Z(R_\alpha) - F^r(\bar{R} - R_\alpha)$ for every $R_\alpha \in [0, \bar{R}]$. Hence $\hat{F}$ satisfies A 2.8iii.

(4) We presupposed that Z and F^r are concave functions. Therefore it follows from (3) that $D_{\hat{F}}$, the projection of $\hat{Y}^{\alpha+\beta}$ into the (R, S)-plane, is a convex set[1]. In order to show that $\hat{F}$ is a concave function, we consider two arbitrary points $(-R^j_{\alpha+\beta}, Q^j_\alpha, S^j_{\alpha+\beta}) := [-(R^j_\alpha + R^{rj}_\beta), Q^j_\alpha, S^{pj}_\alpha - S^{rj}_\beta)]$ (j = 1,2) in the set $\hat{Y}^{\alpha+\beta}$ and we define the convex combinations $-R^\lambda_{\alpha+\beta} := -[\lambda R^1_{\alpha+\beta} + (1-\lambda)\ R^2_{\alpha+\beta}]$ etc. First we observe that for all $\lambda \in [0,1]$ we have $(R^\lambda_{\alpha+\beta}, S^\lambda_{\alpha+\beta}) \in D_{\hat{F}}$, since $D_{\hat{F}}$ is convex. We have to prove however, that with the resource allocation $R^\lambda_{\alpha+\beta}$ it is possible (a) to obtain the net emissions $S^\lambda_{\alpha+\beta}$ and (b) to

1) Note, that the convexity of $\hat{Y}^{\alpha+\beta}$ implies the convexity of the transformation space in the gross emissions approach under the assumptions of lemma 2.4.

produce at least as much as $Q_\alpha^\lambda := \lambda Q_\alpha^1 + (1 - \lambda)\, Q_\alpha^2$. Since F is assumed to be concave, it follows $F(R_\alpha^\lambda) \geq Q_\alpha^\lambda$ (with $R_\alpha^\lambda := \lambda R_\alpha^1 + (1 - \lambda)\, R_\alpha^2$), which proves (b). Consider now $S'_{\alpha+\beta} := Z(R_\alpha^\lambda) - F^r(R_\beta^{r\lambda})$. By the linearity of Z and by the concavity of $F^{r\beta}$ we obtain $Z(R_\alpha^\lambda) = \lambda Z(R_\alpha^1) + (1 - \lambda)\, Z(R_\alpha^2)$, $F^r(R_\beta^{r\lambda}) \geq \lambda F^r(R_\beta^{r1}) + (1 - \lambda)\, F^r(R_\beta^{r2})$ and hence $S'_{\alpha+\beta} \leq S_{\alpha+\beta}^\lambda := \lambda S_{\alpha+\beta}^1 + (1 - \lambda)\, S_{\alpha+\beta}^2 := \lambda Z(R_\alpha^1) + (1 - \lambda)\, Z(R_\alpha^2) - \lambda F^r(R_\beta^{r1}) - (1 - \lambda)\, F^r(R_\beta^{r2})$. We know from 2.15 that if $S'_{\alpha+\beta}$ is a feasible net emission, then every element of the interval $[Z(R_\alpha^\lambda), S'_{\alpha+\beta}]$ is feasible[1]. Since $S_{\alpha+\beta}^\lambda$ is an element of this interval , the claim (a) from above is shown to be valid. This completes the proof of lemma 2.4.

q.e.d.

The relevance of lemma 2.4 is to show the close relationship between the gross and net emissions approaches. The only majo divergence in assumptions concerns the gross emissions function Z. While in 2.2 it is allowed to be strictly convex (or linear), in lemma 2.4 linearity must be assumed in order to establish convexity of $D_{\hat{F}}$ and concavity of $\hat{F}$. The major reason for insisting on the assumption of "convex technology" is, in turn, to make our models suitable for the standard competitive equilibrium analysis.

The basic idea of lemma 2.4 is illustrated in diagram 2.8. The line OC is the graph of the function Z - as the lines OB in diagram 2.4 and 2.5. Uniquely associated to every point on OC there is a production level Q, starting with $Q = 0$ at the origin and monotonely increasing with increasing distance from the origin. Let P in diagram 2.8 be a point on OC with the coordinates $(\hat{R}, \hat{S}^p)$ and define $\hat{S}^p := Z(\hat{R})$. Then

$$\tilde{R} = \hat{R} + R^r = Z^{-1}(\hat{S}^p) + F^{r(-1)}(\hat{S}^p - S)$$

determines the isoquant PQ in diagram 2.8. Since such an

1) Alternatively, the resources could be shifted from abatement to production without changing the overall resource input. Thus the conditions (a) and (b) can be eventually satisfied.

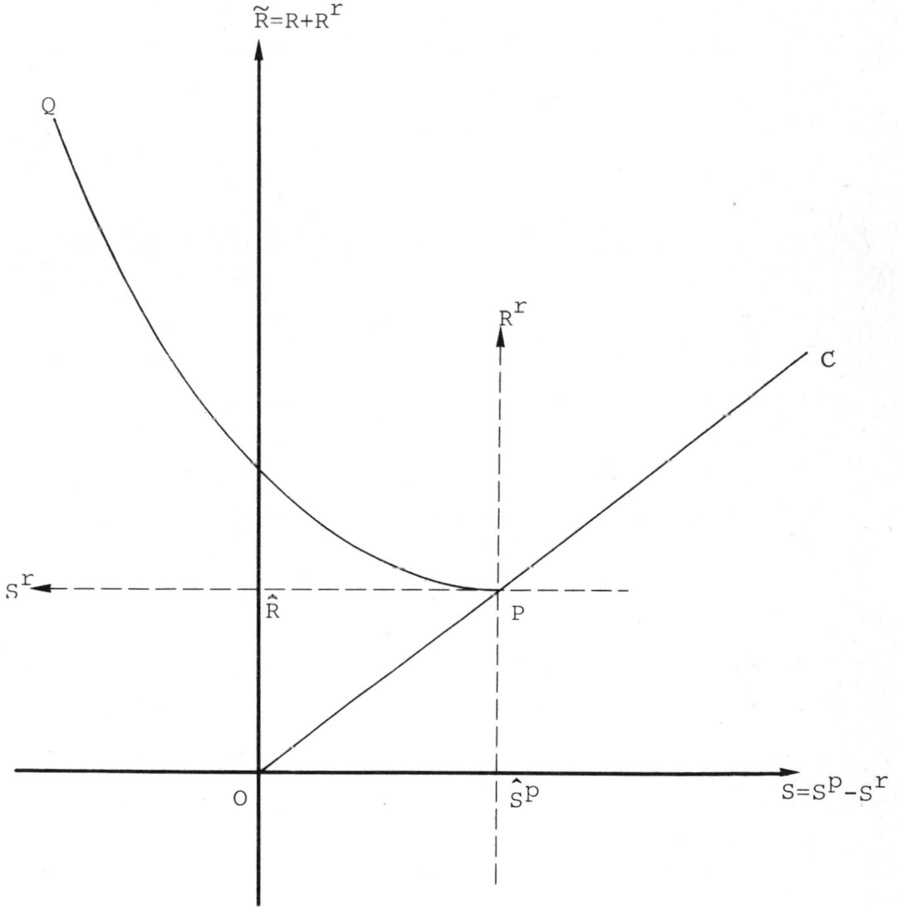

Diagram 2.8

isoquant is defined for every point on OC in diagram 2.8, the plane to the left of OC is densely covered by isoquants. These considerations also illustrate the by-product property of primary waste. Suppose, we select some point in diagram 2.8 on OC or to the left of OC and then move to the left parallel to the horizontal axis. Then we pass isoquants of continuously decreasing levels of production. Hence primary waste is a by-product in the process of producing the consumption good according to the assumption A 2.8i in section 2.2.

Summarizing our comparison between the gross and net emission approaches up to now we observe that the only difference consists in the properties of the function Z from lemma 2.4 and the function Z^i from equation 2.2. In order to show the analytical implication of the convexity of the function Z^i we will now adopt this assumption for Z and ask what kind of net production function will result. For this purpose we introduce the following notation:

$$Y_1^{\alpha} := \{y_{\alpha} := (-R_{\alpha}, Q_{\alpha}, S_{\alpha}^p, V_{\alpha}) \in \mathbb{R}^4 \mid R_{\alpha}, Q_{\alpha} \text{ and } S_{\alpha}^p \text{ satisfy } 2.1'' \text{ and } 2.2''; V_{\alpha} := 0 \text{ and } R_{\alpha}, Q_{\alpha}, S_{\alpha}^p \geq 0\}$$

where

$$Q_{\alpha} \leq F(R_{\alpha}) \text{ and} \tag{2.1''}$$

$$S_{\alpha}^p \geq Z(R_{\alpha}) \tag{2.2''}$$

with $F(0) = Z(0) = 0$

The inequality 2.2'' is not acceptable on technological grounds since it is not possible by mass balance considerations to produce arbitrarily large amounts of an output from a finite amount of input. So 2.2'' must be considered as an auxiliary assumption which is only justified if the inequality sign can be shown not to be effective in the relevant analytical situations. We further define

$$\hat{Y}_1^{\alpha+\beta} := \{(R + R^r, Q, S^p - S^r) \mid (R + R^r, Q, S^p - S^r, V) \in Y_1^{\alpha+\beta} \text{ and } (R + R^r, \bar{Q}, S^p - S^r, V) \notin Y_1^{\alpha+\beta}, \text{ if } \bar{Q} > Q\},$$

where $Y_1^{\alpha+\beta} := Y_1^{\alpha} + Y^{\beta}$ (Y^{β} as introduced above).

Lemma 2.5: If F, Z and F^r from 2.1'', 2.2'' and 2.15 are strictly monotonicly increasing, if F and F^r are concave functions and if Z is a convex function, then the set $\hat{Y}_1^{\alpha+\beta}$ is the graph of a function $\hat{\hat{F}} : \hat{\hat{D}}_F \longrightarrow \mathbb{R}_+$ such that $\hat{\hat{F}}$ satisfies the properties A 2.8i, A 2.8ii and A 2.8iv.

Proof: The properties A 2.8i and A 2.8ii are straightforward from the first part of the proof of lemma 2.4. To show that A 2.8iv also holds we first observe that under the presuppositions of lemma 2.5 Y_1^α and Y^β are convex sets. Hence $Y_1^{\alpha+\beta} := Y_1^\alpha + Y^\beta$ is a convex set and the set of its "upper boundary points", $\hat{Y}_1^{\alpha+\beta}$, is therefore the graph of a concave function.

q.e.d.

In lemma 2.5 we have not established that $\hat{\hat{F}}$ satisfies the assumption A 2.8iii. In fact, it is easy to see from the inequalities 2.2'' and 2.15 that $\hat{\hat{D}}_F \supset \mathbb{R}_+^2$ and hence that A 2.8iii is violated. Diagram 2.9 shows how according to the function $\hat{\hat{F}}$ the output of the consumption good changes with increasing waste production for given $\tilde{R} > 0$.

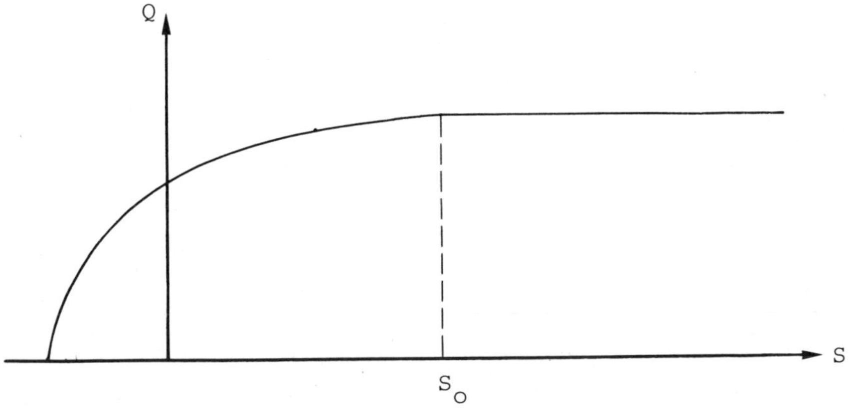

Diagram 2.9

The horizontal line beyond S_o in diagram 2.9 implies that 2.2'' holds with inequality, whereas on the left of S_o 2.2'' is satisfied as an equality. Therefore the net production function $\hat{\hat{F}}$ can be used without harm as long as the analysis is restricted to that part of its domain where $\hat{\hat{F}}_S > 0$. This is always the case when waste is abated, that is when a positive emission tax is levied.

Appendix 2.1

1. The function $U = \Phi(Q_1, Q_2)$ is concave if the Hessian determinant

$$D = \begin{vmatrix} \dfrac{\partial^2 U}{\partial U_1^2} & \dfrac{\partial^2 U}{\partial Q_1 \partial Q_2} \\ \\ \dfrac{\partial^2 U}{\partial Q_2 \partial Q_1} & \dfrac{\partial^2 U}{\partial Q_2^2} \end{vmatrix}$$

is negative semidefinite or negative definite. If the principal minors are $D_1 < 0$ and $D_2 = D > 0$, the determinant is negative definite and the function Φ is strictly concave. From the equations

$$S = H^1(Q_1) + H^2(Q_2) - \Sigma S_i^r$$

$$R_i = F^{i^{-1}}(Q_i)$$

$$S_i = F^{ri}(R_i^r)$$

$$R = \Sigma R_i + \Sigma R_i^r$$

$$U = G(S)$$

we have

$$U = G[H^1(Q_1) + H^2(Q_2) - F^{r1}(R_1^r) - F^{r2}(R - \Sigma F^{i^{-1}}(Q_i) - R_1^r)]$$

2. The procedure is to determine the elements of the Hessian determinant. Compare H. Siebert (1978a, p. 52 - 58).

PART II

MODELS WITH EXPLICIT ABATEMENT

In this part of the book we will analyze how the economy reacts to environmental policy and to what extent trade is influenced. Throughout this part we use the gross-emissions approach that explicity allows for abatement activities. The frame of reference is a two-sector model where pollutants are a joint output of production. In order to simplify the analysis we consider one resource only and consequently do not distinguish between capital and labour. The resource may be used in both production activities and in the abatement activities of the two sectors.

Chapter 3 analyzes how environmental policy will affect the closed economy, i.e. the allocation of resources, national income and relative price which, for a given autarky price of the foreign country, determines comparative advantage. In chapter 4 we consider the small-country case where the small country cannot influence the relative price and has to accept a given price from the world market. Here our interest is on the change of the initial trade equilibrium when environmental policy is introduced in the small country. Although the relative price remains fixed, allocation effects occur and the interesting question arises whether environmental policy will lead to a reduction in the gains from trade.

Chapter 5 analyzes the two-country case with p_{12} being endogenously determined and being influenced by the home country. The allocation effects, the problem of a reduction in the gains from trade, and the terms-of-trade effect are analyzed.

In chapter 6 we discuss the relationship between environmental quality and the gains from trade. It is argued that trade does not only lead to gains from trade in the traditional sense but may also be accompanied by a loss of environmental quality if the country exports the pollution-intensively produced commodity. Also, the incidence of environmental policy on the gains from trade is studied.

3. The Closed Economy

Chapter 3 analyzes which repercussions environmental policy will have in an autarky situation. The main interest is to study the effects of environmental policy on the allocation of resources, national income, and relative price. By deriving results on relative price we also receive information on alterations in comparative price advantage. Section 3.1 specifies the assumptions of the analysis. Then we study the profit maximizing factor demand conditions and how factor demand changes with alterations in the emission tax, assuming a constant relative price (section 3.2). Section 3.3 describes the structure of the two-sector equilibrium model with p_{12} being endogenously determined. The implications of the model are analyzed and interpreted in section 3.4 with 3.5 stressing the effects on relative price and comparative advantage. We specify conditions for an increase in resource use in abatement, for a reduction of resource use in the emission-intensively producing sector, for a decline in national income and for a rise in the relative price of the emission-intensively produced commodity. The final section summarizes the results and indicates possible extensions.

3.1 Assumptions

In addition to the assumptions A 2.1 - A 2.7 we now have to specify the behaviour of economic agents such as environmental policy makers, firms, and households. Also market equilibrium conditions have to be taken into account.

A 3.1 Environmental policy. Environmental policy instruments include moral suasion, subsidies, emission norms for individual firms and permit systems specifying emissions, locations, production or abatement technologies, licenses and emission taxes. We here assume that the government levies an emission tax p_S (in nominal terms) on net emissions S_i, with p_S being changed parametrically.

A 3.2 Profit maximization. Firms maximize profits and regard commodity prices p_i, factor prices p_R, and the emission tax p_S as given.

A 3.3 Consumer behaviour. Commodity demand is given by

$$Q_i^d = D^i(p_{12}, Y) \tag{3.1}$$

where $p_{12} = p_1/p_2$ is the relative price. Additionally, it could be assumed that quantities demanded also depend on environmental quality, i.e. if private goods are substitutes for environmental quality (air conditioning in a smog-region) or if they are complementary to it (binoculars and good visibility in beautiful setting).

A 3.4 National income. Income Y is defined from the production side. There are no savings. In order to close the model, we assume that the government spends the tax income received (i.e. emission taxes) in form of transfers to the households. Consequently disposable income of the households is identical to net national income at market prices and is defined as

$$Y = p_{12}Q_1 + Q_2 \tag{3.2}$$

Observe that Y includes transfers not explicitly shown and that p_{12} is consumers price and not producers price. If Y would be defined with respect to producers price $\tilde{p}_{12}$ emission taxes (and transfers) would appear explicitly on the right side of equation 3.2.

A 3.5 Market equilibrium. Markets must be in equilibrium. Consequently the resource constraint 2.7 must be read as an equality. Also commodity markets must be in equilibrium so that

$$Q_i = Q_i^d \tag{3.3}$$

3.2 Factor Demand for Given Commodity Prices

1. Factor demand by the profit maximizing firm is given by maximizing

$$L_i = p_i Q_i - p_R(R_i + R_i^r) - p_S S_i$$

$$\begin{aligned} \text{s.t. } & Q_i - F^i(R_i) \leq 0 \\ & H^i(Q_i) - S_i^p \leq 0 \\ & S_i^r - F^{ri}(R_i^r) \leq 0 \\ & - S_i + S_i^p - S_i^r \leq 0 \end{aligned}$$

where p_R denotes the resource price in nominal terms. Assuming that production takes place in both sectors, i.e. that we have a meaningful problem, and defining $p_{12} = p_1/p_2$, $p_{R2} = p_R/p_2$ and $p_{S2} = p_S/p_2$ the conditions for profit maximizing factor demand are given as

$$\begin{aligned} p_{R2} &= (p_{12} - p_{S2}H_Q^1)F_R^1(R_1) \\ p_{R2} &= (1 - p_{S2}H_Q^2)F_R^2(R_2) \\ p_{R2} &= p_{S2}F_R^{ri}(R_i^r) \end{aligned} \tag{3.4}$$

The firm will demand the resource R up to a point where the resource price is equal to the marginal value product of the resource (marginal productivity evaluated at the net price). Note that p_{12} is market or consumers price and that $p_{12} - p_{S2}H_Q^1$ (or $1 - p_{S2}H_Q^2$) indicates producers price, namely market price minus pollution generated by one unit of output multiplied with the emission tax. In abatement activities, the resource is demanded up to a point where $p_{R2}/F_R^{ri} = p_{S2}$, i.e. where the emission tax is equal to marginal costs of abatement[1]. Note that $1/F_R^{ri}$ is the first derivative of the input function in abatement (i.e. the inverse $R_i^r = F^{ri^{-1}}(S_i^r)$ to the abatement function) and denotes inputs needed per unit abated. Consequently p_{R2}/F_R^{ri} is marginal abatement cost.

2. Assume p_{S2} is changed parametrically. How is the allocation of resources affected? Consider the five equations 2.7 (resource constraint) and 3.4 (factor demand conditions) with the six variables p_{12}, p_{R2}, R_i, R_i^r and p_{S2} being changed exogenously. Assume for simplicity that p_{12} is fixed. Then equation 3.5 gives us a first answer on the direction of the allocation effects

$$\begin{bmatrix} a_1 & 0 & 0 & 1 \\ 0 & a_2 & 0 & 1 \\ 0 & 0 & -p_{S2}F_{RR}^{r1} & 1 \\ p_{S2}F_{RR}^{r2} & p_{S2}F_{RR}^{r2} & p_{S2}F_{RR}^{r2} & 1 \end{bmatrix} \cdot \begin{bmatrix} dR_1 \\ dR_2 \\ dR_1^r \\ dp_{R2} \end{bmatrix} = \begin{bmatrix} -Z_R^1 dp_{S2} \\ -Z_R^2 dp_{S2} \\ F_R^{r1} dp_{S2} \\ F_R^{r2} dp_{S2} \end{bmatrix} \qquad (3.5)$$

with $a_i = p_{S2}Z_{RR}^i - p_x F_{RR}^i > 0$ and $p_x = \begin{cases} p_{12} : & i = 1 \\ 1 \quad : & i = 2 \end{cases}$

We have the following results:

i) With environmental policy resources used in abatement will increase ($dR_1^r/dp_{S2} > 0$ with no condition attached to it).

1) The same condition holds in monopoly. Consequently emission taxes will work in monopolistic markets. H. Siebert (1976, p. 679-682)

Since this result does not require sector 1 to be the emission-intensive sector, we can also expect that abatement of sector 2 will increase.

ii) Resource use in the emission-intensive sector 1 will decline since we have

$$Z_R^1 > Z_R^2 \Rightarrow \frac{dR_1}{dp_{S2}} < 0.$$

iii) Resources will be shifted from production to abatement since $\Sigma dR_i/dp_{S2} < 0$ and consequently $\Sigma dR_i^r/dp_{S2} > 0$.

iv) Resource use in the less emission-intensive sector 2 may be reduced or may be increased. If it is reduced both sectors lose to abatement; if resource use in sector 2 increases, the emission-intensive sector 1 loses resources to abatement and to sector 2[1]. Among other factors, the reaction of Q_2 is influenced by $Z_R^1 - Z_R^2$ and the magnitude of p_{S2}. If sector 1 is relatively very emission-intensive compared to sector 2, there is a greater chance for Q_2 to rise. Also with a higher emission tax, there is a greater probability for Q_2 to rise.

v) Since resource use in production will decline and resource use in abatement will increase, net emissions will become smaller and environmental quality increases.

vi) Equation 3.5 implicitly defines a price isoquant $F(Q_1, Q_2 p_{R2}, \bar{p}_{12}, p_{S2}) = 0$ for alternative p_{S2} on the transformation space. The properties of that price isoquant are not easily established. We know that with increasing p_{S2} output of sector 1 will decline. Output of sector 2 may fall or increase. As can be seen from equation 3.1.7 in the appendix some conditions must be met to have $d(Q_1/Q_2)/dp_{S2} < 0$.

---

1) Assume we redefine sectorial resource use as $R_i = R_i + R_i^r$. Then we can only specify that as a sufficient condition $dR_i/dp_{S2} < 0$ if $a_2 \geq a_1$, $|F_{RR}^{r1}|_2 > |F_{RR}^{r2}|$ and $p_{12}F_R^1 > F_R^2$ which is equivalent to $Z_R^1 > Z_R^2$. On $a_2 \geq a_1$ compare below.

In diagram 3.1 we have assumed a fixed price $\bar{p}_{12}$. At point A, the emission tax is zero and no resources are used for abatement. If the emission tax is gradually increased the tangency solutions of the given price line will indicate lower levels of Q_1 and lower (or possible higher) levels of Q_2. For simplicity we have assumed increasing Q_2.

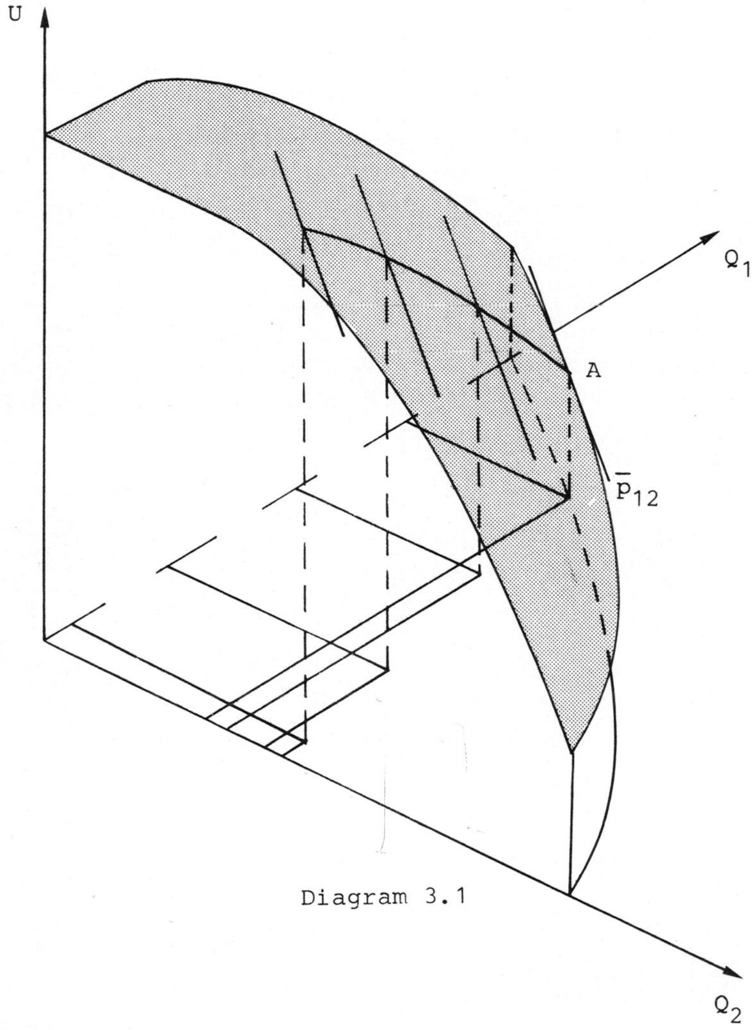

Diagram 3.1

3.3 Structure of the Two-Sector Equilibrium Model

1. Whereas in section 3.2 the commodity price p_{12} was given exogenously we now enlarge the model and let p_{12} be determined endogenously. The model consists of the 18 equations 2.1 - 2.7, 3.1 - 3.4 and the 17 variables S_i^p, S_i, S_i^r, Q_i, R_i, R_i^r, Q_i^d, p_{12}, Y and p_{R2}. The definition of Y in equation 3.2 states that total demand is equal to income, so that in a two-sector model the equilibrium condition for one of the product markets is redundant (Walras law) and should be omitted. By substitution the system can be simplified to

$$
\begin{aligned}
&F^1(R_1) = D^1(p_{12}, p_{12}F^1(R_1) + F^2(R_2)) && \text{(i)} \\
&p_{R2} = p_{S2}F_R^{ri}(R_i^r) && \text{(ii-iii)} \\
&p_{R2} = (p_{12} - p_{S2}H_Q^1)F_R^1(R_1) && \text{(iv)} \qquad (3.6) \\
&p_{R2} = (1 - p_{S2}H_Q^2)F_R^2(R_2) && \text{(v)} \\
&R = R_1 + R_2 + R_1^r + R_2^r && \text{(vi)}
\end{aligned}
$$

Total differentiation and substitution of 3.6vi into (i) - (v) yields

$$
\begin{bmatrix}
a_1 & 0 & 0 & 1 & -F_R^1 \\
0 & a_2 & 0 & 1 & 0 \\
0 & 0 & -p_{S2}F_{RR}^{r1} & 1 & 0 \\
p_{S2}F_{RR}^{r2} & p_{S2}F_{RR}^{r2} & p_{S2}F_{RR}^{r2} & 1 & 0 \\
b_1F_R^1 & -D_Y^1F_R^2 & 0 & 0 & -b_2
\end{bmatrix}
\cdot
\begin{bmatrix}
dR_1 \\ dR_2 \\ dR_1^r \\ dp_{R2} \\ dp_{12}
\end{bmatrix}
=
\begin{bmatrix}
-H_Q^1F_R^1dp_{S2} \\ -H_Q^2F_R^2dp_{S2} \\ F_R^{r1}dp_{S2} \\ F_R^{r2}dp_{S2} \\ 0
\end{bmatrix}
\qquad (3.7)
$$

The coefficients are defined as follows

$$b_1 = 1 - p_{12}D_Y^1 = D_Y^2$$

$$b_2 = D_p^1 + D_Y^1Q_1 < 0.$$

$b_2 < 0$ follows from Slutsky's rule. Let $D^1_{p_{comp.}}$ denote the pure substitution effect. We have

$$D^1_p = D^1_{p_{comp.}} - D^1_Y D^1 \text{ or } D^1_{p_{comp.}} = D^1_p + D^1_Y F^1(R_1) = b_2 < 0,$$

since the pure substitution effect is always negative. Note that equation 3.7 contains equation 3.5 as its subsystem.

2. The structure of the model is represented in diagram 3.2 including commodity markets, the resource market, and the environmental system. The political system compares the actual environmental quality with the desired environmental quality and sets an emission tax p_{S2}. The emission tax influences resources used in abatement processes R^r_i and increases emissions abated S^r_i. Also the emission tax affects producers price and resources used in production R_i and consequently output Q_i. Total demand for resources and supply determine resource price p_{R2} in the resource market, and the resource price has a feed back on abatement and production. Supply and demand determine relative price which has an effect on both production and consumption. Relative commodity price determines comparative price advantage. Quantities produced specify gross emissions S^r_i which together with abated emissions result in net emissions and environmental quality. Finally national income Y at market prices is given by quantities Q_i produced and relative price p_{12} and the receipts from the emission tax; in turn income determines commodity demand.

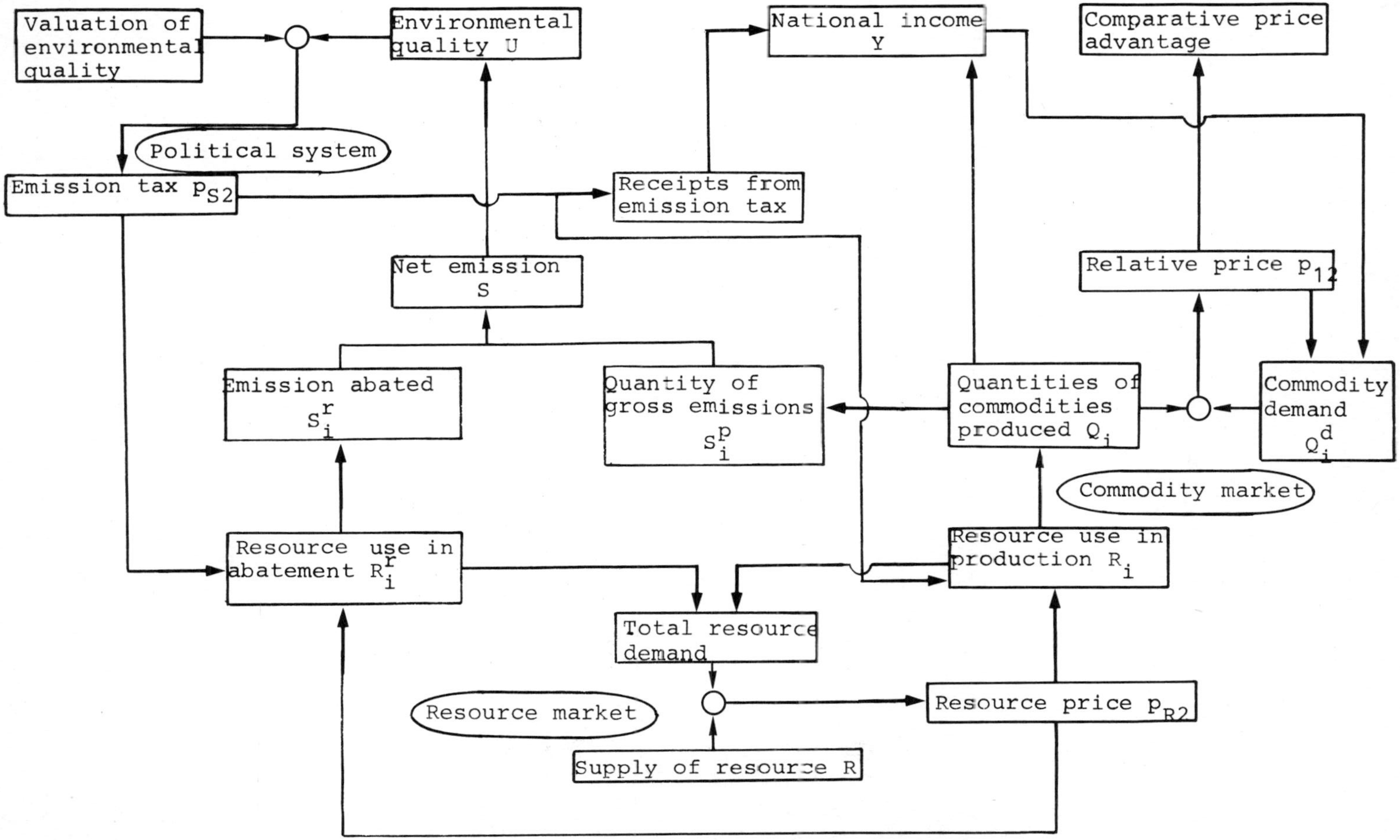
Valuation of environmental quality
Environmental quality U
National income Y
Comparative price advantage
Political system
Emission tax p_{S2}
Receipts from emission tax
Net emission S
Relative price p_{12}
Emission abated S_i^r
Quantity of gross emissions S_i^p
Quantities of commodities produced Q_i
Commodity demand Q_i^d
Commodity market
Resource use in abatement R_i^r
Resource use in production R_i
Total resource demand
Resource market
Resource price p_{R2}
Supply of resource R

Diagram 3.2

3.4 Effects of Environmental Policy in a Closed Economy

1. We are interested to know how environmental policy will affect the variables of the system. How does environmental policy influence commodity price p_{12}, the allocation of resources, production and abatement, consumer demand, environmental quality and national income? Equation 3.7 answers all these questions. Since relative price in a closed economy represents autarky price and since differences in autarky prices are an underlying cause of trade, our model also answers the question to what extent environmental policy affects comparative advantage. We have the following results.

2. For the determinant $\bar{\Delta} > 0$ we have as sufficient conditions

$$\left.\begin{array}{l} D_Y^2 \geq 0 \\ D_Y^1 F_R^2 + D_Y^2 F_R^1 \geq 0 \end{array}\right\} \Rightarrow \bar{\Delta} > 0 \qquad (3.8i)$$

In the following we assume that both commodities are not inferior, i.e. that their marginal propensities to consume are nonnegative ($D_Y^i \geq 0$). Note that this is a sufficient condition and that from equation 3.2.1 in appendix 3.2 other constellations will also guarantee $\bar{\Delta} > 0$, even if one of the commodities is inferior. Similarly the conditions to follow are sufficient conditions.

3. If both commodities are not inferior, resource use in the abatement of sector 1 will increase

$$D_Y^1 F_R^2 + D_Y^2 F_R^1 \geq 0 \Rightarrow \frac{dR_1^r}{dp_{S2}} > 0 \qquad (3.8ii)$$

This result holds without sector 1 being classified as the emission-intensive sector. Consequently, it must also hold for sector 2. An emission tax will increase the resource used in abatement and consequently augment the quantity of emissions abated.

4. Resource use in the emission-intensive sector 1 will be reduced if commodity 1 is not inferior.

$$\left.\begin{array}{l} D_Y^1 \geq 0 \\ z_R^1 > z_R^2 \end{array}\right\} \Rightarrow \frac{dR_1}{dp_{S2}} < 0 \qquad (3.8iii)$$

The non-inferiority of commodity 1 ensures that demand for the emission-intensively produced commodity does not react inversely: We can expect that national income will fall as a consequence of environmental policy (this will be shown below). If in this case $D_Y^1 < 0$, the declining income would increase the demand for the emission-intensively produced commodity and - this effect - necessitates some increase in R_1. $D_Y^1 \geq 0$ excludes this effect.

5. In the less emission-intensively producing sector 2, resource use may increase or decrease. The model allows both cases. Thus, in one case sector 1 and sector 2 lose resources to the abatement activity, whereas in the other case, sector 1 loses resources to sector 2 and the abatement activity.

6. Resource use in both production activities will be reduced ($\Sigma dR_i/dp_{S2} < 0$) and both abatement activities will be increased. Environmental policy shifts sector structure in favor of the abatement activities. Consequently, net emissions will be reduced and environmental quality will improve.

7. For the effect of environmental policy on national income we have

$$\left.\begin{array}{l} z_R^1 > z_R^2 \\ -\eta_{1p} > \alpha > 1 \end{array}\right\} \Rightarrow \frac{dY}{dp_{S2}} < 0 \qquad (3.8v)$$

with $\alpha = \dfrac{1}{1 - \dfrac{F_R^2}{p_{12}F_R^1}}$ and $\eta_{1p} = D_p^1 p_{12}/Q_1$

Net national product at market prices is affected by environmental policy in two ways:

- Resource use in production will decrease, so that for a given price p_{12} national income will fall (withdrawal effect).
- The emission-intensively produced commodity has to be revalued since market price must include the social costs of production. The revaluation-effect runs counter to the withdrawal effect.

National income will fall if the withdrawal effect outweighs the revaluation effect. This is the case, when the price elasticity of demand for the emission-intensively produced commodity is sufficiently large, i.e. $-\eta_{1p} > \alpha > 1$. (Condition 3.8v). A high price elasticity of demand for commodity 1 makes sure that the emission-intensively producing sector will lose large demand quantities, so that the revaluation effect will not be too high.

From the definition of α we have an interesting interrelation between demand conditions and the condition of emission intensity.

First, assume sector 1 is strongly emission-intensive[1) so that α is close to unity. Then the price elasticity does not have to be too high if the withdrawal effect is to be strong. A high emission-intensity of sector 1 means that production costs rise strongly in sector 1, relative price will rise, and sector 1 will lose demand quantities, even if the price elasticity of demand is not too high.

Secondly, if sector 1 is only "weakly" emission-intensive compared to sector 2, α is higher than unity, and the demand for the emission-intensively produced commodity must be very elastic for demand quantities to decline. In other words, in condition 3.8v a high price elasticity

1) Note that $p_{12}F_R^1 = p_{R2} + p_{S2}H_Q^1F_R^1$ and $F_R^2 = p_{R2} + p_{S2}H_Q^2F_R^2$, s that $H_Q^1F_R^1 > H_Q^2F_R^2$ implies that $F_R^2/p_{12}F_R^1 < 1$.

of demand for the emission-intensively produced commodity may be substituted by a strong emission-intensity of sector 1.

8. Structural policy will become an important issue in Western European countries in the future. It is therefore of interest to determine how environmental policy will influence sectoral structure. We have already shown that the production sectors will be reduced and the abatement activities will increase. Measuring sector structure s in terms of resources used in the two sectors, i.e. $s = R_1/R_2$, we know that $ds/dp_{S2} < 0$ if $dR_2/dp_{S2} > 0$, since $dR_1/dp_{S2} < 0$. This means that environmental policy will change sector structure to the disadvantage of the pollution-intensive sector structure. Since $dR_2/dp_{S2} < 0$ cannot be ruled out, we are not sure, however, whether demand conditions are such that the pollution-intensively producing sector 1 may expand with environmental policy relative to another sector. From 3.2.7 in the appendix it can be seen that sector structure measured in resource units will change in favour of sector 2 (for given p_{12}), if

$$R_2F_R^2p_{12}D_Y^1 > R_1p_{12}F_R^1D_Y^2 \tag{3.8vi}$$

Assuming identical sector weights in the initial situation, i.e. $R_1 = R_2$, we have as a sufficient condition for sector 1 to decline relatively that $p_{12}D_Y^1 > D_Y^2$ where the difference must be large enough to offset $p_{12}F_R^1 > F_R^2$.

3.5 Environmental Policy and Comparative Advantage

1. The change in relative price as a consequence of environmental policy is of central interest for the relationship between environmental policy and trade. One of the basic hypotheses for trade to take place is that a country has a comparative price advantage relative to the rest of the world. Let p_{12} indicate the price of the home country in autarky and let p_{12}^* denote the autarky price of the foreign country (rest of the world).

Then $p_{12} \lesseqgtr p^*_{12}$ indicates the existence of comparative price advantage with $p_{12} < p^*_{12}$ indicating a situation in which the home country has a comparative price advantage in commodity 1 and the foreign country in commodity 2 (note that $p_{12} = p_1/p_2$). If we can establish conditions under which environmental policy will affect relative price in a closed economy we have also found an answer as to how comparative price advantage is influenced.

2. As result we have

$$\left.\begin{array}{l} Z^1_R > Z^2_R \\ \\ a_2 D^2_Y (F^1_R)^2 p_{12} \geq a_1 D^1_Y (F^2_R)^2 \end{array}\right\} \Rightarrow \frac{dp_{12}}{dp_{S2}} > 0 \qquad (3.8iv)$$

3. Condition 3.8iv for a rise in the relative price can be split into two sufficient conditions[1].

First it is required, that the demand for the emission-intensively produced commodity 1 is less income elastic than for commodity 2, $D^2_Y \geq p_{12} D^1_Y$. Under the conditions specified above, national income will decline as a consequence of environmental policy. A high income elasticity of demand for the emission-intensively produced commodity would mean that sector 1 loses large quantities of demand, and this has a dampening effect on relative price. $D^2_Y \geq p_{12} D^1_Y$ guaranties that the demand for the emission-intensively produced commodity 1 is reduced less than the demand for commodity 2. This difference in the income effect of the two commodities represents a tendency for the relative price of the emission-intensively produced commodity to rise.

---

1) Note that $F^1_R p_{12} > F^2_R$ follows from $Z^1_R > Z^2_R$.

Secondly it is required that $a_2 \geq a_1$. From

$$a_2 \geq a_1 \quad \Leftrightarrow \quad \left|\frac{dR_1}{dp_{R2}}\right| > \left|\frac{dR_2}{dp_{R2}}\right|$$

we see that this condition[1)] specifies that (for given p_{12} and p_{S2}) sector 1 is more sensitive to changes in resource price than sector 2; we may also say that sector 1 is more dependent on the resource R. This condition can be interpreted as a rudimentary form of a factor-intensity condition in a one-factor model. We can expect that this condition unfolds into a set of factor intensity conditions in a multifactor model. As a result we have:

The relative price of the pollution-intensively produced commodity will rise if the marginal propensity for this commodity to consume is lower than the less pollution-intensively produced commodity and if the pollution-intensively producing sector depends heavily on the resource R.

3. Sufficient conditions for a rise in the relative price can partly substitute each other. Assume sector 1 is "very" pollution-intensive. Then the relative price of commodity 1 may rise even if it has a high income elasticity of demand and loses demand quantities with a decline in income. Or for identical pollution-intensities of both sectors, the relative price will rise, if sector 1 has a sufficiently smaller propensity to consume and thus loses a smaller quantity in demand requiring a higher adjustment in relative price. Finally, assume sector 2 heavily depends on resource R. Then p_{12} can rise nevertheless, if sector 1 is sufficiently more pollution-intensive or if sector 1 has a sufficiently lower income elasticity.

---

1) Differentiate the factor demand conditions 3.4 for given p_{12} and p_{S2} with respect to p_{R2}

$$\frac{dR_i}{dp_{R2}} = \frac{1}{-p_{S2}Z^i_{RR} + p_x F^i_{RR}} = -\frac{1}{a_i} \text{ with } p_x = \begin{cases} p_{12}: x = 1 \\ 1: x = 2 \end{cases}$$

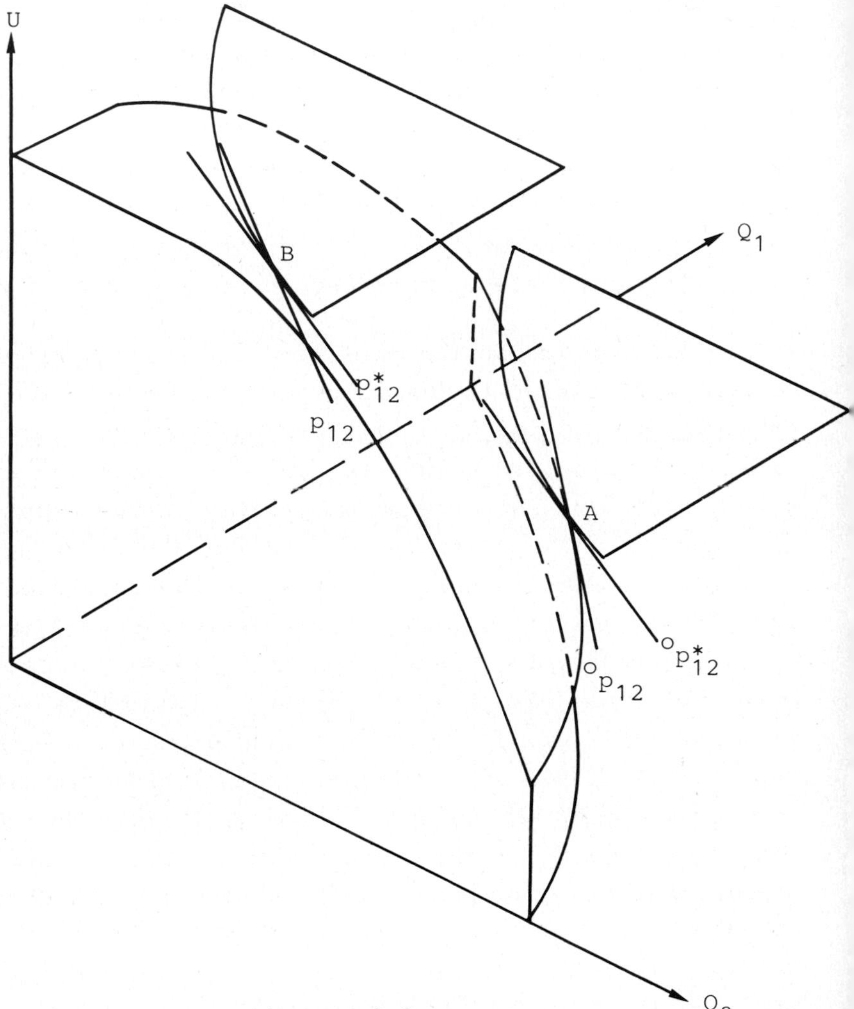

Diagram 3.3

4. $dp_{12}/dp_{S2} > 0$ indicates that environmental policy will under the conditions indicated affect the comparative price advantage of a country. Assume a country exports the pollution-intensively produced commodity 1. Then environmental policy will reduce the comparative price advantage of that country. This case is illustrated in diagram 3.3. Point A depicts the autarky situation of both countries. Assume the foreign country does not pursue environmental policy so that its transformation space can be represented by the traditional transformation curve. This curve lies horizontally in the U-Q_1-Q_2-diagram. At point A, the home country does not undertake environmental policy so that it is located on the lowest part of its transformation space.

The autarky prices differ with ${}^{o}p_{12}$ indicating the price prevailing in the home country and ${}^{o}p_{12} < {}^{o}p^{*}_{12}$ indicating a comparative advantage of the home country in the emission-intensive commodity 1. If the home country now introduces an emission tax, its relative price will increase, so that the p_{12}-line now is less steep. Since the autarky price of the foreign country has not changed, the comparative advantage of the home country has been reduced. There is now a lower potential for trade.

It is possible, that comparative advantage is completely offset by environmental policy, so that $p_{12} = p^{*}_{12}$ and no trade will take place. Also it is conceivable that due to $dp_{12}/dp_{S2} > 0$ the original situation ${}^{o}p_{12} < {}^{o}p^{*}_{12}$ may be reversed into $p_{12} > p^{*}_{12}$. In this case the home country has obtained a comparative advantage in the less emission-intensive commodity 2.

Assume contrary to diagram 3.3 that the home country has a comparative price advantage for the less emission-intensive commodity, i.e. ${}^{o}p_{12} > {}^{o}p^{*}_{12}$. If it undertakes environmental policy, its comparative price advantage will increase due to environmental policy.

Consider two countries with a different abundance of environmental services. Assume environmental policy is able to find the "correct" shadow price for environmental use so that $p_{S2} > p^*_{S2}$ adequately reflects the difference in endowment with p^*_{S2} indicating the emission tax of the foreign country. If all other factors influencing the autarky prices are identical in the two countries we have from $p_{S2} > p^*_{S2}$ that $p_{12}(p_{S2}) > p^*_{12}(p^*_{S2})$ which implies that the country abundant in environmental services will have a comparative price advantage and will export the pollution-intensively produced commodity.

In the real world where emission taxes are determined in the political process we may expect that emission taxes differ from "correct" shadow prices that incidently are not known. We can also expect that some basic factors determining environmental abundance or scarcity will eventually have an impact on the emission taxes. Environmental scarcity is determined by the following factors

- the assimilative capacity of the environment, i.e. the quantities of pollutants an environmental system can absorb without a deterioration in its quality
- the demand for assimilative services, i.e. the net emissions that are entered into the environment. For given environmental policy the quantity of emissions depends on production, pollution and abatement technology, consumption technology, industrial structure, level of development, product mix of the economy
- the evaluation of the environment as public good where such factors enter as level of income per capita since we can expect that with rising per capita income the demand for environmental quality increases density of population, regional agglomerations, value patterns with respect to nature and technology, etc.

3.6 Summary and Extensions

1. As results we have for the closed economy

Theorem 3.1 Under conditions 2.1 - 2.7, and 3.1 - 3.5 and for non-inferior commodities environmental policy will lead to an increase in abatement activities, a reduction in the output of the emission-intensively producing sector, an increase in relative price if the demand for the emission-intensively produced commodity is relatively less elastic than the other commodity and $a_2 \geq a_1$, and a decline in national income for high price elasticity of the emission-intensively produced commodity and/or a strong emission-intensity. The sufficient conditions for the changes discussed are summarized in diagram 3.4.

Theorem 3.2 Assume environmental policy is able to find the correct shadow price for environmental use. Consider two countries with $p_{S2} > p_{S2}^*$. This implies $p_{12}(p_{S2}) < p_{12}^*(p_{S2}^*)$ ceteris paribus. The country with an abundance in environmental services will have a comparative price advantage for the emission intensively produced commodity and will export that commodity.

2. The effects of environmental policy on comparative advantage will vary with the type of policy instrument used. Subsidies will not affect comparative advantage strongly since they principally will not implement the polluter-pays-principle and will not attribute all social costs to private units. Permit systems specifying locational requirements, production or abatement technology have an implicit price and can consequently be treated as an emission tax. The use of permits assumes that governmental agencies are able to specify the state of the art and consequently represent a very static approach to the pollution-problem. The auctioneering of pollution licenses has similar effects as emission taxes and it also has the advantage of determining a given quantity of emissions in advance. The auctioneering process, however, may represent an instrument for a large firm in a region to

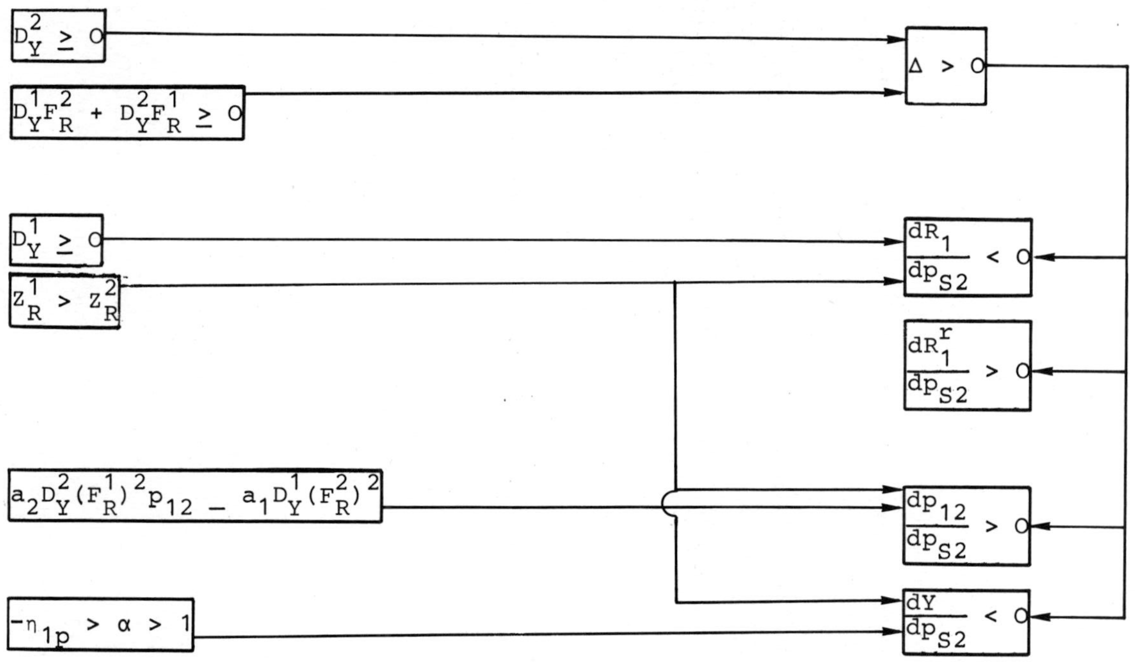

Diagram 3.4 Sufficient conditions

prevent other firms from entering the region or keeping the output of existing firms down to a certain limit which would imply that equal access to the regional labour market may be impeded[1].

3. From empirical studies we know that the emission-intensive sectors generally tend to be basic industries, often involved in the processing of raw materials (chemicals, pulp and paper, refineries); they tend to be energy-intensive and capital-intensive. Whereas the capital-intensitivity characteristic is welcome because it ameliorates possible negative employment effects, the two other traits create problems. Especially, countries do not wish their industrial basic to be too much affected. Consequently, there is some tendency to not apply PPP (the Polluter-Pays-Principle) too strictly.

4. In the allocation model used it is implicitly assumed that firms behave as if they were perfect competitors. Although it can be shown that the incentive function of emission taxes also exists in a monopoly[2], relative price, factor price and allocation will be affected if one of the sectors or both are monopolistic.

5. It is implicitly assumed in the model that industry size can vary easily without affecting the results. In the real world, we can expect large and small firms in an industry, and consequently environmental policy may affect the structure of an industry. It can be expected that if small firms are characterized by an older technology, they will have more problems than large firms. They may have greater difficulty in finding additional capital and in financing R & D for abatement technology. If concentration occurs, an effect on prices is likely.

1) On this argument see H. Siebert (1978b, p. 36-40)
2) H. Siebert, (1976 , p. 679-682)

6. In the real world we have not the one-product firm but multi-product firms. Within these firms we can expect similar allocation processes as in our model since in the long run the firm must revise its internal price system and charge environmental costs to those products that caused them. Temporarily or for reasons of product mix and marketing, however, the individual firm may deviate from an internal application of the PPP-principle to its different products.

7. One type of reaction a firm or an industry has at its disposal is relocation. Comparative price advantage is not only an indicator for potential trade, but it also denotes a location advantage. If the home country exports the emission intensively produced commodity, environmental policy will reduce its comparative price advantage. This also means that the location advantage of the home country is reduced. The effect of environmental policy can be so strong, that $p_{12} < p^*_{12}$ is changed into $p_{12} > p^*_{12}$ and the comparative advantage shifts to the foreign country. This means that the home country now will import the emission-intensive commodity that will now be produced in the foreign country. The change in trade flows is accompanied by a relocation of industry.

8. The model of chapter 3 is a static model assuming given technologies of production and abatement. Consequently it does not account for the most important function of emission taxes, to stimulate research for abatement and to implement improved abatement production technologies. If new technology will be developed, the allocation and price effects are less pronounced; also it is quite conceivable that environmental policy may have the side effect of improving production technology, incorporating better knowledge in vintage capital and thus increasing the comparative advantage. In France for instance, environmental policy seems to have the objective of improving the environment and at the same ti to modernize industry, thus preparing a long-run export potential and advantage of French industries. In a dynamic setting, we also would have to account for a new abatement

sector establishing a comparative advantage in a new line of products.

9. Finally, the model can be extended in two different ways. First, in equation 3.1 the demand for private commodities also depends on environmental quality if the commodities considered are substitutes or complements to each other. This aspect is introduced in chapter 9. Also our general-equilibrium model is partial in the sense that the emission tax p_{S2} is given exogenously as a policy parameter. The model could be enlarged by explicitly considering the political process in which the emission tax is determined. Also we could set a fixed target for environmental quality $\bar{U}$ and let a quasi--market determine the emission tax.

Appendix 3.1

The determinant of equation 3.5 is

$$\Delta = a_1\{a_2 p_{S2}(-F^{r1}_{RR} - F^{r2}_{RR}) + p^2_{S2}F^{r1}_{RR}F^{r2}_{RR}\} + a_2 p^2_{S2}F^{r1}_{RR}F^{r2}_{RR} > 0 \quad (3.1.1)$$

Define Δ_1 and Δ_2 as

$$\Delta_1 = (F^{r1}_{RR} + F^{r2}_{RR})a_2 p_{12}F^1_R - p^2_{S2}F^{r1}_{RR}F^{r2}_{RR}(Z^1_R - Z^2_R)$$

$$\Delta_2 = (F^{r1}_{RR} + F^{r2}_{RR})a_1 F^2_R + p^2_{S2}F^{r1}_{RR}F^{r2}_{RR}(Z^1_R - Z^2_R).$$

$$\frac{dR_1}{dp_{S2}} = \frac{\Delta_1}{\Delta} \quad (3.1.2)$$

$$\frac{dR_2}{dp_{S2}} = \frac{\Delta_2}{\Delta} \quad (3.1.3)$$

$$\frac{dR^r_1}{dp_{S2}} = \frac{\Delta_3}{\Delta} = -\frac{F^{r2}_{RR}}{\Delta}(a_1 F^2_R + a_2 p_{12}F^1_R) > 0 \quad (3.1.4)$$

$$\frac{dp_{R2}}{dp_{S2}} = \frac{p_{R2}}{p_{S2}} + p_{S2}F^{r1}_{RR}\frac{dR^r_1}{dp_{S2}} \quad (3.1.5)$$

$$\frac{dR_1}{dp_{S2}} + \frac{dR^r_1}{dp_{S2}} = \frac{1}{\Delta}\{a_2 p_{12}F^1_R F^{r1}_{RR} - a_1 p_{12}F^2_R F^{r2}_{RR} - p^2_{S2}F^{r1}_{RR}F^{r2}_{RR}(Z^1_R - Z^2_R)\} \quad (3.1.6)$$

$$\frac{d(Q_1/Q_2)}{dp_{S2}} = \frac{1}{Q^2_2\Delta}\{(F^{r1}_{RR} + F^{r2}_{RR})[a_2 p_{12}(F^1_R)^2 Q_2 - a_1(F^2_R)^2 Q_1] - p^2_{S2}F^{r1}_{RR}F^{r2}_{RR}(Z^1_R - Z^2_R)[F^1_R Q_2 - F^2_R Q_1]\} \quad (3.1.7)$$

$$\frac{dR^r_2}{dp_{S2}} = -\frac{F^{r1}_{RR}}{\Delta}(a_2 p_{12}F^1_R + a_1 F^2_R) > 0 \quad (3.1.8)$$

Appendix 3.2

$$\bar{\Delta}=-b_2\Delta-a_2D_Y^2(F_R^1)^2p_{S2}(F_{RR}^{r1}+F_{RR}^{r2})+p_{S2}^2F_R^1F_{RR}^{r1}F_{RR}^{r2}(D_Y^1F_R^2+D_Y^2F_R^1)$$

Define

$$\bar{\Delta}_1 = - b_2\Delta_1 + F_R^1(F_R^2)^2D_Y^1(F_{RR}^{r1} + F_{RR}^{r2})$$

$$\bar{\Delta}_2 = - b_2\Delta_2 + F_R^2(F_R^1)^2D_Y^2(F_{RR}^{r1} + F_{RR}^{r2})$$

$$\frac{dR_1}{dp_{S2}} = \frac{\bar{\Delta}_1}{\bar{\Delta}} \qquad (3.2.1)$$

$$\frac{dR_2}{dp_{S2}} = \frac{\bar{\Delta}_2}{\bar{\Delta}} \qquad (3.2.2)$$

$$\frac{dR_3}{dp_{S2}} = \frac{\bar{\Delta}_3}{\bar{\Delta}} \qquad (3.2.3)$$

$$\bar{\Delta}_3 = - b_2\Delta_3 - F_R^1F_R^2F_{RR}^{r2}(D_Y^1F_R^2 + D_Y^2F_R^1) \qquad (3.2.4)$$

$$\frac{dp_{12}}{dp_{S2}} = \frac{\bar{\Delta}_4}{\bar{\Delta}} \quad \text{with} \qquad (3.2.5)$$

$$\bar{\Delta}_4 = - D_Y^1F_R^2\Delta_2 - D_Y^2F_R^1\Delta_1$$

$$\frac{dY}{dp_{S2}} = \frac{1}{\bar{\Delta}}\{(F_{RR}^{r1} + F_{RR}^{r2}(F_R^1)^2(F_R^2)^2 + (b_2 - Q_1D_Y^1)(-p_{12}F_R^1\Delta_1 + F_R^2\Delta_2) - $$
$$- F_R^1\Delta_1Q_1\} \qquad (3.2.6)$$

$$\frac{d(R_1/R_2)}{dp_{S2}} = \frac{1}{R_2^2\bar{\Delta}}\{-b_2(R_2\Delta_1 + R_1\Delta_2) +$$
$$+ F_R^1F_R^2(F_{RR}^{r1} + F_{RR}^{r2})(R_2F_R^2D_Y^1 - R_1F_R^1D_Y^2)\} \qquad (3.2.7)$$

4. The Small-Country Case

Whereas in chapter 3 we considered a closed economy, i.e. the autarky situation, we now start with a trade equilibrium in the initial situation, so that we allow for exports and imports. In order to simplify the analysis, we assume in chapter 4 that the home country is small. This implies that relative price p_{12} is given for the home country. In chapter 5 this assumption will be relaxed. Section 4.1 specifies the assumptions. The condition of market equilibrium in the closed economy is now substituted by the balance of payments equilibrium. The model is developed in section 4.2 and its implications are discussed in section 4.3. We analyse the allocation effects of environmental policy in the home country, and the influence on trade flows.

4.1 Assumptions

In addition to the equations 2.1 - 2.5, 2.7, 3.1 - 3.4 we specify the model as follows.

A 4.1 Small country. The home country is small compared to the rest of the world so that after trade takes place the relative price p_{12} in the home country is determined in the world market.

A 4.2 Balance of payments equilibrium. The balance of payments of the home country must be in equilibrium. Define excess demand as

$$E_i = Q_i^d - Q_i \qquad (4.1)$$

with $E_i > 0$ denoting imports and $E_i < 0$ exports. Then the balance of payments (i.e. balance of trade) is defined as

$$Z = -(p_{12}E_1 + E_2).$$

Z denotes the balance in terms of commodity 2. It can easily be seen that this definition holds. Assume the home country exports commodity 1 and imports commodity 2, so that $E_1 < 0$ and $E_2 > 0$. Then we have $-p_{12}E_1 = X$ and $E_2 = M$ with X and M denoting export and import "value" in terms of commodity 2. Assume, on the contrary, the home country exports commodity 2 and imports commodity 1. Then $E_2 < 0$ and $E_1 > 0$ and we have $-E_2 = X$ and $p_{12}E_1 = M$.

The balance of payments equilibrium requires that

$$p_{12}E_1 + E_2 = 0 \qquad (4.2)$$

Equation 4.2 substitutes the equilibrium condition A 3.5 for the national commodity markets.

4.2 The General Equilibrium Model for the Small Country

In order to analyze how environmental policy in the small country influences the variables of the economy we use the

19 equations 2.1 - 2.5, 2.7, 3.1 - 3.4, 4.1 and 4.2 with the 18 variables S_i^p, S_i, S_i^r, Q_i, R_i, R_i^r, Y, Q_i^d, p_{R2}, E_1 and E_2, with p_{12} determined by the world market. The definition of Y states that the total demand is equal to income, and the balance of payments equilibrium requires that the excess demand of the economy expressed in terms of commodity 2 is equal to zero, so that in a two-sector-model the definition of E_2 is redundant and can be omitted. Substituting and differentiating with respect to p_{S2} we have

$$\begin{bmatrix} a_1 & 0 & 0 & 1 & 0 & 0 & 0 \\ 0 & a_2 & 0 & 1 & 0 & 0 & 0 \\ 0 & 0 & -p_{S2}F_{RR}^{r1} & 1 & 0 & 0 & 0 \\ p_{S2}F_{RR}^{r2} & p_{S2}F_{RR}^{r2} & p_{S2}F_{RR}^{r2} & 1 & 0 & 0 & 0 \\ F_R^1 D_Y^2 & -F_R^2 D_Y^1 & 0 & 0 & 1 & 0 & 0 \\ -p_{12}F_R^1 D_Y^2 & -F_R^2 D_Y^2 & 0 & 0 & 0 & 0 & 1 \\ 0 & 0 & 0 & 0 & p_{12} & 1 & 0 \end{bmatrix} \cdot \begin{bmatrix} dR_1 \\ dR_2 \\ dR_1^r \\ dp_{R2} \\ dE_1 \\ dE_2 \\ dQ_2^d \end{bmatrix} = \begin{bmatrix} -Z_R^1 dp_{S2} \\ -Z_R^2 dp_{S2} \\ -F_R^{r1} dp_{S2} \\ -F_R^{r2} dp_{S2} \\ 0 \\ 0 \\ 0 \end{bmatrix}$$

Note that equation 4.3 contains equation 3.5 as a subsystem.

4.3 Implications

In the following we assume that the home country exports the emission-intensive commodity 1 and imports commodity 2 in the initial situation. Although relative price is fixed and not influenced by the small country, environmental policy will affect the allocation of resources between the two sectors and between production and allocation. Also trade flows are affected. We have the following results.

With respect to the allocation of resources we have exactly the same results as in model 3.5. Resource use in both abatement activities will rise, resource use in the emission-intensive sector will fall, and in both production activities together it will fall. Resource use in the less emission-intensive sector may fall or increase.

From the results we can infer that it is relative price p_{12} together with p_{S2} that solely determines at which point on the transformation space the country produces so that the production point is completely determined once p_{12} and p_{S2} are fixed. In this case p_{R2} adjusts until equilibrium in the resource market is reached.

Demand conditions enter the picture only in so far as they determine which quantity of the commodities is consumed at home and which quantity is left for export. The balance of payments equilibrium then determines together with the given price p_{12} the quantities to be imported. Whereas p_{12} and p_{S2} determine the production point, the consumption point and consequently excess demand are determined by the demand conditions.

National income will fall (compare equation 4.1.5). This can be easily explained. Resources are withdrawn from production and less is produced (withdrawal effect). There is no revaluation effect as in the autarky case since p_{12} is given. Consequently national income falls.

For the change in exports and imports we have

$$\left.\begin{aligned} & z_R^1 > z_R^2 \\ & F_R^1 D_Y^2 + F_R^2 D_Y^1 > 0 \\ & a_2 p_{12} F_R^1 D_Y^2 > a_1 F_R^2 p_{12} D_Y^1 \end{aligned}\right\} \Rightarrow \frac{d(-E_1)}{dp_{S2}}, \frac{dE_2}{dp_{S2}} < 0$$

Assume sector 1 is emission-intensive[1] and $a_2 \geq a_1$. Then exports will decline if $D_Y^2 > p_{12} D_Y^1$, i.e. if commodity 1 has a lower income elasticity of demand. Note that with falling national income a low income elasticity of demand for the emission-intensive commodity implies that this commodity relatively does not lose too much home demand. Since home demand does not fall too strongly, but production of the commodity is reduced, exports must be smaller.

1) This is also equivalent to $p_{12} F_R^1 > F_R^2$.

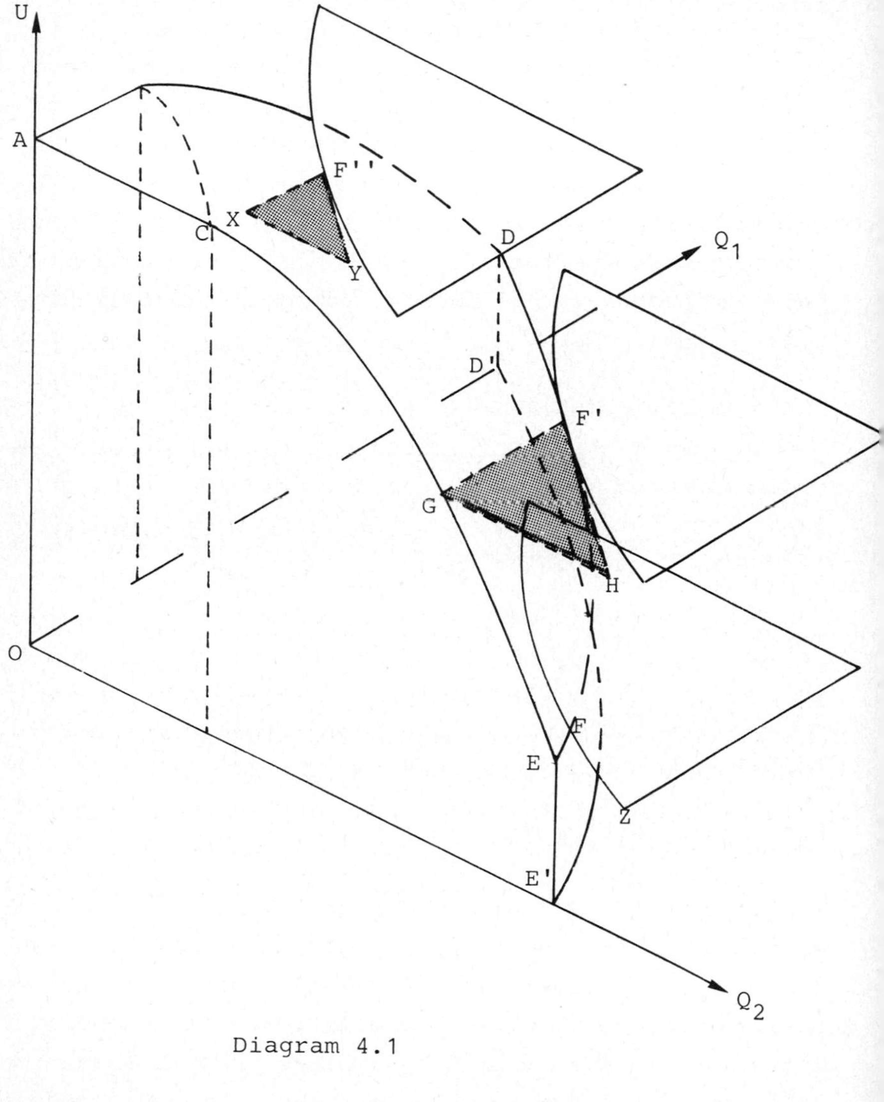

Diagram 4.1

We could also allow the special case that commodity 1 is inferior, i.e. $D_Y^1 < 0$ as long as $D_Y^2 > p_{12}D_Y^1$. With declining income, home demand for commodity 1 would rise in this case and exports would decline; $D_Y^2 > p_{12}D_Y^1$ makes sure that home demand for commodity 2 and consequently imports adjust appropriately.

Home demand for commodity 2 will decline if a positive income elasticity prevails, i.e.

$$\left.\begin{array}{l} Z_R^1 > Z_R^2 \\ \\ D_Y^2 > 0 \end{array}\right\} \Rightarrow \frac{dQ_2^d}{dp_{S2}} < 0$$

Diagram 4.1 illustrates the argument geometrically. The autarky situation is depicted by point F with no trade taking place and $p_{12} < p_{12}^*$. Note that the production block of the foreign country is drawn smaller in order not to overload the diagram. If trade takes place and no environmental policy is undertaken, the relative price of the rest of the world determines the equilibrium price (situation F'). Exports of the home country are indicated by GF' and imports by GH. If now the small country undertakes environmental policy, it will move up the transformation space along a price isoquant since p_{12} remains constant. In the new trade situation we consequently have the same relative price, but exports and imports will be reduced. The trade triangle will become smaller. We will come back to diagram 4.1 when we discuss the gains from trade in chapter 6.

Appendix 4.1

The determinant of equation 4.3 is identical to the determinant Δ of equation 3.5 as defined in 3.1.1 with $\Delta > 0$.

The solutions for resource use are

$$\frac{dR_1}{dp_{S2}} = \frac{\Delta_1}{\Delta}$$

$$\frac{dR_2}{dp_{S2}} = \frac{\Delta_2}{\Delta}$$

$$\frac{dR_1^r}{dp_{S2}} = \frac{\Delta_3}{\Delta}$$

with Δ_i as being defined by equations 3.1.2 - 4.

$$\frac{dE_1}{dp_{S2}} = -\frac{1}{\Delta}\{F_R^1 D_Y^2 \Delta_1 - F_R^2 D_Y^1 \Delta_2\} \quad (4.1.1)$$

$$\frac{dE_2}{dp_{S2}} = \frac{p_{12}}{\Delta}\{F_R^1 D_Y^2 \Delta_1 - F_R^2 D_Y^1 \Delta_2\} \quad (4.1.2)$$

$$\frac{dQ_2^d}{dp_{S2}} = \frac{D_Y^2}{\Delta}\{p_{12} F_R^1 \Delta_1 + F_R^2 \Delta_2\} \quad (4.1.3)$$

$$\frac{dp_{R2}}{dp_{S2}} = \frac{1}{\Delta}\{a_1 a_2 p_{S2}(-F_{RR}^{r1} F_R^{r2} - F_{RR}^{r2} F_R^{r1}) - p_{S2}^2 F_{RR}^{r1} F_{RR}^{r2}(a_1 Z_R^2 + a_2 Z_R^1)\} \quad (4.1.4)$$

$$\frac{dY}{dp_{S2}} = \frac{1}{p_{12}}\{p_{12} F_R^1 \Delta_1 + F_R^2 \Delta_2\} < 0 \quad (4.1.5)$$

5. The Two-Country Case

In this chapter we release the assumption of a given relative price. The home country no longer is a small country but it now affects the relative price in the world market. In addition to equations specifying production and demand conditions in the home country we now also have to specify production and demand conditions in the foreign country. Also we must identify equations that link the two countries together. In section 5.1 the assumptions are specified. In order to keep the model manageable we assume that environmental policy is undertaken in the home country only. The equilibrium condition for commodities now relates to the world market. The model is presented in section 5.2. Results with respect to the allocation of resources, national income in both countries, exports and imports, and relative price (i.e. the terms of trade) are derived in section 5.3. We specify the conditions for an increase in resource use in abatement and a decline in the emission-intensive sector, for a fall in national income of the home country and a rise in relative price. In section 5.4 we compare the results in the closed economy, small country and two-country case.

5.1 Assumptions

In addition to equations 2.1 - 2.5, 2.7, 3.1 - 3.4 and 4.1 we have:

A 5.1 No emission tax in foreign country. The foreign country does not undertake environmental policy so that $p^*_{S2} = 0$ where an asterisk denotes the variable of the foreign country. Consequently factor demand conditions in the foreign country are reduced to

$$p^*_{R2} = p^*_{12}F^{1*}_R \qquad \text{(i)} \qquad (5.1)$$
$$p^*_{R2} = F^{2*}_R$$

and no resources will be used in abatement, i.e. $R^{r*}_i = 0$. The other characteristics of the foreign country are

$$Q^*_i = F^{i*}(R^*_i) \qquad \text{(ii)}$$
$$Q^{d*}_i = D^{i*}(p^*_{12}, Y^*) \qquad \text{(iii)}$$
$$Y^* = p^*_{12}Q^*_1 + Q^*_2 \qquad \text{(iv)} \qquad (5.1)$$
$$R = R^*_1 + R^*_2 \qquad \text{(v)}$$

Also the emission function, the abatement function,the definition of net emissions and the damage function hold for the foreign country.

A 5.2 World market equilibrium. World market for commodity 1 has to be in equilibrium

$$E_1 + E^*_1 = 0 \qquad (5.2)$$

Observe that the budget restraint must hold for the world as a whole and for each individual country. From the budget restraint for the world

$$p_{12}E_1 + E_2 + p^*_{12}E^*_1 + E^*_2 = 0$$

we have due to $E_1 + E^*_1 = 0$, that $E_2 + E^*_2 = 0$, i.e. the world market for commodity 2 is in equilibrium. Equilibrium in the world market for commodity 1 ensures equilibrium in the world market for commodity 2 (Walras law) so that an additional equation for equilibrium in the world market for commodity 2 would be redundant.

Note that $p_{12}E_1 + E_2 = 0$, i.e. equilibrium in the balance of trade, is not asked for explicitly. From the budget restraint we have $Y = p_{12}Q_1^d + Q_2^d = p_{12}Q_1 + Q_2$, so that $p_{12}(Q_1^d - Q_1) + Q_2^d - Q_2 = p_{12}E_1 + E_2 = 0$ and the balance of trade is in equilibrium[1].

5.2 The Model

The system of equations 2.1 - 2.5, 2.7, 3.1 - 3.4, 4.1, 5.1 and 5.2 contains 23 equations and the 23 variables Q_i, Q_i^*, R_i, R_i^r, R_i^*, S_i^p, S_i^r, S_i, Q_i^d, p_{R2}, p_{R2}^* and p_{12}. Due to Jevons law of the indifference of prices we must have a common price in trade equilibrium so that we do not have to distinguish between p_{12} and p_{12}^*. Factor price, however, may differ between countries. Observe that production (emission and abatement technology) may differ between the two countries.

The model can be reduced to the following system of equations:

$$E_i = D^i[p_{12}, p_{12}F^1(R_1) + F^2(R_2)] - F^i(R_i) \qquad \text{(i,ii)}$$

$$-E_1 = D^{1*}[p_{12}, p_{12}F^{1*}(R_1^*) + F^{2*}(R^* - R_1^*)] - F^{1*}(R_1^*) \qquad \text{(iii)}$$

$$E_2^* = D^{2*}[p_{12}, p_{12}F^{1*}(R_1^*) + F^{2*}(R^* - R_1^*)] - F^{2*}(R^* - R_1^*) \qquad \text{(iv)}$$

$$p_{R2} = (p_{12} - p_{S2}H_Q^1)F_R^1(R_1) \qquad \text{(v)}$$

$$p_{R2} = (1 - p_{S2}H_Q^2)F_R^2(R_2) \qquad \text{(vi)}$$

1) If $p_{12}E_1 + E_2 = 0$ is introduced explicitly in the system of equations, one of the demand functions Q_i^d is redundant.

$$p_{R2} = p_{S2}F_R^{r1}(R_1^r) \qquad \text{(vii)}$$

$$p_{R2} = p_{S2}F_R^{r2}(R - R_1^r - \Sigma R_i) \qquad \text{(viii)}$$

$$p_{R2}^* = p_{12}F_R^{1*}(R_1^*) \qquad \text{(ix)} \qquad (5.3)$$

$$p_{R2}^* = F_R^{2*}(R^* - R_1^*) \qquad \text{(x)}$$

The system 5.3 contains ten equations and the ten variables E_i, E_2^*, R_i, R_1^r, R_1^*, p_{R2}, p_{R2}^*, p_{12} with p_{S2} being fixed as a policy parameter in the home country.

We now assume a change in the emission tax of the home country and analyze how the variables will change. Differentiating equation 5.3 totally with respect to p_{S2} we have[1)]

1) Equation 5.3i has been multiplied with p_{12} and added to 5.3ii in order to obtain 5.3i'
$-(b_2 + p_{12}b_1)dp_{12} + p_{12}dE_1 + dE_2 = 0.$
Similarly equation 5.3iii has been multiplied with p_{12} and added to 5.3iv.

$$\begin{bmatrix} a_1 & 0 & 0 & 1 & 0 & 0 & -F_R^1 & 0 & 0 & 0 \\ 0 & a_2 & 0 & 1 & 0 & 0 & 0 & 0 & 0 & 0 \\ 0 & 0 & -p_{S2}F_{RR}^{r1} & 1 & 0 & 0 & 0 & 0 & 0 & 0 \\ p_{S2}F_{RR}^{r2} & p_{S2}F_{RR}^{r2} & p_{S2}F_{RR}^{r2} & 1 & 0 & 0 & 0 & 0 & 0 & 0 \\ 0 & 0 & 0 & 0 & -p_{12}F_{RR}^{1*} & 1 & -F_R^{2*} & 0 & 0 & 0 \\ 0 & 0 & 0 & 0 & F_{RR}^{2*} & 1 & 0 & 0 & 0 & 0 \\ 0 & 0 & 0 & 0 & 0 & 0 & -b_2-p_{12}b_1 & p_{12} & 1 & 0 \\ -p_{12}D_Y^2F_R^1 & p_{12}D_Y^1F_R^2 & 0 & 0 & 0 & 0 & -b_2 & 0 & 1 & 0 \\ 0 & 0 & 0 & 0 & 0 & 0 & -b_2^*-p_{12}b_1^* & -p_{12} & 0 & 1 \\ 0 & 0 & 0 & 0 & -p_{12}[D_Y^{2*}F_R^{1*} + D_Y^1F_R^{2*}] & 0 & -b_2^* & 0 & 0 & 1 \end{bmatrix} \begin{bmatrix} dR_1 \\ dR_2 \\ dR_1^r \\ dp_{R2} \\ dR_1^* \\ dp_{R2}^* \\ dp_{12} \\ dE_1 \\ dE_2 \\ dE_2^* \end{bmatrix} = \begin{bmatrix} -Z_R^1 dp_{S2} \\ -Z_R^2 dp_{S2} \\ F_R^{r1} dp_{S2} \\ F_R^{r2} dp_{S2} \\ 0 \\ 0 \\ 0 \\ 0 \\ 0 \\ 0 \end{bmatrix} \quad (5.4)$$

In equation 5.4 the coefficients b_i^j with j denoting the home country and the foreign country are defined as

$$b_1^j = D_p^{1j} + D_Y^{1j} Q_1 < 0 \qquad \text{with } j = \text{country I, II}$$

$$b_2^j = D_p^{2j} + D_Y^{2j} Q_1 > 0 \qquad \text{with } j = \text{country I, II}$$

$b_1^j < 0$ follows from Slutsky's rule[1]. $b_2^j > 0$ results from the following. Observe that from $Y = p_{12}Q_1^d + Q_2^d$, we have $(p_{12}D_Y^1 + D_Y^2 - 1)dY + (Q_1 + p_{12}D_p^1 + D_p^2)dp_{12} = 0$ where the first bracket (Engel aggregation) and the second bracket (Cournot aggregation) are zero. $p_{12}b_1 + b_2 = Q_1(p_{12}D_Y^1 + D_Y^2) + p_{12}D_p^1 + D_p^2 = 0$ (Cournot aggregation). Consequently $b_2 = -p_{12}b_1$ and from $b_1 < 0$ it follows that $b_2 > 0$. A more intuitive argument is: In a two-commodity world, the two commodities must be substitutes. Consequently $D_p^2 > 0$. Also for our solutions we will assume $D_p^{ij} \geq 0$. Consequently $b_2^j > 0$.

Note that a subsystem of equation 5.4 is the equation 3.5, i.e. the allocation submodel for given commodity prices. This submodel is an element to all models discussed in part II of the book.

5.3 Implications

1. We are interested in the following problem. How does environmental policy in the home country affect the variables of the system? How will environmental policy affect sector structure and the allocation of resources in an open economy? How will the results for a closed economy be changed if trade is introduced? How will environmental policy influence the terms of trade?

---

1) Compare section 3.3.

2. As a sufficient condition for a positive determinant we have from equation 5.1.1 in appendix 5.1

$$D_Y^{ij} \geq 0 \Rightarrow \Lambda > 0 \qquad i = 1,2; \quad j = \text{country I, II} \qquad (5.5i)$$

i.e. the two commodities are not inferior in both countries. This condition is analogous to the conditions for the closed economy.

Note that in the two-country case, the noninferiority of both commodities guarantees stability of the world market. Assume that $dp_{12} \gtrless 0$ if $E_1^W = E_1 + E_1^* \gtrless 0$ where the reaction of p_{12} to excess world demand denotes a market characteristic. Stability in the world market is given if $\frac{dE_1^W}{dp_{12}} = \frac{dE_1}{dp_{12}} + \frac{dE_1^*}{dp_{12}} < 0$, i.e. if the Oniki-Uzawa-offer curves for both countries are sloped negatively. From the factor demand conditions we know that $dR_1/dp_{12} > 0$ and $dR_2/dp_{12} < 0$. From $b_1 = D_p^1 + D_Y^1 Q_1 < 0$ and $D_Y^1 \geq 0$ we have $D_p^1 < 0$. From $b_2 = D_p^2 + D_Y^2 Q_1 > 0$ and $D_Y^2 \geq 0$ we know $D_p^2 > 0$. Consequently we have $\frac{dE_1}{dp_{12}} = D_p^1 + \frac{dQ_1}{dp_{12}} < 0$ and in analogy $\frac{dE_1^*}{dp_{12}} < 0$.

3. With respect to the allocation of resources, our results are very similar to those already known from the other chapters. If the commodities are noninferior, resource use in the abatement activities will increase, and resource use will decrease in both production activities combined. As a consequence environmental quality will improve.

$$D_Y^{ij} \geq 0 \Rightarrow \frac{dR_i^r}{dp_{S2}} > 0, \quad \frac{\Sigma dR_i}{dp_{S2}} < 0 \qquad (5.5ii)$$

Resource use in the emission-intensive sector 1 ($Z_R^1 > Z_R^2$) will be reduced if the commodities are not inferior.

$$\left. \begin{array}{l} Z_R^1 > Z_R^2 \\ D_Y^{ij} \geq 0 \end{array} \right\} \Rightarrow \frac{dR_1}{dp_{S2}} < 0 \qquad (5.5iii)$$

In the less emission-intensively producing sector of the home country it cannot be specified that resource use will decline or increase. The model allows both cases. Thus, in one case sector 1 and sector 2 lose resources to the abatement activity, whereas in the second case, sector 1 loses resources to sector 2 and the abatement activity.

4. With respect to national income two different effects have to be distinguished: i) the withdrawal-effect will reduce national income since resources are withdrawn from production. For given $\bar{p}_{12}$, national income will decline (compare equation 5.1.12 in appendix 5.1). ii) The revaluation effect works in the opposite direction. The revaluation effect indicates the change in relative price due to environmental policy. In equation 5.5v below we specify conditions for the relative price to rise or the terms of trade to improve (if the home country exports the emission-intensively produced commodity). Although the revaluation effect is positive[1], we have sufficient conditions for a declining national income from 5.1.12i and ii in the appendix:

$$\left.\begin{array}{l} z_R^1 > z_R^2 \\ -\eta_{1p} > \alpha > 1 \end{array}\right\} \Rightarrow \frac{dY}{dp_{S2}} < 0 \qquad (5.5iv)$$

This result is identical to the one in the closed economy. If sector 1 is strongly emission-intensive (compared to sector 2), α is close to unity and the price elasticity of demand does not have to be much above 1 to let national income fall. Apparently, the strong emission-intensity of sector 1 is sufficient so that sector 1 loses large demand quantities. This, in turn, makes sure that the withdrawal effect outweighs the revaluation effect. If

1) Note that the revaluation (or terms of trade effect) as defined in equation 5.1.7 represents the first term in 5.1.11. Note that this term is positive.

sector 1 is only weakly emission-intensive (compared to sector 2), α is higher than unity, and the demand for the emission-intensively produced commodity must be very elastic for demand quantities to decline (and for a strong withdrawal effect).

5. Condition 5.5iv specifies the changes in relative price, in exports and imports and resource use in sector 1 of the foreign country.

$$\left.\begin{array}{l} Z_R^1 > Z_R^2 \\ a_2 > a_1 \\ D_Y^2 \geq p_{12} D_Y^1 \end{array}\right\} \Rightarrow \begin{array}{l} \dfrac{dp_{12}}{dp_{S2}} > 0 \\ \dfrac{dR_1^*}{dp_{S2}} > 0 \\ \dfrac{dE_1}{dp_{S2}} > 0 \\ \dfrac{dE_2}{dp_{S2}} < 0 \\ \dfrac{dE_1^*}{dp_{S2}} < 0 \end{array} \qquad (5.5v)$$

Assume $a_2 \geq a_1$, $Z_R^1 > Z_R^2$ and let the home country export the emission-intensively produced commodity. Also assume $D_Y^2 \geq p_{12}D_Y^1$, i.e. the demand for the emission-intensively produced commodity is less elastic than for the less pollution-intensively produced commodity 2. Then the exports of the emission-intensively produced commodity will decline. Note that $dE_1/dp_{S2} > 0$ implies $d(-E_1)/dp_{S2} < 0$ where $-E_1$ are positive export quantities. The relatively low income elasticity of demand for commodity 1 implies that with declining national income home demand will fall not too strongly (compared to commodity 2). Also we know that quantities produced will become smaller; consequently excess supply available for exports falls.

Under the same conditions 5.5v, imports will also fall. Home demand for commodity 2 is reduced with declining income due to the relatively high income elasticity for commodity 2. Although we do not know whether the quantities produced will increase or fall, the reduction in imports is compatible with the other results of the model.

Resources used in sector 1 of the foreign country will rise; less resources will be used in sector 2. Also excess demand of the foreign country for commodity 1 becomes smaller, since more of that commodity is produced there.

6. Relative price p_{12} which represents the terms of trade of the home country, will increase under condition 5.5v. $D_Y^2 \geq p_{12}D_Y^1$ will lead to a reduction of excess supply of commodity 1 in the home country since with declining income home demand does not fall too strongly and since production of the emission-intensively produced commodity is reduced. With positive income-elasticities of the foreign country, the terms of trade of the home country will improve.

From equation 5.1.7 in appendix 5.1, the terms of trade of the home country may worsen if $Z_R^1 < Z_R^2$, $a_2 < a_1$ and $D_Y^2 < p_{12}D_Y^1$. Let the home country export commodity 1; let commodity 2 be produced emission-intensively and let sector 2 be more heavily dependent on the resource. Then environmental policy will worsen the terms of trade of the home country, export quantities will increase, import demand will increase and the terms of trade will fall. In this case environmental policy will improve environmental quality, national income will increase.

7. In the foreign country, national income will increase (equation 5.1.13)[1]. Also sector structure is shifted in favour of sector 1. Since there is no environmental policy in the foreign country, i.e. p_{S2}^* is assumed to be zero, emissions will increase and environmental quality will decline.

---

1) Note that for the foreign country the factor demand conditions imply $p_{R2}^* = p_{12}F_R^{1*} = F_R^{2*}$.

8. Diagram 5.1 summarizes the sufficient conditions for the changes indicated.

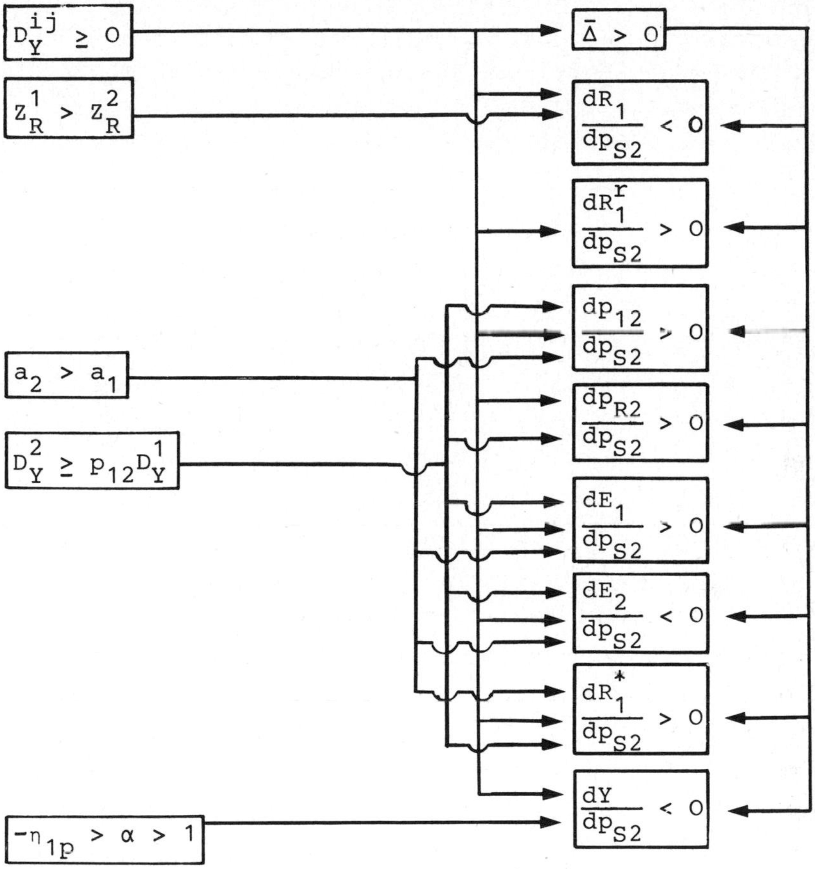

Diagram 5.1: Sufficient conditions

Diagram 5.1 points out the strategic role of some of the assumptions for the results. The assumptions imply non-inferiority of commodities, the relative emission-intensity of sector 1, higher sensitivity of sector 1 with respect to resource price, a lower income elasticity of demand, and either a high price elasticity for the emision-intensive commodity or a strong emission-intensity of sector 1.

9. In diagram 5.2 the argument is illustrated geometrically. The concave transformation space of the home country is given by OADE. The production block of the foreign country is given by XYZ. It is assumed for simplicity that the foreign country does not undertake environmental policy. The initial trade equilibrium is point F where the production block of the foreign country is tangent to the transformation space of the home country.

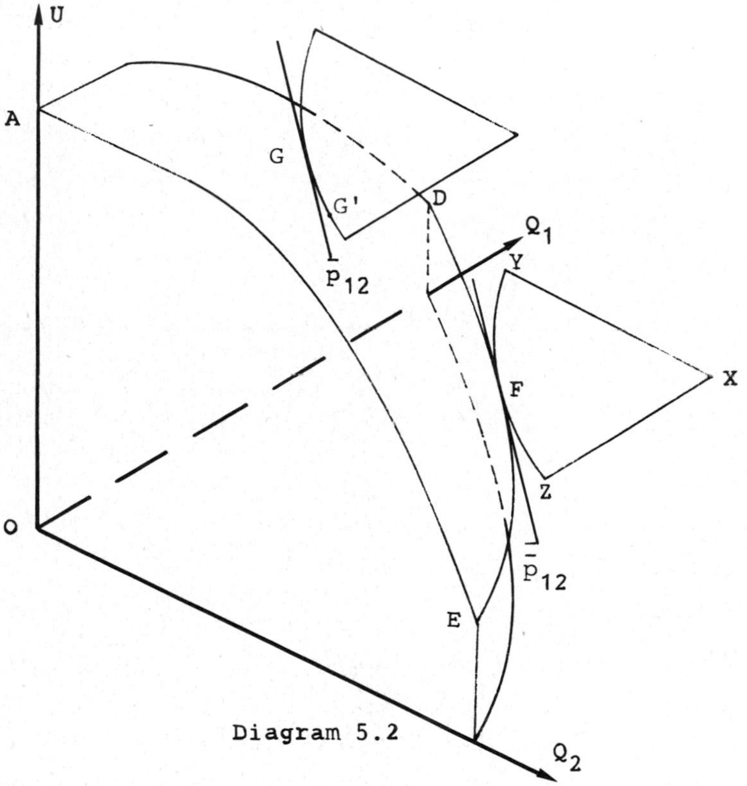

Diagram 5.2

If the home country increases the emission tax, environmental quality will be improved, and income will be reduced for given $\bar{p}_{12}$. This effect is illustrated by a movement from F to G. The terms of trade effect is illustrated by a movement from G to G', so that the overall change stemming from environmental policy can be split into a withdrawal effect and a terms of trade effect. Whereas the withdrawal effect reduces Q_1, ΣR_i, and increases ΣR_i^r and improves environmental policy, the terms of trade effect improves the terms of trade and changes sectoral structure in favour of the pollution-intensively produced commodity 1. From our analysis we also know that under the conditions specified, the new trade equilibrium at G' is associated with a lower national income, a smaller production quantity of Q_1 (compared to F), and smaller export and import quantities. The trade triangle associated with point G' (not drawn in the diagram) is smaller than in the original situation F (not drawn). In the foreign country, the new terms of trade require an increased specialization towards commodity Q_1. This is due to the fact that environmental policy in the home country reduces the home country's comparative advantage for its export commodity 1 (which is produced pollution-intensively). Consequently, environmental quality in the foreign country will be reduced.

5.4 Comparison of the Implications

The reader may have noticed that the models presented in this part have some elementary subsystems as a common element. It is therefore not surprising that similar sufficient conditions arise for some of the results. It seems worth while to compare the main conditions for the different cases.

In table 5.1 we distinguish the closed economy (autarky), the small country, and the two-country case. It can be seen that some conditions hold for all cases. For instance, the non-inferiority of the commodities ensures that the determinants of the different models are positive. Also $z_R^1 > z_R^2$ is a relevant condition for resource use of the pollution-intensively producing sector 1 to decline. The condition $-\eta_{1p} > \alpha > 1$ holds for the decline of national income in the closed economy (with variable p_{12}) and in the two-country case. Also, in both cases, the condition for an increase in relative price is identical.

cases / variables	closed economy 1 a constant p_{12}	 b variable p_{12}	small country 2	two country cas 3
$\Delta, \bar{\Delta}, \Lambda > 0$	n. c.	$D_Y^i \geq 0$	Identical to case 1 a	$D_Y^{ij} \geq 0$
$dR_1/dp_{S2} < 0$	$Z_R^1 > Z_R^2$	$Z_R^1 > Z_R^2$ $D_Y^i \geq 0^{x)}$		$Z_R^1 > Z_R^2$ $D_Y^{ij} \geq 0^{x)}$
$dR_1^r/dp_{S2} > 0$	n. c.	$D_Y^i \geq 0^{x)}$		$D_Y^{ij} \geq 0^{x)}$
$\Sigma dR_i/dp_{S2} < 0$	n. c.	$D_Y^i \geq 0^{x)}$		$D_Y^{ij} \geq 0^{x)}$
$dY/dp_{S2} < 0$	n. c.	$Z_R^1 > Z_R^2$ $-\eta_{1p} > \alpha > 1$		Identical to case 1 b
$dQ_2^d/dp_{S2} < 0$			$Z_R^1 > Z_R^2$ $D_Y^2 > 0^{x)}$	
$d(-E_1)/dp_{S2}$ dE_2/dp_{S2} dE_1^*/dp_{S2} $dR_1^*/d(-p_{S2})$ < 0	–	–	$Z_R^1 > Z_R^2$ $D_Y^i \geq 0$ $D_Y^2 > p_{12} D_Y^1$ $a_2 > a_1$	Identical to case 2
$dp_{12}/dp_{S2} > 0$	-	$Z_R^1 > Z_R^2$ $D_Y^i \geq 0$ $D_Y^2 \geq p_{12} D_Y^1$ $a_2 > a_1$	-	Identical to case 1 b

n. c.: no condition. Result holds in any case.

x) : Reprinted, although already required for a positive determinant.

Table 5.1: Comparison of results.

Theorem 5.1: Let the assumptions describing the two-sector economy of chapters 2 - 5 hold. Assume non-inferior commodities. Assume sector 1 is the emission-intensively producing sector. Then environmental policy will reduce resources used in the emission-intensively producing sector, and in both production activities. Resource use in abatement will increase. This holds for the closed economy, the small-country and the two-country case. For a given relative commodity price national income will decline. If the relative price is variable, national income will decline if either the emission-intensity of a sector is relatively high or if it has a high price elasticity of demand. If the demand for the emission-intensively produced commodity is less income elastic than for the other commodity and if $a_2 > a_1$ (sector 1 is "dependent" on the resource R) the relative price emission-intensively produced commodity will rise and exports as well as imports of the home country will fall.

Appendix 5.1.

Define expressions Δ, Δ_1, Δ_2 and Δ_3 as in appendix 3.1. Define the following expressions as

$$M = (b_1 + b_1^*)(p_{12}F_{RR}^{1*} + F_{RR}^{2*}) + (D_Y^{2*}F_R^{1*} + D_Y^{1*}F_R^{2*})F_R^{1*}$$

$$D_Y^{ij} \geq 0 \quad \Rightarrow M > 0 \qquad\qquad i = 1,2;\ j = I,II$$

$$L = F_R^1 F_R^2 (p_{12}F_{RR}^{1*} + F_{RR}^{2*})(F_{RR}^{r1} + F_{RR}^{r2}) > 0$$

$$K = p_{S2}^2 F_{RR}^{r1} F_{RR}^{r2}(D_Y^1 F_R^2 + D_Y^2 F_R^1)(Z_R^1 - Z_R^2) -$$
$$- (F_{RR}^{r1} + F_{RR}^{r2})(a_2 D_Y^2 p_{12}(F_R^1)^2 - a_1 D_Y^1 (F_R^2)^2)$$

$$\left.\begin{array}{l} Z_R^1 > Z_R^2 \\ a_2 > a_1 \\ D_Y^2 \geq p_{12}D_Y^1 \end{array}\right\} \Rightarrow K > 0$$

Then we have the following solutions

$$\Lambda = \Delta M + F_R^1\{p_{S2}^2 F_{RR}^{r1} F_{RR}^{r2}(D_Y^2 F_R^1 + D_Y^1 F_R^2) - - D_Y^2 F_R^1 p_{S2}(F_{RR}^{r1} + F_{RR}^{r2})\} \tag{5.1.1}$$

$$\frac{dR_1}{dp_{S2}} = \frac{1}{\Lambda}\{M\Delta_1 - D_Y^1 F_R^2 L\} \tag{5.1.2}$$

$$\frac{dR_2}{dp_{S2}} = \frac{1}{\Lambda}\{M\Delta_2 - D_Y^2 F_R^1 L\} \tag{5.1.3}$$

$$\frac{dR_1^r}{dp_{S2}} = \frac{1}{\Lambda}\{M\Delta_3 - F_R^1(D_Y^1 F_R^2 + D_Y^2 F_R^1)(p_{12}F_{RR}^{1*} + F_{RR}^{2*}) (Z_R^1 + p_{R2}/p_{S2})\} \tag{5.1.4}$$

$$\frac{dp_{R2}}{dp_{S2}} = \frac{1}{\Lambda}\{M[p_{S2}^2 F_{RR}^{r1} F_{RR}^{r2}(a_2 Z_R^1 - a_1 Z_R^2) - a_1 a_2 p_{R2}(F_{RR}^{r1} + F_{RR}^{r2})] - F_R^1(p_{12}F_{RR}^{1*} + F_{RR}^{2*})[p_{S2}^2 F_{RR}^{r1} F_{RR}^{r2}(D_Y^1 F_R^2 + D_Y^2 F_R^1)Z_R^2 - D_Y^2 F_R^1 a_2 p_{R2}(F_{RR}^{r1} + F_{RR}^{r2})]\} \tag{5.1.5}$$

$$\frac{dR_1^*}{dp_{S2}} = F_R^{1*}\frac{R}{\Lambda} \qquad (5.1.6)$$

$$\frac{dp_{12}}{dp_{S2}} = -(p_{12}F_{RR}^{1*} + F_{RR}^{2*})\frac{K}{\Lambda} \qquad (5.1.7)$$

$$\frac{dE_1}{dp_{S2}} = \{b_1^*(p_{12}F_{RR}^{1*} + F_{RR}^{2*}) + (D_Y^{1*}F_R^{2*} + D_Y^{2*}F_R^{1*})\}\frac{K}{\Lambda} \qquad (5.1.8)$$

$$\frac{dE_2}{dp_{S2}} = -\{p_{12}M + b_2(p_{12}F_{RR}^{1*} + F_{RR}^{2*})\}\frac{K}{\Lambda} \qquad (5.1.9)$$

$$\frac{dE_2^*}{dp_{S2}} = -\{(p_{12}b_1 + b_2 + p_{12}b_1^*)(p_{12}F_{RR}^{1*} + F_{RR}^{2*}) + p_{12}F_R^{1*}(D_Y^{2*}F_R^{1*} + D_Y^{1*}F_R^{2*})\}\frac{K}{\Lambda} \qquad (5.1.10)^{1)}$$

$$\frac{dY}{dp_{S2}} = \frac{1}{\Lambda}\{-Q_1(p_{12}F_{RR}^{1*} + F_{RR}^{2*})K + M(p_{12}F_R^1\Delta_1 + F_R^2\Delta_2) - F_R^1F_R^2L\} \qquad (5.1.11)$$

$$\left(\frac{dY}{dp_{S2}}\right)_{\overline{p}_{12}} = \frac{1}{\Lambda}\{M(p_{12}F_R^1\Delta_1 + F_R^2\Delta_2) - F_R^1F_R^2L\} < 0 \qquad (5.1.12)$$

due to

$$Z_R^1 > Z_R^2 \Rightarrow p_{12}F_R^1\Delta_1 + F_R^2\Delta_2 < 0$$

Inserting the expressions for Δ_1, Δ_2, K, L, M we have a sufficient condition for $dY/dp_{S2} < 0$ (assuming $D_Y^{ij} \geq 0$ (which implies $\overline{\Delta} > 0$) and $Z_R^1 > Z_R^2$):

$$(p_{12}F_{RR}^{1*} + F_{RR}^{2*})(F_{RR}^{r1} + F_{RR}^{r2})a_2p_{12}(F_R^1)^2[Q_1D_Y^2 + (b_1 + b_1^*)p_{12}] < 0$$

or

$$-\eta_{1p} = \frac{p_{12}D_p^1}{Q_1} > 1 \qquad (5.1.12i)$$

and

1) Note that $p_{12}b_1 + b_2 = 0$

$$(Z_R^1 - Z_R^2)p_{S2}F_{RR}^{r1}F_{RR}^{r2}\{(p_{12}F_{RR}^{1*} + F_{RR}^{2*})[- Q_1(D_Y^2F_R^1 + D_Y^1F_R^2)$$

$$- (b_1 + b_2)(p_{12}F_R^1 - F_R^2)] - F_R^{1*}(D_Y^{2*}F_R^{1*} + D_Y^{1*}F_R^{2*})$$

$$(p_{12}F_R^1 - F_R^2)\} < 0$$

or - as sufficient condition - the bracketed term [ ] must be positive. Using $D_Y^2 = 1 - p_{12}D_Y^1$ and $b_1 = D_p^1 + D_Y^1Q_1$ we have as a sufficient condition

$$-\eta_{1p} = \frac{p_{12}D_p^1}{Q_1} > \alpha = \frac{1}{1 - \dfrac{F_R^2}{p_{12}F_R^1}} \qquad (5.1.12ii)$$

$$\frac{dY^*}{dp_{S2}} = \frac{1}{\Lambda}\{- Q_1^*(p_{12}F_{RR}^{1*} + F_{RR}^{2*}) + F_R^{1*}(p_{12}F_R^{1*} - F_R^{2*})\} \qquad (5.1.13)$$

6. Environmental Quality and the Gains from Trade

When countries trade, they expect gains from trade. When a country exports the emission-intensively produced commodity it will experience a deterioration of its environmental quality. Consequently the overall gains from trade will be smaller than traditionally assumed. What are the gains from trade if environmental quality is explicitly considered in the welfare function? Section 6.1 develops the concept of traditional gains from trade with environmental quality not being taken into account. In section 6.2 we analyse how trade affects environmental quality if a country is opened up for trade. In section 6.3 an initial trade equilibrium is assumed and we study how environmental policy of the home country will affect the net gains from trade, including environmental repercussions. A result is derived that specifies how the emission-tax should be set in an open economy. In section 6.4 we look at the adjustment processes in the foreign country and the "pollute-thy-neighbour-via-trade-theses". Finally (6.5), some thoughts on equalizing tendencies in the emission tax are added.

6.1 The Traditional Gains from Trade

1. The basic motivation for countries to engage in trade is that trade is in the interest of individuals and of countries. The interest of individuals is shown as follows. For the individual consumer it is rational to import commodity 2 from abroad if ${}^{o}p_2 > {}^{o}p_2^{*}w$ where ${}^{o}p_i$ denote autarky prices and w is the exchange rate ($ per unit of foreign currency). Such an absolute price advantage indicates that the product can be supplied by the foreign country at a lower price. If with respect to commodity 1 we have ${}^{o}p_1 < {}^{o}p_1^{*}w$, individuals of the foreign country will demand commodity 2. Assuming that demand for foreign currency arises from import demand and that the supply of foreign currency stems from exports and assuming stability of the foreign exchange market, we can show that the exchange rate will be determined in the autarky price range

$$\frac{{}^{o}p_1}{{}^{o}p_1^{*}} < w < \frac{{}^{o}p_2}{{}^{o}p_2^{*}}$$

from which we have ${}^{o}p_{12} = \dfrac{{}^{o}p_1}{{}^{o}p_2} < \dfrac{{}^{o}p_1^{*}}{{}^{o}p_2^{*}} = {}^{o}p_{12}^{*}$

Consequently the principle of comparative advantage can be interpreted as expressing individual rationality.

2. It can also be shown that trade is in the interest of an individual country. Whereas in the closed economy the consumption point cannot lie outside the transformation curve, trade permits a consumption point outside the production possibility curve. This means that in a trade-situation a country can consume more commodities than in autarky. As Ricardo put it: "It is quite as important to the happiness of mankind, that our enjoyments should be increased by the better distribution of labour, by each country producing those commodities for which by its situation, its climate, and its other natural or artificial advantages it is adapted, and by their exchanging them for the commodities of other

countries...".[1] The division of labour, or specialization on the product being intensively produced with the relatively abundant factor of production leads to welfare gains for the individual country.

3. Assume a welfare function

$$W = W(Q_1^d + Q_2^d) \tag{6.1}$$

The change in welfare is given by

$$dW = W_{Q_2^d} \left(\frac{W_{Q_1^d}}{W_{Q_2^d}} dQ_1^d + dQ_2^d \right)$$

In the situation after trade we know that the relation of marginal utilities correspond to the relative price, i.e. $W_{Q_1^d}/W_{Q_2^d} = p_{12}$. Note that we here consider the price of the situation after trade since marginal utilities, i.e. the evaluation of the consumption bundle, also relate to the new situation. Substitute $Q_i^d = E_i + Q_i$ and take into account that from $p_{12}E_1 + E_2 = 0$ we have $p_{12}dE_1 + E_1dp_{12} + dE_2 = 0$ with $E_1 = 0$, since there is no trade in the initial situation. This simplifies our expression to

$$dW = W_{Q_2^d} \left(p_{12}dQ_1 + dQ_2\right) \tag{6.1i}$$

Assuming a positive marginal utility of commodity 2, $W_{Q_2^d} > 0$, we have as a condition for gains from trade

$$p_{12}dQ_1 + dQ_2 > 0 \quad \Rightarrow \quad dW > 0 \tag{6.1ii}$$

4. For the interpretation of equation 6.1ii we have to distinguish whether $dQ_1 \gtrless 0$. Assume $dQ_1 > 0$, then the condition for gains from trade is (compare diagram 6.1):

$$tg\beta = p_{12} > -\frac{dQ_2}{dQ_1} = tg\alpha \qquad \Rightarrow \qquad dW > 0 \tag{6.1iii}$$

Welfare will increase from opening up a country for trade, i.e. we have gains from trade, if the relative price is higher than the marginal rate of transformation. If condition 6.1iii

---

1) D.Ricardo (1817, p.153)

is given, the optimum condition $p_{12} = -dQ_2/dQ_1$ is not fulfilled and welfare may be increased by moving the economy towards the optimum.

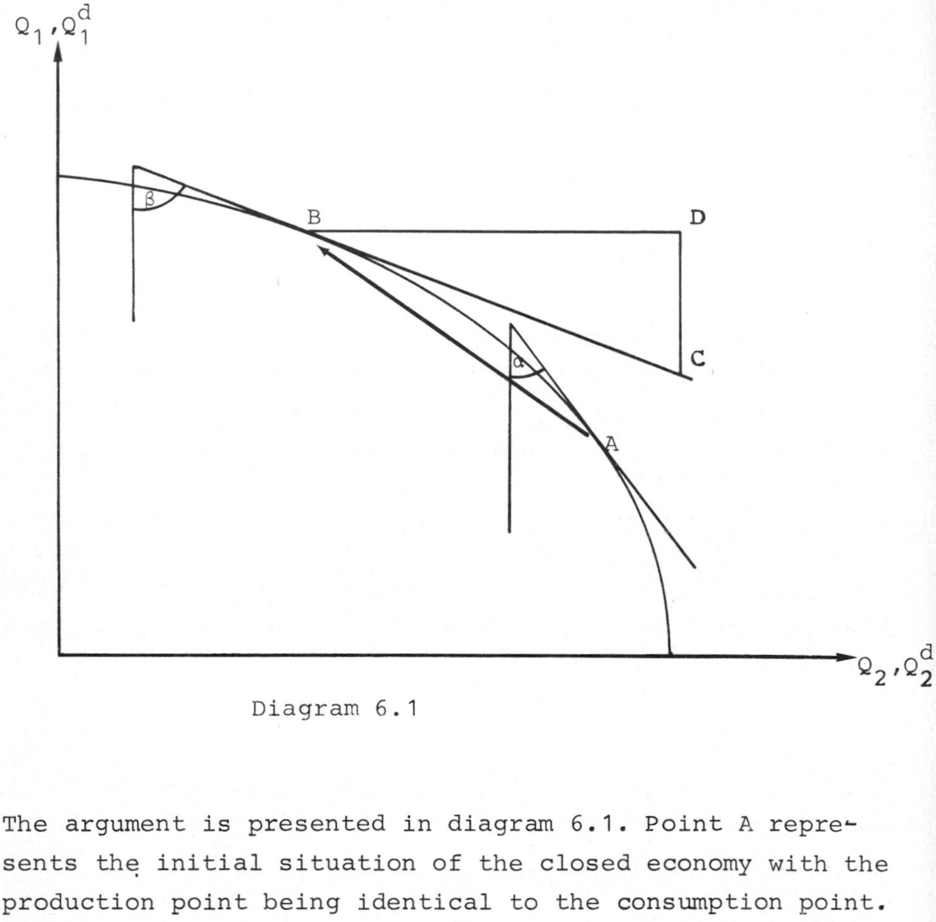

Diagram 6.1

The argument is presented in diagram 6.1. Point A represents the initial situation of the closed economy with the production point being identical to the consumption point. The movement AB along the transformation curve denotes the specialization of the country after trade with $dQ_1 > 0$ and due to the negative marginal rate of transformation $dQ_2 < 0$. The country produces at B but consumes at C with CD exports and BD imports. The consumption point C lies outside the transformation curve. If the production point lies below B, the country has not yet reached its optimum, it still can increase its welfare. Assume for instance the country produce in A, so that $-dQ_2/dQ_1(A) = {}^op_{12}$ where ${}^op_{12}$ denotes the autarky price. Then $p_{12} < -dQ_2/dQ_1(A) = {}^op_{12}$ denotes the well-known condition for trade to take place.

5. If $dQ_1 < 0$ and $dQ_2 > 0$ we have as condition $p_{12} < -dQ_2/dQ_1$ and a diagram analogous to 6.1 may be used.

6.2 Gains from Trade and Environmental Losses

1. Trade like other fields of economic theory so far has not taken into account environmental quality. Does this imply that the results on the welfare gains from trade have to be revised? Assume a two-commodity world with commodity 1 being produced emission-intensively. Let the home country have a comparative price advantage in commodity 1 and - after trade has taken place - let the home country specialize in the production of the emission-intensively produced commodity. As a result of trade then emissions will increase and, with no environmental policy taking place, environmental quality in the home country will decline. Environmental deterioration will reduce the overall benefits to society from trade, and a priori, it cannot be ruled out that the environmental losses may overcompensate the conventional gains from trade.

Consider the situation described above. The welfare function must now be defined as

$$W = W(Q_1^d, Q_2^d, U) \tag{6.2}$$

Taking into account the emission functions, the damage function and the balance of payments conditions

$$dW = W_{Q_2^d}(p_{12}dQ_1 + dQ_2) + W_U G_S (H_Q^1 dQ_1 + H_Q^2 dQ_2) \tag{6.3}$$

2. Comparing equation 6.3 with equation 6.1i we see that changes in environmental quality influence the gains from trade. Consider again the two cases $dQ_1 > 0$ and $dQ_1 < 0$.
i) Assume the country specializes in the production of commodity 1 after trade ($dQ_1 > 0$), i.e. the country has a comparative advantage in commodity 1. With respect to the second term, note that $G_S < 0$. Here two subcases have to be distinguished. First, if $(H_Q^1 dQ_1/dQ_2 + H_Q^2) > 0$ or, due to $dR_2 = -dR_1$, $Z_R^1 < Z_R^2$ commodity 2 is the emission-intensive commodity since Z_R^i measures the marginal tendency of pollution of using a resource in sector i. The result is

as follows: If a country specializes in the production of the less pollution-intensively produced commodity, the usual gains from trade are increased by an improvement in environmental quality. The country reduces the output of the pollution-intensively produced commodity 2, the conventional gains from trade are enhanced by an improvement in environmental quality, and the country exports pollutants via trade to the rest of the world.

Second, if $Z_R^1 > Z_R^2$, the second term in equation 6.3 is negative. As a result we have the following outcome: If a country specializes in the production of the emission-intensively produced commodity the welfare gains from trade (in the usual definition) are (partly) offset by a deterioration in environmental quality. A priori it cannot be ruled out that the welfare loss associated with the deterioration in environmental quality may overcompensate the conventional gains from trade. This result may be conceived when we have a strong preference for environmental quality and a high marginal damage (in the physical sense) due to high levels of pollutants already in the environment.

Consider diagram 4.1 in chapter 4 and assume a no-trade situation F with both the home country and the rest of the world undertaking no environmental policy and $p_{12} < p_{12}^*$. If trade takes place gains from trade occur as shown by the trade triangle associated with point F'. Environmental quality for the home country, however, has declined, since a movement along the curve ED represents a reduction in environmental quality.
ii) If $dQ_1 < 0$ and if the country specializes in the production of commodity 2, analogous results hold. If the commodity 2 is pollution-intensive, environmental quality will decline and the gains from trade have to be connected for environmental disruption. If commodity 2 is not pollution-intensive the shift in sector structure will improve environmental quality.

3. Another way of looking at the problem is that comparative price advantage is not expressed correctly if not all social

costs of production are considered. With no environmental policy being undertaken, as assumed here, environmental costs of production are not attributed to the emission-intensive commodity. Consequently this commodity experiences a hidden protection (or subsidy), and a bias in the allocation of resources occurs. Too many resources are used in the emission-intensive sector, in both production activities (compared to abatement where no resources are used), and the environment is used to a too large extent as a waste receiver. In order to prevent a deterioration of environmental quality, environmental policy must be undertaken.

6.3 The Effects of Environmental Policy on the Net Gains from Trade

1. In section 6.2 we asked the question how the net gains from trade are affected if a country is opened up for trade. The analysis centered on a comparison of the autarky situation with a trade equilibrium. We now assume a trade equilibrium in the initial situation and let the home country implement environmental policy. Then the problem arises, how the net gains from trade (and the traditional gains from trade) are affected.

2. Start with equation 6.2 and substitute the equations of the two-country case. In contrast to the derivation of equation 6.1i we now do not assume $E_1 = 0$ but trade takes place in the initial situation. We have as a result for a change in welfare from environmental policy (compare appendix 6.1):

$$\frac{dW}{dp_{S2}} = \left(W_{Q_2^d} + W_U \frac{G_S}{p_{S2}}\right)\left(\frac{dY}{dp_{S2}}\right)_{\bar{p}_{12}} - W_{Q_2^d} E_1 \frac{dp_{12}}{dp_{S2}} \qquad (6.4)$$

Consider a situation F' in diagram 4.1 with the home country levying an emission tax and the rest of the world having no environmental policy. In this case our results indicate that Q_1 will decrease. U will increase and Q_2 may rise or fall. If we define a price isoquant for varying p_{S2}, we know that this line will move in such a direction that $dQ_1/dp_{S2} < 0$ and $dU/dp_{S2} > 0$. If internal demand for commodity 1 does not fall too much, which we have ruled out, exports of the home country are reduced and the quantity of imports falls. National income falls whereas environmental quality improves. Two cases must be distinguished:

i) In the small-country case, analyzed in chapter 4, p_{12} is given and $dp_{12}/dp_{S2} = 0$ so that the economy moves along a price-isoquant from F' to F'' if environmental policy is undertaken. The terms of trade are not affected by environmental policy, but the trade triangle has become smaller (compare trade triangles F'GH and F''XY in diagram 4.1). The country still can reach a consumption point Y outside its production space, but the chances of moving beyond the production space decrease with the size of the trade triangle In an intuitive sense, the traditional gains from trade are reduced by environmental policy.

Note that for the small-country case expression 6.4 contains two effects: $W_{Q_2^d} (\frac{dY}{dp_{S2}})_{\bar{p}_{12}}$ indicates the evaluated loss of national income, namely in terms of units of commodity 2, evaluated at the marginal utility of that commodity. We call this the evaluated withdrawal effect. From $1/p_{S2} =$ $= Z_R^2/(F_R^2 - p_{R2})$ we have for the second term

$W_U \frac{G_S Z_R^2}{(F_R^2 - p_{R2})} (\frac{dY}{dp_{S2}})_{\bar{p}_{12}} > 0$. This expression indicates the improvement in environmental quality, more precisely the evaluated prevented damage of emissions from reducing national income (in units of commodity 2)[1]. Let us call this the environmental quality effect.

ii) In the two-country case the home country influences relative price and $dp_{12}/dp_{S2} > 0$ if sector 1 is emission-

---

1) Note that $Z_R^2/(F_R^2 - p_{R2}) = \frac{1}{p_{S2}}$ denotes a relation of price of commodity 2 to the emission tax per unit of output.

intensive[1)2)]. This means that in the two-country case we have three different effects on welfare

-the evaluated withdrawal effect
-the environmental quality effect and
-the terms-of-trade effect.

Consider diagram 5.1. Whereas the trade triangle for the small country is at F'', the trade triangle in the two-country case is at G. We know that the terms of trade are better for the home country, i.e. the trade triangle has a greater angle α than in diagram 4.1. We also know that in the two-country case exports and imports will decline. In diagram 6.2 let F'GH denote the trade triangle in the initial trade situation with a zero emission tax where F'G indicate exports and GH imports with tg α denoting the

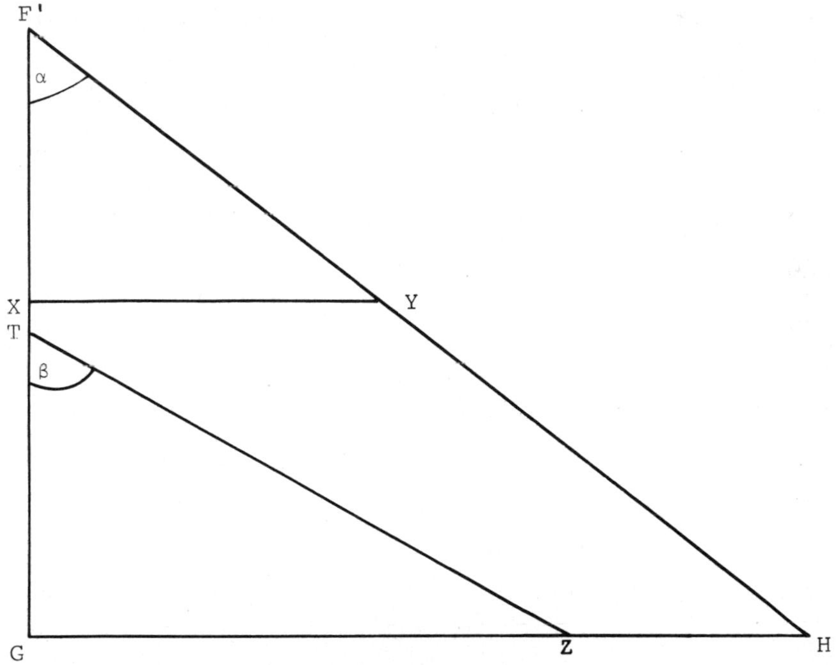

Diagram 6.2

1) Compare the other conditions for this result in chapter 5.
2) Note that $-E_1 > 0$ if the country exports commodity 1.

relative price. In the small-country case the relative price remains constant and the trade triangle is reduced to F'XY. In the two-country case we know that both exports and imports are reduced so that the new trade triangle must be smaller than the initial one. Relative price, however, changes (tg ß) so that the trade triangle for the two-country case may be indicated by TGZ.

3. It is important to note that environmental policy may improve the terms of trade for a country that is exporting the emission-intensively produced commodity. In the everyday discussion of environmental policy in an open economy, it is argued that environmental policy reduces the comparativ advantage of emission-intensively producing sectors, that it consequently affects export changes negatively, and that i endangers employment in the pollution-intensively producing sectors. From this point of view it is argued that environmental policy should consider these opportunity costs (define as reduction in achievement levels of policy targets). The basic recommendation of this argument is that environmental pol cy should be less strict. This argument, however, is based on mercantilistic motivation of international trade. We here can show that environmental policy of the home country reduces exports and consequently leads to an improvement in the terms of trade. Since gains from trade are the ultimate motivations for trade, environmental policy can be beneficial to the home country. Moreover, environmental quality is improved. Under t conditions specified, environmental policy helps in reaching two policy targets.

4. In chapters 4 and 5 the emission tax is changed parametrically so that the triple (Y, U, p_{S2}) indicates environment quality and national income for a given p_{S2}. An increase in p_{S2} will improve environmental quality. National income is reduced with p_{S2} increasing, and the terms of trade effect dampens the decline in income. From the point of view of an overall optimum, p_{S2} must be chosen such that national welfar $W = W(Y,U)$ is maximized. This means that both the gains from trade (affecting Y) and the improvement in environmental poli must be considered as determinants of p_{S2}. Observe that the

change in the gains from trade are determined both by the improvement in the terms of trade and in the reduction of export and import quantities. The optimum is reached where in diagrams 4.1 or 5.1 a three-dimensional social welfare function $W = W(Q_1^d, Q_2^d, U)$, i.e. an indifference lid, will be tangential to the transformation space. Although our model is not an optimization model we can expect a result as to how high the emission tax can be set in order to reach the maximum welfare. This result is now discussed.

5. For the small country case we have from equation 6.4

$$p_{S2} W_{Q_2^d} \lesseqgtr -W_U G_S \Rightarrow \frac{dW}{dp_{S2}} \gtreqless 0 \qquad (6.5)$$

The term on the right side of equation 6.5 indicates prevented marginal environmental damage. The term on the left side denotes the emission tax in value terms, namely the emission tax p_{S2} in real terms (i.e. in quantity units of commodity 2) evaluated with the marginal utility of commodity 2. Welfare will increase if in the initial situation the emission tax in value terms is lower than prevented marginal environmental damage. Welfare will not increase if the emission tax in a given situation is set according to prevented marginal environmental damage. And welfare will fall if in the initial situation the emission tax is set higher than prevented marginal damage.

This result confirms the well-known rule for the setting of the emission tax in a closed economy according to prevented marginal damage for an open economy. It should be pointed out that equation 6.5 is the result of an explanation model and not an optimization model.

Since $p_{S2} = \dfrac{F_R^2 - p_{R2}}{Z_R^2}$ and $p_{S2} = \dfrac{p_{12}F_R^1 - p_{R2}}{Z_R^1}$ equation 6.5

can also be expressed as

$$W_{Q_2^d} < W_{Q_2^d} \frac{p_{R2}}{F_R^2} - W_U G_S H_Q^2 \Rightarrow \frac{dW}{dp_{S2}} > 0 \qquad (6.5i)$$

or

$$W_{Q_2^d} p_{12} < W_{Q_2^d} \frac{p_{R2}}{F_R^1} - W_U G_S H_Q^1 \Rightarrow \frac{dW}{dp_{S2}} > 0 \qquad (6.5ii)$$

In equation 6.5i the right side indicates the social costs of producing commodity 2, namely private marginal costs in real terms (p_{R2}/F_R^2) evaluated with the marginal social utility of commodity 2 and environmental damage attributable to commodity 2. The right side of equation 6.5ii denotes the social costs of producing commodity 1. The left side of both equations denotes the marginal social value of the two commodities.

Welfare will increase with environmental policy if in the initial situation (before environmental policy is undertaken) the marginal social costs of producing a commodity (private plus environmental costs) are higher than the value of that commodity. Since for $p_{S2} = 0$ the relative price must be equal to private marginal costs of production, environmental costs are not accounted for. Introducing an emission tax will reduce R_1, whereas F_R^1 will rise and marginal private costs of production will fall. Also emissions of sector 1 will be reduced, marginal damage will be reduced due to a lower quantity of emissions and the marginal evaluation of the environment will fall since its quality increases (making the usual assumptions about welfare functions). Consequently, after all adaptions have taken place, the commodity price and the social costs of production will be equal.

If in equations 6.5i and 6.5ii the evaluation of a commodity is higher than its social costs of production before environmental policy is pursued, environmental policy cutting back production and decreasing emissions will reduce social costs even further. In this case, welfare will decline and environmental policy should not have been pursued in the first place.

6. Assume now that p_{12} is not fixed. Then the home country may experience an improvement of her terms of trade. From equation 6.4 we have[1)]

$$W_{Q_2} dp_{S2} \lesseqgtr -W_U G_S \alpha \Rightarrow \frac{dW}{dp_{S2}} \gtreqless 0 \qquad (6.6)$$

$$\text{with } \alpha = \frac{\left(\frac{dY}{dp_{S2}}\right)_{\bar{p}_{12}}}{\left(\frac{dY}{dp_{S2}}\right)_{\bar{p}_{12}} - E_1 \frac{dp_{12}}{dp_{S2}}}$$

Assume the home country exports commodity 1 so that $E_1 < 0$. Then $\alpha > 1$. Consequently prevented environmental damage is adjusted upward since with an increase in environmental quality there is also an improvement in the gains from trade.

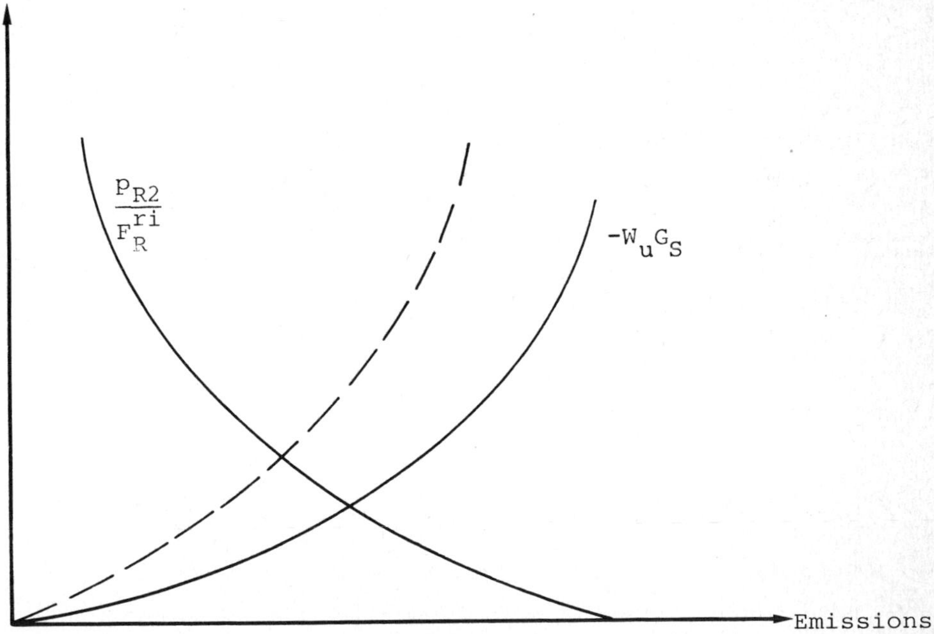

Diagram 6.3

1) Observe that the expression has been divided by $dY/dp_{S2} < 0$.

Consider the well-known diagram with marginal abatement costs and marginal damage prevented. Marginal abatement costs are given by p_{R2}/F_R^{ri} and marginal damage prevented by $-W_U G_S$. Then the emission tax should be set so as to equal marginal abatement costs and marginal damage prevented. If there is an improvement in the terms of trade, marginal benefits do not only consist of prevented environmental damage, but also of the improvement of the terms of trade. Consequently the marginal benefit curve must be adjusted upward.

Compared to the small-country case, the emission tax can be set higher in the home country (in the two-country case) if $dp_{12}/dp_{S2} > 0$. This indicates that the improvement in the terms of trade gives additional leeway for environmental policy in open economies. If there are other costs of environmental policy such as frictional or permanent unemployment or inflationary pressures, these negative effects on policy variables should be taken into consideration in setting the emission tax. In this case the marginal benefit of preventing emissions would have to be adjusted downward so that eventually the emission tax would have to be set lower.

6.4 Pollute-Thy-Neighbour via Trade

1. We have seen so far: If the home country introduces environmental policy its environmental quality will improve and its national income will decline. What happens to the foreign country which is assumed not to undertake environmental policy?

The comparative price advantage of the home country in the emission-intensive commodity will be reduced. Consequently, production of that commodity will increase in the foreign country, and, with given resources, production of the less emission-intensive commodity will decrease. Emissions rise and environmental quality is negatively affected. The foreign country has experienced a welfare loss on the environmental account and emissions, though not having crossed the border, were so to say imported to the foreign country by an increased specialization in the production of the emission-intensive commodity. Note that this effect occurs with resources being internationally immobile. If we allow the mobility of resources, such as capital, the foreign country may attract resources for the expansion of emission-intensive sector which will also increase emissions. Note that in contrast to the deterioration of environmental quality the foreign country experiences an increase in its national income.

2. This outcome of decreasing environmental quality may be interpreted by the country affected as a "pollute-my-neighbour policy" of the country with a high evaluation of the environment. This interpretation, however, is wrong. Assume the country "importing" pollution by international specialization (and factor mobility) is not willing to accept the welfare loss due to its decline in environmental quality. Then the country affected can make its own environment more scarce. Its newly gained production and location advantage is then partly diminished, and the original trade and location shift is partly reduced. The foreign country can even restore the original situation in terms of environmental quality and reduce the improvement in the price advantage completely by choosing an appropriate emission tax. In that case environmental quality will improve and - as an opportunity cost to this improvement - national income will fall.

Observe that one country making the environment more scarce does not initiate a "pollute-thy-neighbour" with possible cumulative retaliation such as in the case of a tariff or devaluation. This can be ascribed to the fact that a country can gain in environmental quality (and consequently export pollution) only at the opportunity cost of a reduction in national income. Empirical evidence suggests that abatement costs rise progressively with improvements in environmental quality. The progressively rising economic costs of environmental quality disprove the "pollute-thy-neighbour" policy thesis.

6.5 Tendencies for an Equalization of the Emission Tax

The previous sections point to some factors that in the long run will work towards an equalization of the emission tax. Before looking at such tendencies let us state under what circumstances the emission tax would be identical between countries. This would be the case if two countries have

- identical assimilative capacities
- identical preference with respect to environmental quality implying the same evaluation of environmental quality for a given income
- same population density since population density may influence the evaluation
- identical political processes for the evaluation of environmental quality and for setting emission taxes
- identical production functions and sector structure
- identical abatement technology.

Assume now that the political process finds the correct shadow price in both countries and both countries have the same evaluation function for environmental quality. And let production and abatement technology be identical. Let the assimilative capacity vary so that the foreign country does not have to introduce an emission tax and let the home country introduce environmental policy. The following processes represent a tendency for an equalization of the emission taxes:

i) National income in the home country decreases so that environmental quality may be valued lower.

ii) Emissions in the foreign country increase by specialization towards the pollution-intensively produced commodity so that environmental quality there declines.

iii) If factors of production are mobile internationally, production of the emission-intensively good in the foreign country is likely to expand even stronger.

iv) National income in the foreign country will increase so a higher value is put on environmental quality.

It is interesting to note that these equalizing tendencies in the emission tax are only operative if environmental policy can be characterized as fixing the emission tax. Assume on the contrary, that environmental policy uses a standard--price approach and sets a fixed target, i.e. a standard of pollutants ambient in the environment. In this case, the policy target represents a restriction that cannot be violated. This means that the shadow price of pollutants and emissions will have to be adjusted so that they satisfy a given target. From this observation follows that the equalization of emission taxes cannot be postulated if a specific environmental quality target is set. In that case, the home country limits $U \geq \bar{U}$ whereas in the foreign country (with no environmental policy) $\bar{U}^* \geq 0$. This means that p^*_{S2} rises and p_{S2} is zero.

Appendix 6.1

Equation 6.4 is derived as follows. Differentiate equation 6.2 with respect to p_{S2}.

$$\frac{dW}{dp_{S2}} = W_{Q_2^d} \left(\frac{W_{Q_1^d}}{W_{Q_2^d}} \frac{dQ_1^d}{dp_{S2}} + \frac{dQ_2^d}{dp_{S2}} \right) + W_U G_S \frac{dS}{dp_{S2}} \qquad (6.1.1)$$

The first expression can be simplified by using the definitions for E_i and taking into account that $p_{12}dE_1 + E_1 dp_{12} + dE_2 = 0$. In contrast to the derivation of equation 6.1i in the text we now do not consider the case when a country is opened up for trade (with $E_1 = 0$ in the initial case of autarky). We consider an initial trade equilibrium so that $E_1 \neq 0$. Therefore we have for the first expression[1)]

$$\left(p_{12} \frac{dQ_1^d}{dp_{S2}} + \frac{dQ_2^d}{dp_{S2}} \right) = p_{12} \frac{dQ_1}{dp_{S2}} + \frac{dQ_2}{dp_{S2}} - E_1 \frac{dp_{12}}{dp_{S2}} =$$

$$= \left(\frac{dY}{dp_{S2}} \right)_{\bar{p}_{12}} - E_1 \frac{dp_{12}}{dp_{S2}} \qquad (6.1.2)$$

For dS/dp_{S2} we have

$$\frac{dS}{dp_{S2}} = Z_R^1 \frac{dR_1}{dp_{S2}} + Z_R^2 \frac{dR_2}{dp_{S2}} - F_R^{r1} \frac{dR_1^r}{dp_{S2}} - F_R^{r2} \frac{dR_2^r}{dp_{S2}}$$

Substituting the resource constraint 2.7 and the factor demand conditions 3.4 we have

$$\frac{dS}{dp_{S2}} = \frac{1}{p_{S2}} \left(\frac{dY}{dp_{S2}} \right)_{\bar{p}_{12}} \qquad (6.1.3)$$

Substituting 6.1.2 and 6.1.3 into 6.1.1 we have equation 6.4 in section 6.3.

---

1) Note that $Y = p_{12}Q_1 + Q_2$ or $Y = p_{12}Q_1^d + Q_2^d - (p_{12}E_1 + E_2)$.

Part III

Models with Implicit Abatement Technology

In this part we discuss the allocative effects of environmental policy using the implicit abatement technology (net emissions approach) developed in part I. In order to link the subsequent analysis to part II we start by studying a simple model with one resource only. This procedure allows us to compare its basic structure and main implications to those of the one-resource model of part II. But it also serves to prepare the basis of the extended two-factor model that is the central issue of part III.

In chapter 7 and 8 we do not aim at covering the contents of part II systematically but rather try to deepen the insight into the common analytical structure of the models under consideration. We therefore postpone several complicating theoretical details to subsequent chapters; in particular, the demand side of the model is treated in a very rudimentary way - mainly for heuristic reasons. Our main objective in chapters 7 and 8 is to show the close relationship of our analysis to the standard neoclassical pure trade theory. This can already be demonstrated for the equilibrium concepts and the comparative statics in the closed economy (chapter 7), but it is even more evident in chapter 8 where we show the close relationship of our model to the traditional theory of technological comparative advantage as well as to the Heckscher-Ohlin-Samuelson-type of pure trade theory.

In chapter 9 we examine the problem of pollution control in an economy endowed with two conventional factor resources and one natural resource: environmental services. The adequate formulation of the net emission technology in this context allows to demonstrate several distinct cases in relation to the concept of strong factor intensity. We analyze the incidental effects on sector structure, factor rewards and relative commodity prices if an environmental policy is undertaken. Information deficits forces environmental policy to carry out a so-called standard-price-approach which takes the special form of an auction process of limited quantities of emission rights. The pricing of the environment caused by fixed quality targets leads to a reduction of the emission--intensively producing sector. We analyze the determinants of the relative autarky price in the context of a two-factor model and we confirm the result that the relative price of th emission-intensively produced commodity will rise. The result are also affected by special demand conditions. In the last section we demonstrate under different economic regimes the possible trade patterns which are induced by environmental policy. In chapter 10 we regard the effects of pollution control on international trade flows and terms-of-trade. First we examine the change of trade flows in a small country model All possible effects are classified. In the following section we use the well-known two-country model of trade. We will pro that free trade with fixed environmental quality targets enab the acting country to improve its terms-of-trade if exports a produced emission-intensively. We also give conditions for ot cases depending on different factor intensities.

7. The Closed Two-Sector-One-Factor Economy

In order to elaborate the principal determinants of comparative advantage in trade between two countries it is important to fully understand the working of the closed economy with and without environmental management being applied. We therefore introduce two different equilibrium concepts: The "laissez-faire equilibrium" refers to situations where no environmental policy action is taken, i.e. where the environment serves as a costless waste receptor. The "price and standard equilibrium", on the other hand, analytically expresses the economy's state, either when a market in emission licenses is established or when an emission tax is implemented. It is shown that under the assumptions chosen these two types of equilibria exist and are unique. We then focus our attention on the properties of price and standard equilibria as well as on the allocative effects of parametric changes in the emission standard. Among other things the well-known least-cost (or: efficiency) property of this "market approach" to environmental management is established.

7.1. Equilibrium Concepts

While in section 3.1 the demand side of the model was represented by commodity demand functions D^i satisfying the assumption A 3.3, we now model the demand side with the help of a social welfare function:

A 7.1 Social welfare function. We assume that the consumers' preferences can be aggregated and represented by a social welfare function[1) $W: R_+^3 \rightarrow R_+$, such that $W := W(Q_1^d, Q_2^d, U)$ is the economy's welfare index, where Q_1^d and Q_2^d are the quantities of goods 1 and 2 available for consumption and where U is the environmental quality. We require W to be quasi-concave and non-decreasing in Q_1^d, Q_2^d and U. Moreover, throughout the chapters 7 and 8 W will be specified by

$$W(Q_1^d, Q_2^d, U) = \min(c_1 Q_1^d U, c_2 Q_2^d U) \qquad (7.1)$$

where c_1 and c_2 are given positive real numbers.

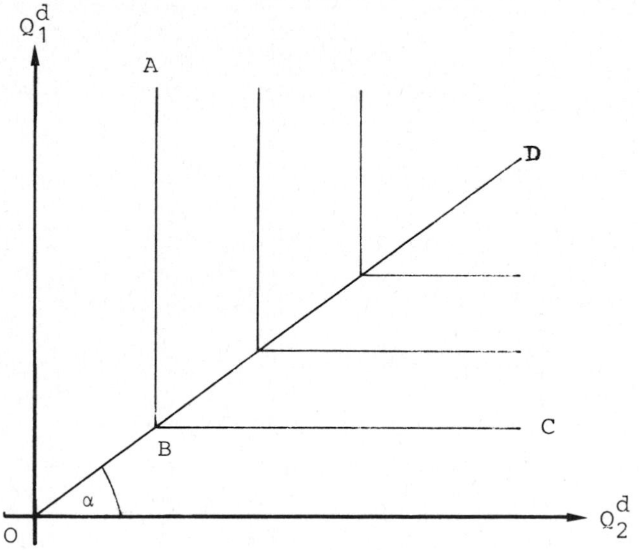

Diagram 7.1

1) The difficulties associated with the attempt to deduce or interprete social welfare functions as aggregated consumers' preferences are well-known since K.J.Arrow (1951). An adequate treatment of these issues is beyond the scope of this book. Note however, that commodity demand functions D^i from A 3.3 can always be "rationalized" as being deduced from some social welfare function.

Diagram 7.1 shows the domain of this welfare function, where $\tan \alpha = c_2/c_1$ and where the lines like ABC represent welfare indifference curves. Equation 7.1 implies that the two consumption goods are assumed to be strictly complementary: Whenever commodity prices are positive, the consumers will demand both commodities in fixed proportion c_2/c_1. Hence given A 7.1, the environmental policy does not bring about changes in sector structure which is an important allocative effect in models of different chapters of this book. The assumption A 7.1 is by no means essential; its adoption in chapters 7 and 8 is exclusively motivated by the considerable analytical simplifications it allows.

We now turn to describe the equilibrium concept to be employed. In principle, we study an economy with competitive markets. But the market mechanism will be amended by environmental policy in case that markets fail to optimally allocate resources. In a first step we show the nature of this market failure. Therefore we ask for the market allocation at environmental "laissez-faire", i.e. when no environmental policy is implemented.

Definition D 7.1 Laissez-faire equilibrium:

An allocation $a := (Q_i^d, Q_i, \tilde{R}_i, S_i, U)$ $(i = 1,2)$

and a price vector $p := (p_1, p_2, p_R, p_S, p_u) \in R_+^5$ with $p_u = 0$

are said to constitute a laissez-faire equilibrium, if

(i) the markets for the consumption goods and for the resource are cleared:

$$Q_1 = Q_1^d, \; Q_2 = Q_2^d, \; \tilde{R}_1 + \tilde{R}_2 = R$$

(ii) for the production sectors i = 1,2 the production activity $(Q_i, \tilde{R}_i, S_i)$ satisfies $Q_i = F^i(\tilde{R}_i, S_i)$ and is profit maximizing relative to p_i

(iii) for the consumption sector the commodity consumption (Q_1^d, Q_2^d) is welfare maximizing for given $U = G(S)$ under the budget constraint $p_1\tilde{Q}_1^d + p_2\tilde{Q}_1^d \leq p_2 Y :=$ $p_1 Q_1 + p_2 Q_2$

(iv) $S := S_1 + S_2$ maximizes $[p_u G(\tilde{S}) + p_S \tilde{S}]$ on R_+

The explicit consideration of prices for emmisions p_S, the price p_u for environmental quality as well as the condition D 7.1iv appear to be highly artificial, but they help to provide some interesting insight into the "logic" of environmental economics. One can look at the damage function G as a technological relation transforming the "input" S (emissions), into the "output" U (ambient quality). Suppose, there were markets for both, emissions and ambient quality, with market prices p_u and p_S. Then $\pi^S(S) := p_u G(S) + p_S S$ is the profit of the "environmental production sector". It follows from $p_u = 0$ and from the assumption A 2.5 that there does not exist a maximum for $\pi(S)$ on R_+ - and hence no laissez-faire equilibrium unless $p_S = 0$. $p_S = 0$ means that in an environmental laissez-faire state emissions can be discharged at zero costs. We require $p_u = 0$ in D 7.1 in order to indicate that the competitive market does not operate for the public good "environmental quality"[1]. The public good property of U is specified in D 7.1iii by the fact that the consumers take the "prevailing" environmental quality as given. They believe that they cannot influence U even though it is ultimately their own consumption decisions with respect to goods 1 and 2 which determine the level of environmental quality. The consumers' total money income $p_2 Y$ consists of their wages factor income $p_R (\tilde{R}_1 + \tilde{R}_2)$, the profits $\pi_i := p_i Q_i - p_R \tilde{R}_i - p_S S_i$ of the two industries and transfer payments $p_S (S_1 + S_2)$ from the environmental agency (which are zero for $p_S = 0$). Thus the value of production is equal to the income received by the consumption sector:

$$p_2 Y = p_1 Q_1 + p_2 Q_2 = p_R (\tilde{R}_1 + \tilde{R}_2) + p_S (S_1 + S_2) + \\ + \pi_1 + \pi_2, \tag{7.3}$$

---

1) One could alternatively presuppose $p_u \geq 0$ in D 7.1. But $p_u > 0$ could not perform a significant allocative role, since it does not appear as a parameter in the producers or consumers optimization procedures. In our view $p_u = 0$ is the natural counterpart of the assumption (implicit in D 7.1iii) that the consumers enjoy the public good "environmental quality" costlessly.

The welfare maximizing consumer behaviour from D 7.1iii implies, when combined with A 7.1 that the demand for consumption goods is strictly complementary: If for arbitrary values of U a commodity bundle $(\bar{Q}_1^d, \bar{Q}_2^d)$ does not satisfy the equation

$$Q_1 = \frac{c_2}{c_1} Q_2 \tag{7.4}$$

then $(\bar{Q}_1^d, \bar{Q}_2^d)$ is not demanded by the consumers' sector. Hence 7.2 is a necessary condition for a demand side equilibrium.

It is easy to show that under the assumptions A 2.8 and A 7.1 the economy has a unique laissez-faire equilibrium[1]. One important property of this equilibrium is that the equilibrium production point (Q_1, Q_2) always satisfies the commodity transformation curve $Q_1 = T^1(Q_2, S_o)$ for some sufficiently large S_o. Hence the laissez-faire equilibrium point $(\bar{Q}_1, \bar{Q}_2, \bar{U})$ is a point on the line BC in diagram 2.3.

The welfare maximal allocation $(Q_1', Q_2', \bar{U}')$ is attained by maximizing W on the transformation space T (as defined in section 2.2). In fact, under A 2.8, A 2.9 and A 7.1 a welfare maximal allocation exists and is unique. Hence the problem of market failure under environmental laissez-faire boils down to the question whether $(\bar{Q}_1, \bar{Q}_2, \bar{U}) \neq (Q_1', Q_2', U')$. Environmental economists typically appear to presuppose this inequality, in particular $\bar{U} < U'$. It is, however, not at all easy, to find straightforward sufficient conditions for $\bar{U} < U'$ within our model, and we will not elaborate on this issue here. We join the environmentalist's view, instead and assume that $\bar{U} < U'$. It follows, that environmental controls are desirable. In the ideal case they should be implemented to restore the welfare maximal allocation (Q_1', Q_2', U'). But it is widely agreed that

1) This result would not be so generally valid if, contrary to the above assumptions, environmental disruption had adverse feed back effects on the production technology or on the resource quality (labourers' health). See, for example, R. Pethig (1975, p.99-124).

the information costs for an environmental protection agency (EPA), to find the optimal value U' are extremely high[1].

Therefore we do not require the EPA to have information on the welfare maximal environmental quality but we ask the EPA instead to pursue the less ambitious objective of implementing an "acceptable" environmental quality standard, which is to be established by some (analytically unspecified) collective decision procedure.

The principle target variable of environmental policy is the environmental quality (and not emissions or an emissions tax rate). But since the damage function G from A 2.5 is strictly monotonely increasing, every environmental quality standard U^S is equivalent to the emission standard $S^S = G^{-1}(U^S)$. In the sequel we will mainly talk about emission standard for analytical convenience.

Among the various possible environmental policy instruments to implement a predetermined emission standard, we consider only those, which have become known as environmental price and standard systems[2].

Definition D 7.2. Price and standard equilibrium.

An allocation $a := (Q_i^d, Q_i, \tilde{R}_i, S_i, U)$ $(i = 1,2)$

and a price vector $p := (p_1, p_2, p_R, p_S, p_u) \in \mathbb{R}_+^5$ with $p_u = 0$

are said to constitute a price and S^S-standard equilibrium, i

(w) = D 7.1w for w = i, ii, iii

(iv) $S := S_1 + S_2$ maximizes $[p_u G(\tilde{S}) + p_S \tilde{S}]$ over the interval $[0, S^S]$

1) See, for example, W.J. Baumol (1972, p.307-322), who also argues, that the existence of multiple welfare maxima may worsen the informational dilemma. In addition, consumers have strong incentives not to reveal their true preferences for environmental quality; see R. Pethig (1978).

2) See T.H. Tietenberg (1973a); W.J. Baumol and W.E. Oates (1975) denote these policy instruments as "environmental charges and standards approach".

There are two distinct institutional interpretations that can alternatively be attached to an environmental price and standard system:

(α) Market in emission licenses. The EPA is assumed to establish a market for emission rights, where the total demand $S_1 + S_2$ for "discharge services" is equated to the EPA's fixed "supply" S^s by a non-negative market price p_S.

(β) Emission tax solution. The EPA raises an emission tax p_S and fixes the tax rate at such a level that the total emission demand $S_1 + S_2$ matches the tolerable emission level S^s.

Note that in both cases the EPA's revenue $p_S (S_1 + S_2)$ is typically positive and is redistributed to the consumers by assumption. The principal difference between the license and tax interpretation is that in the first case the direct policy variable of the EPA is the emission standard while the equilibrium price for emissions is "found" by the market mechanism. In the emission tax case the EPA has to adjust the tax rate in a trial and error procedure until the target emission standard is attained[1].

7.2 Equilibrium Implications and Elementary Comparative Statics

The equilibrium definitions D 7.1 and D 7.2 are closely related. In fact, they only differ from each other in condition iv: In D 7.1iv the "profit" $\pi^S(S)$ is to be maximized over the unbounded interval $\mathbb{R}_+$ while in D 7.2iv $\mathbb{R}_+$ is replaced by the bounded interval $[0, S^s]$. An immediate implication of D 7.2iv is that in a price and S^s-standard equilibrium one obtains

$$p_S \left\{\begin{smallmatrix} = \\ > \end{smallmatrix}\right\} 0 \quad \Rightarrow \quad S \left\{\begin{smallmatrix} \leq \\ = \end{smallmatrix}\right\} S^s \tag{7.5}$$

$$\text{and} \quad S < S^s \quad \Rightarrow \quad p_S = 0 \tag{7.6}$$

From 7.6 it follows that if (a, p) is a price and S^s-stan-

1) It should be noted that along a dynamic adjustment path the different institutional settings may well become relevant. The analysis of comparative dynamics is, however, beyond the scope of this book.

dard equilibrium such that $S < S^s$, then (a, p) coincides with the (unique) laissez-faire equilibrium. Hence D 7.2 contains D 7.1 as a special case.

It is also clear that there is an emission standard whose associated price and standard equilibrium is welfare maximal. But we noted already that due to insufficient information EPA cannot identify this standard with certainty. The implementation of some emission standard S^s may be regarded as a second best solution, at best being a satisfactory approximation to the (unknown) optimal solution. If this view is accepted one may still want to implement a "least cost" environmental quality in the sense, that some given environmental quality $G(S^s)$ is achieved at minimum possible resource cost. This efficiency property is, in fact, satisfied by the environmental price and standard system[1]. The proof will be given, combined with an affirmative answer to the existence question in

Theorem 7.1: Suppose the assumptions A 2.8, A 2.9 and A 7.1 hold. For every $S^s > 0$ there exists a unique price and S^s-standard equilibrium (a, p), such that a is efficient relativ to S^s (according to definition D 2.1).

Proof: Denote by (Q_1^o, Q_2^o) the commodity bundle which satisfies equations 7.4 and 2.9 and by $(\tilde{R}_1^o, \tilde{R}_2^o, \tilde{S}_1^o, \tilde{S}_2^o)$ the factor allocation that is uniquely associated to (Q_1^o, Q_2^o) via the production functions F^i. By satisfying equation 2.9 (Q_1^o, Q_2^o) is efficient relative to S^s, i.e. we have $S_1^o + S_2^o \leq S^s$, $\tilde{R}_1^o + \tilde{R}_2^o = R$ and [2]

$$\frac{F_R^1(\tilde{R}_1^o, S_1^o)}{F_S^1(\tilde{R}_1^o, S_1^o)} = \frac{F_R^2(\tilde{R}_2^o, S_2^o)}{F_S^2(\tilde{R}_2^o, S_2^o)}$$

---

1) This efficiency property was already established by W.J. Baumol and W.E. Oates (1971); compare also T.H. Tietenberg (1973a).

2) Using the subsequent equality we neglect corner solutions that play a role in the case of condition 2.11. This condition does not change our results qualitatively.

Now choose $p \in \mathbb{R}^5_+$ such that $p_u = 0$ and for $i = 1,2$

$$\frac{p_R}{p_i} = F^i_R(\tilde{R}^o_i, S^o_i) \text{ and } \frac{p_S}{p_i} = F^i_S(\tilde{R}^o_i, S^o_i).$$

This price vector p together with the allocation $(Q^d_i = Q^o_i, Q^o_i, \tilde{R}^o_i, S^o_i, G(S^o_1 + S^o_2))$ which is efficient relative to S^s, constitute the unique price and S^s-standard equilibrium.

q.e.d.

Theorem 7.1 can easily be illustrated with the help of diagram 2.7b. Suppose, that the dotted ray OP' in diagram 2.7b 2.7b represents equation 7.4 (i.e. $\tan \beta = c_2/c_1$). The intersection point H (or G or P') between this ray and the commodities transformation curve DE (either CP''B or AP'B) characterizes the commodity bundle (Q^o_1, Q^o_2) as defined in the proof of theorem 7.1. From the point H in diagram 2.7b we can trace back the associated factor allocation in a box diagram like that of diagram 2.8. The factor allocation related to H in diagram 2.7b is represented in diagram 2.8 by a point such as H' on the dotted efficiency curve. The remaining arguments in the proof of theorem 7.1 are well known from standard neoclassical theory.

We now focus our attention on allocative effects induced by changes of environmental policy variables. By A 7.1 we excluded structural changes between the consumption goods sectors. But what is the relationship between the equilibrium values of p_S and alternative emission standards S^s?

<u>Lemma 7.1:</u> Under the assumptions A 2.8, A 2.9 and A 7.1, let (a, p) be a price and S^s-standard equilibrium, such that $S_1 + S_2 = S^s$. Suppose further, that (a', p') is a price and $S^{s}{}'$-standard equilibrium such $p_{SR} := p_S/p_R$ from (a, p) is smaller than $p'_{SR} := p'_S/p'_R$ from (a', p'). Then $S^{s}{}' < S^{\bar{s}}$.

Proof: The assumptions A 2.9ii and iii when combined with marginal productivity pricing imply that a commodity supply (Q_1, Q_2) satisfies, for $p_{SR} \geq 0$, the equation

$$Q_1 = \frac{Rf^1[B^1(p_{SR})]}{B^1(p_{SR})} - \frac{B^2(p_{SR})\ f^1[B^1(p_{SR})]}{B^1(p_{SR})\ f^2[B^2(p_{SR})]}\ Q_2, \qquad (7.7)$$

where the functions B^i are defined in A 2.9iii. Let p_{SR} and p'_{SR} be relative emission taxes such that $0 \leq p_{SR} < p'_{SR}$ and let (Q_1, Q_2) and (Q'_1, Q'_2) be the coordinates of the point of intersection between 7.7 and 7.4 for p_{SR} and p'_{SR} and p'_{SR}, respectively. One can show that $Q_i > Q'_i$ for $i = 1,2$. Now we choose two positive real numbers S^s and $S^{s}{'}$ such that (Q_1, Q_2) satisfies the transformation function T^1 from 2.9 for S^s and (Q'_1, Q'_2) satisfies T^1 for $S^{s}{'}$. Then $S^s > S^{s}{'}$ by lemma 2.4.

q.e.d.

Lemma 7.1 shows that an increase in p_{SR} reduces the aggregate emission level. This effect, which should be viewed as the "normal reaction", is compatible with the findings in the model of sections 3.3 and 3.4 where an increase in p_{S2} also implies a reduction of $S = S_1 + S_2$.

At the first glance lemma 7.1 only applies to the emission tax version of a price and standard system, since p_{SR} is explicitly taken as the (primary) policy variable. But if we recall that price and standard equilibria are unique independent of the interpretation chosen, lemma 7.1 tells us also that the equilibrium price p_{SR} is a (strictly) monotone increasing function of S^s.

Diagram 7.2 shows the working of price and standard systems for alternative emission standards. Part III contains the functions B^i from A 2.9iii. The curve in part II captures the result from lemma 7.1 and part I shows the relationship between equilibrium values of p_{12} and p_{SR} being valid under A 2.8, A 2.9 and under marginal productivity pricing. Parts I and III together are exactly what is known as the "Harrod-Johnson-Diagram" in the standard trade theory[1]. In our model this diagram has a straightforward interpretation: If the relative emission tax p_{SR} increases the consumption good, whose production is relative emission intensive, becomes

1) See, for example, M.C. Kemp (1969, p.8n)

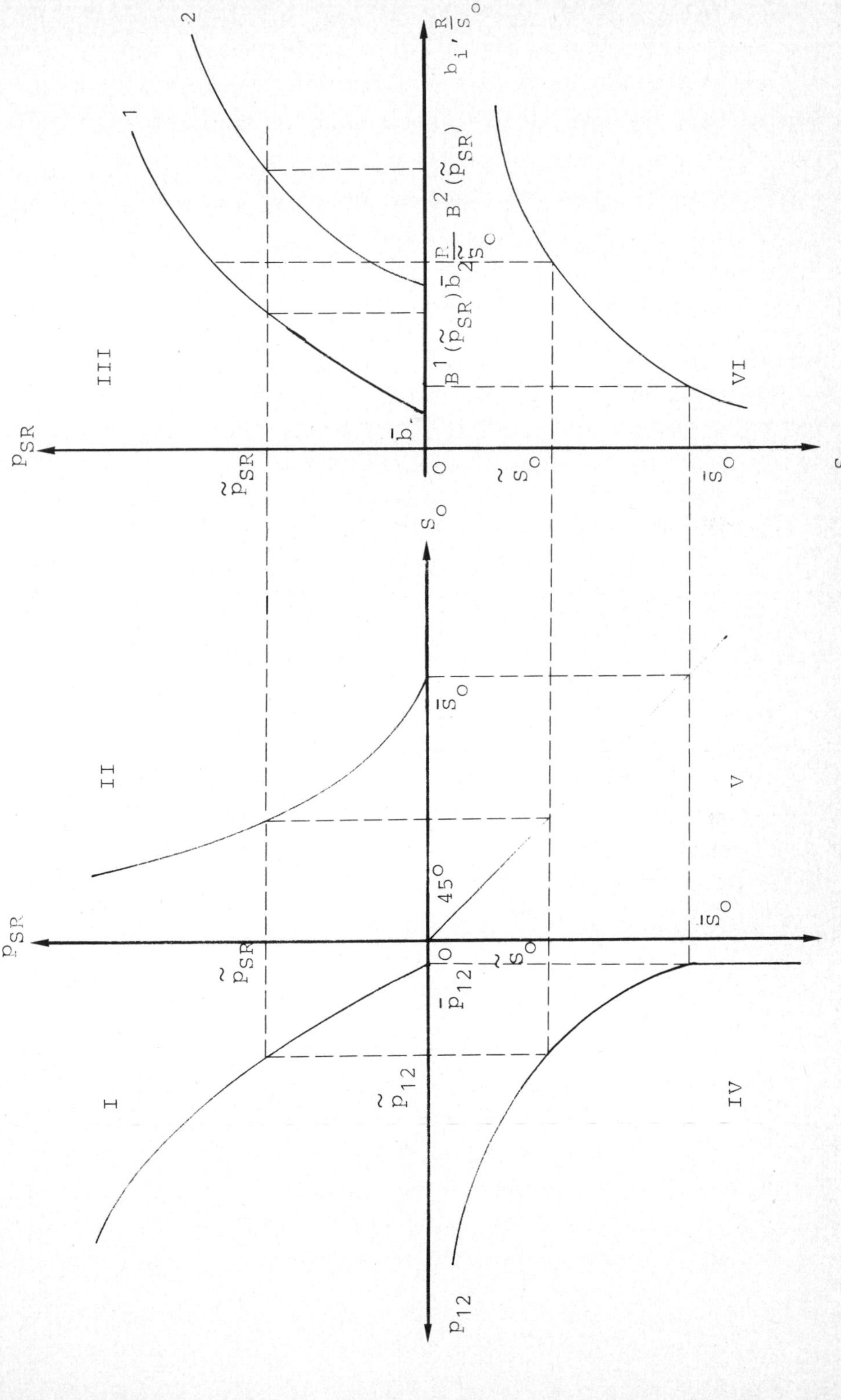

Diagram 7.2

more expensive relative to the other consumption good (i.e. p_{12} increases), the curve in part IV of diagram 7.2 is diagrammatically deduced from parts I, II and V. Finally, in part VI we depicted the symmetric hyperbola $R = S^s\,(R/S)$. In the state of environmental laissez-faire, the economy's equilibrium is characterized in diagram 7.2 by $\bar{p}_{SR} = 0$ and by

$$\bar{p}_{12} := \frac{\bar{b}_2 f^1(\bar{b}_1)}{\bar{b}_1 f^2(\bar{b}_2)} .$$

If EPA implements an emission standard $\tilde{S}^s < \bar{S}^s$, then diagram 7.2 shows the associated values $\tilde{p}_{12}$, $\tilde{p}_{SR}$, $R/\tilde{S}^s$ and $B^i(\tilde{p}_{SR})$. In general p_{SR} and p_{12} will be the greater the more restrictive the (binding) emission standard S^s is chosen.

8. Comparative Advantage, Welfare, and Environmental Policy

We know from the pure trade theory, that a country's comparative advantage may be due to differences in technologies, in endowments or in demand conditions (as compared with the respective conditions of its trading partner). In section 8.1 we investigate different technologies as determinants for comparative advantage. In this context various cases have to be distinguished as to whether no country, one country or both implement or change the restrictiveness of environmental controls. One major result is that under certain conditions technological comparative advantages may be reversed (or overcompensated) by the allocative effects of environmental management. In the remaining part of this chapter we investigate comparative advantage stemming from the countries' differences in relative factor abundance, which include divergencies in endowments and demand conditions. The most interesting feature of this approach is to treat a country's emission standard S^s as if it were a factor endowment. With this interpretation it is possible to apply the traditional Heckscher-Ohlin-Samuelson Theory of Pure Trade to the case of two countries both of which implement an environmental price and standard system. Under some qualifications even the Factor-Price-Equalization theorem carries over insofar as the two countries' relative emission taxes equalize in a trading equilibrium even though the countries pursue restrictive environmental controls in different manners.

8.1 Technological Comparative Advantage

We can now turn to the two-country case. The assumptions A 2.8, A 2.9 and A 7.1 hold for each country. In addition, the production functions are now specified by

A 8.1 Differences in resource productivity:

$$Q_i = F^i(\tilde{R}_i, S_i) =: \lambda_i G^i(\tilde{R}_i, S_i),$$

$$Q_i^* = F^{i*}(\tilde{R}_i^*, S_i^*) =: \lambda_i^* G^i(\tilde{R}_i^*, S_i^*), \tag{8.1}$$

$$\lambda_i > 0, \ \lambda_i^* > 0.$$

Note that the functions G^i are the same for both countries, whereas $\lambda_i \neq \lambda_i^*$ is allowed for.

We wish to know in which way differences in technologies as assumed above influence the pattern of trade. Let us first focus attention to the case of two countries that are not (yet) confronted with severe environmental deterioration, e.g., developing countries, and which therefore have not implemented any environmental controls.

Theorem 8.1: Let the assumptions A 2.8, A 2.9, A 7.1 and A 8.1 be satisfied for both countries, and suppose that no environmental controls are enforced in either country.

(i) The home country specializes its production for export on

$$\left.\begin{array}{l}\text{good } 1\\ \text{no good}\\ \text{good } 2\end{array}\right\}, \text{ if and only if } \frac{\lambda_1}{\lambda_2} \gtreqless \frac{\lambda_1^*}{\lambda_2^*}.$$

(ii) That country which specializes on the production of the emission-intensive good for exports may suffer a welfare loss from trade, whereas the other country always gains from trade.

Proof: By lemma 2.4i both countries have constant rates of transformation. Hence it is obvious that the case of theorem 8.1i is that of the Ricardian theory of trade: Comparative advantages are due to comparative differences in production technologies only.

For the proof of theorem 8.1ii suppose that the home country specializes completely on the production of good 1. Then its autarkic emission S_a increases to the trade equilibrium emission S_t, and its trade equilibrium consumption of both goods increases as well. The welfare in autarky, $W_a = c_i Q_{ia} \; G(S_a)$, is less than the welfare in trade equilibrium, $W_t = c_i Q_{it} G(S_t)$, if the percentage increase of Q_i is higher than the percentage decrease of U. Suppose that $W_t > W_a$ for some given ratio $\bar{\lambda}_1^*/\bar{\lambda}_2^*$ (with $\bar{\lambda}_1^*/\bar{\lambda}_2^* < \lambda_1/\lambda_2$) in the foreign country, and let for $q = 1, 2, 3, \ldots \; (\lambda_1^*/\lambda_2^*)^q$ be a strictly, monotone increasing sequence, starting at $\bar{\lambda}_1^*/\bar{\lambda}_2^*$ and converging at λ_1/λ_2. Associated with this sequence is a strictly monotone decreasing sequence $(Q_i)^q$ of trade equilibrium quantities of good i, starting at Q_{it} and converging to Q_{ia}. Hence there is $\hat{q}$ such that for all $q > \hat{q}$ $\; W_t^q = c_i Q_i^q \; G(S_t) < W_a$.

q.e.d.

The basic idea of the welfare statement in theorem 8.1ii is that under the assumptions made a welfare loss of the country specializing on the emission-intensive good is the more probable (and at some point certain) the less the technological differences between the two countries are. With decreasing technological differences the partial welfare gain from increased commodity consumption tends to zero, whereas the partial welfare loss due to the decrease in environmental quality remains finite, since the home country specializes completely on good 1, whenever $\frac{\lambda_1^*}{\lambda_2^*}$ satisfies $\frac{\bar{\lambda}_1^*}{\bar{\lambda}_2^*} \geq \frac{\lambda_1^*}{\lambda_2^*} > \frac{\lambda_1}{\lambda_2}$.

More generally, a welfare loss from trade occurs to one of the countries, (a) if it specializes on the emission-intensive good (necessary condition) and (b) if the welfare loss due to the decreased environmental quality overcompensates the welfare gain from the increased quantities of private consumption goods after trade (sufficient condition).

Although theorem 8.1i is very simple, it has considerable relevance from the point of view of environmental economics: One may interpret the possibility of waste discharges into the environment as an environmental service. If in both countries the "supply" of this environmental service is large relative to the "demand", like in the case of environmental laissez-faire, the analysis leads straight to the Ricardo results, as if the environment were not at all included in the model. The degree of environmental disruption and the size of the environmental assimilative capacity have no influence on the trade allocation. This result should be viewed as a substantial qualification, or even contradiction, of d'Arge's and Kneese's conjecture that the Theorem of Comparative Advantage as being established in the well-known Heckscher-Ohlin theory immediately carries over to the case of trading economies with polluting industries. They claim more specifically, that "... countries with relatively large environmental assimilative capacities (EAC) should, other things being equal, produce commodities with relatively high wasteloads per unit of production for export and import commodities with relatively low wasteloads in their production[1]", where a country's environmental assimilative capacity is defined by them as its "environment's capacity to assimilate and neutralize waste residuals" which is one of a country's "unique attributes in terms of productive resources[2]".

At some cost of simplification one may classify economies being confronted with severe environmental pollution in the absence of environmental management as industrialized countries, while countries with moderate environmental disruption in the laissez-faire states may be called developing countries. If one of the countries (or both) is industrialized, we will assume that it already adopted an environmental price and standard system with a strictly binding emission standard.

1) See R.C. d'Arge and A.V. Kneese, (1972, p.434).

2) Ibidem; such a definition suggests that the environmental assimilated capacity must be conceived of as a country's natural endowment with environmental assimilative services. Possibly d'Arge and Kneese do not intend to apply their comparative advantage statement to environmental laissez-faire situations, although they do not make this explicit. They may, instead, think of the environmental assimilative capacity to be an environmental policy variable so that it is the environmental capacity which is to be allotted to residuals discharge. Compare ibidem, (p. 427).

In the sequel we study the trade pattern between two countries when the home country (developed country) adopted a price and standard system whereas the other country does not implement environmental controls. What are the trade effects of alternatively restrictive environmental control in the home country?

Theorem 8.2: Let the assumptions A 2.8, A 2.9, A 7.1 and A 8.1 hold for both countries and let environmental controls be absent in the foreign country.

(i) Suppose, the home country implements a price and S^s-standard system. It exports and specializes on good 2, if

$$\frac{\lambda_1}{\lambda_2} < \frac{\lambda_1^*}{\lambda_2^*} .$$

(ii) There exist two real numbers, $r \leq 0$ and $\hat{S}^s > 0$ such that the home country exports and specializes on the production of good 2 for all emission standards $S^s < \hat{S}^s$, if $(\lambda_1/\lambda_2) > (\lambda_1^*/\lambda_2^*) > -r$.

Proof: If $(\lambda_1/\lambda_2) < (\lambda_1^*/\lambda_2^*)$, then by theorem 8.1i the home country would export good 2 if it would not enforce environmental controls. Let p_{12}^a denote the home country's commodity price ratio in autarkic laissez-faire equilibrium, and let $(p_{12})_S$ be the relative price in autarky, when a price and S^s-standard equilibrium is established. Then $(p_{12})_S \geq p_{12}^a$ for every $S^s > 0$ by lemma 7.1 in connection with the structural relationships underlying diagram 7.2. This proves theorem 8.2i.

In order to show the validity of theorem 8.2ii, it suffices to define r. Denote $d^n := (Q_1^n, Q_2^n, S_o^n)$ and let $\{d^n\}$ for $n = 1, 2, \ldots$ be a sequence of vectors d^n such that $S^n \longrightarrow 0$ for $n \longrightarrow \infty$ and (Q_1^n, Q_2^n) satisfies 7.4 and 2.9 for $S_o = S_o^n$ for every $n = 1, 2, \ldots$ Uniquely associated with the sequence $\{d^n\}$ there is a sequence $\left\{ \frac{\partial T^1 (Q_2^n, S_o^n)}{\partial Q_2} \right\}$. Clearly, this sequence is non-positive and increasing by lemma 2.4 and by the Rybczynski theorem[1]. Hence it converges to a non-positive

1) T.M. Rybczynski (1955)

number, which we denote by r.

q.e.d.

Theorem 8.2i spells out the intuitively expected result that a country's technological comparative advantage for the less emission-intensive good 2 is strengthened by environmental controls. On the other hand, if one country has a technologic comparative advantage for the emission intensive good 1 before trade, according to theorem 8.2ii it can (with a minor technologically determined qualification) overcompensate this advantage by choosing a sufficiently restrictive emission standard. In other words, if the home country exports and specializes on the emission intensive good, it can, in genera switch the trade flows by enforcing sufficiently restrictive environmental controls.

Theorem 8.2 can be illustrated by diagram 8.1 that reproduces part IV of diagram 7.2. In diagram 8.1 the home country's laissez-faire equilibrium price p_{12}^{a} is equal to OB. The line DGHK shows how equilibrium good prices respond to alternative emission standards in the home country. Observe that standard S^{s} > OL are not binding; but if S^{s} < OL and if S^{s} is successively strengthened, then the relative price of the emission-intensive good continuously increases. The situation of theorem 8.2i is demonstrated in diagram 8.1 if we let p_{12}^{a*} be equal to OA, where p_{12}^{a*} denotes the commodity price ratio i the foreign country's autarkic laissez-faire equilibrium.

If p_{12}^{a*} = OB = p_{12}^{a} then no trade takes place unless the home country enforces a (binding) emission standard S^{s} < OL in which case it achieves a comparative advantage for the less emission intensive good 2. Theorem 8.2ii is illustrated in diagram 8.1, if we set p_{12}^{a*} = OC. In this case, the home country has a comparative advantage for good 1 as long as its emission standard is greater than OF. For S^{s} = OF no trade takes place whereas for S^{s} < OF the home country obtain a comparative advantage for good 1. If p_{12}^{a*} = OE, the home country's comparative disadvantage for good 2 cannot be turne over by enforcing a price and standard system. Whether such a constellation of technological differences between countries is relevant would have to be decided on on empirical grounds.

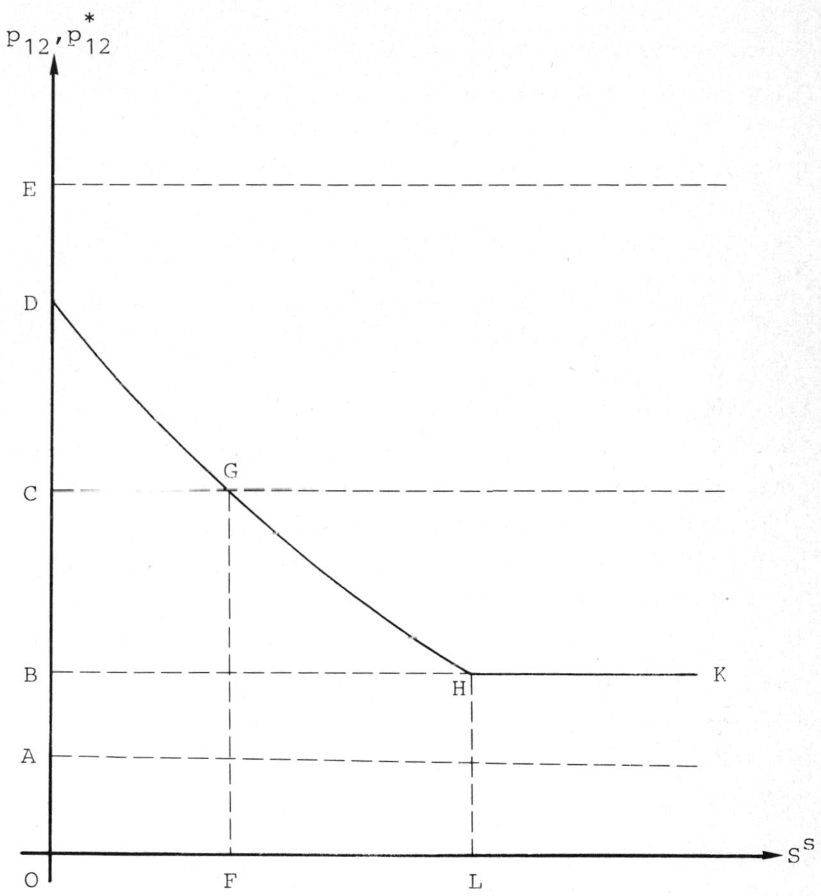

Diagram 8.1

It is not plausible to assume that developing countries have substantial technological comparative disadvantage in the production of the emission-intensive good. Thus in trade with industrialized countries they will typically export and specialize on the production of emission-intensive goods[1) (in particular, if the industrialized countries already enforce environmental controls).

As indicated in theorem 8.1, this is a necessary condition for a welfare loss unless the developing countries implement environmental controls themselves.

8.2 The Heckscher-Ohlin-Samuelson Theory of Pure Trade in an Environmental Setting

This leads us to discuss the pattern of trade between two (industrialized) countries (a) both of which established a price and standard system and (b) both of which do not differ from each other with respect to production technologies. The latter assumption is well known from the standard pure trade theory as developed by Heckscher, Ohlin and Samuelson, in particular. Central to this theory is the concept of (relative) factor abundance. Formally we apply this concept in our present model. But we attach to it a completely different interpretation, since it is used to compare the intensity of the countries' environmental protection. More specifically we introduce

Definition D 8.1: The environmental control by a price and standard system is said to be less restrictive in the home country than in the foreign country,

(i) if $S^S/R > S^{S*}/R^*$ (criterion of relative emission standards)

or alternatively but not equivalently

(ii) if $p_{SR} < p^*_{SR}$ (criterion of relative emission taxes),

where p_{SR} and p^*_{SR} denote autarkic equilibrium values.

---

1) Similar conclusions are drawn by R.C. d'Arge and A.V. Kneese (1972, p.434), A. Majocchi (1972, p. 458-479) and H.Siebert (1974c).

Observe that the definitons 8.1i and ii are a complete formal analogue to the factor abundance concepts, the endowment criterion and the factor price criterion, respectively, in pure trade theory. With the help of these analytical indicators of comparative restrictiveness of environmental controls we now derive two more results which are comparable to the well-known two versions of the standard Heckscher-Ohlin theorem.

Theorem 8.3: Let the assumptions A 2.8, A 2.9 and A 7.1 hold for both countries.

(i) The home country exports and specializes on the production of the emission-intensive good 1,
- if in A 7.1 $c_i = c_i^*$ for i = 1,2 and
- if its environmental control is less restrictive than in the foreign country according to the criterion of relative emission standards (D 8.1i).

(ii) The home country exports and specializes on the production of the emission-intensive good 1,
- if and only if its environmental control is less restrictive according to the criteria of relative emission taxes (D 8.1ii).

Proof: The proof proceeds by standard arguments exactly analogous to that of the Heckscher-Ohlin theorem[1].

Theorem 8.3ii can be illustrated with the help of parts I and III of diagram 7.2 (Harrod-Johnson diagram) that we reproduced in diagram 8.2, for convenience.

Suppose that in diagram 8.2 $\bar{p}_{SR}^*$ and $\bar{p}_{SR}$ are the pre-trade equilibrium relative emission taxes. Then diagram 8.2 shows that the associated equilibrium relative commodity prices satisfy $\bar{p}_{12}^* > \bar{p}_{12}$ which leads to the conclusion of theorem 8.3ii. The right hand part of diagram 8.2 reflects the assumption A 2.9iv according to which sector 1 is more emission intensive than sector 2. Even though theorem 8.3 is restricted to this case (for the sake of simple exposition), it can be easily extended to the opposite condition of

1) Compare M.C. Kemp (1969, p.74)

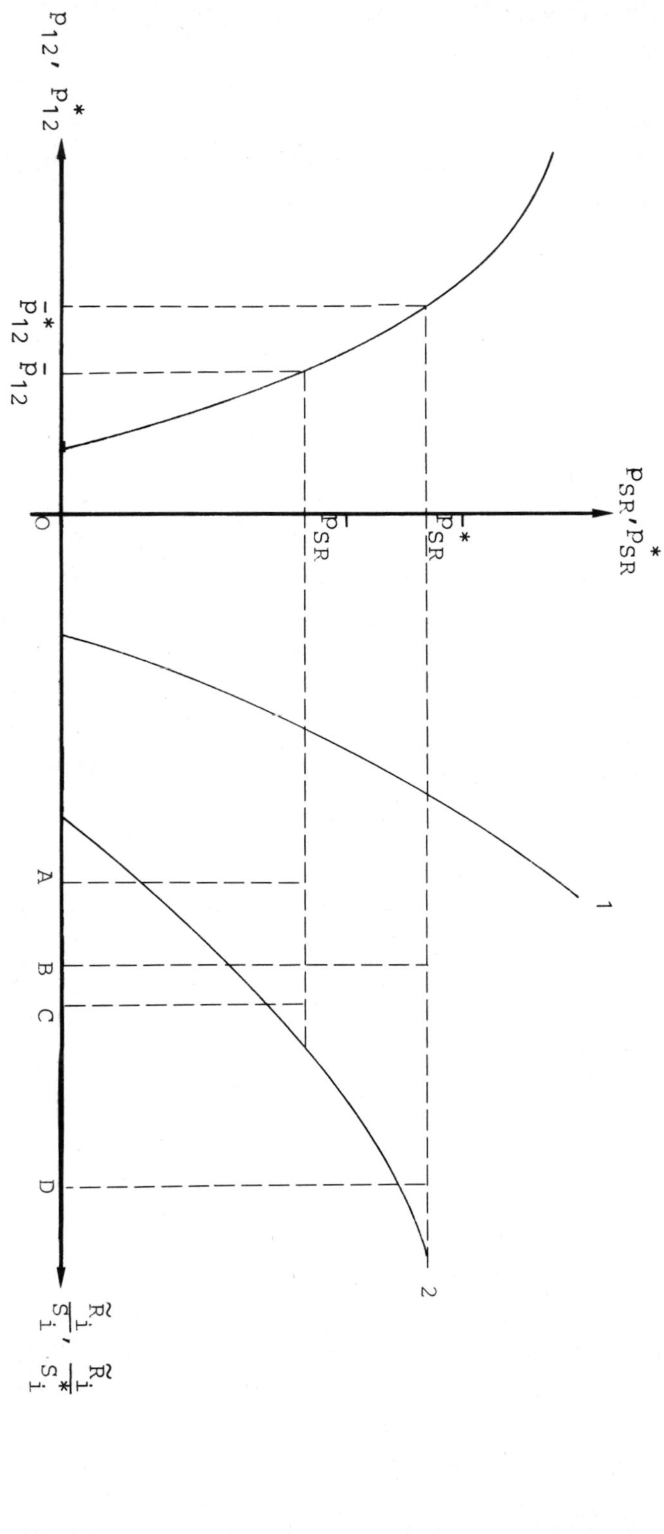
P_{12}, P_{12}^*
$\bar{P}_{12}^*$ $\bar{P}_{12}$
P_{SR}, P_{SR}^*
O
$\bar{P}_{SR}$
$\bar{P}_{SR}^*$
1
2
A
B
C
D
$\frac{\tilde{R}_i}{S_i}$, $\frac{\tilde{R}_i}{S_i^*}$

Diagram 8.2

relative emission-intensity. We need only relabel the commodities in diagram 8.2, i.e. good 1 becomes good 2 and vice versa. It follows immediately that $\bar{p}^*_{SR} > \bar{p}_{SR}$ implies $\bar{p}^*_{21} > \bar{p}_{12}$. Hence the home country exports and specializes on the production of good 2 which by assumption is (again) the emission-intensive commodity.

Since the demand conditions are not treated explicitly in diagram 8.2, this figure cannot be used to illustrate theorem 8.3i. But suppose that in diagram 8.2 R/S^S is equal to OA or OC and R^*/S^{S*} is equal to OD. Then $R/S^S < R^*/S^{S*}$ and the home country which enforces less restrictive environmental controls in the sense of D 8.1i exports the emission intensive good. Alternatively we can assign R/S^S = OC and R^*/S^{S*} = OB in diagram 8.2. In this case, the home country implements the more restrictive price and standard system according to the criterion of relative emission standards, but the less restrictive environmental policy according to definition D 8.1i - and it exports the emission-intensive good. In such a situation theorem 8.3ii still holds while the presupposition of identical demand is not satisfied in theorem 8.3i.

As to the d'Arge and Kneese conjecture on comparative advantage discussed above one may argue that this conjecture is rationalized and rigorously qualified by theorem 8.3, if one interprets the environmental assimilative capacities to be equal to the emission standards S^S and S^{S*}

Obviously, under the assumptions of theorem 8.3, as in the traditional theory, no country can suffer a welfare loss from trade, since by guarantee of the national environmental protection agencies the countries' environmental qualities remain unchanged in the trading equilibrium.

In spite of this similarity to the traditional theory the welfare implications of the model presented here are more intricate, for the emission standards as determinants of welfare clearly are policy decision variables. Let us suppose for the moment that each country has sufficient information to know the best attainable welfare level assigned to each emission standard and that consequently each country realizes its welfare maximum in its autarkic equilibrium. If we now allow for trade while simultaneously requiring the countries to maintain their autarkic emission standards, one country may be able to further increase its welfare position by changing its emission standard provided that the other country leaves its own standard unchanged. Evidently, in a trading world with national environmental controls the partner countries' welfare maximization problems are interdependent: One country's welfare depends on a decision variable (emission standard) of the other country, so that we are analytically confronted with a typical oligopoly problem.

We do not intend to investigate here possible solutions to this problem, but it is interesting to note that the mutual interdependence of trade and environmental policy instruments may cause an unstable international situation where the two countries are involved in a "trade and environmental quality war" in which one country possibly reacts to the other country's attempt to "export" its pollution. In order to avoid such inefficient conflict strategies the politicians should be recommended to try and reach a bargaining solution. In so far the theory indicated here supports the view, that the national governments should cooperate and coordinate their national environmental policies.

It is further important to realize that differences in the restrictiveness of national environmental policies according to definition D 8.1i or ii do not generally imply differences in national environmental qualities. Possible policy divergencies do not only depend on the restrictiveness definition chosen but also on the differences between the national damage functions A 2.5, the qualification of which is an entirely empirical question. Hence it is conceivable (or even likely) that two countries which harmonized their environmental policies in the sense of enforcing the same environmental quality must not apply equally restrictive environmental controls. So we obtain the unexpected result that the pursuit of uniform environmental quality targets - and in the intuitive sense the enforcement of equally restrictive environmental policies - may be the (only) reason for nonzero trade between two countries.

Finally, the analysis of the trade between two countries both of which enforce a price and standard system should be supplemented by an economically interesting re-interpretation of the well-known Factor-Price-Equalization theorem.

Theorem 8.4: Let the assumptions of theorem 8.3 hold and let the relative restrictiveness of the national price and standard systems be measured by the criterion of the relative emission standards (definition D 8.1i)

Then the relative emission prices p_{SR} and p^*_{SR} prevailing in the trading equilibrium are the same for both countries, if the environmental control in one country is not "too" restrictive as compared with that in the other country.

Sketch of the proof: Theorem 8.4 is in both, its presuppositions and conclusion, exactly equivalent to the Factor-Price-Equalization theorem. The relevance of the absolute difference $|(\bar{a}/\varepsilon) - (\bar{a}^+/\varepsilon^+)|$ for theorem 8.4 to hold may best be analyzed by the "cone of diversification method" as exposed by Chipman[1).]

Two remarks seem to be in order in connection with theorem 8.4. Firstly, equalization (or the tendency toward equalization) of relative emission prices implies that the emission prices must change in each country when the emission standards are maintained at their autarkic levels. This price change is performed by the market if the countries implemented the license-version of the price and standard system. If, however, the emission tax approach is adopted, it is the national environmental protection agencies, that have to change the emission taxes adequately when the economies pass from their autarkic equilibria to the trading equilibrium[2)]. If the national

1) For a detailed discussion of the Factor-Price-Equalization theorem see J.S. Chipman (1966, p.20n)

2) The trading equilibrium clearly reflects the long-run allocative displacements of trade and national environmental policies. The comparative static analysis that is applied here leaves completely unspecified the path toward the trading equilibrium and so-called short-run comparative advantages.

emission taxes would remain unchanged, the resultant tradin_ equilibrium would have the property that in one country the emission is less and in the other it is larger than the autarkic emission standard. More generally, the disadvantage of the tax approach as compared with the license approach is that it requires a policy response to every exogenous shock of the economy. It should also be emphasized that in the case of unchanged emission taxes one country may suffer a welfare loss from trade.

Secondly, provided that autarkic emission standards remain unchanged, when trade is allowed for, theorem 8.4 does not support the view that divergent social evaluation of environ mental quality and/or divergent relative emission standards in two trading countries necessarily call for different emission prices in trading equilibrium. Suppose that in a free trading world relative emission taxes are the same in all countries. If in such a situation some countries decide to pursue different national environmental quality targets, the international emission taxes will not diverge (within sc limits and with some analytical qualifications). This trade effect may be considered to be some kind of international harmonization of environmental policies where the harmonizat refers to tools emission taxes but not necessarily to target

9. Pollution Control in a Two-Sector-Two-Factor Economy with Trade

This chapter examines the problem of pollution control in an economy endowed with two conventional factors of production and one natural resource: environmental services. In contrast to chapters 3 and 7 the analysis integrates an additional resource into the problem. We have two producing sectors which offer two consumer goods (Q_i) and emissions (S_i) produced jointly with these two goods. The analysis takes over the net emissions approach developed in part I. We suppose that the initial allocation state $((\bar{Q}_i), \bar{U}(\bar{S}))$ which is the result of a competitive equilibrium is a welfare-inferior-situation. Environmental policy attempts to ration the usage of the environment by implementing an emission standard S^s for the economy. Section 9.1 presents the assumptions and describes the production technology. In section 9.2 we study the supply side of the closed economy. We analyze the incidental effects on factor rewards and sector structure when a given commodity price ratio is assumed. Then we study the impacts of variable commodity prices on sector structure with the help of Samuelson's reciprocity-relation. The closed model will be completed by integration of the demand side in section 9.3. In contrast to the preceding chapters the demand functions also depend on the value of the existing environmental quality. The pricing of the environment caused by binding emission standards leads to a reduction of the emission intensive sector. The decisive criterion is the concept of strong emission and factor intensity. In section 9.4 we get some results about the determinants of the changing autarky price ratio. Finally in section 9.5 we relate environmental policy to international trade. We try to give an answer to the question: To what extent does the scarcity or abundance of the environment, expressed by different international emission standards, determine the trade pattern? The problem will be discussed for a variety of possible cases.

9.1 The Structure of the Closed Economy

9.1.1 Production Technology

1. A representative firm of the two sectors (i=1,2) is regarded as maximizing profit subject to alternative pollution control regimes.

The firm produces two outputs, one of which is a marketable good Q_i and the other a waste product S_i. Both outputs are produced using labour A_i and capital K_i. The firm has a certain flexibility in selecting between a palette of production processes. At given quantities of primary inputs, the technology allows to produce various bundles (Q_i, S_i), because primary treatment of waste production can be carried out internally by the firm. Such a variable production process could be formalized as: [1]

$$Q_i = f^i(A_{i1}, K_i)$$

$$S_i = g^i(A_{i2}, K_i) \quad \text{and } A_{i1} + A_{i2} = A_i \tag{9.1}$$

where f^i is a usual concave production function and g^i is a convex function, which describes the net joint production of waste with $g^i_A < 0$, $g^i_K > 0$. The firm is able to reallocate labour inputs between two internal usages: production and waste treatment. Equation 9.1 shows that the net emissions depend directly on the chosen input mix and indirectly through the joint input K_i on the production level.

For analytical reasons we assume that this technology could be condensed in a single equation by

$$Q_i = F^i(A_i, K_i, S_i) \qquad i = 1,2 \tag{9.2}$$

where S_i can be interpreted as an environmental input (pollution level), although it is in fact a waste output.

---

1) Compare D.K.Whitcomb (1972, p.27).

Equation 9.2 satisfies the assumptions:[1)]

A 9.1 F^i is a strongly quasi-concave function defined on a subset D_{Qi} of input space $\mathbb{R}_+^3$, continuous and nonnegative. The domain

$$D_{Qi} = \{(A_i, K_i, S_i) \mid S_i \leqq \varphi_i(A_i, K_i),\ (A_i, K_i, S_i) \geqq 0\} \text{ is convex.}$$

φ_i is a strongly monotone, increasing function with $\varphi_i(0,0)=0$.

For all $S_i \in \{S_i' \mid S_i' = \varphi_i(A_i, K_i)\}$ we have $F_S^i = 0$.

A 9.2 F^i is at least twofold continuously differentiable, with $F_A^i > 0$, $F_K^i > 0$, $F_S^i \geqq 0$.

A 9.3 F^i is linear homogenous.

A 9.4 $Q_i > 0 \Leftrightarrow (A_i, K_i, S_i) > 0$

Diagram 9.1 illustrates F^i for fixed $\bar{K}_i$.[2)]

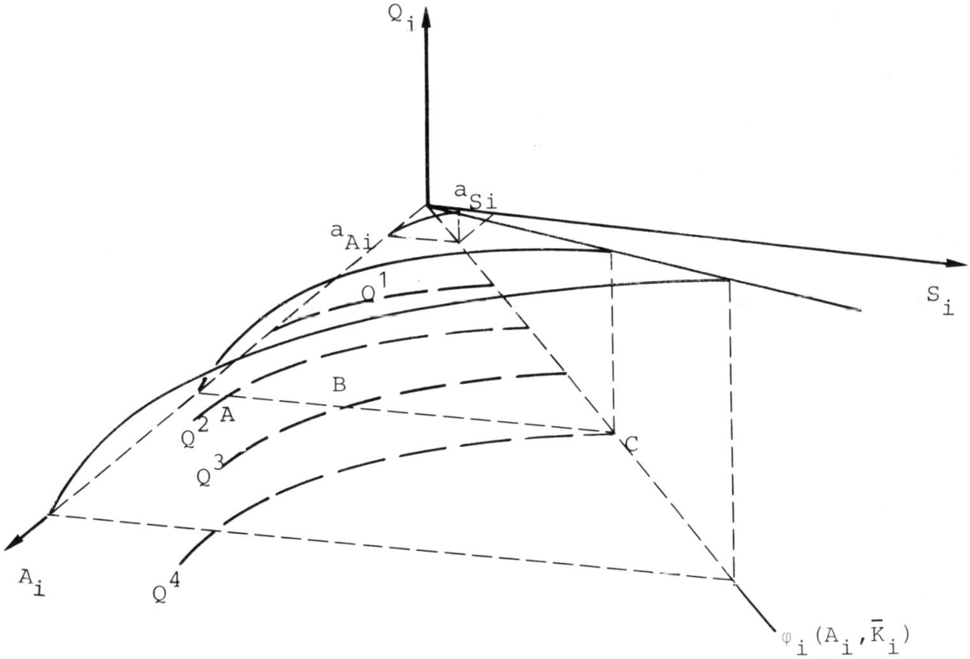

Diagram 9.1

1) Analytical equivalent assumptions are used in part I and in chapter 7 of part III concerning one-factor models.
2) Compare also diagram 2.4 in part I.

2. Expressing the production of Q_i and waste S_i as joint products allows for the possible trade off of Q_i and S_i, while maintaining a specific level of resource utilization. The formalization indicates the ability of the industry to treat its waste products internally. The reduction (avoiding) of S_i is realized by shifting resources out of the production of Q_i into the primary treatment of waste. Assumption A 9.1 ensures that the isoquants are strongly convex and the boundedness of production space for given (A_i,K_i) i.e. for given resources one can produce solely finite quantities. φ_i could be interpreted geometrically as a capacity line which is a collection of maximum $a_{Si} := S_i/Q_i$ - coefficients at alternative Q_i - levels. If the environmental service is a free good, we observe solely a production mix along φ_i. For all $S_i < \varphi_i$ it is possible to reduce the net emission at constant Q_i by increase of (A_i,K_i) or at constant (K_i,A_i) by reducing Q_i. A 9.2 is self explaining and A 9.3 is conventional but improves the analytical handling. A 9.4 denotes that all factors are essentials, and that a total waste avoidance is only compatible with zero production. At constant (A_i,K_i) we can realize a sectoral transformation curve $Q_i = \gamma_i(S_i)$, which shows that the marginal costs of treatment increase with every avoided emission unit.

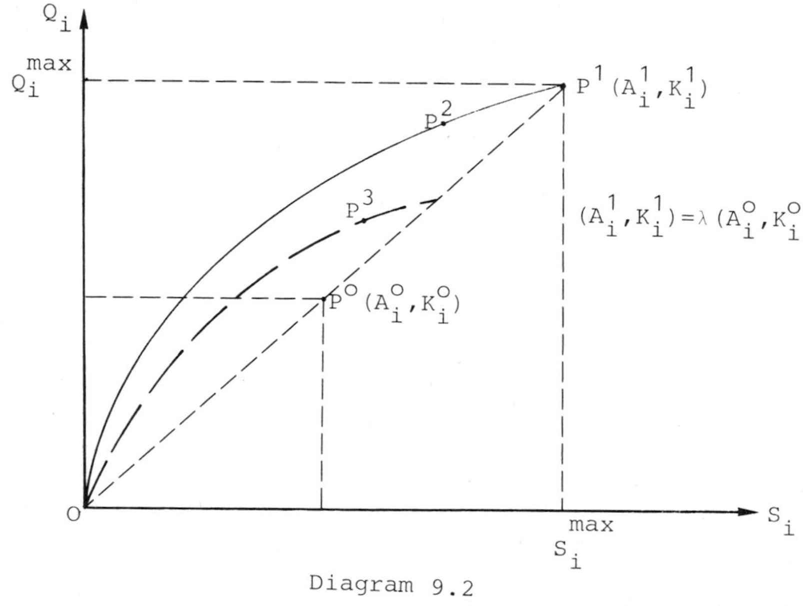

Diagram 9.2

Diagram 9.2 demonstrates clearly the jointness property of equation 9.2. We could imagine at least four possible reactions to pollution control policies:

i) The product and input mix remains constant but the scale level would be reduced. (P^o in diagram 9.2).

ii) At constant $k_i := K_i/A_i$ the product mix is changed. That is an internal reallocation of resources takes place. (P^2 in diagram 9.2).

iii) A combination of i) and ii) (P^3 in diagram 9.2).

iv) The same as in iii) but k_i is variable.

9.1.2 Assumptions and the Complete Model-Structure

Besides we set the additional assumptions:

A 9.5 Perfect competition prevails in all markets. Firms are maximizing profit.

A 9.6 All primary factors (A,K) are inelastically supplied. There exists perfect mobility between sectors and full employment.

A 9.7 Both sectors produce a homogenous waste product with quantities $S_1 + S_2 = S$.

A 9.8 The implemented emission standard $S^s \leq S$ is a binding constraint for the production possibilities of the economy.

There will be established a market in emission rights (licenses), where the total demand S_1+S_2 of polluters (buyers) is equated to the fixed supply S^s by a non-negative market price p_S for an emission right. The emission right directly confers a right to emit waste up to a certain rate per time unit. The actual standard then restricts the total industrial demand of "discharge services".
In total we have besides equations 9.2 the following relations:

$$K_1 + K_2 = K \tag{9.3}$$

$$A_1 + A_2 = A \tag{9.4}$$

$$S_1 + S_2 = S \leq S^s \tag{9.5}$$

$$U = G(S); \qquad U_S < 0, \; U_{SS} < 0 \tag{9.6}$$

$$Y = Q_1 + p_{21}Q_2 = p_A A + p_K K + p_S S^s \tag{9.7}$$

$$Q_i^d = D^i\,(p_{21}, Y, U) \qquad i = 1,2 \tag{9.8}$$

where $U = G(S)$ is the function of environmental quality discussed in part II and Y denotes national income; $p_{21}: = p_2/p_1$ defines the relative commodity price with good one as numeraire; p_j $(j = A,K,S)$ denote factor prices respectively the price of an emmision right. Q_i^d is the aggregate demand for commodity i, depending also on environmental quality because the consumers must take the existing deterioration as given. The firms solve at given prices (p_j) $j = 1,2,A,K,S$ the problem

$$\text{Max } L^i = \pi^i(Q_i,A_i,K_i,S_i) + \alpha_i^1 \; (F^i(A_i,K_i,S_i) - Q_i) + + \alpha_i^2 \; (\varphi_i(A_i,K_i) - S_i)$$

where $\pi^i =: p_iQ_i - p_AA_i - p_KK_i - p_SS_i$.

We get the usual conditions for an interior solution:

$$p_iF_j^i = p_j \qquad i = 1,2 \qquad j = A,K \tag{9.9}$$

In an economy without any environmental policy we have:

$$p_S = 0 \Rightarrow F_S^i = 0 \tag{9.10i}$$

If an effective price and standard-policy is implemented we have:

$$p_iF_S^i = p_S > 0 \tag{9.10ii}$$

9.2 The Supply Side of the Economy

In the following we discuss the comparative-static properties of the supply side where (A,K,p_{21}) are exogenous. We focus on the sector structure effect if the emission standard S^s is restricted.

It will be demonstrated that the sectoral demand of emission rights can be treated similarly as an input and that it depends on all prices. A central aim is to show, what are the effects of increasing prices for emission rights. The analytical difficulties arise from the explicit consideration of a third argument S_i in the production function, as can be studied in the literature[1]. Only in section 9.2 we have the special assumption:

A 9.9 Commodity prices are given exogenously.

1) P.A. Samuelson (1953, p. 1-20), R.W. Jones (1971, p. 3-21), R.N. Batra, F.R. Casas (1976, p. 21-38), R.W. Jones, J.A. Scheinkman (1977, p. 909-935).

9.2.1 The Structural Equations[1)]

1. The linear homogenity allows to formulate:

$$1 = f^i(a_{Ai}, a_{Ki}, a_{Si})$$

where (a_{Ai}, a_{Ki}) are the input requirements per output (input-coefficient) and a_{Si} denotes the waste output per output (emission-coefficient).
At full employment we have:

$$a_{A1}Q_1 + a_{A2}Q_2 = A \qquad (9.11)$$

$$a_{K1}Q_1 + a_{K2}Q_2 = K \qquad (9.12)$$

The total waste quantity of the economy is determined by

$$a_{S1}Q_1 + a_{S2}Q_2 = S \qquad (9.13)$$

The technology of the economy is summarized by the matrix T:

$$T: = \begin{bmatrix} a_{A1} & a_{A2} \\ a_{K1} & a_{K2} \\ a_{S1} & a_{S2} \end{bmatrix}$$

Due to assumptions A 9.3 and A 9.5 we get the price equations with the help of equations 9.9, 9.10:

$$a_{A1}p_A + a_{K1}p_K + a_{S1}p_S = p_1 \qquad (9.14)$$

$$a_{A2}p_A + a_{K2}p_K + a_{S2}p_S = p_2 \qquad (9.15)$$

By reason of A 9.1 - A 9.5, A 9.9 the coefficients a_{ji} are costminimal functions of $(p_A, p_K, p_S) > 0$

$$a_{ji} = A_{ji}(p_A, p_K, p_S) \qquad j = A,K,S; \quad i = 1,2 \qquad (9.16)$$

The eleven equations 9.11 - 9.16 describe the supply side of the economy with eleven endogenous variables $((Q_i), (a_{ji}), (p_j))$ and five exogenous variables (A, K, S^S, p_1, p_2).

---

1) Compare the base structure in R.N.Batra, F.R.Casas (1976, p.22n).

3. After total differentiation of equations 9.11, 9.12 and 9.13 we get:

$$\lambda_{A1}\hat{Q}_1 + \lambda_{A2}\hat{Q}_2 = \hat{A} - (\lambda_{A1}\hat{a}_{A1} + \lambda_{A2}\hat{a}_{A2}) \tag{9.17}$$

$$\lambda_{K1}\hat{Q}_1 + \lambda_{K2}\hat{Q}_2 = \hat{K} - (\lambda_{K1}\hat{a}_{K1} + \lambda_{K2}\hat{a}_{K2}) \tag{9.18}$$

$$\lambda_{S1}\hat{Q}_1 + \lambda_{S2}\hat{Q}_2 = \hat{S}^s - (\lambda_{S1}\hat{a}_{S1} + \lambda_{S2}\hat{a}_{S2}) \tag{9.19}$$

where $\lambda_{ji} := \frac{a_{ji}Q_i}{j}$ $j = A,K,S$ and $i = 1,2$ denotes the proportion of the total supply of the j-th factor used in the i-th sector. λ_{Si} is the proportion of sector i on total waste production. It may be noted that

$$\lambda_{j1} + \lambda_{j2} = 1 \qquad j = A,K,S$$

Define

$$[\lambda_{jk}] := \begin{bmatrix} \lambda_{j1} & \lambda_{j2} \\ \\ \lambda_{k1} & \lambda_{k2} \end{bmatrix} \qquad j,k = A,K,S \text{ as the relevant sub-matrices.}$$

Total differentiation of equations 9.14, 9.15 with usage of the cost minimization condition[1)] results in:

$$\theta_{A1}\hat{p}_A + \theta_{K1}\hat{p}_K + \theta_{S1}\hat{p}_S = \hat{p}_1 \tag{9.20}$$

$$\theta_{A2}\hat{p}_A + \theta_{K2}\hat{p}_K + \theta_{S2}\hat{p}_S = \hat{p}_2 \tag{9.21}$$

where θ_{ji} is the distributive share of the j-th factor in the i-th sector, with

$$\theta_{ji} = \frac{a_{ji}p_j}{p_i} \qquad \begin{matrix} j = A,K,S \\ i = 1,2 \end{matrix}$$

Whereas θ_{Si} is to be interpreted as that portion of cost which stems from the demand for emission rights (emission cost) and $\theta_{Ai} + \theta_{Ki} + \theta_{Si} = 1 \quad i = 1,2.$

1) A necessary condition for a minimum is:
$p_A da_{Ai} + p_K da_{Ki} + p_S da_{Si} = 0$ or $\theta_{Ai}\hat{a}_{Ai} + \theta_{Ki}\hat{a}_{Ki} + \theta_{Si}\hat{a}_{Si} = 0$

Define

$$[\theta_{jk}] := \begin{bmatrix} \theta_{j1} & \theta_{k1} \\ & \\ \theta_{j2} & \theta_{k2} \end{bmatrix} \qquad j,k = A,K,S \text{ as the relevant sub-matrices.}$$

We have the intention to shock the system for changes in (p_A, p_K, p_S). That is why we must express the change of a_{ji} in terms of price changes.

3. Let us define the partial elasticity of substitution[1)]σ^i_{jk} when we have the production function $Q_i = F^i(V^i_1, V^i_2, V^i_3) := F^i(A_i, K_i, S_i)$ as:

$$\sigma^i_{jk} = \frac{\sum_{h=1}^{3} F^i_h V^i_h}{V^i_j V^i_k} \frac{H_{jk}}{H} = \frac{Q_i}{V^i_j V^i_k} \frac{H_{jk}}{H} \qquad \begin{matrix} i = 1,2 \\ j,k = 1,2,3 \end{matrix}$$

where H denotes the determinant of the Hessian matrix and H_{jk} is the cofactor of the j,k element in H. We can reformulate this as

$$\sigma^i_{jk} = \frac{\partial V^i_j}{\partial p_k} \frac{p_k}{V^i_j} \frac{1}{\theta_{ki}}$$

With this formulation σ^i_{jk} shows, how a relative change of p_k affects the relative input j, when the factor price change is weighted by its distributive share θ_{ki}.

4. After total differentiation of equations 9.16 and observing the homogenity of degree zero[2)] of A_{ji} we get for the input demand:

1) Compare R.G.D. Allen (1938, p. 503n).
2) Since A_{ji} is homogenous of degree zero, we have:
$\theta_{Ai}\sigma^i_{Ak} + \theta_{Ki}\sigma^i_{Kk} + \theta_{Si}\sigma^i_{Sk} = 0;$ $\quad k = A,K,S \quad i = 1,2$

$$\hat{a}_{Ai} = -\ \theta_{Ki}\sigma^{i}_{KA}\ (\hat{p}_A-\hat{p}_K) - \theta_{Si}\sigma^{i}_{SA}\ (\hat{p}_A-\hat{p}_S)$$

$$\hat{a}_{Ki} = \ \theta_{Ai}\sigma^{i}_{AK}\ (\hat{p}_A-\hat{p}_K) - \theta_{Si}\sigma^{i}_{SK}\ (\hat{p}_K-\hat{p}_S) \quad i = 1,2 \quad (9.2$$

$$\hat{a}_{Si} = \ \theta_{Ai}\sigma^{i}_{AS}\ (\hat{p}_A-\hat{p}_K) + \theta_{Ki}\sigma^{i}_{KS}\ (\hat{p}_K-\hat{p}_S)$$

9.2.2 The Concept of Factor Intensity

1. For the following analysis we need the subsequent definition of intensity:

Definition D 9.1: For all $(p_A,\ p_S,\ p_K) > 0$ we call sector 1

a) relatively strong emission intensive if:

$$\frac{a_{S1}}{a_{K1}} > \frac{a_{S2}}{a_{K2}} \quad \text{and} \quad \frac{a_{S1}}{a_{A1}} > \frac{a_{S2}}{a_{A2}}$$

b) relatively weak emission intensive if:

$$\frac{a_{K1}}{a_{S1}} > \frac{a_{K2}}{a_{S2}} \quad \text{and} \quad \frac{a_{A1}}{a_{S1}} > \frac{a_{A2}}{a_{S2}}$$

The analogue applies to the other inputs.
We can deduce the following implications:

i) A sector is strongly intensive in one factor usage and weakly intensive in another one; the third factor being a nonintensive one.

ii) A sector is weakly intensive in the usage of that factor, which is used strongly in the other sector.

2. In this chapter we distinguish three cases:

case (1) sector 1 is strongly emission intensive and sector 2 is strongly capital intensive.

case (2) sector 1 is strongly emission intensive and
sector 2 is strongly labour intensive.

case (3) sector 1 is strongly capital intensive and
sector 2 is strongly labour intensive.

Definition D 9.1 and the assumed cases determine various constellations, which differ in the signs of the sub-determinants obtained from the matrices $[\lambda_{jk}]$ and $[\theta_{jk}]$.

We have:

$$\text{sign } |\lambda_{jk}| = \text{sign } (a_{j1}a_{k2} - a_{j2}a_{k1}) \text{ and}$$

$$\text{sign } |\lambda_{jk}| = \text{sign } |\theta_{jk}| \qquad j,k = A,K,S^{1)}$$

with $|\theta_{jk}| = \theta_{j1}\theta_{k2} - \theta_{j2}\theta_{k1}$, where $|\theta_{kj}| = - |\theta_{jk}|$.

If we consider the above relations we get the subsequent table of cases for the intensities:

case	signs of sub-determinants			cost shares
(1)	$\|\lambda_{SK}\| > 0$	$\|\lambda_{SA}\| > 0$	$\|\lambda_{KA}\| < 0$	$\theta_{S1} > \theta_{S2}$
	$\|\theta_{SK}\| > 0$	$\|\theta_{SA}\| > 0$	$\|\theta_{KA}\| < 0$	$\theta_{K2} > \theta_{K1}$
(2)	$\|\lambda_{SK}\| > 0$	$\|\lambda_{SA}\| > 0$	$\|\lambda_{AK}\| < 0$	$\theta_{S1} > \theta_{S2}$
	$\|\theta_{SK}\| > 0$	$\|\theta_{SA}\| > 0$	$\|\theta_{AK}\| < 0$	$\theta_{A2} > \theta_{A1}$
(3)	$\|\lambda_{KS}\| > 0$	$\|\lambda_{AS}\| < 0$	$\|\lambda_{KA}\| > 0$	$\theta_{K1} > \theta_{K2}$
	$\|\theta_{KS}\| > 0$	$\|\theta_{AS}\| < 0$	$\|\theta_{KA}\| > 0$	$\theta_{A2} > \theta_{A1}$

Table 9.1

1) It can be shown easily for example:

$$\text{sign } |\lambda_{SK}| = \frac{Q_1Q_2}{SK} [a_{S1}a_{K2} - a_{S2}a_{K1}] \text{ and}$$

$$\text{sign } |\theta_{SK}| = \frac{\theta_S\theta_K}{\theta_1\theta_2} \text{ sign } |\lambda_{SK}|$$

We should mention that it can be proved, that if a sector is strongly intensive (weakly intensive) in the usage of a factor, then the costshare of that factor θ_{ki} is greater (lower) than the corresponding share in the other sector.(We observe this fact in the last column of table 9.1.)
This means in economic terms for example: If a sector is declared as relatively emission intensive in physical units, the sector will also be intensive in that "factor" when we measure in cost shares. Finally it is important to notice that it is impossible to draw any conclusion about the factor which is neither strongly nor weakly intensive. For example, we cannot deduce in case (1) if $\theta_{A1} \lesseqgtr \theta_{A2}$.

9.2.3 <u>Emission-Standard Policy and Factor Rewards at Constant Commodity Prices</u>

1. Next we study the implications for factor prices if the environmental standard is enforced. Unlike in the usual (2x2) - model, the alteration of an endowment parameter affects the factor prices and therefore the costminimal input-mix[1].
The policy decides to shorten the minimum acceptable level of waste emission so that $\hat{S}^S < 0$. This means a reduction of the supply level of emission rights. The compatibility of supply and demand is reached by exclusion of potential emitters at a rising price p_S.

2. After executing some cumbersome analytical steps (appendix 9.1) we are able to compact the information given in 9.17 - 9.21 in a matrix-system, where C_1, C_2, C_3 represent some coefficients defined in appendix 9.1:

$$\begin{bmatrix} \theta_{A1} & \theta_{K1} & \theta_{S1} \\ \theta_{A2} & \theta_{K2} & \theta_{S2} \\ C_1 & C_2 & C_3 \end{bmatrix} \begin{bmatrix} \hat{p}_A \\ \hat{p}_K \\ \hat{p}_S \end{bmatrix} = \begin{bmatrix} \hat{p}_1 \\ \hat{p}_2 \\ B \end{bmatrix} \qquad (9.23)$$

1) The first systematic analysis of complex cases with more factors and goods can be found in P.A. Samuelson (1953, p. 1 - 20).

The determinant of coefficients of 9.23 is given by D:[1)]

$$D = -(\theta_{K1}-\theta_{K2})^2 \frac{1}{\theta_K} \sum_{\substack{i=1\\ i\neq 1}}^{2} \lambda_{Ai}\,\lambda_{Si}\,\theta_1\,\sigma^i_{AS}$$

$$-(\theta_{S1}-\theta_{S2})^2 \frac{1}{\theta_S} \sum_{\substack{i=1\\ i\neq 1}}^{2} \lambda_{Ai}\,\lambda_{Ki}\,\theta_1\,\sigma^i_{AK}$$

$$-(\theta_{A1}-\theta_{A2})^2 \frac{1}{\theta_A} \sum_{\substack{i=1\\ i\neq 1}}^{2} \lambda_{Ki}\,\lambda_{Si}\,\theta_1\,\sigma^i_{KS}$$

Inspection of D shows, that the sign of D depends only on the signs of σ^i_{jk}, since the terms before the sum terms are quadratic and all the coefficients are positive.
We can therefore point out under the assumption of weak substitutes that:[2)]

$$\sigma^i_{jk} > 0 \ (j = A,K,S,\ i = 1,2) \ \Rightarrow D < 0$$

3. We want to get information on the influences on factor prices (p_A, p_K) and emission prices p_S, if the emission standard is a binding constraint at given commodity prices. On account of A 9.6 we have $\hat{A} = \hat{K} = 0$ and $B = |\lambda_{AK}|\ \hat{S}^s$ in 9.23.

With A 9.6, A 9.9 and equation system 9.23 we compute:

$$\hat{p}_A = \frac{|\theta_{SK}|\ \ |\lambda_{KA}|}{D}\ \hat{S}^s \tag{9.24}$$

$$\hat{p}_K = -\frac{|\theta_{SA}|\ \ |\lambda_{KA}|}{D}\ \hat{S}^s \tag{9.25}$$

$$\hat{p}_S = \frac{|\theta_{KA}|\ \ |\lambda_{KA}|}{D}\ \hat{S}^s \tag{9.26}$$

---

1) The definitions of θ_k and θ_i i = 1,2, k = A,K,S are given in appendix 9.1.
2) It can be shown that one $\sigma^i_{jk} < 0$ (at most one) is compatible with D < 0. See the proof in R.N. Batra, F.R. Casas (1976, p. 24).

Equations 9.24 - 9.26 imply some economic results which are summarized for cases (1) - (3) in theorems 9.1 and 9.2:

Theorem 9.1 [1]: If A 9.1 - A 9.9 are given, intensifying the emission standard involves a rising price of emission rights
Proof: In all cases (1) - (3) we have sign $|\lambda_{AK}|$ = sign $|\theta_{AK}$
Since D < 0 we get with 9.26: $\hat{p}_S/\hat{S}^s < 0$.

The influence of the environmental policy on the prices of the primary factors can be shown with the help of 9.24, 9.25 and table 9.1 as:

$$\begin{aligned} &\text{case (1):} \quad \hat{p}_A / \hat{S}^s > 0 \text{ and } \hat{p}_K / \hat{S}^s < 0 \\ &\text{case (2):} \quad \hat{p}_A / \hat{S}^s < 0 \text{ and } \hat{p}_K / \hat{S}^s > 0 \qquad (9.27) \\ &\text{case (3):} \quad \hat{p}_A / \hat{S}^s > 0 \text{ and } \hat{p}_K / \hat{S}^s > 0 \end{aligned}$$

The economic results in respect to the changes of factor rewards are summarized in theorem 9.2.

Theorem 9.2: If A 9.1 - A 9.9 are valid, then the restrictio of the emission standard $\hat{S}^s < 0$ results in:

a) an increase (reduction) of the reward of capital and a reduction (increase) of the wage rate, if either sector is strongly emission intensive and the other sector is strongly capital intensive (labour intensive).
b) a reduction of both factor rewards, if neither of the sec tors produces relatively emission intensively.

Proof: Obvious with 9.24, 9.25 and table 9.1.

One should compare these results with the one-factor models in part II.

4. We focus our attention on the economic interpretation of case (1), so that the economic content should become obvious It is clear that the relatively "dirty" sector is attacked quite harder by the environmental policy, because its emissi cost per production unit θ_{S1} is greater than in the other sector.

1) The analysis gives us also some insights, if we would enforce an emission tax policy instead.

This becomes obvious if we reformulate 9.20, 9.21 as:

$$\theta_{Ai}\hat{p}_A + \theta_{Ki}\hat{p}_K = \hat{p}_i - \theta_{Si}\hat{p}_S \qquad i = 1,2 \qquad (9.28)$$

In the initial equilibrium we have an equality between commodity price and unit factor cost. We have found out that at constant commodity prices the policy activity causes a rise of p_S which forces an alternation in the input mix of the firms and therefore in the factor costs. We will prove later that sector 1 must reduce his production whereas sector 2 expands. Since sector 1 which is also labour intensive offsets relatively more labour than capital during the cut-down process, we must have divergencies in the factor-market-quantities at the initial factor prices because sector 2 demands capital services in greater proportions. These divergencies could be eliminated by higher capital rewards and lower wage rates as demonstrated in theorem 9.2 a). In accordance with this process - it will be later shown - the sectoral capital intensities[1] are lowered.

9.2.4 Factor Demand- and Sector Structure-Effects of Environmental Policy

1. In the following we study the involved implications for output structure, when factor demand responds in sequel of changed factor prices. We want to show how the sector structure is changed via substitution processes, if the commodity prices are given. We should mention explicitly, that in this framework the number of "factors" (j=3) exceeds the number of commodities (i=2). This results formally in a functional dependence of factor prices and endowments unlike in the usual (2x2)-model.[2]

1) Analytically we can tackle the interpretation problem by use of the famous Stolper-Samuelson theorem. With the help of equation 9.28 the reader is able to see that the impact of the policy can be treated similarly as a reduction of commodity prices (right-hand side). Since sector 1 is hit harder than the capital intensive sector 2 ($\theta_{S1} > \theta_{S2}$), we derive a raising of the rate of the relatively intensive factor capital etc.

2) Compare the analysis given by P.A. Samuelson (1953).

2. We rewrite 9.24 - 9.26 in the form of relative factor price changes and substitute the resulting expressions into system 9.22. We obtain for the change in costminimal factor demands:

$$\hat{a}_{Ai} = -\frac{|\lambda_{AK}|}{D}\{\theta_{Ki}\sigma^i_{AK}[\theta_{S2}-\theta_{S1}] + \theta_{Si}\sigma^i_{AS}[\theta_{K1}-\theta_{K2}]\}\hat{S}^s \quad (9.29)$$

$$\hat{a}_{Ki} = \frac{|\lambda_{AK}|}{D}\{\theta_{Ai}\sigma^i_{AK}[\theta_{S2}-\theta_{S1}] - \theta_{Si}\sigma^i_{KS}[\theta_{A2}-\theta_{A1}]\}\hat{S}^s \quad (9.30)$$

$$\hat{a}_{Si} = \frac{|\lambda_{AK}|}{D}\{\theta_{Ai}\sigma^i_{AS}[\theta_{K1}-\theta_{K2}] + \theta_{Ki}\sigma^i_{KS}[\theta_{A2}-\theta_{A1}]\}\hat{S}^s \quad (9.31)$$

We are able to give a unique qualitative statement about the reallocative effects only if we have information about the magnitude of shares of those factors, which are neither strongly nor weakly intensive in usage.

For instance in case (1) we have no data about sign $(\theta_{A2}-\theta_{A1})$ in case (2) we know nothing about sign $(\theta_{K1}-\theta_{K2})$ and finally in case (3) we have no knowledge about sign $(\theta_{S2}-\theta_{S1})$. It is possible, however, to get some information about the σ^i_{jk} with the given assumptions of strict quasi-concavity and linear homogenity after some tricky manipulations[1) (See appendix 9.2).
These inequalities must be properly substituted for those σ^i_{jk} which are multiplied with the unspecifiable term $(\theta_{j2}-\theta_{j1})$ j = A,K,S in the cases (1), (2) or (3).
Finally we are interested in getting a formula for the change of capital intensities: $\hat{k}_i = \hat{a}_{Ki} - \hat{a}_{Ai}$. We obtain from 9.29 and 9.30:

$$\hat{k}_i = \frac{|\lambda_{AK}|}{D}\{\sigma^i_{AK}[\theta_{S2}-\theta_{S1}]\,[\theta_{Ai}+\theta_{Ki}] - \theta_{Si}\sigma^i_{AS}[\theta_{K2}-\theta_{K1}] - \theta_{Si}\sigma^i_{KS}[\theta_{A2}-\theta_{A1}]\}\hat{S}^s \qquad i = 1,2 \quad (9.32)$$

If we check case (1) we get after substitution of inequality 9.2.1 of appendix 9.2 into 9.29 - 9.32 the results:

1) Compare F.R. Casas (1972, p. 199).

a) $\hat{a}_{Ai} > 0$ b) $\hat{a}_{Ki} < 0$

c) $\hat{a}_{Si} >$ (negative number); but $\hat{a}_{Si} < 0 \Leftarrow \sigma^{i}_{AS} = \sigma^{i}_{KS}$ (9.33)

d) $k_i < 0$

In case (2) we use 9.2.2 of appendix 9.2 and obtain

a) $\hat{a}_{Ai} >$ (negative number), therefore no unique statement

b) $\hat{a}_{Ki} > 0$ c) $\hat{a}_{Si} < 0$ (9.34)

d) $\hat{k}_i > 0$

Finally, if we check (3) we are unable to give clear statements about $\hat{a}_{Ki}$. But we succeed in deriving sufficient conditions for diminishing capital intensities if we use 9.2.3 of appendix 9.2 in 9.32. (Compare relation 9.2.4 in appendix 9.2).

Since $|\lambda_{AK}|$, D, $\hat{S}^s < 0$ we have as a sufficient condition for $\hat{k}_i < 0$: $\sigma^{i}_{AS} \geq \sigma^{i}_{KS}$,
which means in economic terms that the technology in both sectors allows an easier substitution of waste through labour. We get the following results in case (3):

a) $\hat{a}_{Ai} > 0$ b) $\hat{a}_{Ki} <$ (positive number); no result.

(9.35)

c) $\hat{a}_{Si} < 0$ d) $\hat{k}_i < 0 \Leftarrow \sigma^{i}_{AS} \geq \sigma^{i}_{KS}$ $i = 1,2$

All the results demonstrate that the response to a pollution policy (at constant factor endowment and prices p_i) is a shift in the production mix indicated by $\hat{a}_{Si}$ and in the input mix indicated by $\hat{k}_i$. The direction of the shift depends on the intensity constellations shown by 9.33 - 9.34.
We observe a shrinkage in the emission-coefficients which is a intuitive clear result if one considers $\hat{p}_S > 0$. The lowering (raising) of the capital intensities becomes obvious if one notices the factor price effects in theorem 9.2.

3. The next step is to show how the supply side of the economy is affected. We substitute equations 9.29 - 9.31

into 9.1.1 of appendix 9.1. After some intricate transformations we get[1] for i = 1,2:

$$\hat{Q}_i\Big|_{\substack{\hat{p}_i=0\\ \hat{A}=\hat{K}=0}} = (-1)^{i-1}\frac{\hat{S}^s}{\theta_1\theta_2}\frac{1}{D}\{(\theta_{S2}-\theta_{S1})(\theta_{Ai}+\theta_{Ki})\theta_i\sum_{\substack{i=1\\ i\neq l}}^{2}\lambda_{Ai}\lambda_{Ki}\theta_l\sigma^i_{AK}$$

$$-(\theta_{A2}-\theta_{A1})\theta_S\lambda_{Ai}\sum_{\substack{i=1\\ i\neq l}}^{2}\lambda_{Ki}\lambda_{Si}\theta_l\sigma^i_{KS} \qquad (9.36)$$

$$+(\theta_{K1}-\theta_{K2})\theta_S\lambda_{Ki}\sum_{\substack{i=1\\ i\neq l}}^{2}\lambda_{Ai}\lambda_{Si}\theta_l\sigma^i_{AS}\} \qquad i,l=1,2 \quad i\neq l$$

We observe that the changes in Q_1 and Q_2 have opposite directions: sign $\hat{Q}_1$ = - sign $\hat{Q}_2$.
But we are unable to specify definitely the signs of $\hat{Q}_i$ because we have no information - as before - about the factor shares of the non-intensive factors.[2] If we take into consideration the inequalities 9.2.1 or 9.2.2 or 9.2.3 of appendix 9.2 corresponding to the unspecified term in 9.36, we will obtain after some cumbersome transformation, a unique qualitative result[3]. In case (1) we consider inequality 9.2.1 and derive for i = 1:[4]

$$\hat{Q}_1 < \frac{\hat{S}^s}{D} F < 0 \qquad (9.37)$$

where $F < 0$ denotes a complicated term defined in appendix 9.2. Because $\hat{S}^s < 0$, $D < 0$ and $F < 0$, we see that the right-hand side of the inequality is negative, so that we can conclude unambiguously $\hat{Q}_1 < 0$ or $\hat{Q}_1/\hat{S}^s > 0$.
Through corresponding operations[4] we can show that for i = 2 in 9.36:

$$\hat{Q}_2 > -\frac{\hat{S}^s}{D} F' > 0 \qquad (9.38)$$

1) See R. Gronych (1980).
2) The result is unequivocal if we assume capital being almost exclusively used in the waste treatment process and labour is negligible for substitution: $\sigma^i_{KS} > 0$ and $\sigma^i_{AS} = 0$.
3) In the other case we consider inequality 9.2.2 and get an analogous result.
4) See equation 9.2.5 in appendix 9.2.

where F' < 0 denotes an analogous term as F in 9.37. Therefore we can repeat the economic effects of cases (1) and (2) in theorem 9.3.

Theorem 9.3[1]: If A 9.1 - A 9.9 are valid, the restriction of the emission standard reduces the output of the relatively emission intensive sector and increases the output of the other sector.

Proof: Obvious with 9.37 and 9.38. The other case (2) can be shown in the same way.

This central result makes it thoroughly clear that the policy involves a sectoral change of the economy if we ignore the demand side. We have seen in the foregoing discussion, which reallocative processes have taken place to fulfil the environmental goal. We observe equivalent results in the case of an emission tax policy in part II.

4. In the following sections we are interested in changes of relative commodity supply. With equation 9.2.6 in appendix 9.2 we are able to evaluate possible structure effects. For the moment we want to know the effects if $\hat{p}_i = 0$. By taking the difference $\hat{Q}_1 - \hat{Q}_2$ with the help of 9.36 we obtain equation 9.2.7 in appendix 9.2. We see that:

i) the intersectoral differences in the factor cost shares $\theta_{k1} - \theta_{k2}$ determine the direction of the sectoral change and

ii) the extent of the change depends on the magnitude of the standard change as well as on the size of the "dirty" industry and on the technical characteristics of production (e.g. partial substitution elasticities)

It can be shown that the most polluting industry must reduce more than proportional if the sector is relatively unimportant[2].

1) Theorem 9.3 could be generalized. It can be shown that at constant p_i an increase in the supply of one factor increases the output of the commodity using the increased factor relative intensively, while the other output will decrease. The well-known Rybczynski-theorem is also valid in this extended neoclassical model. R.N. Batra, F.R. Casas (1976, p. 34); R.W. Jones, J.A. Scheinkman (1977).

2) A sufficient condition for this result is: $\lambda_{A1} + \lambda_{K1} + \lambda_{S1} < 1$. See R.W. Jones; J.A. Scheinkman (1977, p. 932).

5. We want to demonstrate graphically the allocative effects in factor space and commodity space. We neglect the factor capital and consider the case (1), where sector 1 is strongly emission intensive. If the economy is richly endowed with environmental services, so that the industries do not exhaust the assimilative capacity in a no-policy situation (or the existing standard) we have no restrictions for the production possibilities of the economy. No single industry exceeds the capacity (or standard) at complete specialization:

$$S^S > a_{S1}Q_1^V > a_{S2}Q_2^V \text{ where } Q_i^V := \max[Q_1(A,K), Q_2(A,K)].$$

In the conventional Edgeworth-Bowley-box [1] with dimensions (A,S^S), all industries produce along expansion paths where $F_S^i = 0$. That is to say, we have an "excess-supply" of emission possibilities. The reader could imagine this situation in diagram 9.3 when the dimension of S^S is enlarged. In commodity space we get a projection in (Q_1,Q_2)-space of the generalized transformation function $Q_1 = T(Q_2,S^S)$. In the

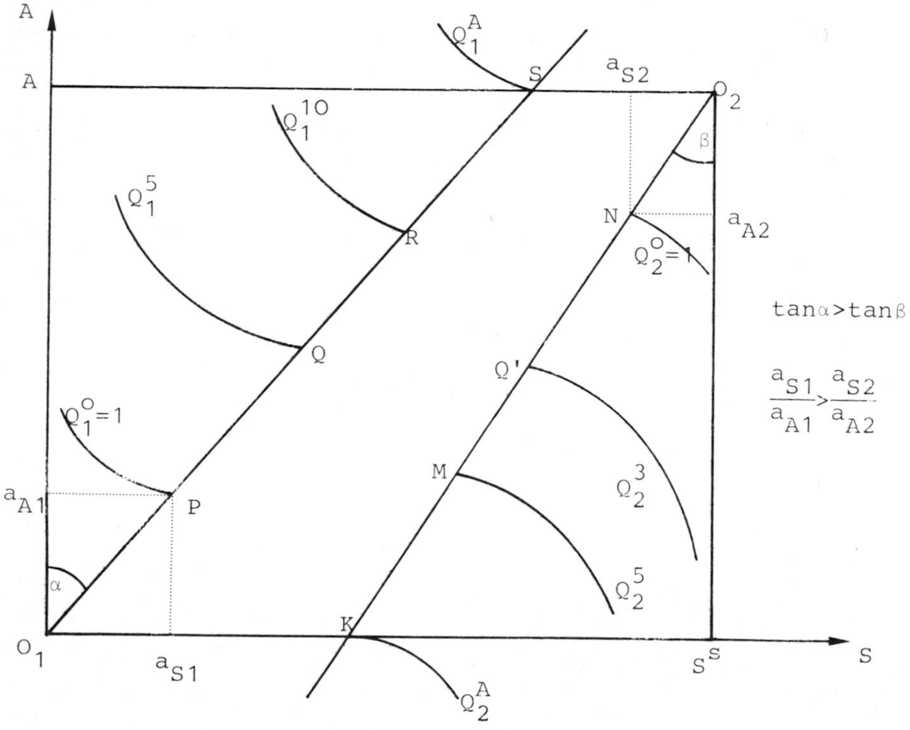

Diagram 9.3

1) Compare the geometrical description on page 43.

no policy case we have $p_S = 0$, and the resultant curve denotes the maximum reachable output combinations (diagram 9.4).
If $p_{21} := \frac{p_2}{p_1}$ is given, we select a special allocation drawn as R and N resp. A in diagram 9.4.

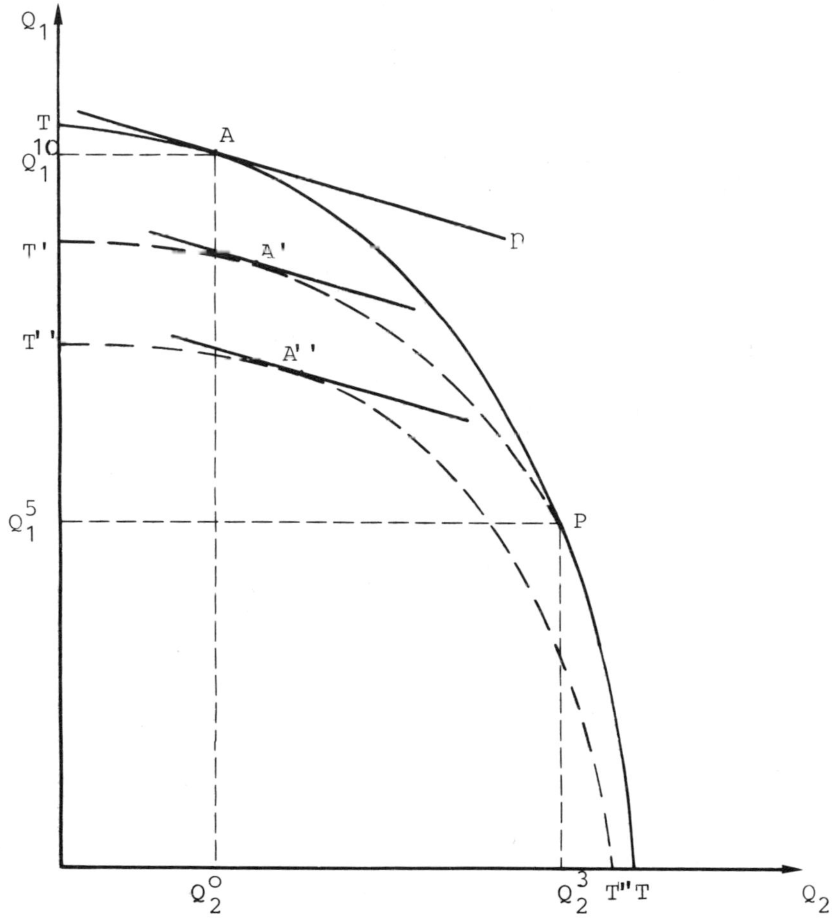

Diagram 9.4

The restriction of S^S gives rise to a shift of point 0_2 to the left. The now existing S^S could be an effective restriction at certain p_i's. That is to say, the excess "supply" of emission rights disappears and we observe a positive p_S for the now scarce resource. Observe T'T if S^S is fixed effectively. It is possible that at some other relative prices the existing norm is not effective. See points M,M' in diagram 9.5 and segment PT in diagram 9.4. Diagram 9.5 demonstrates the case $a_{S2}Q_2^v < S^s < a_{S1}Q_1^v$ which causes an efficiency locus PRO_2.

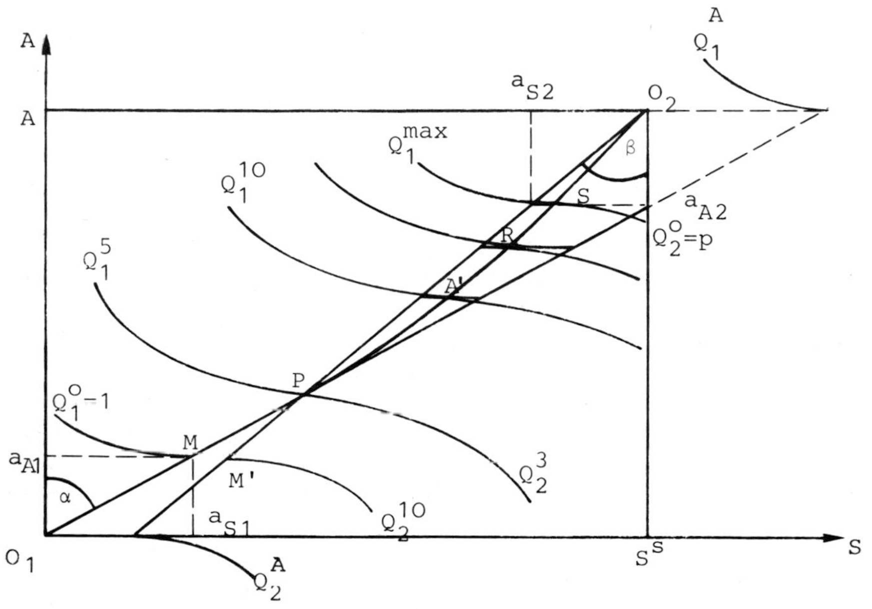

Diagram 9.5

Only if S^s is a binding constraint for all p_{21}, we generate a monotone increasing efficiency locus and an inward shift of the transformation graph.[1)] We denote the resulting curve as the transformation curve relative to S^s. We notice at given p_{21} and $\hat{S}^s < 0$ a shift of supply from A' to A'' in diagram 9.4 which visualizes the Rybczynski-effect.

6. In case (3) we observe that no industry is strongly intensive in the usage of the environment.

1) $S^s < a_{S2}Q_2^v < a_{S1}Q_1^v$

After diverse manipulations we have expression 9.2.8 in appendix 9.2. Depending on our assumptions $\theta_{K1} > \theta_{K2}$ and $\theta_{A2} > \theta_{A1}$, we conclude $\hat{Q}_1/\hat{S}^s < 0$, if the sufficient conditions a), b) are fulfilled:

$$\text{a) } \sigma^1_{AS}\lambda_{K2}\lambda_{A1} \geqq \sigma^1_{KS}\lambda_{A2}\lambda_{K1} \quad \text{resp. } 1 > \frac{\lambda_{K2}\lambda_{A1}}{\lambda_{A2}\lambda_{K1}} \geqq \frac{\sigma^1_{KS}}{\sigma^1_{AS}};^{1)} \qquad (9.39)$$

and

$$\text{b) } \sigma^2_{AS} \geqq \sigma^2_{KS}$$

A symmetric condition holds if $\theta_{A1} > \theta_{A2}$ and $\theta_{K2} > \theta_{K1}$ (the opposite case) and $\hat{Q}_1/\hat{S}^s < 0$:

$$\text{a) } \sigma^1_{AS}\lambda_{K2}\lambda_{A1} \leqq \sigma^1_{KS}\lambda_{A2}\lambda_{K1} \quad \text{resp. } \frac{\sigma^1_{KS}}{\sigma^1_{AS}} \geqq \frac{\lambda_{K2}\lambda_{A1}}{\lambda_{A2}\lambda_{K1}} > 1 \qquad (9.40)$$

and

$$\text{b) } \sigma^2_{KS} \geqq \sigma^2_{AS}$$

The economic results are stated in theorem 9.4:

<u>Theorem 9.4:</u> If A 9.1 - A 9.9 are valid, the restriction of S^s brings about a rise in the output of the capital intensive (labour intensive) sector, if it is much more difficult to substitute capital (labour) in both sectors against waste than the other factor.

Proof: 9.36 in connection with inequality 9.2.3 in appendix 9.2

The cases consider the technological possibility that both sectors are able to reduce their net production of waste much easier through additional labour input (capital input).

The economic content is as follows. The higher p_S for emission rights forces both sectors to use the remaining factors intensively. The resulting adjusting process is a mixture of price- and quantity-changes, since the policy influences

---

1) Notice $\frac{\lambda_{K2}\lambda_{A1}}{\lambda_{A2}\lambda_{K1}} := \frac{k_2}{k_1} < 1$

the factor price in a way which is described in theorem 9.2. At constant p_{21} we get a backward incidence on the factor rewards (theorem 9.2b) as well as a reduction of sectoral capital-intensities if labour is easier to substitute ($\sigma^i_{AS} \geqq \sigma^i_{KS}$).

Therefore the output of the sector falls which uses the now relative scarce resource labour intensively. In case (3) this has been sector 2.

7. Now we make a little digression to point out a property of the generalized, concave transformation function $Q_1 = T(Q_2,S)$ If $S=S^s$ is fixed we have geometrically speaking a cut of the function in $\mathbb{R}^3_+$ and get a projection into (Q_1,Q_2)--space. We call the endowment-triplet now as $V:=(A,K,S^s)$. We want to know something about this conventional transformation-curve:

<u>Lemma 9.1:</u> a) If A 9.1 - A 9.4 are valid and A 9.6, A 9.8 holds, the transformation curve $Q_1 = T(Q_2,V)$ relative to a given standard S^s has a concave shape.
b) If the input vectors of the sectors are linearly independent for all (p_k), k=A,K,S, then $T(Q_2,V)$ is strongly concave for all $V \geqq 0$.[1)]

Proof: The leading idea of the proof could be found in[2)] K.Lancaster (1969, p. 127n)

<u>Lemma 9.2:</u> Reciprocity relation [3)]
If $Q_1 = T(Q_2,V)$ is a strongly concave function, then the following relations are valid:

$$\text{i)}\ \frac{\partial p_S}{\partial p_i} = \frac{\partial Q_i}{\partial S^s} \qquad \text{ii)}\ \frac{\partial p_A}{\partial p_i} = \frac{\partial Q_i}{\partial A} \qquad \text{iii)}\ \frac{\partial p_K}{\partial p_i} = \frac{\partial Q_i}{\partial K} \qquad i=1,2 \qquad (9.41)$$

Proof: See R.W.Jones; J.A.Scheinkman (1977, p.921n)

The relations 9.41 give us a link between the allocation

1) In this (2x3)-case the condition demands, that the factor- and emission intensities defined by definition D 9.1 are different between sectors for all (p_k).
2) A thorough proof will be given in R. Gronych (198o)
3) see P.A.Samuelson (1953, p. 1-2O)

effects and the price effects of a change in endowment. should point out that this equivalence is given by the duality relation of the Rybczynski-theorem and the Stolper-Samuelson-theorem.

The precise understanding of these partial derivatives is important. On the right-hand side of each equation we are concerned with a change in output, when the endowments of one of the three inputs changes with the relative goods price ratio p_{21} being fixed. On the left-hand side we are concerned with the change in an input price (in money terms) when one of the goods prices p_i has changed.

9.2.5 The Impacts of Variable Output Prices

1. In this section now we fix the endowment vector inclusively S^S. We are able to compute the reactions of the system at varying commodity prices by equation system 9.23, but the analysis is much easier, if we use the just obtained reciprocity-relations in equations 9.41.

2. We redefine 9.41 in terms of "hat"-variables as:[1]

$$\frac{\hat{p}_S}{\hat{p}_i} = \frac{\theta_i}{\theta_S}\frac{\hat{Q}_i}{\hat{S}^S}\Bigg|_{\hat{p}=0} \quad (9.42i) \qquad \frac{\hat{p}_A}{\hat{p}_i} = \frac{\theta_i}{\theta_A}\frac{\hat{Q}_i}{\hat{A}}\Bigg|_{\hat{p}=0} \quad (9.42ii)$$

$$\frac{\hat{p}_K}{\hat{p}_i} = \frac{\theta_i}{\theta_K}\frac{\hat{Q}_i}{\hat{K}}\Bigg|_{\hat{p}=0} \quad (9.42iii)$$

We now reformulate 9.42i as a relation which shows the change in real emission price caused by relative goods price changes:[2]

$$\frac{\hat{p}_S-\hat{p}_2}{\hat{p}_2-\hat{p}_1} = -\frac{\hat{Q}_1}{\hat{S}^S}\frac{\theta_1}{\theta_S}\Bigg|_{\hat{p}=0} \quad \text{resp.} \quad \frac{\hat{p}_S-\hat{p}_1}{\hat{p}_2-\hat{p}_1} = \frac{\hat{Q}_2}{\hat{S}^S}\frac{\theta_2}{\theta_S}\Bigg|_{\hat{p}=0} \qquad (9.43)$$

1) The notation on the right-hand side symbols explicitly the given goods price ratio.
2) A formal proof can be found in R. Gronych (1980).

We easily see that 9.43 allows to make some statements about changes of real emission prices, since we have some information about the terms on the right-hand side given by theorem 9.3.

If p_S is an endogenous variable in the model and S^S is the instrument variable, then we can deduce the following result:

Theorem 9.5: If A 9.1 - A 9.8 are valid, then a raise of the relative commodity price of a good causes an increase of the real price of emission rights if the concerned good is strongly emission intensive.

Proof: By theorem 9.3 we have $\hat{Q}_i/\hat{S}^S > 0$ and $\hat{Q}_j/\hat{S}^S < 0$ if $\theta_{Si} > \theta_{Sj}$ and $\hat{S}^S < 0$.

With i=1 (i=2) and $\hat{p}_{21} = \hat{p}_2 - \hat{p}_1 < 0$ (>0) we obtain with equation 9.43 $\hat{p}_S - \hat{p}_i > 0$ q.e.d.

We are able to show that the real price of the nonintensive input declines.[1]

3. We know that if both goods are produced and A 9.3, A 9.5 are valid, then the goods prices reflect unit costs.
In the case of exogenously given p_S[2] (policy fixes emission taxes), we can also get a statement about the change in supply price ratio. With 9.42i i = 1,2 we obtain:

$$\hat{p}_{21} := \hat{p}_2 - \hat{p}_1 = \theta_S \, C \, \hat{p}_S \tag{9.44}$$

where $C := \left[\dfrac{1}{\theta_2 \left.\dfrac{\hat{Q}_2}{\hat{S}^S}\right|_{\hat{p}=0} - \theta_1 \left.\dfrac{\hat{Q}_1}{\hat{S}^S}\right|_{\hat{p}=0}} \right]$ and sign $\hat{p}_{21}$ = sign C.

It should be noticed that equation 9.44 reflects the information how relative supply-price is changed and not how the autarky-price is changed.

1) The Stolper-Samuelson statement seems to be valid also in this extended model.
2) In this case then S is an endogenous variable.

Theorem 9.6[1]: If A 9.1 - A 9.8 are valid, we have an increase in relative supply price (=unit cost) of the strongly emission intensive good, if the emission tax is raised.

Proof: Obvious with the help of 9.44 and application of theorem 9.3.
Compare also the results in part II with an emmision tax policy.

4. The reciprocity relations in the formulation of 9.43 can be used to check the sensitivity of sector structure at varying commodity prices and constant endowments. For this, we need some information about the changes of relative input prices.
We compute for $\hat{V} = (\hat{A},\hat{K},\hat{S}^S) = 0$ the expressions 9.3.1 - 9.3.2 in appendix 9.3.

After substitution of equations 9.3.1 - 9.3.3 of appendix 9.3 into 9.2.6 of appendix 9.2, we yield after some lengthy transformations[2] the important result:

$$\left.\frac{\hat{Q}_1-\hat{Q}_2}{\hat{p}_{21}}\right|_{\hat{V}=0} = \frac{1}{D}\{\theta_K S_{AK} S_{KS} + \theta_A S_{AS} S_{AK} + \theta_S S_{KS} S_{AS}\} := \frac{H}{D} \qquad (9.45)$$

$$S_{jk} := \sum_{i=1}^{2} \frac{\lambda_{ji}\lambda_{ki}}{\theta_i} \sigma^i_{jk} > 0 \qquad j,k = A,K,S \quad j \neq k$$

where H > 0 denotes the remaining braced term.

Since D < 0 and $S_{jk} > 0$ we get the important economic result:

Theorem 9.7: If we have an economy with incomplete specialisation and given A 9.1 - A 9.8, the output of the sector raises, that realizes an increase of its relative goods price while the other sector's output declines (normal price output response).[3]

---

1) Analogous results can be obtained under different intensity assumptions.
2) See R. Gronych (1980).
3) The algebra of 9.45 confirms the strongly concave shape of the transformation locus relative to a fixed emission standard.

5. At this stage we are able to summarize the effects, which influence the relative commodity supply of the economy given by 9.2.7 in appendix 9.2 and 9.45 denoted by the functions g and h:

$$\hat{Q}_1-\hat{Q}_2 = g(\hat{S}^s, (\theta_{S2}-\theta_{S1}), (\theta_{K2}-\theta_{K1}), (\theta_{A2}-\theta_{A1})) + h(\hat{p})$$

We have demonstrated by theorems 9.3, 9.7 that the sector structure depends on the emission intensity respectively factor intensity and on the given commodity price ratios.

9.3 The Demand Side of the Economy

In the next step we close the model by integrating the demand side of the economy. Remembering that aggregate demand is influenced parametrically by the environmental quality, we get for total change of 9.8:

$$\hat{Q}_1^d = \eta_{1p}\hat{p}_{21} + \eta_{1Y}\hat{Y} + \eta_{1U}\varepsilon_{US}\hat{S}^s$$

$$\hat{Q}_2^d = -\eta_{2p}\hat{p}_{21} + \eta_{2Y}\hat{Y} + \eta_{2U}\varepsilon_{US}\hat{S}^s$$

where $\eta_{ip} > 0$, η_{iY} denote price elasticities resp. income elasticities of demand, while $\varepsilon_{US} := \frac{dU}{dS}\frac{S}{U} < 0$ represents the reaction of environmental quality to changes of waste disposal, and $\eta_{iU} \gtrless 0$ symbols the substitutional/complementar character of U to consumption good i.
The latter dependency is usually ignored since it complicates the analysis. Only in the case $\eta_{iU} = 0$ or $\eta_{1U} = \eta_{2U}$ we are allowed to ignore the influence.

With regard to

$$\sigma_D := \frac{\partial(Q_1^d/Q_2^d)}{\partial p_{21}} \frac{p_{21}}{Q_1^d/Q_2^d} = \eta_{1p}+\eta_{2p} > 0, \text{ we receive}$$

for relative demand:

$$\hat{Q}_2^d - \hat{Q}_1^d = - \sigma_D\hat{p}_{21} + (\eta_{2Y} - \eta_{1Y})\hat{Y} + \varepsilon_{US}(\eta_{2U} - \eta_{1U})\hat{S}^s \quad (9.4$$

which reveals that the demand structure depends on changes of price ratios, real income and environmental quality.

In contrast to usual models we have three different kinds of demand characteristics.

9.4 Determinants of the Autarky Price Ratio

1. The supply side could be formalized in an analogous way through 9.2.7 in appendix 9.2 and with 9.45 as:

$$\hat{Q}_2 - \hat{Q}_1 = -\hat{p}_{21}\frac{H}{D} - \hat{S}^s\frac{G}{D} = \hat{p}_{21}\sigma_S - \hat{S}^s\frac{G}{D} \tag{9.47}$$

where $\sigma_S := -\frac{H}{D} > 0$ is called as the elasticity of commodity substitution along the transformation curve.[1]

Market equilibrium after the disturbance requires:

$\hat{\bar{Q}}_i - \hat{Q}_i^d = 0 \ (i = 1,2)$.

We obtain from 9.46 - 9.47 for the equilibrium price change:

$$\hat{p}_{21} = \frac{1}{(\sigma_S+\sigma_D)}\{\varepsilon_{US}(\eta_{2U}-\eta_{1U}) + \frac{G}{D}\}\hat{S}^s + \frac{(\eta_{2Y}-\eta_{1Y})}{(\sigma_S+\sigma_D)}\hat{Y} \tag{9.48}$$

Equation 9.48 enables us to point out the determinants of the autarky price ratio. The first term reflects the influence of environmental policy while the second term covers the induced effects of real income shifts. We see that the incidence of policy measures depends on the one hand on technological constellations (G) and on the other hand on behavioural characteristics of the demand side.

2. We will study the problem under the assumption of homothetic preferences in Q_i^d, so that $\eta_{1Y} = \eta_{2Y} = 1$.[2]

If we consider the relation $\eta_{1U}\theta_1 + \eta_{2U}\theta_2 = 0$ with $\theta_i > 0 \ (i = 1,2)$, then we can conclude that always one good is complementary ($\eta_{iU} > 0$) and the other one is a substitute ($\eta_{jU} < 0$) to U or both goods are independent of existing U($\eta_{iU} = 0$).

We can therefore deduce from 9.48 if $\hat{S}^s < 0$:

$$\hat{p}_{21} \gtrless 0 \quad \Leftrightarrow \quad \varepsilon_{US}(\eta_{2U}-\eta_{1U}) + \frac{G}{D} \lessgtr 0 \tag{9.49}$$

When we limit our attention to cases (1) and (2), we have:

---

1) R.W. Jones (1965).

2) Later we will discuss cases with the assumption dropped.

Theorem 9.8: If A 9.1 - A 9.8 are valid and $\eta_{1Y}=\eta_{2Y}$ holds and sector 1 is strongly emission intensive, then follows:

$$\hat{p}_{21} < 0 \quad \Leftarrow \quad \eta_{1U} \geq \eta_{2U}$$

Proof: In cases (1), (2) we have $G < 0$.[1] Since $\varepsilon_{US} < 0$, $D < 0$ and $\eta_{1Y}=\eta_{2Y}=1$, we can deduce immediately theorem 9.8 from 9.48. q.e.d.

3. In economic terms theorem 9.8 means that the equilibrium price ratio of the "waste intensive" good raises if the improved environment does not cause a reduction of relative demand in that good. In other words, the demand effect shoul not be "perverse" in that it works against the falling suppl resulting through the policy. A sufficient condition for a "normal" result is that the relative demand raises or remains constant.[2] The opposite case is only possible if the demand for the "dirty" good 1 falls very much since $\eta_{1U} < 0$ and $\eta_{2U} > 0$ (compare 9.49). Table 9.2 summarizes the possible outcomes.

case	(1) sector 1 emission intensive sector 2 capital intensive $G < 0$	(2) sector 1 emission intensive sector 2 labour intensive $G < 0$	(3) sector 1 capital intensive sector 2 labour intensive $G > 0$
a) $\eta_{1U}>\eta_{2U}$	$\hat{p} < 0$	$\hat{p} < 0$	$\hat{p} \gtrless 0$
b) $\eta_{2U}>\eta_{1U}$	$\hat{p} \gtrless 0$	$\hat{p} \gtrless 0$	$\hat{p} > 0$
c) $\eta_{1U}=\eta_{2U} = 0$	$\hat{p} < 0$	$\hat{p} < 0$	$\hat{p} > 0$

Table 9.2

1) Observe that sign $\hat{Q}_1 \big|_{\hat{p}=0}$ = sign $(\hat{Q}_1-\hat{Q}_2) \big|_{\hat{p}=0}$. That is why the sign of coefficient F in 9.37 is qualitatively comparabl with the sign of G in 9.2.7 in appendix 9.2.

2) Compare the results obtained in part II without the effect of environmental quality. The above results are directly comparable if we use $\hat{p}_{21} = -\hat{p}_{12}$.

Only in cases (1)a), (1)c), (2)a), (2)c) we observe a priori unique outcomes of the policy. In cases (1)b), (2)b), the sufficient condition is not fulfilled. We cannot exclude the possibility of an increasing p_{21} caused by raising demand of good 2.
If we have a growing relative damand for good 2, then the relative strength of the two opposite forces is decisive. The increasing supply of good 2 or the growing demand of good 2 can dominate the price determination. Equation 9.48 reveals additionally that the absolute extent of relative change is influenced by the height of price-elasticities of supply and demand (σ_S, σ_D). The more elastic the relative supply is or the more the elastic relative demand is, the smaller will be the absolute change.

4. We are able to give a compact geometric illustration[1] (diagram 9.6) the technique of which is familiar from R.E. Caves, R.W. Jones (1973)

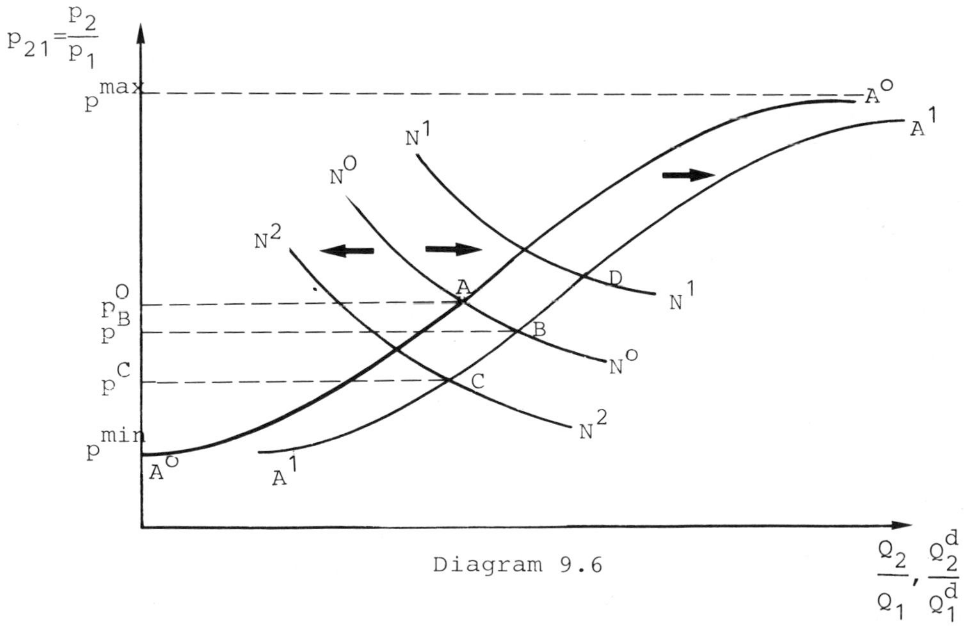

Diagram 9.6

1) The geometric presentation is only partial, since we neglect the income effects and consider only parametric variations of s^S.

In the initial situation, autarky price ratio OP^o is determined by the cut of relative supply curve[1.)] A^oA^o and the relative demand curve N^oN^o. The policy activity brings about a shift to the right of the relative supply curve A^1A^1. In case of $\eta_{iU} = 0$, and $\eta_{iY} = 1$, demand remains at the old curve and we realize a smaller equilibrium price ratio $OP^B < OP^o$. On the contrary if demand pattern changes in favour of the environment intensive good 1, then the tendency of falling price ratios will be reinforced, $OP^C < OP^B < OP^o$. Both cases confirm theorem 9.8. The unusual outcome, which has been mentioned , can be shown by a rightward shift of relative demand (N^1N^1) so that the final price ratio could be higher (point D). Column 3 of table 9.2 contains the possible outcomes if all the productive sectors are not strongly emission intensive.

5. If we drop the assumption of neutral income effects, by inspection of equation 9.48 we confirm that the income effects are able to reinforce or to reverse the described outcomes.
In case of $\eta_{2Y} > \eta_{1Y}$ (i.e. the "dirty" good is relatively inelastic to income changes), the typical price effect is reinforced $(\hat{p}_{21} < 0)$. The other cases will be able to soften or reverse the price effect of environmental policy, if the waste intensive consumption good possesses relatively high income elasticities. The mentioned determinants will then have a decisive influence on specialization pattern in trade. This aspect will be dealt with in the next section.

9.5 Pollution Policy and Comparative Advantage

9.5.1 Assumptions and Scarcity Concepts

1. The foregoing constructions will now be integrated in the well-known Heckscher-Ohlin-Samuelson theory (HOS) to identify the trade specialization pattern of two countries. Our special intention is to show, that differing environmental targets or differing natural endowments in environmental

1) On account of the shape of the transformation curve, we have for $p \rightarrow p^{max}$ an asymptotic shape of Q_2/Q_1, since Q_1 becomes zero.

resources (assimilative capacity) could be decisive factors of existing comparative unit cost differentials on account of the influence on production possibilities of each country. That is why international differences in relative factor endowments (incl. environment) determine the marginal cost differentials which guide the trade pattern.

2. To make the following discussion precise, let us state some assumptions.

A 9.10 The quantities of primary inputs A,K in both countries are fixed and absolutely immobile between countries but perfectly mobile inside each country.
A 9.11 Each country possesses a production technology described by 9.2. The sectoral production function is internationally identical but intersectorally different.
A 9.12 The factor intensities and emission intensities of all sectors have always the same constellation for all factor price relations (i.e. non-reversal for intensities).
A 9.13 The preferences are identical and homothetic in Q_i^d in both countries.[1)]

It seems to be worthwile to distinguish the following different situations labelled (α), (β), (γ):

(α) Two trading countries are assumed to have no environmental problems. They are relatively rich endowed physically with environmental resources, if we have in both nations: $S^a > S^{max}(A,K)$. S^a indicates the value of the waste limit at which the eco-system begins to react in form of environmental quality losses ($U(S \leq S^a) = U^{max}$), and $S^{max} := \max\ [a_{S1}Q_1(A,K);\ a_{S2}Q_2(A,K)]$ denotes the maximum of waste emissions which could ever be realized.

We can interpret this situation as one where the "supply" of natural environmental resources is greater than the maximum demand. The total demand of environmental services expressed as waste emissions could be absorbed by the ecosphere without detoriations. The availibility of natural resources therefore represents no restriction for production possibilities. Alternatively it can comprise the case, where both countries

1) Foreign variables are labelled with "*".

realize autarky equilibria with no policy, since society and/ or executive do not place any priority to environmental goals: $S^{max}(K,A) \leq S^{\ddagger}$ where $S^{\ddagger}$ symbols the value of that waste limit beyond which the ecological-economic system collapses.[1)]

(β) The foreign country is richly endowed with S in the physical sense of (α). The home country carries out a price-standard-policy because the actual emissions are perceived as a policy problem. Environmental policy selec an emission standard out of the interval: $S^a < S^s \leq S^{\ddagger}$.

(γ) Both nations carry out a price-standard-policy: $S^a < S^s \leq S^{\ddagger}$ and $S^{a*} < S^{s*} \leq S^{\ddagger *}$

To make the intensity of the policy measures in both countries comparable we assume, that the maximum allowable emission per input unit is greater in the foreign country:[2)]

$$S^{s*}/K^* > S^s/K \text{ and } S^{s*}/A^* > S^s/A \text{ and } S^{s*}/k^* > S^s/k \quad (9.50)$$

where $k := K/A$

We say the emission norm is relatively more restrictive in th home country. We call this the criterion of relative emission standards.

Finally we make the additional assumptions:

A 9.14 The foreign country is relatively richly endowed with natural resources according to the criterion of 9.50. Both nations have identical relative primary factor endowments: $k=k^*$.

A 9.15 S^s, S^{s*} are binding constraints, $S^s < S^{min} < S^{max}$ and $S^{s*} < S^{min*} < S^{max*}$. $S^{min} := \min[a_{S1}Q_1(A,K),\ a_{S2}Q_2(A,K)]$.

A 9.16 The demand structure is independent from existing U:

$$\eta_{iU} = 0, \quad i = 1,2$$

On account of A 9.13, A 9.16 we have for all given $\bar{p} = \bar{p}^*$:[3)]

$$Q_1^d(\bar{p},Y) \,/\, Q_2^d(\bar{p},Y) = Q_1^{d*}(\bar{p},Y^*) / \, Q_2^d(\bar{p},Y^*)$$

we take into consideration the various situations (α), (β), (γ)

1) $S^{\ddagger}$ indicates therefore a minimum value in the preference set of society to sustain life.
2) A comparable criterion is given in chapters 7 and 8.
3) At the same price ratio the demand pattern is identical and independent of the height of Y.

we are able to give information about the resulting trade patterns after entering trade.

9.5.2 Trade under Alternative Policy Regimes

1. Theorem 9.9: If we have situation (α) and A 9.1 - A 9.8, A 9.10 - A 9.13, A 9.16 are valid, then a country will export (import) the good, which uses the relatively rich (scarce) primary factor relative intensively.

Proof: In this no policy-situation the relative-cost divergencies are determined by divergencies in (K,A).

From equation system 9.23 we receive with $\hat{p}_i=\theta_{S1}=\theta_{S2}=0$: $(\hat{p}_A-\hat{p}_K)/B\overset{!}{=}0$. The analysis confirms that the endowment has no more any influence on factor price ratios. The situation (α) which reflects a low degree of economic development of the countries is contained in the foregoing analysis as a special case with $p_S=\hat{p}_S:=0$ and $\theta_{S1} = \theta_{S2} = 0$. Since $\theta_S = 0$ and $\hat{A} = \hat{K} = \hat{S}^S = 0$, we get from 9.45 the price-output response given by 9.4.1 in appendix 9.4. Since all sum-terms are nonnegative in 9.4.1 and D < 0, we rewrite:

$$\hat{Q}_2-\hat{Q}_1=-\frac{C}{D\theta_1\theta_2}\hat{p}_{21}=\sigma_S\hat{p} \quad \text{where } \sigma_S:=-\frac{C}{\theta_1\theta_2 D}>0 \tag{9.51}$$

Otherwise if $\hat{p}_{21}=p_S=\theta_{S1}=\theta_{S2}=0$ we are able to compute the output effects at varying endowments. From equations 9.1.1 in appendix 9.1 and equations 9.22 we get 9.42 in appendix 9.4:

$$\hat{Q}_2-\hat{Q}_1\Big|_{\hat{p}_{21}=0} = \frac{1}{|\lambda_{AK}|}\{(\hat{K}-\hat{A}) - (\hat{p}_A-\hat{p}_K)(\delta_A+\delta_K)\} \tag{9.52}$$

Therefore we obtain with 9.51 and 9.52: $\hat{Q}_2-\hat{Q}_1=\frac{\hat{K}-\hat{A}}{|\lambda_{AK}|}+\sigma_S\hat{p}_{21}$

Under A 9.13, A 9.16 the demand side brings about: $\hat{Q}_2^d-\hat{Q}_1^d = -\sigma_D\hat{p}_{21}$

An equilibrium calls for $\hat{Q}_i = \hat{Q}_i^d$ i = 1,2; so we get

$$\hat{p}_{21} = -\frac{1}{\sigma_S+\sigma_D}\frac{(\hat{K}-\hat{A})}{|\lambda_{AK}|}$$

with sign $\hat{p}_{21}/(\hat{K}-\hat{A})$ = sign $|\lambda_{AK}|$ = sign (k_1-k_2)

We can state therefore:

$$k_1 \lesseqgtr k_2 \;\Leftrightarrow\; \hat{p}_{21}/(\hat{K}-\hat{A}) \lesseqgtr 0$$

In case of $({}^{K}/A) \gtrless ({}^{K^*}/A^*)$, we can conclude $p \gtrless p^*$ which induces the trade pattern mentioned in theorem 9.9

q.e.d.

2. Next we want to demonstrate that differing emission targets can influence the direction of trade flows by affecting the international competitive situation (pollution policy as a determinant of trade).

Theorem 9.10: If we have situation (γ) and let A 9.1 - A 9.8, A 9.10 - A 9.16 be given, then a country exports the strongly emission intensive good, if its emission norm is relatively less restrictive than the one of the other country.

Proof: From equation system 9.23 we obtain with $\hat{p}_i = 0$:

$$\begin{aligned} \hat{p}_A - \hat{p}_K &= \frac{1}{D}[\theta_{S2} - \theta_{S1}]\, B \\ \hat{p}_A - \hat{p}_S &= \frac{1}{D}[\theta_{K1} - \theta_{K2}]\, B \\ \hat{p}_K - \hat{p}_S &= \frac{1}{D}[\theta_{A2} - \theta_{A1}]\, B \end{aligned} \tag{9.53}$$

$$\begin{aligned} \text{With } B :&= |\lambda_{KS}|\hat{A} + |\lambda_{SA}|\hat{K} + |\lambda_{AK}|\hat{S}^s \\ &= -\lambda_{K1}(\hat{S}^s - \hat{A}) + \lambda_{A1}(\hat{S}^s - \hat{K}) + \lambda_{S1}(\hat{K} - \hat{A}) \end{aligned}$$

On account of A 9.14 we have: $\hat{A} = \hat{K}$, which assures k to be constant.

$$B = -|\lambda_{AK}|[\hat{K}\underbrace{(\lambda_{S1} + \lambda_{S2})}_{=1}] + |\lambda_{AK}|\hat{S}^s = |\lambda_{AK}|\;(\hat{S}^s - \hat{K}) \tag{9.54}$$

From equation 9.2.6 in appendix 9.2 we get with $\hat{A}=\hat{K}$ and the relations 9.53, 9.54

$$\hat{Q}_2 - \hat{Q}_1 \Big|_{\hat{p}_{21}=0} = \frac{-B}{D|\lambda_{AK}|}G = -\frac{[\hat{S}^s - \hat{K}]}{D}G \tag{9.55}$$

where G is a sum term as in 9.2.7 in appendix 9.2.

The change of relative demand is given by:

$\hat{Q}_2^d - \hat{Q}_1^d = -\sigma_D \hat{p}_{21}$ if A 9.13, A 9.16 holds.

It follows:

$$\hat{p}_{21} = \frac{1}{\sigma_S+\sigma_D} \frac{G}{D|\lambda_{AK}|} B = \frac{1}{\sigma_S+\sigma_D} \frac{G}{D} (\hat{S}^s-\hat{K}) \qquad (9.56)$$

In case (1) we have $\theta_{S1}>\theta_{S2}$ and $\theta_{K2}>\theta_{K1}$, whereas in case (2) we have $\theta_{S1}>\theta_{S2}$; but $\theta_{A2}>\theta_{A1}$; all cases lead to $G < 0$. For that reason a reduction of S^s/K by $(\hat{S}^s-\hat{K}) < 0$ induces a raise of the relative price of the waste intensive good 1 (i.e. $\hat{p}_{21} < 0$).

By reason of A 9.14 $\frac{S^{s*}}{K^*} > \frac{S^s}{K} \Rightarrow p^*_{21} > p_{21}$ which in fact leads to a trade pattern described in theorem 9.10. The country which is relatively richly endowed with environmental resources exports the relatively emission intensive good 1.

q.e.d.

At differing national endowments in emission possibilities relative to primary factor bundles which have a constant structure, we obtain from equation 9.56 differing autarky price ratios. Or equivalently we can say that the foreign country can produce relatively more of the emission intensive good 1: $(Q_1/Q_2)^* > (Q_1/Q_2)$ for every p_{21} in the interior of the nonspecialization interval (compare equation 9.55).

3. In the following our intention is to analyze a sequence of potential situations for the home country. We assume a starting situation which is described as follows. The foreign country has not exceeded the assimilitative services by its emission activity. The foreign country is relatively rich in environmental resources.[1] The home countrv may have at the same moment an emission standard S^s_o, but S^s_o is no binding constraint at existing price ratios: $S^{max} < S^s_o$.

Additionally, we suppose the home country to be relatively capital rich ($K/A > K^*/A^*$) and the production technology fulfils the assumptions of case (2), i.e. sector 1 is relatively emission intensive and sector 2 is relatively labour intensive. On account of this situation we have

1) Our aim is a comparison with the value of S of the home country, so we take as a value of reference the maximum extent of usage $S^{a*} = S^{S*}_o$.

$p_S = p_S^* = 0$ and consequently $\theta_{S1} = \theta_{S2} = \theta_{S1}^* = \theta_{S2}^* = 0$; theorem 9.9 holds. The capital-rich home country possesses an export base for the capital intensive good 1.[1)]

Because $K/A > K^*/A^* \Rightarrow p_{21} > p_{21}^*$. The convential HOS-theorem is valid, if the endowment of environmental resources has no pecuniary influence on comparative costs.

The described situation is represented in diagram 9.7 through the autarky equilibria P^I and P^* with price ratios $p_{AUT}^I > p_{AUT}^*$. The transformation locus relative to S_o^s of the home country is labelled through TT. T^*T^* denotes the other country. It should be noticed that the boundaries are solely determined by primary factor restrictions. From the analysis of the supply side it is evident that the labour-rich foreigners can produce relatively more of the labour intensive commodity for all given p than the capital-rich home country[2)]:

$Q_2^*(\bar{p})/Q_1^*(\bar{p}) > Q_2(\bar{p})/Q_2(\bar{p})$.

In other words, we can say, that identical quantity ratios $Q_2/Q_1 = Q_2^*/Q_1^*$ could be produced with different opportunity-costs, i.e. the labour-intensive good 2 of the home country will be offered relatively more expensive:

$p_{21} > \tilde{p}_{21}^*$ in productions points P^I and $\tilde{P}^*$ in diagram 9.7.[3)]

If we reconsider that both countries have the same demand quantity ratios at alternative $\bar{p}$, we recognize that the foreign country must export the second good and the home country exports the first good, when we reach a free trade equilibrium.

In a following situation we suppose a stricter emission standard of the home country with $S_n^s < S^{max}(K,A) < S_o^s$ (n=1,2...) so that we now have the situation (β).

The restriction of S^s is drawn geometrically as T^nT^n. The curve shows a biased shrinkage against the capital intensive and strongly emissions intensive Q_1 (see diagrams 9.7, 9.8).

---

1) Observe that good 1 is capital intensive, since $a_{K1}/a_{A1} > a_{K2}/a_{A2}$.

2) Compare the quantity relations for $p=p^I$ in the points P^I and Q^* in diagram 9.7.

3) Notice the potential price ratios along the ray $\overline{OS}$ in diagram 9.7.

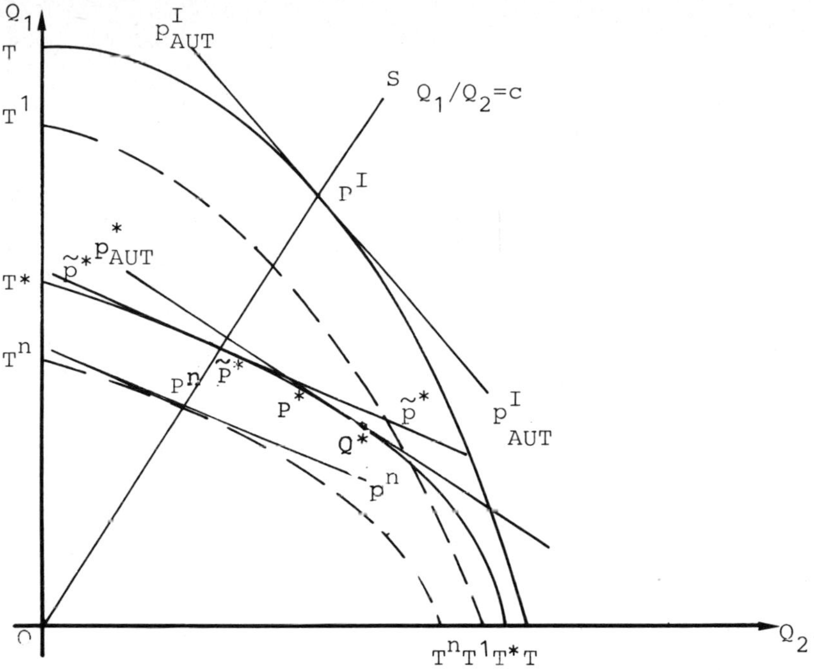

Diagram 9.7

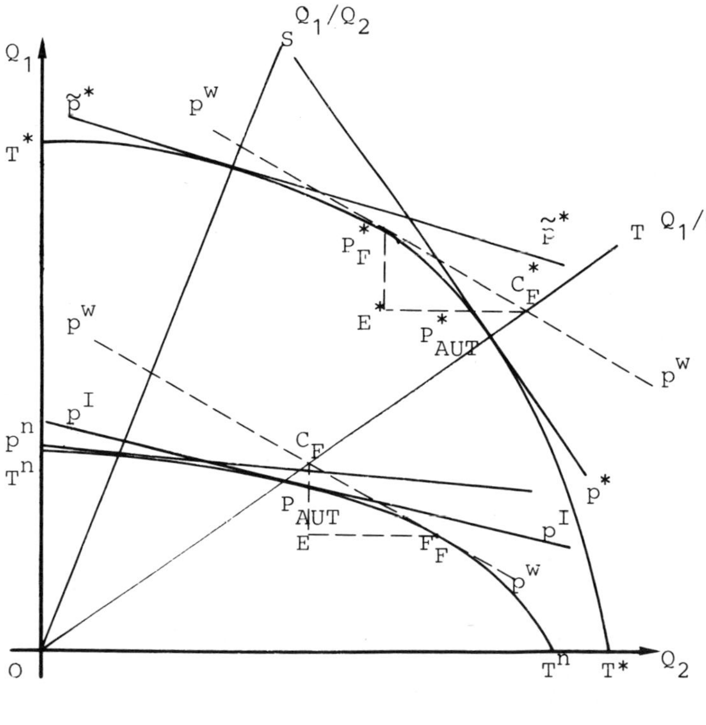

Diagram 9.8

We denote T^nT^n as the projection of the generalized output locus at fixed S^s_n and call this as transformation curve relative to S^s_n: $Q_1 = T(Q_2;S^s_n)$ with $n=1,2...; S^s_o>S^s_1>...$

If we regard for the moment the output structure of the autarky situation as fixed, then we observe raising opportunity costs of the "dirty" Q_1.[1)]
Let us formalize this as a sequence of price ratios:

$$\left|\frac{\partial Q_1(Q_2;S^s_n)}{\partial Q_2}\right| := \left(\frac{p_2}{p_1}\right)_n < \left|\frac{\partial Q_1(Q_2;S^s_{n-1})}{\partial Q_2}\right| := \left(\frac{p_2}{p_1}\right)_{n-1}$$

with $n = 1,2,...$

We can state the following theorem.

Theorem 9.11: Let $G \geq 0$ be the limit of the sequence $\{|\partial Q_1(Q_2;S^s_n)/\partial Q_2| \; S^s_{n-1} > S^s_n;\; n \in I;\; Q_1/Q_2 = c\}$
The initial situation in autarky is described by:

$$\left(\frac{p_2}{p_1}\right)_o > \left(\frac{p_2}{p_1}\right)^*_o$$

If $(p_2/p_1)^* > G$, then there exists $u \in I$ with $S^s_u > 0$ such that for all $S^s_n < S^s_u$ we have $(p_2/p_1)^* > (p_2/p_1)$: The home country has a comparative advantage in the production of the relatively "clean" Q_2 under the assumptions A 9.13 - A 9.16.

Proof: obvious

In economic terms the theorem indicates that a sufficiently restrictive standard S^s_u exists which equalizes the opportunity costs in both countries along $\overline{OS}$.
Finally for all sequential $S^s_n < S^s_u$ we get a comparative advantage in the labour intensive and non emission intensive production of Q_2 $(\tilde{p}^* > p^n)$. In other words, the foreign country offers at identical supply price ratios a relatively greater quantity of Q_2 than the home country.
For all states with $S^s_n < S^s_u$ we can expect a free trade situation with an equilibrium price ratio p^w, which generates

1) For clarity of the exposition, we have not drawn the social indifference curves in the tangential points.

a foreign excess supply of the emission intensive good 1 and an excess demand of Q_2. Just the opposite can be stated for the home country. It's quite clear that the trade triangles ($P_F^* E^* C_F^*$ and $P_F E C_F$) have the same extent at p^w in diagram 9.8. The environmental actions of the home land bring forth the foreign comparative advantage in natural endowment. The direction of specialization has reversed.

Since[1)] $S^{s*}/k^* > S^s/k$ the environment rich foreign country now exports the emission intensive Q_1 and imports the labour intensive Q_2. The foregoing expressed idea has shown that the richness of a nation in environmental resources lead necessarily to a production-specialization in wasteful production. Only if a sufficient strong control policy is undertaken in the other country, the endowment advantage plays a significant role.

1) Because we have no existing foreign norm, we substitute the greatest possible emission quantity $S^{a*} = S^{s*}$

Appendix 9.1

We get from 9.17, 9.18 under the assumption

$$[\lambda_{AK}] := \begin{bmatrix} \lambda_{A1} & \lambda_{A2} \\ \lambda_{K1} & \lambda_{K2} \end{bmatrix} \quad \text{is nonsingular:}$$

$$\hat{Q}_1 = \{\lambda_{K2}(\hat{A} + \beta_A) - \lambda_{A2}(\hat{K} + \beta_K) \quad / \ |\lambda_{AK}|$$

$$\hat{Q}_2 = \{\lambda_{A1}(\hat{K} + \beta_K) - \lambda_{K1}(\hat{A} + \beta_A) \quad / \ |\lambda_{AK}| \qquad (9.1.1)$$

where $\beta_j := -[\lambda_{j1}\hat{a}_{j1} + \lambda_{j2}\hat{a}_{j2}]$ $\qquad j = A,K,S$

after substitution of 9.1.1 into 9.19 we have:

$$\frac{\lambda_{S1}\ \lambda_{K2}(\hat{A}+\beta_A)-\lambda_{S1}\lambda_{A2}(\hat{K}+\beta_K)+\lambda_{S2}\ \lambda_{A1}(\hat{K}+\beta_K)-\lambda_{S2}\ \lambda_{K1}(\hat{A}+\beta_A)}{|\lambda_{AK}|}=\hat{S}^S+\beta_S$$

or equivalently under consideration of:

$$|\lambda_{jK}| = \lambda_{j1}\ \lambda_{k2} - \lambda_{j2}\ \lambda_{K1} = \lambda_{j1} - \lambda_{k1} = \lambda_{k2} - \lambda_{j2},$$

$j,k = A,K,S$ $(j \neq k)$ we will get:

$$|\lambda_{KS}| \quad (\hat{A}+ \beta_A) + |\lambda_{SA}|(\hat{K} + \beta_K) + |\lambda_{AK}| \ (\hat{S}^S + \beta_S) = 0$$

We substitute $\hat{\beta}_i$ and obtain:

$$\sum_{i=1}^{2}\{|\lambda_{KS}|\ \lambda_{Ai}\ \hat{a}_{Ai} + |\lambda_{SA}|\ \lambda_{Ki}\ \hat{a}_{Ki} + |\lambda_{AK}|\ \lambda_{Si}\ \hat{a}_{Si}\}$$

$$= |\lambda_{KS}|\hat{A}+|\lambda_{SA}|\hat{K}+|\lambda_{AK}|\hat{S}^S := B$$

Finally if we integrate the expressions $\hat{a}_{ji}$ of 9.22, we will get after some cumbersome manipulations[1]:

$$\hat{p}_A \sum_{i=1}^{2} [\sigma^i_{AS} \ R^i_K - \sigma^i_{AK} \ R^i_S] + \hat{p}_K \sum_{i=1}^{2} [\sigma^i_{AK}\ R^i_S - \sigma^i_K \ R^i_A] \qquad (9.1.2)$$

$$+\hat{p}_S \sum_{i=1}^{2} [\sigma^i_{KS}\ R^i_A - \sigma^i_{AS} \ R^i_K] = B$$

1) Compare also R.N.Batra, F.R.Casas (1976, p.25).

with

$$R_K^i := |\lambda_{AK}|\ \lambda_{Si}\theta_{Ai} - |\lambda_{KS}|\lambda_{Ai}\theta_{Si} = \lambda_{Ai}\lambda_{Si}\theta_S\ (\theta_{K2}-\theta_{K1})/\theta_K$$

$$R_A^i := |\lambda_{SA}|\ \lambda_{Ki}\theta_{Si} - |\lambda_{AK}|\lambda_{Si}\theta_{Ki} = \lambda_{Ki}\lambda_{Si}\theta_S\ (\theta_{A2}-\theta_{A1})/\theta_K$$

$$R_S^i := |\lambda_{KS}|\ \lambda_{Ai}\theta_{Ki} - |\lambda_{SA}|\lambda_{Ki}\theta_{Ai} = \lambda_{Ai}\lambda_{Ki}\theta_S\ (\theta_{S2}-\theta_{S1})/\theta_S$$

and $\theta_l := \dfrac{p_l Q_l}{Y}$ (l = 1,2) denotes the share of production value from good l in real income whereas $\theta_k := \dfrac{p_k k}{Y}$ (k=A,K,S) denotes the factor share resp. emission revenue in real income.

If we reduce the structural relations 9.20, 9.21 and 9.1.2 we will form the matrix system 9.23, where C_1, C_2, C_3 represent the coefficients of $\hat{p}_k$ in 9.1.2.

Appendix 9.2

On account of $\theta_{Ai}\sigma^i_{AK} + \theta_{Ki}\sigma^i_{Kk} + \theta_{Si}\sigma^i_{Sk} = 0 \quad k=A,K,S;\ i=1,2$ we are able to show:

$$\sigma^i_{AA} = \frac{1}{\theta^2_{Ai}}[\theta_{Ki}\ \theta_{Si}]\begin{bmatrix}\sigma^i_{KK} & \sigma^i_{KS}\\ \sigma^i_{KS} & \sigma^i_{SS}\end{bmatrix}\begin{bmatrix}\theta_{Ki}\\ \theta_{Si}\end{bmatrix} < 0$$

Since $\theta_{ki} > 0$ (k=A,K,S) the quadratic form is negativ definit. This implies for determinant $|\sigma_{jk}| > 0$, which allows to say:

$$\sigma^i_{KS} > -\frac{\theta_{Ai}\sigma^i_{AK}\sigma^i_{AS}}{\theta_{Ki}\sigma^i_{AK}+\theta_{Si}\sigma^i_{AS}} \tag{9.2.1}$$

$$\sigma^i_{AS} > -\frac{\theta_{Ki}\sigma^i_{AK}\sigma^i_{KS}}{\theta_{Ai}\sigma^i_{AK}+\theta_{Si}\sigma^i_{KS}} \tag{9.2.2}$$

$$\sigma^i_{AK} > -\frac{\theta_{Si}\sigma^i_{KS}\sigma^i_{AS}}{\theta_{Ai}\sigma^i_{AS}+\theta_{Ki}\sigma^i_{KS}} \tag{9.2.3}$$

$$\hat{k}_i < \frac{|\lambda_{AK}|}{D[\theta_{Ai}\sigma^i_{AS}\ \ \theta_{Ki}\sigma^i_{KS}]}\{\theta_{Si}(\sigma^i_{AS}-\sigma^i_{KS})(\sigma^i_{KS}\theta_{Ki}(\theta_{A2}-\theta_{A1})- -\sigma^i_{AS}\theta_{Ai}(\theta_{K2}-\theta_{K1}))\}\hat{S}^S \tag{9.2.4}$$

With the help of 9.2.1 and 9.36 we get the following inequality:

$$\begin{aligned}\hat{Q}_1 < \frac{\hat{S}^S}{D}\{&\frac{1}{C_1}[\sigma^1_{AK}(\theta_{S2}-\theta_{S1})\theta_{K1}+\sigma^1_{AS}(\theta_{K1}-\theta_{K2})\theta_{S1}]\\ &[\sigma^1_{AK}(\lambda_{A2}\lambda_{K1}\theta_{A1}+\lambda_{K2}\lambda_{A1}\theta_{K1})+\sigma^1_{AS}\lambda_{K2}\lambda_{A1}\theta_{S1}]\\ &+\frac{1}{C_2}[\sigma^2_{AK}(\theta_{S2}-\theta_{S1})\theta_{K2}+\sigma^2_{AS}(\theta_{K1}-\theta_{K2})\theta_{S2}]\\ &[\sigma^2_{AK}(\lambda_{A2}\lambda_{K2}\theta_{A2}+\lambda_{A2}\lambda_{K2}\theta_{K2})+\sigma^2_{AS}\lambda_{A2}\lambda_{K2}\theta_{K2}]\}:=\frac{S^S}{D}F\end{aligned} \tag{9.2.5}$$

where $C_i := \theta_{Ki}\sigma^i_{AK} + \theta_{Si}\sigma^i_{AS} > 0 \qquad i = 1,2$

For the change in relative commodity supply we get from 9.1.1 in appendix 9.1 and equations 9.22 with $\hat{A}=\hat{K}=0$ after some manipulations:

$$\hat{Q}_1-\hat{Q}_2=\frac{\beta_A-\beta_K}{|\lambda_{AK}|}=\frac{1}{|\lambda_{AK}|\theta_1\theta_2}\{(\hat{p}_A-\hat{p}_K)[(\theta_K+\theta_A)\sum_{\substack{i=1\\ i\neq 1}}^{2}\lambda_{Ai}\lambda_{Ki}\theta_1\sigma^i_{AK}]$$

$$(\hat{p}_A-\hat{p}_S)[\theta_S\sum_{\substack{i=1\\ i\neq 1}}^{2}\lambda_{Ai}\lambda_{Si}\theta_1\sigma^i_{AS}] \qquad (9.2.6)$$

$$-(\hat{p}_K-\hat{p}_S)[\theta_S\sum_{\substack{i=1\\ i\neq 1}}^{2}\lambda_{Ki}\lambda_{Si}\theta_1\sigma^i_{KS}]\}$$

If we consider equation 9.36 for i=1,2 we obtain for $\hat{p}_i=0$, $\hat{A}=\hat{K}=0$:

$$\hat{Q}_1-\hat{Q}_2\Big|_{\substack{\hat{p}=0\\ \hat{A}=\hat{K}=0}}=\frac{\hat{S}^S}{\theta_1\theta_2\,D}\{[\theta_{S2}-\theta_{S1}][\theta_K+\theta_A]\sum_{\substack{i=1\\ i\neq 1}}^{2}\lambda_{Ai}\lambda_{Ki}\theta_1\sigma^i_{AK}$$

$$+[\theta_{K1}-\theta_{K2}]\theta_S\sum_{\substack{i=1\\ i\neq 1}}^{2}\lambda_{Ai}\lambda_{Si}\theta_1\sigma^i_{AS} \qquad (9.2.7)$$

$$-[\theta_{A2}-\theta_{A1}]\theta_S\sum_{\substack{i=1\\ i\neq 1}}^{2}\lambda_{Ki}\lambda_{Si}\theta_1\sigma^i_{KS}\}:=\frac{\hat{S}^S}{D}G$$

where G stands for the remaining term.

$$\hat{Q}_1>\frac{\hat{S}^S}{D}\{\frac{\theta_{S1}}{G_1}[\sigma^1_{AS}(\theta_{K1}-\theta_{K2})\theta_{A1}+\sigma^1_{KS}(\theta_{A2}-\theta_{A1})\theta_{K1}]$$

$$[\sigma^i_{AS}\lambda_{K2}\lambda_{A1}-\sigma^1_{KS}\lambda_{A2}\lambda_{K1}]+[\frac{\lambda_{AS}\lambda_{K2}\theta_{S2}}{G_2}] \qquad (9.2.8)$$

$$[\sigma^2_{AS}(\theta_{K1}-\theta_{K2})\theta_{A2}+\sigma^2_{KS}(\theta_{A2}-\theta_{A1})\theta_{K2}][\sigma^2_{AS}-\sigma^1_{KS}]\}$$

where

$$G_i:=\theta_{Ai}\sigma^i_{AS}+\theta_{Ki}\sigma^i_{KS}>0$$

Appendix 9.3

From 9.42 we are able to compute:

$$\left.\frac{(\hat{p}_A-\hat{p}_K)}{\hat{p}_{21}}\right|_{\hat{V}=0} = \theta_1 \left.\left[\frac{1}{\theta_K}\frac{\hat{Q}_1}{\hat{K}} - \frac{1}{\theta_A}\frac{\hat{Q}_1}{\hat{A}}\right]\right|_{\hat{p}=0} \quad (9.3.1)$$

$$\left.\frac{(\hat{p}_A-\hat{p}_S)}{\hat{p}_{21}}\right|_{\hat{V}=0} = \theta_1 \left.\left[\frac{1}{\theta_S}\frac{\hat{Q}_1}{\hat{S}^s} - \frac{1}{\theta_A}\frac{\hat{Q}_1}{\hat{A}}\right]\right|_{\hat{p}=0} \quad (9.3.2)$$

$$\left.\frac{(\hat{p}_K-\hat{p}_S)}{\hat{p}_{21}}\right|_{\hat{V}=0} = \theta_1 \left.\left[\frac{1}{\theta_S}\frac{\hat{Q}_1}{\hat{S}^s} - \frac{1}{\theta_K}\frac{\hat{Q}_1}{\hat{K}}\right]\right|_{\hat{p}=0} \quad (9.3.3)$$

Appendix 9.4

With $\theta_S, \theta_{S1}, \theta_{S2} = 0$ and $\hat{A} = \hat{K} = \hat{S}^s = 0$ we compute with 9.45

$$\frac{\hat{Q}_1 - \hat{Q}_2}{\hat{p}_{21}} = \frac{1}{|\lambda_{AK}|\theta_1\theta_2 D}\left\{\sum_{\substack{i=1\\ i\neq 1}}^{2} \lambda_{Ai}\lambda_{Ki}\theta_1\sigma^i_{AK}\left[\sum_{i=1}^{2} R^i_K\sigma^i_{AS} - \sum_{i=1}^{2} R^i_A\sigma^i_{KS}\right]\right\}$$

with $R^i_K = |\lambda_{AK}|\lambda_{Si}\theta_{Ai}$ and $R^i_A = -|\lambda_{AK}|\lambda_{Si}\theta_{Ki}$.

$$\frac{\hat{Q}_1 - \hat{Q}_2}{\hat{p}_{21}} = \frac{1}{D\theta_1\theta_2} \underbrace{\sum_{\substack{i=1\\ i\neq 1}}^{2} \lambda_{Ai}\lambda_{Ki}\theta_1\sigma^i_{AK}\left[\sum_{i=1}^{2}\lambda_{Si}\theta_{Ai}\sigma^i_{AS} + \sum_{i=1}^{2}\lambda_{Si}\theta_{Ki}\sigma^i_{KS}\right]}_{:=C} \quad (9.4.1)$$

Since p_S, p_{21}, θ_{S1}, θ_{S2} are all zero, we get from 9.1.1 and 9.22 the following reactions at varying endowment:

$$\left.\hat{Q}_2 - \hat{Q}_1\right|_{\hat{p}_{21}=0} = \frac{1}{|\lambda_{AK}|}[(\hat{K} - \hat{A}) + (\beta_K - \beta_A)] =$$

$$= \frac{1}{|\lambda_{AK}|}\{(\hat{K} - \hat{A}) - (\hat{p}_A - \hat{p}_K)(\delta_K + \delta_A)\} \quad (9.4.2)$$

where

$$\beta_K = -\sum_{i=1}^{2}\lambda_{Ki}\hat{a}_{Ki} = -(\hat{p}_A - \hat{p}_K)\sum_i \theta_{Ai}\sigma^i_{AK} := -(\hat{p}_A - \hat{p}_K)\,\delta_A$$

$$-\beta_A = \sum_{i=1}^{2}\lambda_{Ai}\hat{a}_{Ai} = -(\hat{p}_A - \hat{p}_K)\sum_i \theta_{Ki}\sigma^i_{AK} := -(\hat{p}_A - \hat{p}_K)\,\delta_K$$

10. The Incidence of Environmental Policy on Trade Flows and the Terms of Trade

In the preceding chapter we shed some light on the incidence environmental policy in a closed economy. We now start from a trade equilibrium and analyze the effects of an emission standard policy on trade flows and the terms of trade. The chapter is divided into two sections. The first section assumes a small country and studies the impacts of the emission standard policy on the supply side and the income- and policy-induced effects on the demand side. In contrast to chapter 4 we also consider the influence of changes of environmental quality on demand structure. It can be shown that the impact of environmental policy depends on special production- and demand-characteristics.

In the second section we give up the assumption of a given world price ratio. The home country is faced with a given offer-curve of the rest of the world. In a two-country model we investigate the analytical link between an environmental policy of the home country and the possible change of the world price ratio. We try to give an answer to the question whether the acting country will be able to share its costs of pollution control with the rest of the world via a terms of trade improvement. On the basis of this analytical technique, it is easy to extend the model with an acting foreign country. The analysis formalizes some geometrical and verbal attempts presented in the literature by Walter (1974a) and Grubel (1976) and makes use of the results in chapter 9 where we discussed a two-good-three-factor model.

10.1 The Small-Country Case

10.1.1 Assumptions

We take over the model structure of the preceding chapter 9. We start by studying the implications of an emission standard policy on trade flows. We assume a small country that is a price taker in the international market. We regard the variable S^S as the main instrument variable of the political system. We suppose that S^S is either introduced or restricted.
In this section we state the following assumptions.
A 10.1 The home country is a small country.
A 10.2 The primary factor endowment is constant.
The emission standard S^S acts as the instrumental variable.
A 10.3 At the initial trade equilibrium described by equation 10.1, commodity 1 is the export good and commodity 2 the import good.
A 10.4 The assumptions of chapter 9 concerning the supply- and demand-side are valid.

The initial trade equilibrium is described by

$$p_{21} = p^*_{21} = p^W \qquad \text{(i)}$$
$$\qquad\qquad\qquad\qquad\qquad\qquad\qquad\qquad (10.1)$$
$$E_i + E_i^* = 0 \qquad i = 1,2 \qquad \text{(ii)}$$

where[1] p^W denotes the given world price ratio and E_i the excess demand function:

$$E_i := Q_i^d(p_{21}, Y, G(S)) - Q_i(p_{21}, S) \qquad (i = 1,2)$$

If we consider the budget constraint $E_1 + p_{21}E_2 = 0$, we can define the implied trade balance equilibrium as:

$$Z := E_1^* - p_{21}E_2 = -(E_1 + p_{21}E_2) = 0 \qquad (10.2)$$

10.1.2 Geometrical Exposition

Before we discuss analytically the implications of an emission standard policy, it seems worthwhile to offer a geometric

---

1) Foreign variables are always indicated by a "*".

illustration (diagram 10.1) [1]. We have the transformation locus (TT) of the home country denoted by $Q_1 = T(Q_2;V)$, where $V:=(A,K,S^s)$ indicates the fixed endowment. The social indifference map is taken for constant environmental quality $G(S^s) = U^s$ with: $Q_1^d = \Psi_1(Q_2^d,U^s)$ and alternative levels of social utility $\overline{W}_l < \overline{W}_{l+1}$ [2].

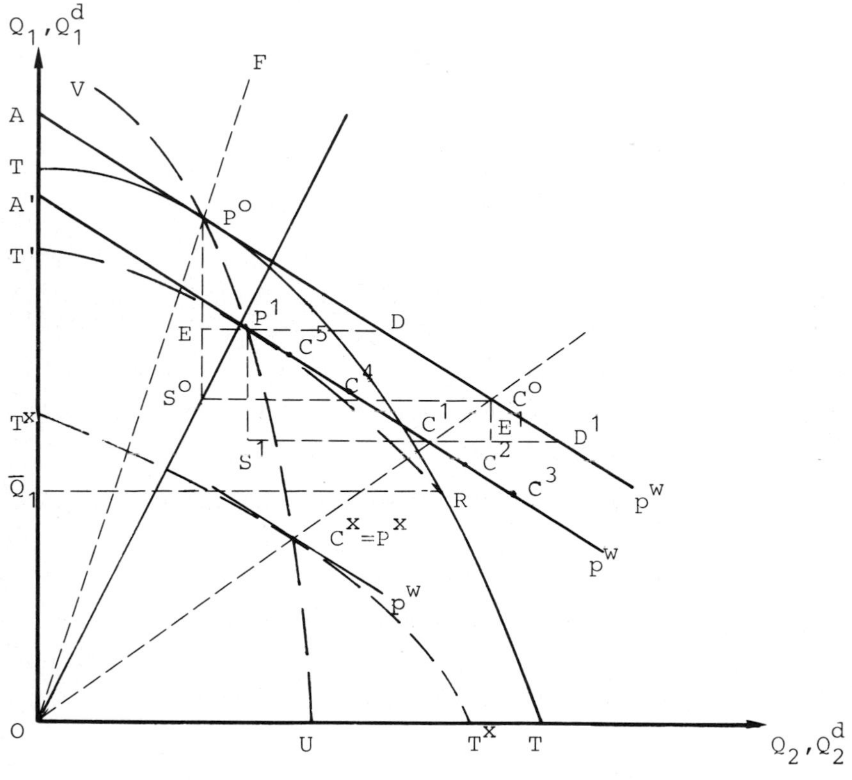

Diagram 10.1

For given p^w the home country realizes an equilibrium at the production point P^o and consumption point C^o. S^oP^o exportables are traded against S^oC^o importables. The analysis of chapter 9 has shown that the reduction of S^s forces the polluting industries to allocate some resources labour and capital in an internal waste abatement activity. We observe a change in the input mix and also an alteration in the

1) A geometric presentation is also given by Grubel (1976).
2) In order to simplify the exposition, the indifference curves are presented only by the tangential points C^l with the price line p^w.

production mix of the output vector (Q_i, S_i). At a constant price ratio equation 10.3 holds[1] if $dS^s < 0$:

$$\left.\begin{array}{l}\dfrac{\partial Q_i}{\partial S^s} > 0 \\[2ex] \dfrac{\partial Q_j}{\partial S^s} < 0\end{array}\right| \Leftrightarrow \left|\begin{array}{l}Q_i \text{ is strongly emission-intensive} \\ \qquad\qquad\text{and} \\ Q_j \text{ is strongly factor-intensive} \\ i,j=1,2 \quad i \neq j\end{array}\right. \tag{10.3}$$

We know that the achievement of the desired quality standard U^s requires the real expenditure of factors which are no more available for production purposes. The primary effect on the supply side leads to a biased inward shrinkage of the production possibility frontier to T'T in case of a strongly emission-intensive production of commodity 1. The common segment RT with the old curve arises from the fact that up to an output $O\bar{Q}_1$ the actual standard [2] of the home country does not form a binding constraint for the production possibilities since: $S^s > a_{S1}Q_1 + a_{S2}Q_2$ for all $Q_1 < \bar{Q}_1$.

The new production point lies to the right of P^o on the monotone decreasing line VU[3] which represents all the (Q_1, Q_2) - vectors at constant p_{21} and alternative decreasing S^s-levels. The positions of the new consumption points C^i $(i=1,\dots,5)$ are determined by the possible reactions of demand caused by reduced disposable income and improved environmental quality. We will see later that the magnitudes of marginal propensities to consumption and the sensitivity of demand in respect to U are decisive. The final total effect on trade volume is therefore a mix of consumption and production effects. The resulting trade triangles become smaller in the observed case of diagram 10.1.

---

1) See the results obtained in chapter 9.
2) Alternatively we can imagine that the assimilative capacity is sufficiently large to guarantee the desired U^s without any emission abatement devices.
3) In the literature this line is called the Rybczynski-line.

10.1.3 The Trade Effects

1. Since we want to examine the effects of pollution abatement on international trade flows, especially the possible structural changes, we now differentiate the excess-demand functions with respect to S^S:

$$\frac{\partial E_i}{\partial S^S} = \frac{\partial Q_i^d}{\partial Y}\frac{\partial Y}{\partial S^S} + \frac{\partial Q_i^d}{\partial U}\frac{dU}{dS^S} - \frac{\partial Q_i}{\partial S^S} \qquad (i=1,2) \qquad (10.4)$$

since $\frac{\partial Y}{\partial S^S} = \frac{\partial Q_1}{\partial S^S} + p_{21}\frac{\partial Q_2}{\partial S^S}$ we can reformulate equation

10.4 with the help of some elasticities which have been defined in the previous chapter. The elasticity

$\eta_{iU} := \frac{\partial Q_i^d}{\partial U}\frac{U}{Q_i^d}$ is a measure of the sensitivity of demand[1) at

varying U and $\varepsilon_{US} := \frac{dU}{dS}\frac{S}{U} < 0$ indicates the sensitivity of U at varying emissions S.

On account of the trade balance equilibrium 10.2, we get after differentiation:

$$\frac{\partial E_1}{\partial S^S} = -p_{21}\frac{\partial E_2}{\partial S^S} \qquad (10.5)$$

That is why we can concentrate on the reactions of one market. We are interested in the variation of home import demand and get from 10.4:

$$\frac{\partial E_2}{\partial S^S} = \frac{m_2}{p_{21}}\frac{\partial Q_1}{\partial S^S} - m_1\frac{\partial Q_2}{\partial S^S} + \eta_{2U}\,\varepsilon_{US}\frac{Q_2^d}{S^S}$$

or alternatively

$$\frac{\partial E_2}{\partial S^S} = \frac{1}{p_{21}}\frac{\partial Y}{\partial S^S}(m_2 - z_2) + \eta_{2U}\,\varepsilon_{US}\frac{Q_2^d}{S^S} \qquad (10.6)$$

---

1) Remember that we have $\eta_{1U}\frac{p_1Q_1^d}{Y} + \eta_{2U}\frac{p_2Q_2^d}{Y} = 0$ from the budget constraint. Compare chapter 9.

where $m_1 := \frac{\partial Q_1^d}{\partial Y}$ and $m_2 := p_{21}\frac{\partial Q_2^d}{\partial Y}$ are marginal propensities to consume exportables and importables whereas

$z_2 := p_{21} \frac{\partial Q_2}{\partial s^s} / \frac{\partial Y}{\partial s^s}$; $z_1 := \frac{\partial Q_1}{\partial s^s} / \frac{\partial Y}{\partial s^s}$ measure the rate of change in the output of importables respectively exportables as a proportion of the rate of change in income[1].

The m's and z's have the following properties:

$m_1 + m_2 = 1$
$z_1 + z_2 = 1$

2. If we utilize the terminology from Johnson (1958, p.76) in the context of factor growth, we can specify the nature of policy effects depending on the various possible values taken by z_1 and z_2. On account of 10.3 we have in case of $z_2 < 0$, $z_1 > 1$ an ultra-anti-trade-bias because the exportable good 1 is strongly emission-intensive. To put it in other words, the emission standard policy causes an absolute decline in the exportable production, so that the fall is proportionally greater than the fall in income[2]. If we consider the opposite case of strongly emission-intensive production of good 2, we state with 10.3 a fall in the production of import-substitutes 2 by more than the real income: $z_2 > 1$, $z_1 < 0$. This case is termed as ultra-pro-trade-biased because the average propensity to produce importables (exportables) shrinks (grows).

Equations 10.5 and 10.6 will give us some information about possible trade reactions. We see that technological constellations as well as influences of changing U and Y on the demand pattern are of crucial importance. We know from

1) One can regard z_i as an indicator showing the sector structure effect of the environmental policy. Since $\partial Y/\partial s^s$ is negative the magnitude z_i indicates the production bias of the standard policy.

2) If we denote $\theta_i := \frac{p_i Q_i}{Y}$ as the average propensity to produce exportables (i=1) respectively importables (i=2), we observe an increasing degree of self-sufficiency in producing import substitutes, because the extent of production of import substitutes increases: $\frac{\partial \theta_2}{\partial s^s} = \frac{\partial Y}{\partial s^s} \frac{1}{Y}(z_2 - \theta_2) < 0$.

chapter 9 that the impact on the demand structure depends on the substitutional ($\eta_{iU} < 0$) or complementary relation ($\eta_{iU} > 0$) of demand to U and additionally on the income effect

Note that with falling income and both goods being superior ($m_i > 0$), the demand for both goods is reduced. In the case of one inferior commodity ($m_i < 0$), we will have strongly biased demand effects. The demand of the inferior good ceteris paribus grows while the demand of the other good must fall more than proportionally ($m_1 + m_2 = 1$).

3. We are now able to summarize some analytical results:

Theorem 10.1 Let A 10.1 - A 10.4 be given, then the following holds:

$$\text{a)} \quad \frac{\partial E_2}{\partial s^s} \gtreqless 0 \Leftarrow \{m_2 \gtreqless z_2 \text{ and } \eta_{2U} \lesseqgtr 0\}$$

$$\text{b)} \quad \frac{\partial E_1}{\partial s^s} \lesseqgtr 0 \Leftrightarrow \frac{\partial E_2}{\partial s^s} \gtreqless 0 \qquad (10.7)$$

Proof: Follows immediately from 10.5, 10.6 in connection with 10.3.

4. For an economic interpretation of theorem 10.1, we distinguish two cases:

(1) exportable 1 is strongly emission-intensive
importable 2 is strongly factor-intensive

(2) the opposite of (1)

ad (1) The production effect is ultra-anti-trade-biased ($z_1 > 1$, $z_2 < 0$), since the production of exportables is reduced and the degree of self-sufficiency $\theta_2 = \frac{p_2 Q_2}{Y}$ raises. The import demand shrinks (compare 10.6), if no bias on the demand exists which works against the production effect. If the importable is a superior commodity and if additionally the importable is a substitute to $U(\eta_{2U} < 0)$ or is independent of $U(\eta_{2U} = 0)$, then the home demand always declines. In diagram 10.1 we observe that along the straight line OC^0 the consumption effect is neutral and the overall trade effect is shown by the new trade triangle $P^1S^1C^1$. If the economy has a relatively high income elasticity for importables, the demand falls much more than for good 1 (see consumption points C^4 or C^5) and the trade volume indicated by triangles shrinks faster than before. We could also allow the special case that commodity 2 is inferior ($m_2 < 0$). But as long as $|m_2| > |z_2|$, the partial effect of rising demand cannot overcompensate the production effect. (Consumption point C^3 in diagram 10.1). Only if the consumption effect is extremely biased in favour to the importable, i.e. $m_2 < z_2 < 0$ and $\eta_{2U} \geq 0$, one can expect a raising import volume. In the normal case the supply of exportables falls at constant p^w 1), so that the trade volume is reduced by environmental policy 2). We observe overall neutral effects on trade if all cusps of the trade triangles are situated on the ray OS^o. Since the trade triangle $S^1C^1P^1$ is to the right of OS^o, we can classify this as anti-trade-biased. The remaining cases can be easily verified. Additionally diagram 10.1 demonstrates the situation with a sufficient restriction of $S^s = S^s_x$ which is prohibitive for trade at given p^w (see point $C^x=P^x$).

ad (2) The production effect is ultra-pro-trade-biased ($z_2 > 1$, $z_1 < 0$) with the effect of a declining degree of self-sufficiency. What happens? In the case of non-inferiority of demand ($0 < m_i < 1$) and if $\eta_{2U} \geq 0$ the import demand increases. If the importable is an inferior commodity ($m_2 < 0$), we can say, that the income effect supports the pro-trade-bias of the supply side. The overall trade effect must have the same direction. Only in the very extreme case of sufficient biased consumption effect, so that the importable is "ultra-superior" with $m_2 > z_2 > 1$ and $\eta_{2U} \leq 0$, we can state an overall anti-trade-bias caused by the standard policy.

---

1) Compare equation 10.7b. The condition $m_2 > z_2$ is illustrated in diagram 10.1 by the amounts of the vectors $z_2 \hat{=} \frac{EP^1}{P^1D} < 0$ and $m_2 \hat{=} \frac{C^1E^1}{C^1D^1} > 0$.

2) Compare the somewhat different sufficient conditions in chapter 4, where we have a different production technology and demand specification.

5. Summing up we have: If we abstract from inferior goods and accept the assumptions A 10.1 - A 10.4, then a more stringent emission standard causes a reduction (raise) of the trade vol if the exportable (importable) commodity is strongly emission intensive and import demand falls (rises) or remains constant when the environmental quality improves. Without any inferior goods, one can imagine extreme cases only, if the improved environmental quality induces such a shift demand that the normal shift via income effect is overcompensated.

10.2 Terms of Trade Effects of Environmental Policy

Now we relax the assumption of given world price ratio and study the comparative-static implications for the terms of trade in a framework of two trading countries[1]. An existing trade equilibrium described by equation 10.1 is illustrated by the intersection of Meade-type offer curves. This equilibrium is shocked by the initiation of a program to reduce the pollution in the home country. Since the home country is no longer small, the endogenous world price ratio (the terms of trade) is affected by environmental policy. Our aim is to get some information about the likely effects on the terms of trade. A change of the terms of trade may increase or lower the social cost of attaining a given target of environmental quality from what it would have been if the terms of trade had remained constant. We suppose that every country realizes trade points on his offer curve (the law of Walras is valid). Since we are interested in the change of world price ratio, we can tackle the problem analytically as if we have a one-good-trade model of international trade. Throughout the present section, we assume that only the home country undertakes environmental policy[2] and that the environmental quality is independent of foreign pollution[3].

1) A somewhat different method to study the implications of an emission tax on world market is presented in chapter 5.
2) An extended version in case of two acting countries can be found in Gronych (1980).
3) That is no international spillover effects take place.

Before we present the comparative statics, let us elaborate two analytical insights concerning Walras' law in the world market and concerning the local stability of the system.

10.2.1 World Market Equilibrium and Stability

1. We assume given endowment vectors of the economies V, V^*. The aggregate supply functions are represented by:

$$Q_i = A_i(p_{21},V) \quad i=1,2 \qquad (10.8i,ii)$$

Since $Y = Q_1 + p_{21}Q_2$ and $U(S^S)$ is parametrically given, we can formulate the national excess demands as:

$$E_i = Q_i^d - Q_i = H_i(p_{21},V,U(S^S)) \quad i=1,2$$

Therefore rewrite the demand as:

$$Q_i^d = Q_i + E_i = D_i(p_{21}, U(S^S)) \quad i=1,2 \qquad (10.9i,ii)$$

The aggregated world excess demand is defined as:

$$E_i^W := E_i + E_i^* = (Q_i^d + Q_i^{d*}) - (Q_i + Q_i^*) := \Phi_i(p_{21};V,V^*) \qquad (10.10)$$

In a world equilibrium we have:

$$E_i^W(p^W) = 0 \ (i=1,2) \text{ and } p_{21} = p^W \qquad (10.11)$$

The budget restriction of the home country requires:

$$Q_1^d + p_{21}Q_2^d = Q_1 + p_{21}Q_2,$$

so that in trade equilibrium

$$E_1 = -p^W E_2 \qquad (10.12)$$

For the world excess-demand follows:

$$E_1^W = E_1 + E_1^* = -p^W(E_2 + E_2^*) = -p^W E_2^W \qquad (10.13)$$

On account of Walras' law and given E_2^W the excess demand of good 1 is determined. That is why we can concentrate our study on one market. In equilibrium we have $E_2^W = 0$, so that 10.13 can be redefined as a trade balance equilibrium:

$$E_2^* - \frac{1}{p_{21}} E_1 = 0 \qquad (10.14)$$

The whole system is then determined through the equations[1] 10.14, 10.9i, 10.9ii*, 10.8i, 10.8ii* in the five endogenous variables p_{21}, E_1, E_2^*, Q_1, Q_2^* and given V, V^*. It is easy to see that the other variables can be obtained by using the remaining production relations 10.8 and the budget equations. The knowledge of the change in the world price ratio is sufficient to get information about the allocation effects in the two countries, if one uses the result of the closed model in chapter 9.

2. If an equilibrium is shocked by disturbances of parameters, it is necessary to have some conditions about the local stability of the system. As is well known by the correspondence principle, we need stability to make possible a comparative static analysis. In this extended neoclassical model we confirm, that the Hicks conditions for imperfect stability are necessary and sufficient for unique results in comparative statics[3]. Later we will see that an evaluation of some terms is only possible with the knowledge of stability conditions. The literature[4] shows that the static stability analysis à la Hicks corresponds only in limited cases with the conditions gained from a dynamic, local stability procedure. Therefore only the dynami technique is relevant[5]. We now postulate a Walrasian Tâtonne ment-process, which regards the change of excess demands in time.

We have the well-known rules:

i) A nonequilibrium price will be raised (reduced) if the excess demand is positive (negative).

ii) We will have transactions only in an equilibrium.

---

1) The relevant foreign equations are labelled by a "*".
2) We do not need such an expanded system as in chapter 5 wher a two-country analysis is undertaken. In contrast to this analysis, chapter 5 investigates an emission tax policy and uses the gross-emissions approach developed in chapter 2.
3) Compare Takayama (1972, p.362)
4) See for example Gandolfo (1972, p.341n)
5) It can be shown, that the Hicks conditions for static stability are neither necessary nor sufficient for dynamic stability. Compare Gandolfo (1972, p.280), Samuelson (1947).

An adequately formulated reaction hypothesis is as follows[1)2)]:

$$\dot{p}_{21} = \frac{dp_{21}}{dt} = \Psi_2[\Phi_2(p_{21};V,V^*)], \qquad (10.15)$$

where Ψ_2 is a sign preserving function which characterizes the velocity of reaction with sign $\Psi_2[\ldots] = \text{sign}\,[\ldots]$, $\Psi_2(0) = 0, \Psi_2'(\ldots)>0$.

We suppose an existing equilibrium value of p^W so that $\Phi_2\ (p^W\ldots) = 0$. If p_{21} is the current value, then we can approximate 10.15 with the help of a Taylor series expansion about the equilibrium point p^W.

$$\frac{dp_{21}}{dt} = \Psi_2'(\Phi_2(p^W)) + \Psi_2'\ \Phi_2'(p^W)(p-p^W) + \ldots = \Phi_2'(p^W)(p-p^W) \qquad (10.16)$$

Let $\Psi_2' = 1$ in the above formula.

Since $\Phi_2'(p^W) = \frac{\partial E_2}{\partial p_{21}} + \frac{\partial E_2^*}{\partial p_{21}}$, we get:

$$\frac{dp_{21}}{dt} = \left(\frac{\partial E_2}{\partial p_{21}} + \frac{\partial E_2^*}{\partial p_{21}}\right)(p_{21}-p^W) := \Delta(p_{21}-p^W). \qquad (10.17)$$

Equation 10.17 is a differential equation of the first degree in (p_{21},t). With adequate initial conditions this results in

$$p_{21}(t) = p_{21}(0)\ e^{\Delta t} + p^W \qquad (10.18)$$

where $p_{21}(0) = A\ e^{\Delta 0}$ and A = const.

The time path of 10.18 depends on the sign of Δ.

We have $\lim_{t\to\infty} p(t) = p^W \Leftarrow \Phi_2' = \Delta<0$

$\Delta < 0$ is a sufficient condition for local stability of the trade model.

3. The forgone stability condition can be reformulated with the help of some well-known price elasticities and the validity of A 10.3 at given V, V^*. Let us define η_{Mj} as the home country (foreign) import demand elasticity and ε_{Xj} as the home country (foreign) export supply elasticity.

---

1) On account of 1o.13 one could have formulated equivalently $\dot{p}_{21} = -\Psi_1[\Phi_1]$.

2) See G. Gandolfo (1972, p.279n)

a) $\eta_{M2} := -\dfrac{\partial E_2}{\partial p_{21}} \dfrac{p_{21}}{E_2}$ b) $\eta^*_{M1} := \dfrac{\partial E^*_1}{\partial p_{21}} \dfrac{p_{21}}{E^*_1}$

c) $\varepsilon_{X1} := -\dfrac{\partial E_1}{\partial p_{21}} \dfrac{p_{21}}{E_1}$ d) $\varepsilon^*_{X2} := \dfrac{\partial E^*_2}{\partial p_{21}} \dfrac{p_{21}}{E^*_2}$

The foreign budget restriction can be written as:

$$E^*_1 + p_{21}E^*_2 = 0 \tag{10.20}$$

We differentiate 10.20 and substitute 10.19b,d:

$$-\eta^*_{M1} + \varepsilon^*_{X2} + 1 = 0 \text{ or } \varepsilon^*_{X2} = \eta^*_{M1} - 1 \tag{10.21}$$

If we take into consideration 10.19a, 10.19d, 10.17, 10.21, 10.22, we obtain after some manipulations:

$$\Delta = -\frac{E_2}{p_{21}} [\eta_{M2} + \eta^*_{M1} - 1] < 0 \tag{10.22}$$

Inspection of 10.22 shows that the stability condition requires $(\eta_{M2} + \eta^*_{M1} - 1) > 0$, i.e. the absolute sum of the demand elasticities must exceed one.

10.2.2 Implications of Emission Standard Policy

1. In the following we investigate possible changes of p^W exhibiting the home terms of trade resulting from:
i) alternative levels of the emission standard S^S and
ii) alternative assumptions about the pollution technique.
We have seen in the preceding chapter that the environmental policy affects comparative costs in the case of a binding emission standard. We will expect a noticeable influence on international prices if the home country is sufficiently large. We set some additional assumptions beside A 10.1 - A 10.4.

A 10.1': The rest of the world undertakes no environmental policy. This means $dV^* = 0$ and $\dfrac{\partial E^*_2}{\partial S^{S*}} = 0$. 1)

A 10.5: The world market is locally stable.
A 10.6: We have no inferior goods: $0<m_i<1$; $i=1,2$.

1) Geometrically spoken, the foreign offer curve remains const.

2. We want to derive a formula which links the terms of trade change with the change of s^s. With the help of the implicit function theorem[1], we are able to express the price ratio in terms of parameters V,V^*: $p_{21} = p(V,V^*)$ with $\Phi_2(p(V,V^*);V,V^*)=0$ We have $\Phi_2(p_{21};V,V^*)=0$ and $p_{21}=p$ in an equilibrium state. We know $\partial\Phi_2/\partial p_{21} \neq 0$. That is why we can develop p_{21} as a function of the parameters (V,V^*) in a small neighbourhood of the equilibrium.

If A 10.1', A 10.2, A 10.5 hold, then we obtain:[2]

$$\frac{\partial p_{21}}{\partial V} = -\left(\frac{\partial \Phi_2}{\partial p_{21}}\right)^{-1} \frac{\partial \Phi_2}{\partial V} = -\frac{1}{\Delta}\left(\frac{\partial E_2}{\partial V} + \frac{\partial E_2^*}{\partial V}\right) \tag{10.23a}$$

Considering A 10.1' we get:

$$\frac{\partial p_{21}}{\partial s^s} = -\frac{1}{\Delta}\frac{\partial E_2}{\partial s^s} \tag{10.23b}$$

Substitution of 10.6 into 10.24b leads to[3]

$$\frac{\partial p_{21}}{\partial s^s} = -\frac{1}{p_{21}\Delta}\underbrace{\left\{\frac{\partial Y}{\partial s^s}(m_2-z_2) + \eta_{2U}\varepsilon_{US}\frac{p_{21}Q_2^d}{s^s}\right\}}_{:=B} \tag{10.24}$$

We observe under the validity of A 10.5 that sign $\frac{\partial p_{21}}{\partial s^s}$ = sign B holds. On account of A 10.1' we identify a functional dependence between the terms of trade change and the change of home import demand which is induced by the reallocative effects and the income reduction of pollution policy. The evaluation of the terms on the right-hand side is taken at constant prices, because the shift of the offer curve is determined by the change of import demand at constant price ratios.

3. We make a temporary assumption to simplify the process of deducing results.

---

1) Compare for example Intriligator (1971,p.499)
2) Analogous methods are used in problems of growth and trade. Compare Kemp (1969, p.104n), Schittko (1976, p.304n).
3) Equation 10.24 shows the great importance of the stability condition for the comparative statics.

A 10.7 Demand does not react to environmental quality:
$\eta_{iU} = 0$ i=1,2.

Therefore we are able to deduce [1] 10.25, since A 10.5 holds:

$$\frac{\partial p_{21}}{\partial s^S} \gtreqless 0 \Leftrightarrow m_2 \gtreqless z_2. \tag{10.25}$$

Remember $z_2 := p_{21}\frac{\partial Q_2}{\partial s^S} / (p_{21}\frac{\partial Q_2}{\partial s^S} + \frac{\partial Q_1}{\partial s^S})$

We can distinguish only two possible production effects if 10.3 is valid:
i) In case of $z_2<0$, we have an ultra anti-trade-bias, since $\partial Q_2/\partial s^S<0$ and $\partial Q_1/\partial s^S>0$.
ii) In case of $z_2>1$, we obtain an ultra-pro-trade-bias resulting from the bias against the import substitute (i.e. $\partial Q_2/\partial s^S>0$ and $\partial Q_1/\partial s^S<0$).

4. The economic results are summarized in theorem 10.2:

<u>Theorem 10.2:</u> Let the assumptions A 10.1 - A 10.7 be given. Furthermore in the home country an effective emission standard policy is undertaken.

a) Then a shortage of the emission standard always causes an improvement (worsening) of the terms of trade, if the production of the exportable is strongly emission intensive (strongly factor intensive) and the import substitute is strongly factor intensive (strongly emission intensive).
b) The improvement (worsening) effect is maximal in case of inelastic foreign import demand.

Proof: a) Use equation 10.25 and 10.3.
b) Let $0<\eta^*_{M1}<1$, so that Δ ceteris paribus becomes smaller. Then use equation 10.25.

q.e.d.

5. The results presented in theorem 10.2 are consistent with an intuitive understanding of the processes involved[2].

1) This result of an emission standard policy is directly comparable with the effects of an emission tax policy described in chapter 5.
2) In chapter 5 we obtained comparable results in the context of an emission tax policy and where the demand structure is independent of U.

The initiation of a pollution control policy of the home country decreases the relative abundance of good 1 over good 2 and in order to equalize world demand and output the relative price of good 1 has to increase. The home country's terms of trade improve because Q_1 is its export good and because its total output is smaller while that of the foreign country remains constant. We can interprete this result as signifying that trade enables a country which undertakes an environmental policy to transfer a share of its real costs of pollution control generated entirely within its own borders to the rest of the world.

A necessary condition for this outcome is that the export good pollutes much more than the importable. Our results cannot support the view of Grubel (1976) who claims that the terms of trade effect is independent of the polluting characteristic. In the opposite case where the importable is relatively emission-intensive, we obtain a deterioration effect of the terms of trade, which implies an additional component of social cost to achieve the policy goal U^s. It will be quite difficult on informational grounds for the political system to check the likely price effects of international trade. The information cost to set the proper quality target seem to be prohibitive. A departure of this unique effect is only possible if we relax the assumption of noninferior goods and incorporate the effect of U on the demand side (A 10.6, A 10.7). In the preceding section 10.1 we have examined some sufficient conditions which guarentee unique reactions of import demand at constant p^w. The same conditions in connection with 10.24 allow to draw some conclusions for the possible direction of the terms of trade movement. Generally, we can maintain that a raising (reduction) of home import demand at constant prices will lead to a deterioration (improvement) of the country's terms of trade.

For example if the influence of U on demand cannot be ignored, we can support the result in theorem 10.2 under the validity of A 10.1 - A 10.6 if 10.26 holds:

$$\left\{\frac{\partial p}{\partial S^s} \gtrless 0 \Leftrightarrow \frac{\partial E_2}{\partial S^s}\right\} \gtrless 0 \Longleftarrow \{m_2 \gtrless z_2 \text{ and } \eta_{2U} \lesseqgtr 0\} \qquad (10.26)$$

This formulation covers the possible outcome, that the chance for an improvement (deterioration) of the terms of trade are increased, if the ultra-anti-trade (ultra-pro-trade)-biased production effect is assisted by the demand side. This appears when the home import demand is lowered (increased) in case of $\eta_{2U} < 0$ ($\eta_{2U} > 0$).

Otherwise a sufficient biased demand shift is able to render a worsening (improvement) if $m_2 \gtrless z_2$ and $\eta_{2U} \gtrless 0$ contrary to the claim of theorem 10.2. In addition to this we conclude extreme reactions on the demand side caused by inferiority in consumption. In case of inferiority of the importable ($m_2<0$) and $|m_2|<|z_2|$, we obtain a worsening of trade contrary to the result in theorem 10.2. It is easy to construct other constellations which increases the likelihood of an anomalous reaction.

6. We can give a short description of the working of the model. The supply effect is obvious, since the output of that commodity always shrinks which pollutes much more than the other sector. The lowering of real national income induces a decline of both commodity demands if all goods are superior and if the environmental quality does not affect the demand. The resulting excess supply of the less polluting commodity and the excess demand of the polluting commodity enforces an alternation of the price structure. Under the assumption of local stability we get for example a raise of the price of the strongly emission intensive export good.

10.2.3 A Diagrammatical Exposition with Trade-Curves

1. The discussed problems can be reconstructed in a trade curve diagram. Before doing this it seems worthwhile to show how the trade indifference curves are influenced by the introduction of a third argument in the social utility function. Starting from an autarky equilibrium - P^{AUT} in diagram 10.2 - we draw at given $V=(A,K,S^S)$ all export-import combinations which realizes the same social utility-level. The construction of such trade indifference curves H^n is

well known[1]. In our model, one must notice a constant environmental quality to render a proper comparison of commodity bundles[2]. To make possible a graphic presentation in commodity space, one must draw iso welfare lines with a higher quality value of U below a relevant indifference curve with a lower U index but higher bundles.

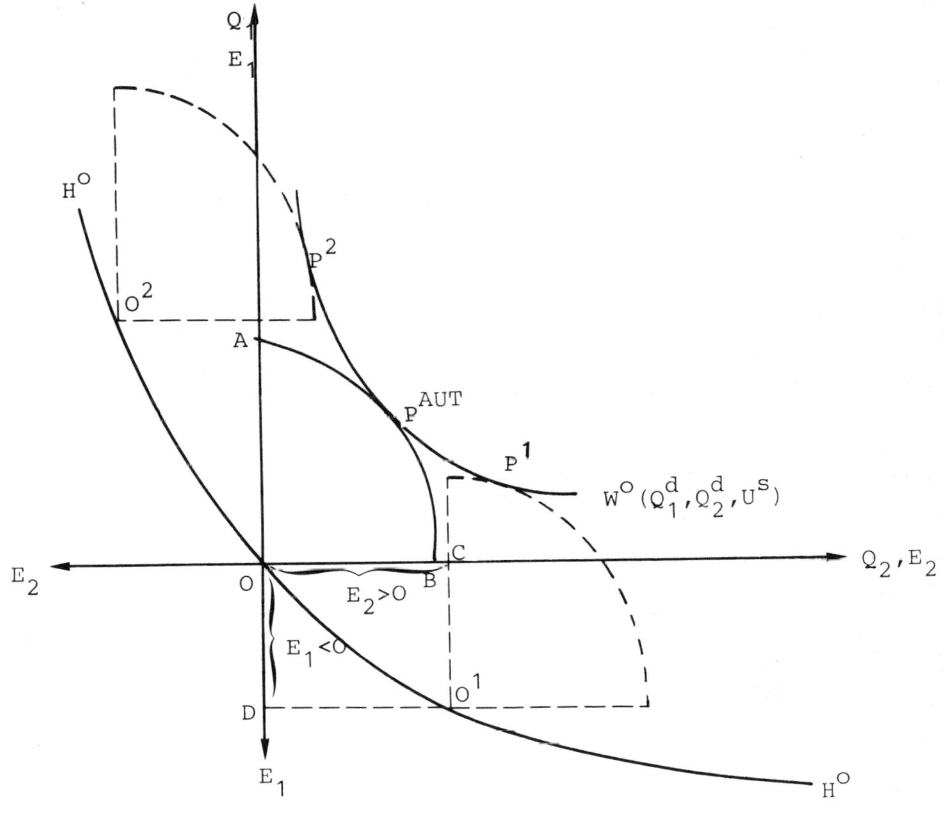

Diagram 10.2

1) Compare J.E.Meade (1952, p.44n) and all better text books of international trade theory.

2) $H^n(V) := \{(E_1,E_2)/(Q_1^d,Q_2^d) - (E_1,E_2) \in \hat{Y}$ and $W(Q_1^d,Q_2^d,U^S) = C_n \,|\, C_n$ const. $n \in N_o\}$

Y denotes the efficiency locus of the production possibility set.

The home country will be indifferent between the points P^1 or P^2 and the autarky point P^{AUT}. Consistency requires at point P^1 an export of OD units and an import of OC units. In P^2 we have a higher price ratio and a inverse trade pattern[1)]. If we shift the production block along social indifference curves with higher levels but the same U-index, we obtain a whole map of trade indifference curves (H^o, H^1, H^2,...) relatively to a constant quality index U^s or constant S^s. With this map one can model with the help of the budget restriction the famous Marshall-Mill-offer-curve.

$$E_1 + p_{21}E_2 = 0 \qquad (10.27)$$

The graph of equation 10.27 expresses a linear function through the origin, the slope of which is given by

$-\frac{dE_1}{dE_2} = p_{21} = -\frac{E_1}{E_2}$ (=world price ratio). At varying p_{21} we obtain the locus of tangential points which cover all optimal trade quantities. Notice that this defines a single offer-curve relative to a given emission norm: $E_1 = \varphi(E_2, S^s)$, the graph of which is given by PNOQRS in diagram 10.3. We hav integrated in diagram 10.3 the foreign offer curve P'OS' which is derived in the same manner. An equilibrium which defines compatible trade plans of both countries is denoted by point R and p^w. We observe an export of OB units of the home country and OC of import units at the equilibrium price ratio p^w. The decrease of the emission standard from S^s_o to S^s_1 leads to an inward shrinkage from TT to T'T' biased against the strong emission intensive good 2 (diagram 10.4). The new equilibrium point is shown as $p^1(S^s_1) > p^o(S^s_o)$.

---

1) It can be shown that the slope of trade indifference curves corresponds with the slope of social indifference curves and transformation curves in appropriate points. It can also be shown that they are strictly convex if the transformation curve and the welfare function are strictly concave.

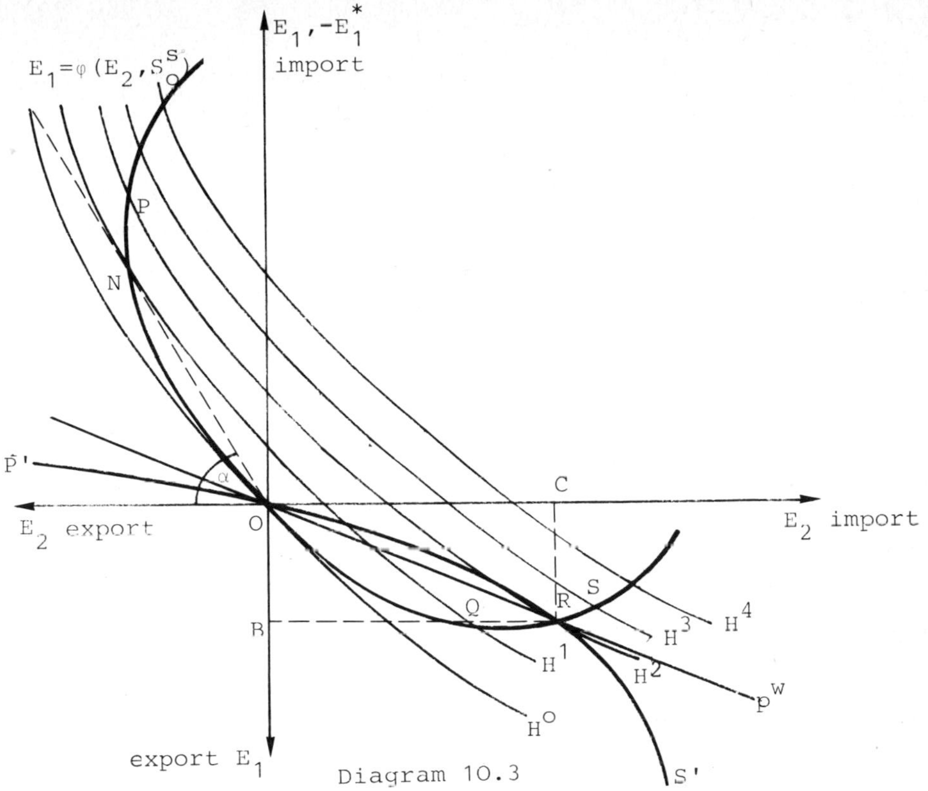

Diagram 10.3

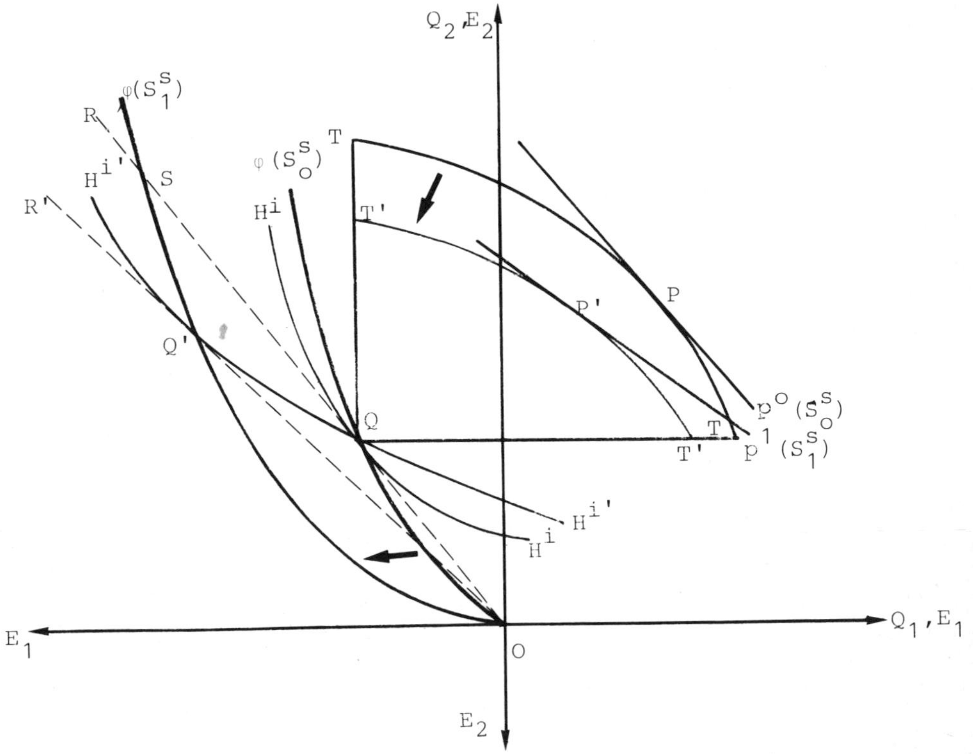

Diagram 10.4

A trade indifference curve H^i passes through the origin of the production block, the slope of which - measured by the price line OR - is equal to the price ratio p^o. The new block T'T' relative to the norm S_1^s touches a social indifference curve in P', the level of which represents a higher welfare. Since the slope in P' is lower than in P, we must have a new trade indifference curve $H^{i'}$ corresponding to the norm S_1^s which has a lower slope in Q. A new price line OR' touches the new curve $H^{i'}$ in Q', therefore Q' denotes a point on the relevant new offer curve $\varphi(S_1^s)$. $\varphi(S_1^s)$ represents the locus of all tangential points of different price lines with the new map of trade indifference curves relative to the norm S_1^s. We discover - under the assumption of emission-intensive production of commodity 2 - an outward shift of the offer curve, so that at a constant price ratio the trade volume is enlarged (ultra-pro-trade-bias). In the fourth quadrant, where commodity 2 denotes an exportable we must have an upward shift of the offer curve. In other words, in case of relatively emission intensive export production the φ-function shifts inward, so that at constant prices the trade volume reduces (ultra-anti-trade-bias).

2. If we suppose case (1) where the export good is relativel waste intensive, we know the trade effect to be ultra-anti-trade-biased in case of non inferior goods. The home country offer curve shifts to the left in case of $S_1^s < S_o^s$ (diagram 10.5). The home import demand evaluated at constant terms of trade ($\hat{=}$OP) reduces from OV to OW resulting in an excess supply of good 2 (VW) and an excess demand of good 1 (PR). A stable market mechanism leads to an increasing price ratio of good 1, this means the terms of trade of the home country indicated by OP' improves. We see that the endogenous change of trade quantities depends on the slope of the foreign offer curve.

We get with the help of 10.19, 10.21, 10.22, 10.23b for the total change:

$$\frac{dE_2}{dS^s} = \frac{\partial E_2}{\partial p_{21}} \frac{\partial p_{21}}{\partial S^s} + \frac{\partial E_2}{\partial S^s} = \{\eta_{M2} \frac{E_2}{p_{21}} \frac{1}{\Delta} + 1\} \frac{\partial E_2}{\partial S^s}$$

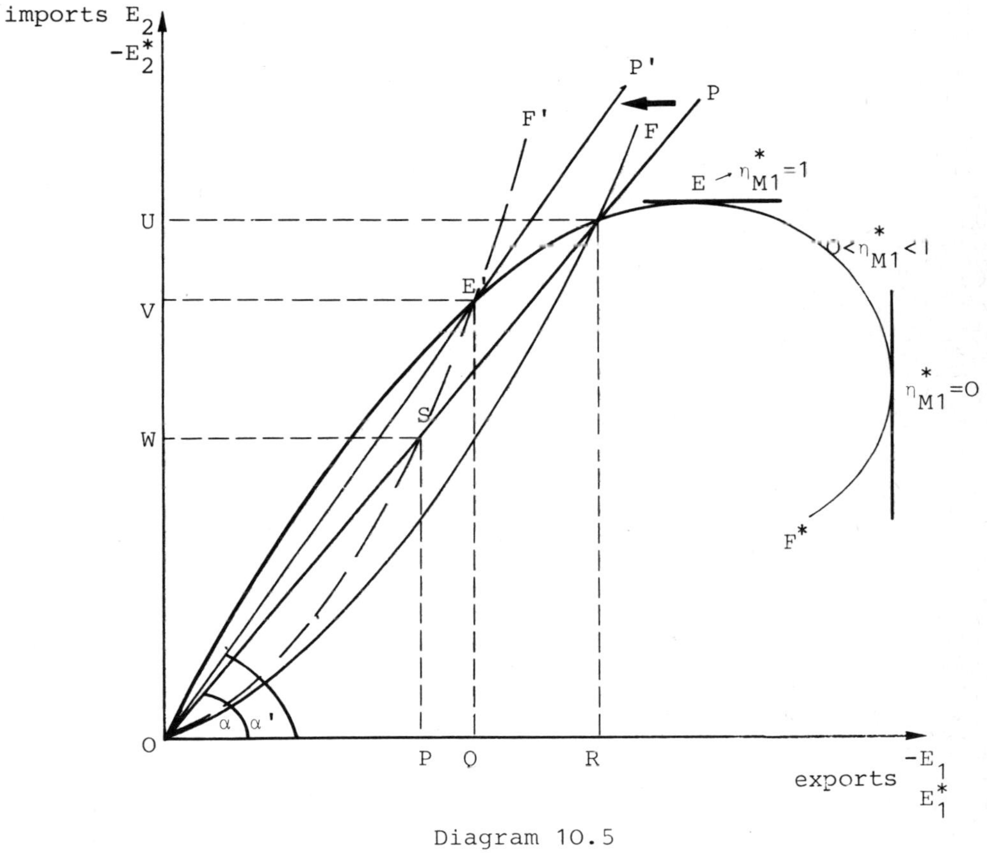
imports E_2
$-E_2^*$
P'
P
F'
F
$E \rightarrow \eta_{M1}^*=1$
U
$0<\eta_{M1}^*<1$
E'
V
$\eta_{M1}^*=0$
S
W
F^*
α
α'
O
P
Q
R
$-E_1$
exports
E_1^*

Diagram 10.5

$$= -\frac{1}{\Delta}\frac{E_2}{p_{21}}(\eta^*_{M1} - 1)\frac{\partial E_2}{\partial s^s} := -\frac{1}{\Delta}\frac{E_2}{p_{21}}\varepsilon^*_{X2}\frac{\partial E_2}{\partial s^s} \tag{10.28}$$

For the export change (=foreign imports) we get:

$$\frac{dE^*_1}{ds^s} = \frac{\partial E^*_1}{\partial s^s}\frac{\partial p_{21}}{\partial s^s} = -\frac{1}{\Delta}E_2\,\eta^*_{M1}\frac{\partial E_2}{\partial s^s} \tag{10.29}$$

In the elastic part of the foreign offer curve ($\eta^*_{M1}>1$), we will observe - under the assumptions A 10.1 - A 10.7 - a trade equilibrium where both export and import levels decrease, denoted by UV and QR in diagram 10.5. In the inelastic part of the foreign offer curve ($0<\eta^*_{M1}<1$) we deduce an increasing import volume and a lowering export volume, whereby the terms of trade improvement will be greater since $|\Delta|$ becomes smaller. Geometrically spoken the equilibrium point falls into the monotone decreasing part of the curve.

Symmetric arguments hold if we consider the case, where the import substitute Q_2 is relatively emission-intensive. Now we obtain the outward shift of the offer curve which induces always a worsening of the terms of trade as long as we have an elastic curve. In the inelastic part, where the import volume shrinks and the export volume increases, we have a drastic deterioration of the terms of trade (compare 10.28, 10.29).

3. Finally it should be noticed that the described terms of trade effects cannot appear, if the emission norm of the home country does not form a binding constraint of the production set at current price ratios. In the relevant part of the offer curve no shift appears with the result of constant terms of trade. Furthermore the analysis assumes a passive foreign country. We must expect in reality that the trade partner would also undertake a control policy so that the outcome on the terms of trade must be reinterpreted. The formal analysis would be much more complicated.

10.3 Summary

In the first part we analyze the effects of production pollution control on international trade under the assumption of a small country. A classification of possible effects of pollution control on trade is undertaken, drawing on the concepts of trade biases from the theory of growth. We focused on the possible factors affecting the direction and magnitude of the change. In the second part we used the well-known two-country model of trade. We proved that free trade with direct pollution control in the form of a emission standard policy enables the acting country to improve its terms of trade if the exportable is relatively emission intensive. We have also given sufficient conditions for special demand effects. Especially we are able to give conditions for a worsening of the terms of trade. The final quantity effects of international trade are seen to depend on the price effect in the world market and on the price elasticity of foreign demand.

PART IV

EXTENSIONS

In the preceding three parts of this book we discussed the analytical framework and studied several basic issues of trade and environment. Although up to now our concept was to elaborate thoroughly and rigorously the most important theoretical questions, many interesting problems of trade and environment have not been dealt with so far. In the following two chapters we focus our attention on two further aspects of environmental control in open economies that extend the previous analysis in two different directions: We wish to study the impacts of environmental controls on trade when capital mobility or recycling is introduced.

Chapter 11 treats the adjustments to the implementation of an emission tax in a two-country, two-sector, two-factor model with capital being an internationally mobile factor. This additional assumption allows us to investigate the reallocation of capital between trading countries as a consequence of national environmental policy. Thus, some of the previously received results will be qualified or modified due to the factor mobility assumption.

In chapter 12 the waste treatment option to avoid environmental disruption is complemented by the possiblity of recycling which we conceive of as the reclamation of a productive input from the (previously useless) by-product with the help of a scarce resource. Recycling is not only an important device for natural resource conservation but it is linked to environmental management as well, and, moreover, it has obvious international dimensions in trading economies. Several conclusions are received with respect to the interdependencies of national environmental policies, changes in the rates of recycling, comparative advantages and trade.

11. Impacts of an Emission Tax in an Open Economy with Capital Mobility

So far there has been an extensive treatment of environmental policy in the traditional two-country, two-commodity and two--factor model of pure trade theory. Nevertheless one important aspect - particularly in the context of the analysis of the impacts of environmental policy - has been neglected: the possibility of international capital allocation. For one would suspect a restrictive environmental policy in one country to be a disincentive for capital allocation there.

This chapter, therefore tries to extend the work of the previous parts by analyzing the impacts of an emission tax within the framework of a neoclassical two-country, two--commodity, and two-factor world with capital movements between both countries. The work of Chipman (1971), Batra and Casas (1976) and Pethig (1976) are basic references of this chapter. While Chipman treats the problem of capital mobility in the standard trade model, Batra and Casas deal with a three factor model and Pethig presents a method of taking pollutants emitted by a production process as an input to that process (see section 2.2).

The following section presents the assumptions concerning the behaviour of consumers and producers and derives the corresponding demand and supply conditions. In the next two sections the complete general equilibrium system is established and some characteristics of the model are discussed. The fourth section specifies the initial equilibrium situation, while section 11.5 deals with the comparative static results. The final section is devoted to some concluding discussions.

11.1 Assumptions

For the development of a fairly adequate model of an economy trying to prevent a further decline of its environmental quality by implementing an emission tax the reactive behaviou of both consumers and producers are of utmost importance. The first two subsections therefore treat the decision process in these sectors, while the exposition of the complete model and a discussion of its properties is given in the next two sections.

11.1.1 Producers

It is impossible to analyze the complex decision problem of a industry, i.e. to take account of the many single decisions taking place in many different and independent firms with regard to various objectives, heterogeneous commodities, and confronted with all sorts of demand and supply conditions on their respective markets, without loosing sight of the partic lar problem of their adjustment to an emission tax. In so far some rather drastically simplifying assumptions seem to be in order.

Producers behaviour is assumed to be the same in all sectors under consideration in this chapter, therefore, in this subsection sector and country sub- and superscripts are omitted for notational convenience. The following assumptions concerning the production set and the behaviour of a representative producer are identical to those of chapter 9. Thus we need no discuss them in detail here.[1)]

A 11.1 Production vector. The production vector consists of one output Q, one pollutant S, and two factors, labour A and capital K, i.e. $(Q,S,A,K) \in R_+^4$

The second assumption concerns the production set. It is assu that the output Q is a function of the inputs and the pollutant S. Thus the pollutant S is treated as an input to the production process.

---

1) Compare particularly section 9.2 and section 9.3.

A 11.2 Production set. Production possibilities are represented by a concave, twice continuously differentiable production function $F: D \rightarrow R_+$

$$Q \leq F(K,A,S) \tag{11.1}$$

with $D := \{(K,A,S) \mid S \leq \Phi(K,A); \Phi_A > 0; \Phi_K > 0\} \subset R_+^3$

and $\forall\ (K,A,S) \in D: \quad S = \Phi(K,A) \Rightarrow F_S(K,A,S) = 0$

where $\Phi_K := \dfrac{\partial \Phi(K,A)}{\partial K}$; $\Phi_A := \dfrac{\partial \Phi(K,A)}{\partial A}$; $F_S(\cdot) := \dfrac{\partial F(\cdot)}{\partial S}$

Finally an assumption concerning the objective of the representative firm has to be formulated.

A 11.3 Firm behaviour. The representative firm behaves as a price taker and maximizes its profits G

$$G = pQ - p_A A - p_K K - p_S S \tag{11.2}$$

where the p, p_A, p_K, p_S denote the commodity price, the input prices and the emission tax (p_S).

A 11.4 Linear homogenity. The production function is homogenous of degree one, i.e.

$$\forall (K,A,S) \in D: F(\lambda K, \lambda A, \lambda S) = \lambda F(K,A,S) \tag{11.3}$$

Assuming further an inner solution to the problem described by the assumptions A 11.1 to A 11.3 then A 11.4 implies that the commodity price and factor intensities are functions of factor prices and the emission tax only and may be written as follows[1]:

$$\left.\begin{aligned} p &= g(p_K, p_A, p_S) && \text{(i)} \\ \frac{K}{Q} &= g_K(p_K, p_A, p_S) && \text{(ii)} \\ \frac{A}{Q} &= g_A(p_K, p_A, p_S) && \text{(iii)} \\ \frac{S}{Q} &= g_S(p_K, p_A, p_S) && \text{(iv)} \end{aligned}\right\} \tag{11.4}$$

1) Compare section 9.3

These equations may be differentiated and transformed into change rates to yield[1]:

$$\hat{p} = \theta_K \hat{p}_K + \theta_A \hat{p}_A + \theta_S \hat{p}_S \qquad \text{(i)}$$

$$\hat{K} = \hat{Q} + \theta_K \sigma_{KK} \hat{p}_K + \theta_A \sigma_{AK} \hat{p}_A + \theta_S \sigma_{SK} \hat{p}_S \qquad \text{(ii)}$$

$$\hat{A} = \hat{Q} + \theta_K \sigma_{KA} \hat{p}_K + \theta_A \sigma_{AA} \hat{p}_A + \theta_S \sigma_{SA} \hat{p}_S \qquad \text{(iii)} \qquad (11.5)$$

$$\hat{S} = \hat{Q} + \theta_K \sigma_{KS} \hat{p}_K + \theta_A \sigma_{AS} \hat{p}_A + \theta_S \sigma_{SS} \hat{p}_S \qquad \text{(iv)}$$

where $\theta_K := \frac{p_K K}{pQ}$; $\theta_A := \frac{p_A A}{pQ}$; $\theta_S := \frac{p_S S}{pQ}$;

and σ_{KK}, σ_{AK}, σ_{SK}, etc. denote the substitution elasticities according to Allen (1938, p. 503-505).

The property of homogenity of degree one is a common assumption in pure trade theory[2]. It facilitates analysis in a way that makes the treatment of complex trade models possible. The most important consequence of it is the relation between commodity and factor prices 11.5i which is independent of the level of output.

11.1.2 Consumers

The main purpose of this section consists in stating an assumption about consumer behaviour which on the one hand retains substitutability and on the other keeps a complex model treatable. Therefore, the following assumption is stated.

A 11.5 Demand. The ratio of expenditures for commodity 1 ($p_1 Q_1^d$) to expenditures of commodity 2 ($p_2 Q_2^d$) is constant, i.e.

$$p_1 Q_1^d = \sigma p_2 Q_2^d \qquad \sigma = \text{constant} \qquad (11.6)$$

---

1) For a detailed derivation refer to section 9.3
2) Compare e.g. Kemp (1969), Takayama (1972).

One easily deduces the following demand functions from assumption A 11.5

$$Q_1^d = \frac{\sigma}{1+\sigma} \frac{E}{p_1}$$

$$Q_2^d = \frac{1}{1+\sigma} \frac{E}{p_2} \qquad (11.7)$$

where E stands for the total expenditure on both commodities.

Demand conditions like those of equation 11.7 may be derived by utility maximization of a representative consumer[1]. The choice of the consumer is restricted to the commodities of the two industries. The possibility of a direct impact on the demand functions by environmental quality is disregarded, because direction as well as scale of such an impact on the demand for highly aggregated commodities are unclear.

Finally the implications of the demand assumption A 11.5 for demand elasticities should be pointed out:

(i) income elasticities equal one,

(ii) own price elasticities equal minus one and

(iii) cross price elasticities are zero.

Particularly this last implication (iii) seems to be justified, if one has in mind industries producing consumption goods or investment goods. Between commodity bundles of this kind it seems reasonable to assume unaffectedness of demand by a small price change of the other commodity.

---

1) Such a demand system may be attained e.g. by maximizing a Cobb-Douglas type utility function - $U = A(Q_1^d)^{\alpha}(Q_2^d)^{\beta}$, with A, α, β denoting parameters-. Thus one arrives at $\sigma=\alpha/\beta$.

11.2 The General Equilibrium System

So far the fundamental assumptions concerning behaviour of consumers and producers are laid down. With the help of four further assumptions the complete model may be drawn up.

A 11.6 Two countries and two commodities. There are two countries, the home country I and the foreign country II, each producing and demanding two commodities. Both commoditie are internationally traded.

A 11.7 Capital mobility. Capital is supplied inelastically in both countries (K,K^*) and offered on a common international market.

$$K + \bar{K} \geq \sum_{i=1}^{2} K_i \qquad (11.8)$$

$$K^* + \bar{K}^* \geq \sum_{i=1}^{2} K_i^*$$

$\bar{K}^*$ and $\bar{K}$ denote capital exports, if negative, and capital imports, if positive, of the respective country[1)].

A 11.8 Labour supply. Labour is supplied in each country inelastically (A,A^*) and is internationally totally immobile.

$$A \geq \sum_{i=1}^{2} A_i \qquad (11.9)$$

$$A^* \geq \sum_{i=1}^{2} A_i^*$$

It is obvious that production is assumed to take place according to assumptions A 11.1 to A 11.4 in both sectors and both countries. Therefore, for each country two systems of equations (as 11.4) describing factor demand and commodity supply conditions are part of the model. Analogously a demand condition (as 11.6) belongs to each country. These equations are discerned by sub- and superscripts refer-

1) Variables and parameters with a superscript * belong to the foreign country.

ring to industries and countries, respectively.

Now excess demand E_i, E_i^*, i = 1,2 may be defined as

$$E_i = Q_i^d - Q_i \qquad i = 1,2$$
$$E_i^* = Q_i^{d^*} - Q_i^* \tag{11.10}$$

and budget constraints of country I and II must hold:

$$\sum_{i=1}^{2} p_i E_i + p_K \bar{K} = 0$$
$$\sum_{i=1}^{2} p_i E_i^* + p_K \bar{K}^* = 0 \tag{11.11}$$

These budget constraints may alternatively be interpreted as balances of payments and show, that a surplus or deficit in the trade balance is only possible in so far as it is compensated by a respective ex- or import of capital. Further these budget constraints together with profit and utility maximizing behaviour guarantee that the inequalities in equations 11.8 and 11.9 are always met with equality. Thus full employment of factors is implied.

A Walrasian equilibrium finally is said to hold, if

$$E_1 + E_1^* = 0$$
$$\bar{K} + \bar{K}^* = 0 \tag{11.12}$$

are satisfied. It is clear, that by Walras' law and market equilibrium conditions an excess demand or supply of commodity 2 is ruled out, i.e.

$$E_2 + E_2^* = 0 \tag{11.12'}$$

is always guaranteed.

Finally, the homogenity of degree zero of all demand and supply functions together with the exclusion of a money market requires a normalization of prices.

$$p_1 = 1 \tag{11.13}$$

Equations in the text	Home country	Foreign Country
*	$\sum_{i=1}^{2} S_i = S$	$\sum_{i=1}^{2} S_i = S^*$
11.4iv	$\frac{S_i}{Q_i} = g_S^i(p_A, p_K, p_S),\ i=1,2$	$\frac{S_i^*}{Q_i^*} = g_S^{i*}(p_A, p_K, p_S),\ i=1,2$
11.4iii	$\frac{A_i}{Q_i} = g_A^i(p_A, p_K, p_S),\ i=1,2$	$\frac{A_i^*}{Q_i^*} = g_A^{*i}(p_A^*, p_K, p_S^*),\ i=1,2$
11.4ii	$\frac{K_i}{Q_i} = g_K^i(p_A, p_K, p_S),\ i=1,2$	$\frac{K_i^*}{Q_i^*} = g_K^{i*}(p_A^*, p_K, p_S^*),\ i=1,2$
11.4i	$p_i = g^i(p_A, p_K, p_S),\ i=1,2$	$p_i = g^{i*}(p_A^*, p_K, p_S^*),\ i=1,2$
11.9	$\sum_{i=1}^{2} A_i - A = 0$	$\sum_{i=1}^{2} A_i^* - A^* = 0$
11.8	$\sum_{i=1}^{2} K_i - K = \bar{K}$	$\sum_{i=1}^{2} K_i^* - K^* = \bar{K}^*$
11.6	$p_1 Q_1^d = \sigma p_2 Q_2^d$	$p_1 Q_1^{d^*} = \sigma^* p_2 Q_2^{d^*}$
11.10	$E_i = Q_i^d - Q_i,\ i=1,2$	$E_i^* = Q_i^{d^*} - Q_i^*,\ i=1,2$
11.11	$\sum_{i=1}^{2} p_i E_i + p_K \bar{K} = 0$	$\sum_{i=1}^{2} p_i E_i^* + p_K \bar{K}^* = 0$
11.12	$\bar{K} + \bar{K}^* = 0$	
	$E_1 + E_1^* = 0$	
11.13	$p_1 = 1$	

Variables: -endogenous: $Q_i, K_i, A_i, S_i, Q_i^d, E_i, \bar{K}, \bar{K}^*, S, S^*, Q_i^*, K_i^*, A_i^*,$
$S_i^*, Q_i^{d*}, E_i^*, p_i, p_K, p_A, p_A^*$

-exogenous: p_S, p_S^*

Parameter: $\sigma, \sigma^*, A, A^*, K, K^*$

Table 11.1: The complete model

Equations 11.8 to 11.13 and the respective demand and supply conditions of consumers and producers - as derived in the preceding section - complete the model. Table 11.1 presents a survey of the total system.

The model as presented in table 11.1 constitutes the typical price-standard-equilibrium[1]. Notice, however, that in this model emission taxes are treated as exogeneous, i.e. as policy instruments, and hence the demand for environmental services S_i, S_i^* is endogeneously determined. Consequently the equations denoted by * may be interpreted as definitions of the total emissions S, S^*. The system of table 11.1, thus, consists of 33 endogeneous variables and 33 equations.

There remains to investigate the logical consistency of the model developed so far. If there exists no solution to the equation system of table 11.1, then further comparative static results are pointless.[2] To derive general conditions for the existence of an equilibrium in this case is, however, beyond the scope of this chapter[3]. Therefore the following assumption is adopted.

A 11.9 Existence. There exists a unique equilibrium to the system of table 11.1.

With this assumption it is possible to proceed. Differentiating the equation system of table 11.1 totally and substituting for the variables $\hat{Q}_i^d$, $\hat{Q}_i^{d*}$, $\hat{A}_i$, $\hat{A}_i^*$, $\hat{K}_i$, $\hat{K}_i^*$, $\hat{S}_i$, $\hat{S}_i^*$ and $\hat{p}_1$ reduces the model to 16 equations. Recall that the system is recursive in the equations determining the total emissions of both countries. Therefore these equations may be omitted. Finally, the remaining system of 12 equations is attained by substitution of $\hat{E}_1^*$ and $\hat{\bar{K}}^*$.

1) Compare chapter 7, definition D 7.2.
2) For the discussion of the existence problem in a related model without emissions, compare Eichberger (1978)
3) A special case will be discussed below, p. 244.

$$
\begin{bmatrix}
0 & y_E^1 & -\sigma y_E^2 & 0 & y_Q^1 & -\sigma y_Q^2 & 0 & 0 & -y^{d1} & 0 & 0 & 0 \\
0 & y_E^{1*} & 0 & -\sigma^* y_E^{2*} & 0 & 0 & y_Q^{1*} & -\sigma^* y_Q^{2*} & -y^{d1*} & 0 & 0 & 0 \\
y_{\bar{K}} & y_E^1 & y_E^2 & 0 & 0 & 0 & 0 & 0 & y_E^2 & 0 & 0 & y_{\bar{K}} \\
y_{\bar{K}}^* & y_E^{1*} & 0 & y_E^{2*} & 0 & 0 & 0 & 0 & y_E^{2*} & 0 & 0 & y_{\bar{K}}^* \\
-y_{\bar{K}} & 0 & 0 & 0 & y_K^1 & y_K^2 & 0 & 0 & 0 & \kappa_A & 0 & \kappa_K \\
0 & 0 & 0 & 0 & y_A^1 & y_A^2 & 0 & 0 & 0 & \alpha_A & 0 & \alpha_K \\
-y_{\bar{K}}^* & 0 & 0 & 0 & 0 & 0 & y_K^{1*} & y_K^{2*} & 0 & 0 & \kappa_A^* & \kappa_K^* \\
0 & 0 & 0 & 0 & 0 & 0 & y_A^{1*} & y_A^{2*} & 0 & 0 & \alpha_A^* & \alpha_K^* \\
 & & & & & & & & 0 & \theta_A^1 & 0 & \theta_K^1 \\
 & \multicolumn{3}{c}{\mathbf{0}_{4\times 4}} & & \multicolumn{3}{c}{\mathbf{0}_{4\times 4}} & -1 & \theta_A^2 & 0 & \theta_K^2 \\
 & & & & & & & & 0 & 0 & \theta_A^{1*} & \theta_K^{1*} \\
 & & & & & & & & -1 & 0 & \theta_A^{2*} & \theta_K^{2*}
\end{bmatrix}
\begin{bmatrix}
\hat{\hat{K}} \\ \hat{E}_1 \\ \hat{E}_2 \\ \hat{E}_2^* \\ \hat{Q}_1 \\ \hat{Q}_2 \\ \hat{Q}_1^* \\ \hat{Q}_2^* \\ \hat{p}_{21} \\ \hat{p}_{A1} \\ \hat{p}_{A1}^* \\ \hat{p}_{K1}
\end{bmatrix}
=
\begin{bmatrix}
0 \\ 0 \\ 0 \\ 0 \\ -\kappa_S \hat{p}_{S1} \\ -\alpha_S \hat{p}_{S1} \\ -\kappa_S^* \hat{p}_{S1}^* \\ -\alpha_S^* \hat{p}_{S1}^* \\ -\theta_S^1 \hat{p}_{S1} \\ -\theta_S^2 \hat{p}_{S1} \\ -\theta_S^{1*} \hat{p}_{S1}^* \\ -\theta_S^{2*} \hat{p}_{S1}^*
\end{bmatrix}
\qquad (11.14)
$$

In the system 11.14 the following notation is used:

(i) $\hat{\bar{K}} := \frac{d\bar{K}}{\bar{K}}$; $\hat{E}_1 := \frac{dE_1}{E_1}$; $\hat{Q}_1 := \frac{dQ_1}{Q_1}$; etc.

(ii) $y_E^1 := p_1 E_1$; $y_Q^1 := p_1 Q_1$; $y_K := p_K \bar{K}$; $y^{d2} := p_2 Q_2^d$; etc.

(iii) $\theta_A^1 := \frac{p_A A_1}{p_1 Q_1}$; $\theta_K^2 := \frac{p_K K_2}{p_2 Q_2}$; etc.

(iv) $\alpha_j := \sum_{i=1}^{2} y_A^i \, \theta_j^i \, \sigma_{jA}^i$; $\kappa_j := \sum_{i=1}^{2} y_K^i \, \theta_j^i \, \sigma_{jK}^i$; $j=K,A,S$

and analogously for the foreign country.

By the normalization of the price $p_1 = 1$ in equation 11.13 now all price changes have to be interpreted as relative price changes. To avoid any misinterpretation change rates of prices are subsequently indexed by 1, e.g. $\hat{p}_{21}$, $\hat{p}^*_{A1}$ etc.

One easily recognizes from 11.14 that our system allows to analyze the impact of a rising emission tax on trade E_1, E_2, capital movements $\bar{K}$ and sector structure Q_1, Q_2 as well as on the terms of trade p_{21} and factor prices. From the changes of outputs and prices the corresponding effects of such a policy on emissions (and as a consequence on environmental quality) may be derived.

Before proceeding to the comparative statics some characteristics of this approach are discussed in the following section.

11.3 Some Characteristics of the Model

1. The basic features of the model developed in the preceding parts are shown in diagram 11.1 where quantity variables are represented by cubes and price variables by circles. Producers in both countries decide about their supply of commodities and the corresponding demand of inputs in the light of the exogeneously given emission taxes (p_S,p_S^*) and a given price vector (p_1,p_2,p_A,p_A^*,p_K). Consumers decide about their demand for commodities with respect to the given price vector (p_1,p_2). These decisions have to be

adjusted to each other on the markets by means of price changes. The question of existence of an equilibrium to the equation system of table 11.1 may thus equivalently be understood as the problem of finding a price vector ($p_1, p_2, p_A, p_A^*, p_K$), such that at given emission taxes and given supplies of labour and capital in each country all decisions of producers and consumers are compatible at these prices.

2. One easily checks from diagram 11.1 , that there are five markets to be considered in this model. The number of independent markets and independent prices reduces to four, however, if Walras' law and price normalization are taken account of. On the other hand the model contains four production functions and by the assumption of homogenity of degree one (A 11.4) for this function there are exactly four equations only between prices - see 11.4i in table 11.1. Consequently one may state, that there exists a solution to our model, if and only if there is a solution to the subsystem 11.4i[1], i.e.

$$1 = g^1(p_{A1}, p_{K1}, p_{S1}) \; ; \; 1 = g^{1*}(p_{A1}^*, p_{K1}, p_{S1}^*) \qquad (11.15)$$
$$p_{21} = g^2(p_{A1}, p_{K1}, p_{S1}) \; ; \; p_{21} = g^{2*}(p_{A1}^*, p_{K1}, p_{S1}^*)$$

for exogenously given p_{S1}, p_{S1}^* and $(p_{21}, p_{A1}^*, p_{A1}, p_{K1}, p_{S1}, p_{S1}^*) >> 0$

Exactly because in general one cannot be sure, that there exists a solution to this system, assumption A 11.9 was necessary. To show, however, that there is at least one class of production functions for which an equilibrium is possible, the following theorem is proved:

Theorem 11.1: Suppose the production functions are all of the Cobb-Douglas type, i.e.

$$Q_i = \mu_i A_i^{\alpha_i} K_i^{\kappa_i} S_i^{\rho_i} \; , \quad \alpha_i + \kappa_i + \rho_i = 1$$
$$\qquad i=1,2 \qquad (11.16)$$
$$Q_i^* = \mu_i^* (A_i^*)^{\alpha_i^*} (K_i^*)^{\kappa_i^*} (S_i^*)^{\rho_i^*} \; , \quad \alpha_i^* + \kappa_i^* + \rho_i^* = 1$$

then there exists a solution $(p_{21}, p_{A1}, p_{A1}^*, p_{K1}) >> 0$ for every

1) Compare for this Chipman (1971), theorem 1, where the related case without emissions and emission taxes is discussed.

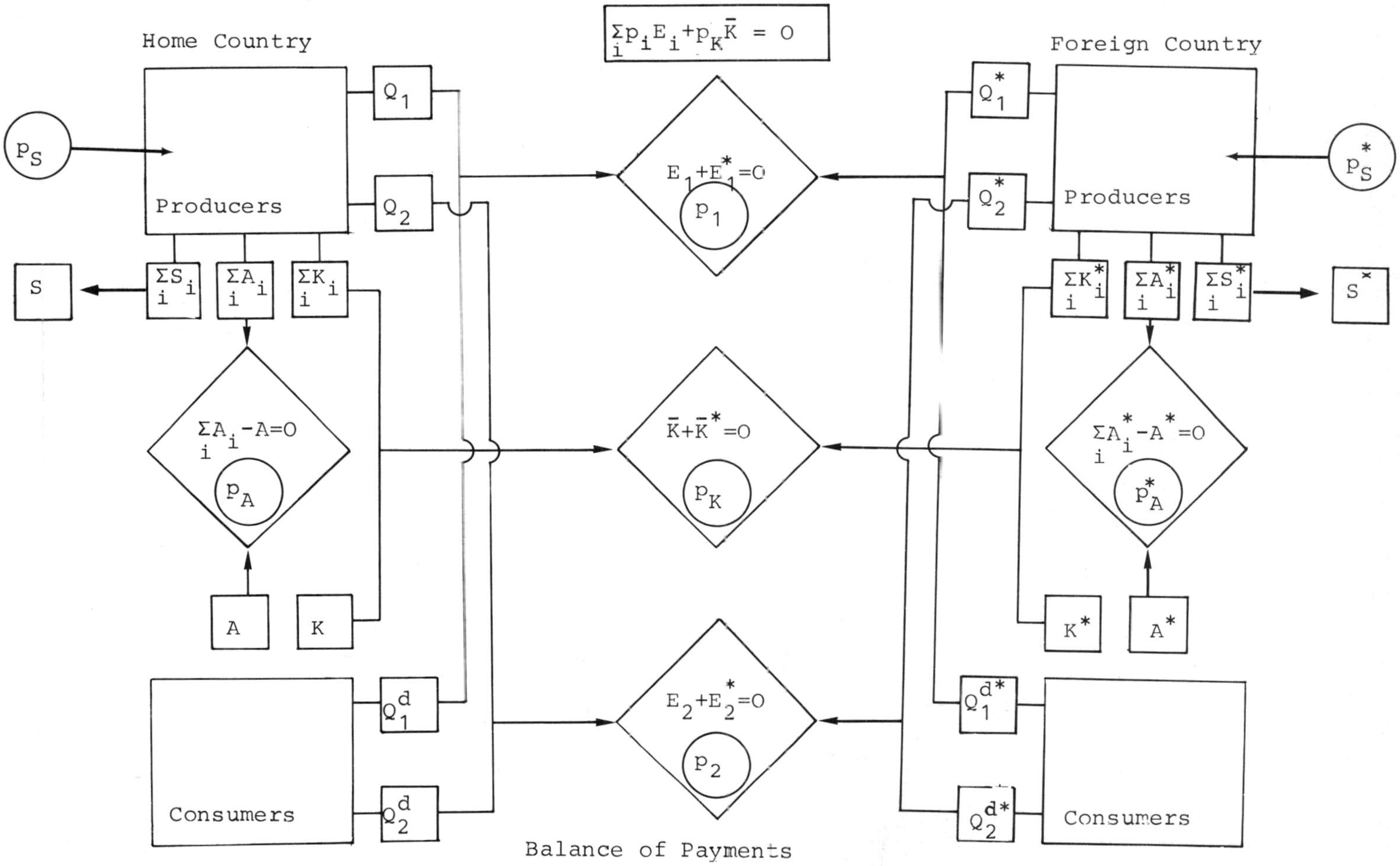
Home Country
Foreign Country
$\sum_i p_i E_i + p_K \bar{K} = 0$
Producers
Producers
Consumers
Consumers
p_S
p_S^*
Q_1
Q_2
Q_1^*
Q_2^*
$\sum_i S_i$
$\sum_i A_i$
$\sum_i K_i$
$\sum_i K_i^*$
$\sum_i A_i^*$
$\sum_i S_i^*$
S
S^*
$E_1 + E_1^* = 0$
p_1
$\sum_i A_i - A = 0$
p_A
$\bar{K} + \bar{K}^* = 0$
p_K
$\sum_i A_i^* - A^* = 0$
p_A^*
A
K
K^*
A^*
$E_2 + E_2^* = 0$
p_2
Q_1^d
Q_2^d
Q_1^{d*}
Q_2^{d*}
Balance of Payments

Diagram 11.1

$(p_{S1}, p^*_{S1}) \gg 0$ to the equation system 11.15, if and only if

$$\alpha^*_1(\kappa_1\alpha_2-\kappa_2\alpha_1) - \alpha_1(\kappa^*_1\alpha^*_2 - \kappa^*_2\alpha^*_1) \neq 0 \qquad (11.16')$$

holds.

Proof[1]: To show this result, it is necessary to derive the related price equations 11.15 from the maximization problem of producers when confronted with production functions 11.16. This derivation is easily performed by substitution of the marginal conditions into the production functions. Some straightforward calculations, then, result in:

$$1 = M_1 p_{K1}^{\kappa_1} p_{A1}^{\alpha_1} p_{S1}^{\rho_1} \; ; \qquad 1 = M^*_1 p_{K1}^{\kappa^*_1} p_{A1}^{*\alpha^*_1} p_{S1}^{*\rho^*_1}$$

$$p_{21} = M_2 p_{K1}^{\kappa_2} p_{A1}^{\alpha_2} p_{S1}^{\rho_2} \; ; \; p_{21} = M^*_2 p_{K1}^{\kappa^*_2} p_{A1}^{*\alpha^*_2} p_{S1}^{*\rho^*_2} \qquad (11.15')$$

where $M_i : = \mu_i^{-1} \kappa^{-\kappa_i} \alpha_i^{-\alpha_i} \rho_i^{-\rho_i}$ and M^*_i is analogously defined.

By taking logarithms one gets the following system of log-linear equations.

$$\begin{bmatrix} 0 & \kappa_1 & \alpha_1 & 0 \\ -1 & \kappa_2 & \alpha_2 & 0 \\ 0 & \kappa^*_1 & 0 & \alpha^*_1 \\ -1 & \kappa^*_2 & 0 & \alpha^*_2 \end{bmatrix} \begin{bmatrix} \ln p_{21} \\ \ln p_{K1} \\ \ln p_{A1} \\ \ln p^*_{A1} \end{bmatrix} = \begin{bmatrix} -\ln M_1 - \rho_1 \ln p_{S1} \\ -\ln M_2 - \rho_2 \ln p_{S1} \\ -\ln M^*_1 - \rho^*_1 \ln p^*_{S1} \\ -\ln M^*_2 - \rho^*_2 \ln p^*_{S1} \end{bmatrix} \qquad (11.$$

Such a system has a solution, if and only if the determinant of the coefficient matrix is non-singular. The value of this determinant, however, is non-zero, if inequality 11.16' holds. This is easily checked by expansion of the coefficient determinant of 11.17.

q.e.d.

It is obvious, that the condition 11.16' rules out identical production functions in both countries, and thus

1) This proof is in the same spirit as that of theorem 5 of Chipman (1971).

internationally identical technologies.

3. The property of equal numbers of independent endogenous prices and linearly homogenous production functions gives rise to the special structure of the coefficient matrix in the comparative static system 11.14. It is a well known[1] property of a decomposable matrix, that its determinant may be expressed as the product of the determinants of its square matrices along the principal diagonal. Denote the determinant of the coefficient matrix in 11.14 by Δ, then expansions will show[2]

$$\Delta = Y\Delta_1\Delta_2 \qquad (11.18)$$

with $Y := y^1_{\bar{K}} y^2_E y^{2*}_E y^1_Q y^2_Q y^{1*}_Q y^{2*}_Q$

$$\Delta_1 := \theta^{1*}_A \theta_{KA} - \theta^1_A \theta^*_{KA}$$

$$\Delta_2 := (1+\sigma^*)\theta^*_{KA}(\theta_{KA}-\Gamma_A) - (1+\sigma)\theta_{KA}(\theta^*_{KA}-\Gamma^*_A)$$

$$\theta_{ij} := \theta^1_i\theta^2_j - \theta^2_i\theta^1_j \;;\quad \Gamma_i := \theta^2_i + \sigma\theta^1_i \qquad i,j=K,A,S;$$

and analogously for the foreign country.

One easily sees, that Δ_1 is the determinant of the coefficient matrix of the differentiated price system. To have a non-vanishing determinant ($\Delta \neq 0$) neither Δ_1 nor Δ_2 must be zero.

Finally, note that fixing factor intensities (i.e. θ_{ij}) as in traditional Heckscher-Ohlin trade models are not sufficient for a particular sign of Δ. There are additional assumptions concerning labour productivity θ^1_A, θ^{1*}_A and demand conditions σ, σ^* necessary to establish the sign pattern of Δ. This problem will be taken up again in section 11.5 below.

11.4. Specification of the Economy

So far the model has been discussed rather generally. To arrive, however, at some coherent propositions about possible impacts of an emission tax, some more detailed information

1) Compare e.g. Fischer (1975, p.147).
2) See appendix 11.1

about the kind of equilibrium one deals with is necessary. To avoid any misunderstanding: if the model would have been specified with explicit production functions and explicit demand conditions, then there would have been no freedom left to choose, what equilibrium the model is in. Consequently trade and capital patterns as well as sector structure would have been determined.

Because of the indeterminateness of the equilibrium position of the model in this section particular properties are assumed with regard to trade patterns, international capital allocation, sector structure and demand conditions.

1. Patterns of trade and capital flows. Suppose, that there exists an equilibrium, where the home country exports commodity 1, imports commodity 2 and exports capital to the foreign country, i.e.

$$E_1 < 0; \quad E_2 > 0 \ ; \ \bar{K} < 0 \tag{11.19}$$

From equation 11.11 this implies the value of imports p_2E_2 to exceed the value of exports p_1E_1.

2. Patterns of demand. It is assumed, that consumers in the foreign country have a relatively stronger preference for commodity 1 than the consumers of the home country. This is in line with taking commodity 1 as the export commodity of the home country.

$$\sigma^* \geq \sigma \tag{11.20}$$

The equality is allowed, because it will sharpen analysis sometimes to assume internationally equal demand patterns. Thus, it is possible to abstract from effects brought about by demand differences.

3. Patterns of productions. For the description of production patterns one generally refers to such concepts as factor productivity and factor intensity differences between countries. However, in this model there are basically three productive factors and factor intensity is not anymore such a clearcut concept; for it is possible that a factor is

intensive with respect to the second, but not intensive with respect to the third factor.

For these reasons "factor intensity" has to be redefined. Following a proposal of Batra and Casas (1976) the notion of "strong factor intensity" is introduced.[1)]

<u>Definition D 11.1</u>: A factor i employed in the production of commodity r (V_{ir}) is used strongly intensive compared to its employment in the production of commodity s (V_{is}), if

$$\frac{V_{ir}}{V_{jr}} > \frac{V_{is}}{V_{js}} \qquad \forall\ j=1\ldots n,\ j \neq i$$

holds.

It follows from this definition for a two-commodity, three-factor framework, that in each sector there is exactly one factor used intensively in the strong sense. For example, assume $\frac{K_1}{A_1} > \frac{K_2}{A_2}$, $\frac{S_1}{A_1} > \frac{S_2}{A_2}$ and $\frac{S_1}{K_1} < \frac{S_2}{K_2}$; then sector 1 produces strongly capital intensive, while sector 2 is strongly labour intensive and no sector is emission intensive.

To specify the production patterns in the light of this definition, four sectors have to be compared pairwise. Therefore one may imagine a great variety of combinations. This set of possible combinations can be reduced, for only a change of the emission tax of the home country will be analyzed. As a consequence - as is shown in the following section - it is possible to disregard the intensity of emissions in the foreign country and to restrict the attention to the comparison of capital-labour ratios there. Hence, in the foreign country only two cases are of interest,

$$\frac{K_1^*}{A_1^*} > \frac{K_2^*}{A_2^*} \quad \text{or} \quad \frac{K_1^*}{A_1^*} < \frac{K_2^*}{A_2^*}.$$

1) Compare for the same definition section 9.2.2, definition D 9.1.

In the home country the analysis of the impact of an emission tax change is confined to the following pattern of strong intensities.

-Sector 1 is strongly emission intensive i.e. $\frac{S_1}{A_1} > \frac{S_2}{A_2}$ and

$$\frac{S_1}{K_1} > \frac{S_2}{K_2}$$

-Sector 2 is strongly capital intensive, i.e. $\frac{K_2}{S_2} > \frac{K_1}{S_1}$ and

$$\frac{K_2}{A_2} > \frac{K_1}{A_1}$$

If the definitions of θ_{KA}, θ_{KA}, θ_{SA} and θ_{SK} in equation 11.1 are recalled, one can easily check, that by the preceding assumptions concerning factor intensities their signs are determined. Take e.g.

$$\theta_{KA} = \theta_A^1 \, \theta_A^2 \, \frac{p_K}{p_A} \left[\frac{K_1}{A_1} - \frac{K_2}{A_2}\right]$$

to see, that from the assumption of strong capital intensity $\theta_{KA} < 0$ holds. In a similar fashion the other θ_{ij} (i,j = K,A will be determined. Table 11.2 presents the assumptions made with respect to the intensity pattern in a more compact way.

	θ_{SA}	θ_{SK}	θ_{KA}	θ^*_{KA}
Case I	+	+	-	+
Case II	+	+	-	-

Table 11.2: Sign patterns of θ_{ij}

The final reason for the choice of exactly these intensity assumptions from the great number of possible combinations is two-fold:

(i) in country A one sector should be strongly emission intensive, thus $\theta_{SA} > 0$, $\theta_{SK} > 0$ were chosen;

(ii) the intensities of capital with respect to labour should in one case be of opposite sign between the countries and in the other of the same; therefore case I and case II were distinguished.

Finally, before proceeding to the presentation of the results, an assumption for the elasticities of substitution σ_{ij} (i,j = K,A,S) should be made.

$$\sigma_{ij} \begin{cases} > 0 & i \neq j \\ < 0 & i = j \end{cases} \qquad i,j = K,A,S \qquad (11.21)$$

One can prove[1)] that $\sigma_{ij} < 0$ if i=j. From homogenity of degree one $\sum_i \theta_i \sigma_{ij} = 0$. Consequently $\sum_{i \neq j} \theta_i \sigma_{ij} = -\theta_j \sigma_{jj} > 0$. holds. In a three factor model therefore at most one of the two substitution elasticities can be negative. It seems a reasonable assumption, however, to regard both substitution elasticities $\sigma_{ij} (i \neq j)$ as positive, because a negative elasticity would describe a complementary relationship, a case which can safely be ruled out, if one deals with such highly aggregated inputs as labour, capital, and environmental services.

11.5. Impacts of an Emission Tax

One of the most convenient features of this model is the decomposable matrix in 11.14. This characteristic allows to treat the impact of taxing the pollutants on the price system separately from the quantity effects.[2)] Thus price effects are discussed in the following subsection, while the impacts on trade and capital movements as well as those on sector structure are dealt with in the second and third subsection.

Because of the symmetrical assumptions for both countries only the case where an emission tax is raised in the home country, will be discussed. The effects of an emission tax change in the foreign country would be identical to those in the home country.

11.5.1 Price Effects

Taking advantage of Cramer's rule the following results

1) See e.g. Allen (1938, p. 503-505)
2) An example for the method of derivation of the effects is given in the appendix 11.1

concerning the price effects are easily obtained.

$$\frac{\hat{p}_{21}}{\hat{p}_{S1}} = \frac{\theta_{SA}}{\theta_A^{1*}} \cdot \Omega$$

+ −
+ ?

$$\frac{\hat{p}_{A1}}{\hat{p}_{S1}} = \frac{\theta_{SK}}{\theta_{SA}} \cdot \left[\frac{\theta_A^{1*}}{\theta_{KA}^{*}} + \frac{\theta_S^{1}}{\theta_{SK}} \right] \cdot \frac{\theta_{SA}}{\theta_A^{1*}} \cdot \Omega$$

+ + + + −
+ − + + ?

$$\frac{\hat{p}_{K1}}{\hat{p}_{S1}} = -\frac{\theta_A^{1*}}{\theta_{KA}^{*}} \cdot \frac{\theta_{SA}}{\theta_A^{1*}} \cdot \Omega$$

+ + −
− + ?

$$\frac{\hat{p}_{A1}^{*}}{\hat{p}_{S1}} = \frac{\theta_K^{1*}}{\theta_{KA}^{*}} \cdot \frac{\theta_{SA}}{\theta_A^{1*}} \cdot \Omega \qquad (11.22)$$

+ + −
− + ?

with $\Omega := \left[\frac{\theta_{KA}}{\theta_{KA}^{*}} - \frac{\theta_A^{1}}{\theta_A^{1*}} \right]^{-1}$

− +
+ +

Where the sign patterns below the terms reflect their signs according to the assumptions chosen in the preceding section: the first row refers to case I and the second to case II of table 11.2.

From the results of 11.22 the crucial importance of the sign of Ω is obvious. Clearly, if the opposite sectors are capital intensive with respect to labour in both countries – as in case I – Ω will always be negative and no other assumption is required for a clearcut solution. However, in case II θ_{KA}, θ_{KA}^{*} are both negative. Consequently the sign of Ω

depends on the relative importance of the capital-labour intensities compared to the relative labour productivities. This can be shown transforming Ω to yield:

$$\Omega = \frac{\theta_A^1}{\theta_A^{1*}} \frac{\theta_A^2}{\theta_A^{2*}} \cdot \frac{p_A^*}{p_A} \cdot \left[\frac{K_1/A_1 - K_2/A_2}{K_1^*/A_1^* - K_2^*/A_2^*} - \frac{Q_2/A_2}{Q_2^*/A_2^*} \right]$$

The difficulty raised by the fact, that in both countries the same sector is capital intensive with respect to labour, reveals a basic feature of this model: beside factor intensity relations also factor productivity matters.

For concreteness it will be assumed, that the intersectoral capital-labour intensity differences are always dominated by the factor productivities of the sectors 2, i.e.

$$\frac{Q_2/A_2}{Q_2/A_2^*} > \frac{K_1/A_1 - K_2/A_2}{K_1^*/A_1^* - K_2^*/A_2^*} \tag{11.23}$$

Consequently $\Omega < 0$ will also hold in case II.

Apart from the effect of the emission tax change on the price of labour in the home country all price effects are determined. But in case II θ_{KA}^* and θ_{SK} are of opposite sign. Therefore it has to be decided, whether or not

$\left|\frac{\theta_A^1}{\theta_{KA}}\right| > \left|\frac{\theta_S^1}{\theta_{SK}}\right|$ holds. To fix the sign of the bracketed term

in the equation of $\hat{p}_{A1}/\hat{p}_{S1}$, the latter may be transformed as follows:

$$\frac{\hat{p}_{A1}}{\hat{p}_{S1}} = \frac{\theta_S^1}{\theta_{SA}} \frac{\hat{p}_{21}}{\hat{p}_{S1}} - \frac{\theta_{SK}}{\theta_{SA}} \frac{\hat{p}_{K1}}{\hat{p}_{S1}} \tag{11.24}$$

Clearly in case I $\hat{p}_{21}/\hat{p}_{S1}$ and $\hat{p}_{K1}/\hat{p}_{S1}$ are of opposite sign. In case II, however, both are negative. A declining relative price of commodity 2 tends to reduce the supply of commodity 2 and hence, because sector 2 is labour intensive compared to sector 1 ($\theta_{SA} > 0$), to reduce the demand for labour. With a fixed supply of labour this will require a declining wage rate. On the other hand a smaller price of capital may induce a rising capital demand in the strongly capital intensive sector 2 at the same time rising demand for labour. This effect runs counter to the first.

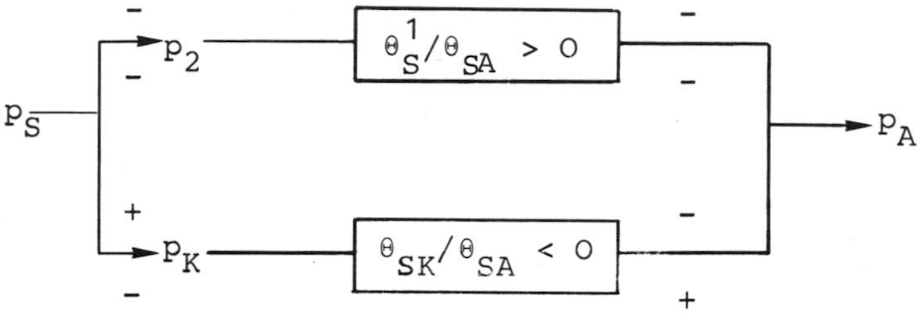

Diagram 11.2

The twofold impact on the wage rate of the home country is shown in diagram 11.2. Thus the further assumption

$$\left|\frac{\theta_A^1}{\theta_{KA}}\right| > \left|\frac{\theta_S^1}{\theta_{SK}}\right| \tag{11.25}$$

-implying $\frac{\hat{p}_{A1}}{\hat{p}_{S1}} > 0$ in case II - may be understood as regarding the lower impact in diagram 11.2 to be the more important.

Now the results with respect to the price system may be stated completely.

<u>Proposition 11.1:</u> Suppose (i) the ratio of the labour productivities in the production of commodity 2 be always greater than the ratio of the differences between the sectoral capital-labour ratios - i.e. condition 11.23 holds -, and (ii) in case II condition 11.25 holds, then the impact of an emission tax change $\hat{p}_{S1}$ on the other prices will display the following sign pattern:

	$\hat{p}_{21}/\hat{p}_{S1}$	$\hat{p}_{A1}/\hat{p}_{S1}$	$\hat{p}_{K1}/\hat{p}_{S1}$	$\hat{p}^*_{A1}/\hat{p}_{S1}$
Case I	-	-	+	-
Case II	-	+	-	+

It should be noticed at this stage that the impacts of an emission tax change on the terms of trade under condition 11.23 are basically the same as in the model of chapter 5, equation 5.5v, if one takes account of the fact that in this chapter the price of commodity 1 is chosen as numeraire as compared to that of commodity 2 in chapter 5. Thus under the qualification of 11.23 the result derived in chapter 5, when only one resource is regarded and the gross-emissions approach is used, that the price of the emission-intensively produced commodity will rise can be extended even to a model where capital mobility as well as the net-emissions approach are integrated.

A particular property with respect to the results 11.22 should finally be pointed out. Without a further condition - neither 11.23 nor 11.25 - the following relations hold:

(i) $$\text{sign}\ \frac{\hat{p}^*_{A1}}{\hat{p}_{S1}} = -\ \text{sign}\ \frac{\hat{p}_{K1}}{\hat{p}_{S1}}$$

(ii) $$\text{sign}\ \frac{\hat{p}^*_{A1}}{\hat{p}_{S1}} = \text{sign}\left[\theta_{KA}\ \frac{\hat{p}_{21}}{\hat{p}_{S1}}\right]$$

Thus it is obvious, that the impact both on the price of capital and on the price of labour in the foreign country depends only on the impact on commodity prices and the capital-labour ratios in this country. Diagram 11.3 summarizes these results in a similar way as diagram 11.2 did.

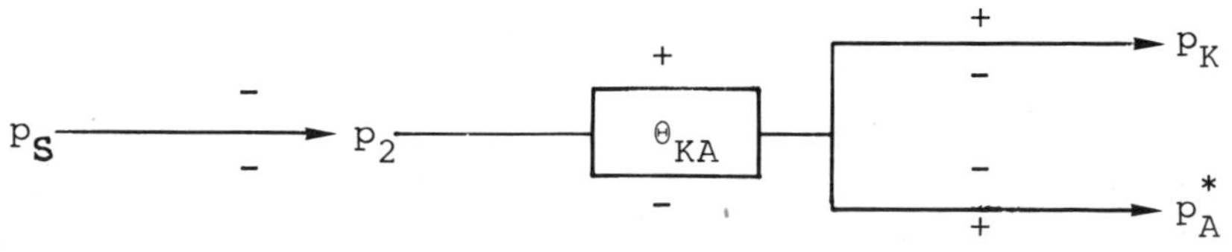

Diagram 11.3

One easily recognizes, that the Stolper-Samuelson theorem holds for the foreign country. This is not surprising, if one is aware of the fact, that only capital-labour ratios of the foreign country are affected, if the environmental policy is not changed in this country. Consequently a decline of the relative commodity price will bring about smaller prices for the relative intensively used factor. It is worth noticing, that even an internationally common capital market will not disturb the validity of this theorem.

To summarize the following price effects may be discerned:

(i) Given the dominant importance of factor productivities condition 11.23 - the relative price of commodity 2 will always decline, when an emission tax is levied, because sector 1 has been defined as strongly emission intensive. This result is well in line with intuition.

(ii) The factor prices of the foreign country adapt to such a change of the relative price according to the Stolper Samuelson theorem, i.e. the price of the intensively used factor will move in the same direction as the relative price, while the price of the less intensively used factor adjusts contrarily. This result holds in spite of the internationally common capital market.

(iii) The most complicated impact concerns the price of labour in the home country. Here two effects have to be regarded, an impact from changed relative price and an impact from changed capital price. These effects may move parallel - as in case I - or contrary to each other - as in case II. Therefore the assumption concerning the importance of these two effects - condition 11.25 - had to be chosen, to guarantee a clearcut result on $\hat{p}_{A1}/\hat{p}_{S1}$.

11.5.2 The Impact on Trade and Capital Movements

In contrast to the rather clearcut results about the effects of an emission tax on the price system, quantity effects are far less conclusive. In general; however, there may be distinguished two channels through which an emission tax can affect the quantity variables. The first impact is the direct adjustment brought about by the tax, while the second runs through a changed price system and the subsequent quantity adaptations to this new price vector.

Computations of these results turned out to be rather tedious.[1] Thus it seems reasonable to give some preliminary results before the statement of the proper solutions.

Table 11.3 presents some terms which will prove convenient for further discussion.

$B:=\sigma\theta_{KA}+\Gamma_A$	$B^*:=\sigma^*\theta^*_{KA}+\Gamma^*_A$	$b:=\sigma^*\theta^*_{KA}\Gamma_A-\sigma\theta_{KA}\Gamma^*_A$
$C:=\Gamma_A-\theta_{KA}$	$C^*:=\Gamma^*_A-\theta^*_{KA}$	$c:=\theta_{KA}\Gamma^*_A-\theta^*_{KA}\Gamma_A$
$D:=(1+\sigma)\theta_{KA}$	$D^*:=(1+\sigma^*)\theta^*_{KA}$	$d:=(\sigma^*-\sigma)\theta_{KA}\theta^*_{KA}$

$$Y:=\theta^*_{KA}y^{d1*}\frac{\hat{p}_{21}}{p_{S1}}-\left(\Sigma^*_A\frac{\hat{p}^*_{A1}}{p_{S1}}+\Sigma^*_K\frac{\hat{p}_{K1}}{p_{S1}}\right)$$

$$X:=\theta_{KA}y^{d1}\frac{\hat{p}_{21}}{p_{S1}}-\left(\Sigma_A\frac{\hat{p}_{A1}}{p_{S1}}+\Sigma_K\frac{\hat{p}_{K1}}{p_{S1}}\right)-\Sigma_S$$

$$Z:=y^2_E\frac{\hat{p}_{21}}{p_{S1}}+y_{\bar{K}}\frac{\hat{p}_{K1}}{p_{S1}}$$

with

$$\Sigma_j:=\Gamma_K\left(\sum_{i=1}^{2}y^i_A\theta^i_j\sigma^i_{jA}\right)-\Gamma_A\left(\sum_{i=1}^{2}y^i_K\theta^i_j\sigma^i_{jK}\right)=\Gamma_K\alpha_j-\Gamma_A\kappa_j$$

where j=K,A,S (analogously for the foreign country denoted by *).

Table 11.3: Some helpful substitutions

1) The way computations have been done is shown in the appendix 11.1.

Some relations between the terms of table 11.3 will be needed later on.

Lemma 11.1: For the terms of table 11.3 the following relations hold:

$$B > 0;\ B^* > 0;\ C > 0;\ C^* > 0 \qquad \text{(i)}$$

$$\text{sign } D = \text{sign } \theta_{KA};\ \text{sign } D^* = \text{sign } \theta^*_{KA} \qquad \text{(ii)}$$

$$D - B + C = 0;\ D^* - B^* + C^* = 0 \qquad \text{(iii)} \quad (11.26)$$

$$\Delta_2 = DC^* - D^*C = b - c - d \qquad \text{(iv)}$$

$$\Sigma_A + \Sigma_K + \Sigma_S = 0;\ \Sigma^*_A + \Sigma^*_K + \Sigma^*_S = 0 \qquad \text{(v)}$$

Proof: The proof is easily accomplished and left to the reader. Note that $\sum_i \theta_i \sigma_{iK} = \sum_i \theta_i \sigma_{iA} = \sum_i \theta_i \sigma_{iS} = 0$[1], $i=K,A,S$.

Thus there remain only the terms Δ_2, X, Y and Z to be discussed. Δ_2 has already been defined in 11.18 and with the lemma stated above it is easily transformed to yield:

$$\Delta_2 = C \cdot C^* \left[\frac{D}{C} - \frac{D^*}{C^*} \right] = C \cdot C^* \left[\frac{1+\sigma}{\Gamma_A/\theta_{KA} - 1} - \frac{1+\sigma^*}{\Gamma^*_A/\theta^*_{KA} - 1} \right] \qquad (11.27)$$

For case I Δ_2 clearly has a negative sign. However, in case II the sign of Δ_2 is indeterminate. Because $\sigma^* \geq \sigma$ (from 11.20) a sufficient condition for $\Delta_2 > 0$ would be a somewhat stronger version of 11.23 namely

$$\frac{\theta_{KA}}{\theta^*_{KA}} < \frac{\Gamma_A}{\Gamma^*_A} \qquad (11.28)$$

Inequality 11.28 states, that the ratio of the differences of the intersectoral capital-labour ratios must always be smaller than the ratio of the demand weighted labour productivities Γ_A/Γ^*_A. Hence $\Gamma^*_A/\theta^*_{KA} > \Gamma_A/\theta_{KA}$ and $\theta^*_{KA} < 0$ imply $\Delta_2 > 0$ for case II.

Compared to Δ_2 the sign pattern of Y can be derived much easier. One sees (from condition 11.21) that $\Sigma^*_A < 0$ and $\Sigma^*_K > 0$ and, consequently,

1) For a proof of this relation refer to Allen (1938, p.503-50

$$\text{sign } Y = -\text{sign } \theta^{*}_{KA} \qquad (11.29)$$

must hold. From the representation of Y in table 11.3 it is obvious, that Y describes the impact which an emission tax increase in the home country will bring about in the foreign country via a changed price framework.

Likewise X can be interpreted as the tax incidence in the home country through price changes and a direct effect Σ_S. The determination of X, however, is far more intricate. From 11.21 again $\Sigma_A < 0$ and $\Sigma_K > 0$ may be derived. But Σ_S remains undetermined. Yet one easily checks, that $X > 0$ holds in case II, provided $\Sigma_S < 0$. On the contrary for case I the factor price effect - the term in brackets in the definition of X in table 11.3 - is certainly negative and hence opposite to the first term ($\theta_{KA} y^{d1} \hat{p}_{21}/\hat{p}_{S1}$). Therefore a unique sign of X in case I might only be attainable at the cost of rather strong assumptions concerning the strength of the price effects in X relative to each other. Thus lets assume $\Sigma_S < 0$ and consequently $X > 0$ in case II, while leaving open the question of the sign of X in case I.

Σ_S deserves a short discussion. From 11.26v one has

$$\Sigma_A + \Sigma_K = -\Sigma_S > 0$$

and hence $-\Sigma_A < \Sigma_K$. The assumption of a negative Σ_S thus implies the global capital substitutability to be absolutely greater than global labour substitutability. One can see the same implication from the definition of Σ_S in table 11.3.

$$\Sigma_S < 0 \Leftrightarrow \Gamma_K\left(\sum_{i=1}^{2} y_A^i \, \theta_S^i \, \sigma_{SA}^i\right) < \Gamma_A\left(\sum_{i=1}^{2} y_K^i \, \theta_S^i \, \sigma_{SK}^i\right)$$

One recognizes that by this assumption the global substitutability of pollutants against capital exceeds that of pollutants against labour.

Finally, the term Z must be determined and interpreted. For case I, clearly $Z < 0$ holds. But for case II the sign of Z is not clear. Simple transformations yield, however,

$$Z = y_{\bar{K}} \cdot \left[\frac{y_E^2}{y_{\bar{K}}} - \frac{\theta_A^{1*}}{\theta_{KA}^{*}} \right] \cdot \frac{\hat{p}_{21}}{\hat{p}_{S1}} \tag{11.30}$$

In 11.30 the first term in brackets is always negative, the second only in case I. Therefore it is assumed

$$\left| \frac{y_E^2}{y_{\bar{K}}} \right| > \left| \frac{\theta_A^{1*}}{\theta_{KA}^{*}} \right| \tag{11.30'}$$

and thus $Z < 0$ always.

To get a better idea about what the term Z really means the balance of payments equation of the home country from table 11.1 is differentiated with respect to the emission tax:

$$y_E^1 \frac{\hat{E}_1}{\hat{p}_{S1}} + y_E^2 \frac{\hat{E}_2}{\hat{p}_{S1}} + y_{\bar{K}} \frac{\hat{\bar{K}}}{\hat{p}_{S1}} = - \left[y_E^2 \frac{\hat{p}_{21}}{\hat{p}_{S1}} + y_{\bar{K}} \frac{\hat{p}_{K1}}{\hat{p}_{S1}} \right] =: -Z \tag{11.31}$$

From 11.31 the interpretation of Z as the reevaluation effect of the balance of payments caused by changed prices is obvious. After this rather extensive discussion of the terms in table 11.3 the results concerning trade and capital movements can be stated.

$$y_{\bar{K}} \frac{\hat{\bar{K}}}{\hat{p}_{S1}} = - \frac{1}{\Delta_2} \{D^* X + D\ Y + d\ Z\}$$

$$\begin{array}{cccc} - & +\ ? & -\ - & +\ - \\ + & -\ + & -\ + & -\ - \end{array}$$

$$y_E^1 \frac{\hat{E}_1}{\hat{p}_{S1}} = \frac{1}{\Delta_2} \{B^* X + B\ Y + b\ Z\} \tag{11.32}$$

$$\begin{array}{cccc} - & +\ ? & +\ - & +\ - \\ + & +\ + & +\ + & -\ - \end{array}$$

$$y_E^2 \frac{\hat{E}_2}{\hat{p}_{S1}} = - \frac{1}{\Delta_2} \{C^* X + C\ Y + c\ Z\}$$

$$\begin{array}{cccc} - & +\ ? & +\ - & -\ - \\ + & +\ + & +\ + & +\ - \end{array}$$

The sign pattern below the equations of 11.32 shows the difficulty of a clearcut solution. Therefore it is indispensable to discuss the single effects in some detail.

The definition of d in table 11.3 shows that the evaluation effect Z has a substantial impact on capital movements between both countries only in a context of divergent demand patterns. Suppose $\sigma = \sigma^*$, then d equals zero and the effect Z vanishes. Thus the assertion can be made that for small differences in international demand patterns in case II $y_{\bar{K}}\hat{\bar{K}}/\hat{p}_{S1}>0$. Hence capital exports of the home country ($y_{\bar{K}}<0$) will be reduced. Case I however, defies such an easy determination. The only unambiguous terms are again the reevaluation effect Z and the impact on foreign allocation Y. While the effect Z clearly tends to raise capital exports, the effect Y rather lowers them. Thus final behaviour of capital movements in this case depends critically on the sign of X which is ambiguous.

Case II reveals a clearcut impact towards reduction of the exports of commodity 1. And in case I apart from the reallocation effect X in the home country all other impacts point to the same direction. Consequently one can conclude that commodity exports tend to decline. As to the imports case II shows that reallocation effects - X and Y - tend to lower them, while the effect Z has a clear positive impact. Case I exhibits the same result with regard to Y and Z. Only X is undetermined. Thus the imports are most likely to decline. The results as indicated by 11.32 are put together in the following proposition.

Proposition 11.2: Suppose

(i) demand-weighted labour productivities dominate the relative capital-labour differences, i.e.

$$\frac{\Gamma_A}{\Gamma_A^*} > \frac{\theta_{KA}}{\theta_{KA}^*} ;$$

(ii) the general substitutability of pollutants with respect to capital is greater than with respect to labour, i.e. $\Sigma_S < 0$;

(iii) the reevaluation effect Z is always negative, and
(iv) demand differences are small,

then the impact of an emission tax change $\hat{p}_{S1}$ on internationa capital movements $\hat{\bar{K}}$ and trade, $\hat{E}_1$ and $\hat{E}_2$, will display the following sign pattern:

	$y_{\bar{K}}\ \hat{\bar{K}}/\hat{p}_{S1}$	$y_E^1\ \hat{E}_1/\hat{p}_{S1}$	$y_E^2\ \hat{E}_2/\hat{p}_{S1}$
Case I	?	(+)	?
Case II	+	+	(-)

An interesting result of proposition 11.2 is the declining capital export of the home country for case II. Yet it has already been shown, that the relative price of commodity 2 will be negatively affected by an emission tax and in consequence the total output of commodity 2, $Q_2+Q_2^*$ will be reducec In case II commodity 2 is produced with a higher capital-labour ratio as commodity 1 in both countries. Thus worldwide demand for capital in the home country will rise, due tc the better substitutability of capital to pollutants. Therefore, at fixed supply of capital, demand for capital in the home country will rise, or at least not decline as much as in the foreign country. By the same argument it is obvious why the result for capital movements is inconclusive in case

As to the impact on trade, there the results from propositior 11.2 seem to be well in line with the adjustments one would suspect from the induced relative price changes. The indeterminateness in case I is due to the same argument as in the case of the capital movements. As far as these trade effects could be established, they seem to point to the same direction as in the model of chapter 5, equation 5.5v.

11.5.3 The Impact on Sector Structure

As in the preceding section the impact of an emission tax on the output in the home country can be broken down into three single effects: the reallocation effect in the home country, the reallocation effect in the foreign country, and the reevaluation effect. The latter two effects remain as before, Z and Y, while the former effect has changed. Analogous to the analysis in the last chapter therefore, at the beginning of this section there is a discussion of the reallocation effects, $\bar{X}$ and $\bar{\bar{X}}$, in the home country.

$$\bar{X} := \left\{ -\theta_A^2 \, y^{d1} \frac{\hat{p}_{21}}{\hat{p}_{S1}} + \Psi_A^2 \frac{\hat{p}_{A1}}{\hat{p}_{S1}} + \Psi_A^2 \frac{\hat{p}_{K1}}{\hat{p}_{S1}} + \Psi_S^2 \right.$$

$$\bar{\bar{X}} := \left\{ -\theta_A^1 \, y^{d1} \frac{\hat{p}_{21}}{\hat{p}_{S1}} + \Psi_A^1 \frac{\hat{p}_{A1}}{\hat{p}_{S1}} + \Psi_K^1 \frac{\hat{p}_{K1}}{\hat{p}_{S1}} + \Psi_S^1 \right\} \qquad (11.33)$$

The similarity of the structure of the terms $\bar{X}$, $\bar{\bar{X}}$ in 11.33 with X as defined in table 11.3 is obvious. Instead of $-\Sigma_j (j=K,A,S)$ now $\Psi_j^i (i=1,2;\ j=K,A,S)$ have to be regarded. These Ψ_j^i are defined as follows:

$$\Psi_j^1 := \left[-\left(\sum_{i=1}^{2} y_A^i \theta_j^i \sigma_{jA}^i \right) + \Sigma_j^1 u \right]$$

$$(j=K,A,S) \qquad (11.34)$$

$$\Psi_j^2 := \left[\sigma \left(\sum_{i=1}^{2} y_A^i \theta_j^i \sigma_{jA}^i \right) + \Sigma_j^2 u \right]$$

where $\Sigma_j^i := \theta_K^i \left(\sum_{i=1}^{2} y_A^i \theta_j^i \sigma_{jA}^i \right) - \theta_A^i \left(\sum_{i=1}^{2} y_K^i \theta_j^i \sigma_{jK}^i \right)$

and $u := \left[1 - \frac{1+\sigma}{1+\sigma^*} + \frac{1+\sigma}{1+\sigma^*} \frac{\Gamma_A^*}{\theta_{KA}^*} \right]$

To get an idea of the sign of Ψ_j^1, Ψ_j^2 notice that the term u is positive for case I, i.e. $\theta_{KA}^* > 0$, because $\sigma^* \geq \sigma$ holds. Though for $\sigma^* = \sigma$ one can establish sign u = sign θ_{KA} in general, for $\sigma^* > \sigma$ such a conclusion cannot be drawn. Yet for case I one easily obtains - recalling the previous condition 11.21 - $\Psi^2_A < 0$. However, similar results concerning the other Ψ^i_j cannot be gained.

A further problem are the terms Ψ^i_S which defy any clearout interpretation. As in 11.26v one can show by writing out and rearranging the whole term that

$$\sum_j \Psi^i_j = 0 \quad (j=K,A,S,\ i=1,2)$$

holds. Therefore Ψ^2_S may be substituted by $-(\Psi^2_A + \Psi^2_K)$. And hence one can state $\bar{X} > 0$ for case I, if the price effect of capital $(\hat{p}_{K1}/\hat{p}_{S1})$ is absolutely greater than one.

Now the results for the impact of an emission taxation on the sector structure can be spelled out.

$$y^1_Q \frac{\hat{Q}_1}{\hat{p}_{S1}} = \frac{1}{\Delta_2} \Big\{ D^*\bar{X} - (1+\sigma)\ \theta^2_A Y - (\sigma^* - \sigma)\ \theta^2_A\ \theta^*_{KA}\ Z \Big\}$$

$$\begin{matrix} - & + + & & - & & + & - \\ + & - ? & & + & & - & - \end{matrix}$$

(11.35)

$$y^2_Q \frac{\hat{Q}_2}{\hat{p}_{S1}} = -\frac{1}{\Delta_2} \Big\{ D^*\bar{\bar{X}} - (1+\sigma)\ \theta^1_A\ Y - (\sigma^* - \sigma)\ \theta^1_A\ \theta^*_{KA}\ Z \Big\}$$

$$\begin{matrix} - & + ? & & - & & + & - \\ + & - ? & & + & & - & - \end{matrix}$$

Equation 11.35 shows apart from $\bar{X}$, $\bar{\bar{X}}$ a totally clear picture: the reevaluation effect as well as the foreign reallocation effect point to a declining output of commodity 1 and a rising output of commodity 2 no matter what case is regarded.

The only problems are the reallocations taking place in the home country. To those, however, it seems hard to attach a particular sign under an interpretable condition. Therefore only for case I $\bar{X} > 0$ may be obtained, thus establishing the result $y^1_Q\ \hat{Q}_1/\hat{p}_{S1} < 0$ for case I.

<u>Proposition 11.3</u>: Suppose conditions (i) and (iii) of proposition 11.2 hold and the capital price effect is greater

than one, i.e. $\left|\frac{\hat{p}_{K1}}{\hat{p}_{S1}}\right| > 1$, then the impact of an emission tax change $\hat{p}_{S1}$ on the sector structure of the home country will exhibit the following sign pattern:

	$y_Q^1\ \hat{Q}_1/\hat{p}_{S1}$	$y_Q^2\ \hat{Q}_2/\hat{p}_{S1}$
Case I	-	(-)
Case II	(+)	(-)

Although according to proposition 11.3 the impact on sector structure cannot be determined clearly, from equation 11.35 at least the feed-back effect of the changed price system from the foreign country as well as the reevaluation effect point in the same direction.

These effects tend to reduce the output of commodity 1 while raising the output of commodity 2. Hence there is a strong tendency to change sector structure towards an expanding sector 2 and a shrinking sector 1. Yet without detailed information about the actual values of the variables and parameters no clearcut conclusion is possible.

Finally, before finishing the discussion of the impacts of an emission tax a brief look upon the impact on the pollution level seems to be in order.

11.5.4 The Impact on Pollution

The target of environmental policy is undoubtedly the level of pollution. Therefore an inquiry into the effectiveness of an emission tax in the framework of an open economy with international capital movements is indispensable. From the analysis of the behaviour of the producers the emission-output ratio has been derived as a function of factor prices and the emission tax - compare equation 11.4iv in table 11.1. Differentiation with respect to the emission tax and transforming into change rates yield for each sector an equation as 11.5iv.

With the help of the definition * in table 11.1, finally, the following relation is attained:

$$\frac{\hat{S}}{\hat{p}_{S1}} = y_S^1 \frac{\hat{Q}_1}{\hat{p}_{S1}} + y_S^2 \frac{\hat{Q}_2}{\hat{p}_{S1}} + \rho_K \frac{\hat{p}_{K1}}{\hat{p}_{S1}} + \rho_A \frac{\hat{p}_{A1}}{\hat{p}_{S1}} + \rho_S \qquad (11.36)$$

$$\begin{array}{ccccccc} - & ? & + & + & + & - & - \\ ? & ? & + & - & + & + & - \end{array}$$

where $\rho_j := \sum_{i=1}^{2} y_S^i \, \theta_j^i \, \sigma_{jS} \quad (j=K,A,S)$

From 11.36 one can see that the impact of an emission tax on emissions in an open economy is not as unambiguously negative, as one may think from intuition. Discussing first the price change impact, it is immediately clear that from $\rho_K + \rho_A + \rho_S = 0$ the last three terms of 11.36 may be transformed to

$$\rho_K \frac{\hat{p}_{K1}}{\hat{p}_{S1}} + \rho_A \frac{\hat{p}_{A1}}{\hat{p}_{S1}} + \rho_S = \rho_K \left(\frac{\hat{p}_{K1}}{\hat{p}_{S1}} - 1\right) + \rho_A \left(\frac{\hat{p}_{A1}}{\hat{p}_{S1}} - 1\right)$$

Consequently, it is obvious that for factor price changes absolutely smaller than one this impact is negative.[1)]

At last the effect of an output variation can be shown to be negative, if $(\theta_S^1 \bar{X} - \theta_S^2 \bar{\bar{X}})$ is positive. As in the case of the determination of the sectoral effects, the feed back effect from the foreign country and the reevaluation effect tend in the expected direction, i.e. towards lowering the amount of pollutants emitted.

Proposition 11.4: Suppose assumption (i) of proposition 11.2 holds, the factor price effects are absolutely smaller than one, i.e. $\left|\frac{\hat{p}_{K1}}{\hat{p}_{S1}}\right| < 1$ and $\left|\frac{\hat{p}_{A1}}{\hat{p}_{S1}}\right| < 1$, and $\theta_S^1 \bar{X} - \theta_S^2 \bar{\bar{X}}$ is positive then the impact of an emission tax on the amount of emitted pollutants S will be negative.

1) Notice that this condition contradicts the condition $|\hat{p}_{K1}/\hat{p}_{S1}| > 1$ in proposition 11.3.

Although the conditions for a reduction of pollutants in the home country are not very severe, it is interesting to see, that there is no general guarantee for the effectiveness of an emission tax at the pursuit of the environmental policy target to reduce pollutants.

11.6 Some Concluding Remarks

The arguments in the chapters 8 and 9 lead to the conclusion that ceteris paribus a country will export the emission intensively produced commodity, if its environmental policy is less severe than in the competing countries. Or, in other words, the restrictiveness of environmental policy is a source of comparative disadvantage. Yet in chapter 5 it had been shown that in a general equilibrium system of two trading countries (with only one input), conclusions concerning adjustments of the economies after the implementation of an emission tax are no longer straightforward. As a consequence some conditions, even if not very restrictive, had to be formulated to ensure the expected results. Thereafter the impact of the emission tax on the trade pattern and the terms of trade could be determined:

- exports of emission intensively produced commodities will decline,
- imports will decline as well - as a consequence of the required trade balance equilibrium and
- the relative price of the emission intensive commodity will rise.

In the model of this chapter treating the impacts of an emission tax in a two-country, two-commodity and two-factor framework with international mobility of capital, the results concerning exports, imports and terms-of-trade could be maintained at least for some cases, however, at the cost of further, qualifying conditions.

The mobility of capital has been introduced into this model to allow for reallocation of capital between both countries. In spite of intuition which leads to suppose a rising capital export from the country with a severe environmental policy to the country without - or with a less restrictive - environmental protection, the result in this chapter points to the opposite adjustment. Clearly, this might be due to the assumptions on the initial equilibrium position, but one can conclude at least that there need not be a strange assumption to bring about such a result.

This counterintuitive conclusion of additional capital allocation in the country exerting an environmental policy, however, may be explained by other arguments. Two basic features of the neoclassical Walrasian equilibrium are the full employment condition for all inelastically supplied factors and the absence of capital as a financial, interest bearing asset. Hence capital can be allocated only according to its marginal productivity between all sectors. It can neither be consumed, nor stored for later activity. As a consequence capital will be allocated where it is most intensively demanded for production. Demand for capital, however, will rise in the country with environmental policy already by the assumption of substitutability of capital against pollutants. On the other hand the full employment condition - brought about by the total flexibility of prices - prevents a too strongly reduced output in any country and a potentially total shift of capital and production from one country to the other. Therefore, a good deal of adjustment to an emission tax takes place at the cost of the revenue of one factor - whether labour or capital will depend on the capital and labour intensities of the initial equilibrium.

The last passage motivates a warning to avoid a misinterpretation. The results of this chapter indicate what changes of prices and quantities must take place to have once again an equilibrium after a rise of an emission tax exhibiting the same properties as the prior equilibrium with the smaller emission tax. These characteristics are (i) full employment of factors, (ii) non-specialization of each country and (iii) balance of payments equilibrium.

Thus, the results of this model rather should be taken as a frame of reference; first, for what should happen after the implementation of an emission tax into a given economic system, if a full employment equilibrium shall be restored, and secondly, for what might be possible supporting policies, if one or the other of these adjustments will not take place by institutional inflexibilities, e.g. if prices will not adjust in the expected way.

Appendix 11.1

From the system 11.14 results may be attained by Cramer's rule. All computations have been done according to the same scheme. Therefore only the derivation of the system determinant Δ and of the effects $\hat{p}_{21}/\hat{p}_{S1}$ and $\hat{\bar{K}}/\hat{p}_{S1}$ will be demonstrated here in the appendix. The computations of all the other effects follow the same pattern.

1. Derivation of Δ

$$\Delta = \Delta_1 \bar{\Delta}_2$$

with
$$\Delta_1 := \begin{vmatrix} 0 & \theta_A^1 & 0 & \theta_K^1 \\ -1 & \theta_A^2 & 0 & \theta_K^2 \\ 0 & 0 & \theta_A^{1*} & \theta_K^{1*} \\ -1 & 0 & \theta_A^{2*} & \theta_K^{2*} \end{vmatrix} = \theta_A^1 [\theta_A^{1*} \theta_K^{2*} - \theta_K^{1*} \theta_A^{2*}] - \theta_A^{1*} [\theta_A^1 \theta_K^2 - \theta_K^1$$

$$= \theta_A^{1*} \theta_{KA} - \theta_A^1 \theta_{KA}^*$$

and
$$\bar{\Delta}_2 := \begin{vmatrix} 0 & y_E^1 & -\sigma y_E^2 & 0 & y_Q^1 & -\sigma y_Q^2 & 0 & 0 \\ 0 & y_E^{1*} & 0 & -\sigma^* y_E^{2*} & 0 & 0 & y_Q^{1*} & -\sigma^* y_Q^{1*} \\ y_{\bar{K}} & y_E^1 & y_E^2 & 0 & 0 & 0 & 0 & 0 \\ y_{\bar{K}}^* & y_E^{1*} & 0 & y_E^{2*} & 0 & 0 & 0 & 0 \\ -y_K & 0 & 0 & 0 & y_K^1 & y_K^2 & 0 & 0 \\ 0 & 0 & 0 & 0 & y_A^1 & y_A^2 & 0 & 0 \\ -y_K^* & 0 & 0 & 0 & 0 & 0 & y_K^{1*} & y_K^{2*} \\ 0 & 0 & 0 & 0 & 0 & 0 & y_A^{1*} & y_A^{2*} \end{vmatrix}$$

$$= Y \left\{ \begin{vmatrix} 1 & -\sigma & 0 \\ -1 & 0 & -\sigma \\ 0 & 1 & 1 \end{vmatrix} \begin{vmatrix} \theta_K^1 & \theta_K^2 & 0 & 0 \\ \theta_A^1 & \theta_A^2 & 0 & 0 \\ \theta_K^1 & \theta_K^2 & \theta_K^{1*} & \theta_K^{2*} \\ 0 & 0 & \theta_A^{1*} & \theta_A^{2*} \end{vmatrix} - \begin{vmatrix} 1 & -\sigma & 0 & 1 & -\sigma & 0 & 0 \\ -1 & 0 & -\sigma^* & 0 & 0 & 1 & -\sigma^* \\ 1 & 1 & 0 & 0 & 0 & 0 & 0 \\ 0 & 1 & 1 & 0 & 0 & 0 & 0 \\ 0 & 0 & 0 & \theta_A^1 & \theta_A^2 & 0 & 0 \\ 0 & 0 & 0 & \theta_K^1 & \theta_K^2 & \theta_K^{1*} & \theta_K^{2*} \\ 0 & 0 & 0 & 0 & 0 & \theta_A^{1*} & \theta_A^{2*} \end{vmatrix} \right\}$$

$$= Y \; \{(\sigma^*-\sigma) \; \theta_{KA} \; \theta_{KA}^* - (1+\sigma^*) \; \theta_{KA}^*(\theta_A^2+\sigma \; \theta_A^1)+(1+\sigma) \; \theta_{KA}(\theta_A^{2*}+\sigma^* \theta_A^{1*})\}$$

$$= Y \; \{(1+\sigma^*) \; \theta_{KA}^* \; (\theta_{KA}-\Gamma_A) \; - \; (1+\sigma) \; \theta_{KA} \; (\theta_{KA}^* - \Gamma_A^*)\}$$

$$= Y \; \Delta_2$$

where θ_{KA}^*, θ_{KA}, Γ_A^*, Γ_A and Y are as defined in 11.18.

2. Derivation of $\hat{p}_{21}/\hat{p}_{S1}$

From Cramer's rule one has ($\hat{p}_{S1}^*=0$)

$$\hat{p}_{21} = \frac{\bar{\Delta}_2 \; \Delta_{p_2}}{Y \; \Delta_1 \; \Delta_2} = \frac{\Delta_{p_2}}{\Delta_1}$$

$$\text{with } \Delta_{p_2} := \begin{vmatrix} -\theta_S^1 \hat{p}_{S1} & \theta_A^1 & 0 & \theta_K^1 \\ -\theta_S^2 \hat{p}_{S1} & \theta_A^2 & 0 & \theta_K^2 \\ 0 & 0 & \theta_A^{1*} & \theta_K^{1*} \\ 0 & 0 & \theta_A^{2*} & \theta_K^{2*} \end{vmatrix} = (\theta_S^1\theta_A^2-\theta_S^2\theta_A^1)(\theta_K^{1*}\theta_A^{2*}-\theta_K^{2*}\theta_A^{1*})\hat{p}_{S1}$$

$$= \theta_{SA}\theta_{KA}^*\hat{p}_{S1}$$

$$\frac{\hat{p}_{21}}{\hat{p}_{S1}} = \frac{\theta_{SA}}{\theta_A^{1*}} \left[\frac{\theta_{KA}}{\theta_{KA}^*} - \frac{\theta_A^1}{\theta_A^{1*}} \right]^{-1} = \frac{\theta_{SA}}{\theta_A^{1*}} \; \Omega$$

3. Derivation of $\hat{\bar{K}}/\hat{p}_{S1}$

$$\hat{\bar{K}} = \frac{\Delta_{\bar{K}}}{\Delta} = \frac{\Delta_{\bar{K}}}{Y\,\Delta_1\,\Delta_2}$$

For $\hat{p}^*_{S1} = 0$, $Y_{\bar{K}} := Y/y_K$ and q,r,s,t,u as defined below computations for $\Delta_{\bar{K}}$ are most easily achieved.

$$q := \begin{vmatrix} 1 & -\sigma & 0 & 1 & -\sigma & 0 & 0 & 0 \\ -1 & 0 & -\sigma^* & 0 & 0 & 1 & -\sigma^* & 0 \\ 1 & 1 & 0 & 0 & 0 & 0 & 0 & 0 \\ 0 & 1 & 1 & 0 & 0 & 0 & 0 & 0 \\ 0 & 0 & 0 & \theta^1_K & \theta^2_K & 0 & 0 & \kappa_S \\ 0 & 0 & 0 & \theta^1_A & \theta^2_A & 0 & 0 & \alpha_S \\ 0 & 0 & 0 & 0 & 0 & \theta^{1*}_K & \theta^{2*}_K & 0 \\ 0 & 0 & 0 & 0 & 0 & \theta^{1*}_A & \theta^{2*}_A & 0 \end{vmatrix}$$

$$= (1+\sigma^*)\ \theta^*_{KA}\ (\Gamma_K\ \alpha_S - \Gamma_A\ \kappa_S) = (1+\sigma^*)\ \theta^*_{KA}\ \Sigma_S = D^*\ \Sigma_S$$

$$r := \begin{vmatrix} 1 & -\sigma & 0 & 1 & -\sigma & 0 & 0 & 0 \\ -1 & 0 & -\sigma^* & 0 & 0 & 1 & -\sigma^* & 0 \\ 1 & 1 & 0 & 0 & 0 & 0 & 0 & 0 \\ 0 & 1 & 1 & 0 & 0 & 0 & 0 & 0 \\ 0 & 0 & 0 & \theta^1_K & \theta^2_K & 0 & 0 & \kappa_A \\ 0 & 0 & 0 & \theta^1_A & \theta^2_A & 0 & 0 & \alpha_A \\ 0 & 0 & 0 & 0 & 0 & \theta^{1*}_K & \theta^{2*}_K & 0 \\ 0 & 0 & 0 & 0 & 0 & \theta^{1*}_A & \theta^{2*}_A & 0 \end{vmatrix}$$

$$= (1+\sigma^*)\ \theta^*_{KA}\ (\Gamma_K\ \alpha_A - \Gamma_A\ \kappa_A) = (1+\sigma^*)\ \theta^*_{KA}\ \Sigma_A = D^*\ \Sigma_A$$

$$s := \begin{vmatrix} 1 & -\sigma & 0 & 1 & -\sigma & 0 & 0 & 0 \\ -1 & 0 & -\sigma^* & 0 & 0 & 1 & -\sigma^* & 0 \\ 1 & 1 & 0 & 0 & 0 & 0 & 0 & 0 \\ 0 & 1 & 1 & 0 & 0 & 0 & 0 & 0 \\ 0 & 0 & 0 & \theta^1_K & \theta^2_K & 0 & 0 & 0 \\ 0 & 0 & 0 & \theta^1_A & \theta^2_A & 0 & 0 & 0 \\ 0 & 0 & 0 & 0 & 0 & \theta^{1*}_K & \theta^{2*}_K & \kappa^*_A \\ 0 & 0 & 0 & 0 & 0 & \theta^{1*}_A & \theta^{2*}_A & \alpha^*_A \end{vmatrix}$$

$$= (1+\sigma)\ \theta_{KA}\ (\Gamma^*_K\ \alpha^*_A - \Gamma^*_A\ \kappa^*_A) = (1+\sigma)\ \theta_{KA}\ \Sigma^*_A = D\ \Sigma^*_A$$

$$t := \begin{vmatrix} 1 & -\sigma & 0 & 1 & -\sigma & 0 & 0 & 0 \\ -1 & 0 & -\sigma^* & 0 & 0 & 1 & -\sigma^* & 0 \\ 1 & 1 & 0 & 0 & 0 & 0 & 0 & y_{\bar{K}} \\ 0 & 1 & 1 & 0 & 0 & 0 & 0 & 0 \\ 0 & 0 & 0 & \theta^1_K & \theta^2_K & 0 & 0 & \kappa_K \\ 0 & 0 & 0 & \theta^1_A & \theta^2_A & 0 & 0 & \alpha_K \\ 0 & 0 & 0 & 0 & 0 & \theta^{1*}_K & \theta^{2*}_K & \kappa^*_K \\ 0 & 0 & 0 & 0 & 0 & \theta^{1*}_A & \theta^{2*}_A & \alpha^*_K \end{vmatrix}$$

$$= (1+\sigma^*)\ \theta^*_{KA}\ \Sigma_K + (1+\sigma)\ \theta_{KA}\ \Sigma^*_K - y_{\bar{K}}\ (\sigma^*-\sigma)\ \theta_{KA}\ \theta^*_{KA}$$

$$= D^*\ \Sigma_K + D\ \Sigma^*_K + d\ y_{\bar{K}}$$

$$
u := \begin{vmatrix}
-y^{d1} & 1 & -\sigma & 0 & 1 & -\sigma & 0 & 0 \\
-y^{d1*} & -1 & 0 & -\sigma^{*} & 0 & 0 & 1 & -\sigma^{*} \\
y_E^2 & 1 & 1 & 0 & 0 & 0 & 0 & 0 \\
0 & 0 & 1 & 1 & 0 & 0 & 0 & 0 \\
0 & 0 & 0 & 0 & \theta_K^1 & \theta_K^2 & 0 & 0 \\
0 & 0 & 0 & 0 & \theta_A^1 & \theta_A^2 & 0 & 0 \\
0 & 0 & 0 & 0 & 0 & 0 & \theta_K^{1*} & \theta_K^{2*} \\
0 & 0 & 0 & 0 & 0 & 0 & \theta_A^{1*} & \theta_A^{2*}
\end{vmatrix}
$$

$$
= \theta_{KA}\, \theta_{KA}^{*}\, [(1+\sigma^{*})y^{d1} + (1+\sigma)y^{d1*} + (\sigma^{*}-\sigma)y_E^2]
$$

$$
= D^{*}\theta_{KA}y^{d1} + D\, \theta_{KA}^{*}y^{d1*} - d\, y_E^2
$$

By interchanging the first with the ninth column of $\Delta_{\bar{K}}$, adding the third and fourth row and expanding along the "new" first column one easily shows:

$$
\left| \begin{array}{cccccccccccc}
0 & y_E^1 & -\sigma y_E^2 & 0 & y_Q^1 & -\sigma y_Q^2 & 0 & 0 & -y^{d1} & 0 & 0 & 0 \\
0 & y_E^{1*} & 0 & -\sigma^{*} y_E^{2*} & 0 & 0 & y_Q^1 & -\sigma^{*} y_Q^{2*} & -y^{d1} & 0 & 0 & 0 \\
0 & y_E^1 & y_E^2 & 0\;0 & 0 & 0 & 0 & 0 & y_E^2 & 0 & 0 & y_{\bar{K}} \\
0 & y_E^{1*} & 0 & y_E^{2*} & 0 & 0 & 0 & 0 & y_E^{2*} & 0 & 0 & y_{\bar{K}}^{*} \\
-\kappa_S \hat{p}_{S1} & 0 & 0 & 0 & y_K^1 & y_K^2 & 0 & 0 & 0 & \kappa_A & 0 & \kappa_K \\
-\alpha_S \hat{p}_{S1} & 0 & 0 & 0 & y_A^1 & y_A^2 & 0 & 0 & 0 & \alpha_A & 0 & \alpha_K \\
0 & 0 & 0 & 0 & 0 & 0 & y_K^{1*} & y_K^{2*} & 0 & 0 & \kappa_A^{*} & \kappa_K^{*} \\
0 & 0 & 0 & 0 & 0 & 0 & y_A^{1*} & y_A^{2*} & 0 & 0 & \alpha_A^{*} & \alpha_K^{*} \\
-\theta_S^1 \hat{p}_{S1} & 0 & 0 & 0 & 0 & 0 & 0 & 0 & 0 & \theta_A^1 & 0 & \theta_K^1 \\
-\theta_S^2 \hat{p}_{S1} & 0 & 0 & 0 & 0 & 0 & 0 & 0 & -1 & \theta_A^2 & 0 & \theta_K^2 \\
0 & 0 & 0 & 0 & C & 0 & 0 & 0 & 0 & 0 & \theta_A^{1*} & \theta_K^{1*} \\
0 & 0 & 0 & 0 & 0 & 0 & 0 & 0 & -1 & 0 & \theta_A^{2*} & \theta_K^{2*}
\end{array} \right.
$$

$$= -Y_{\bar{K}} \{u \, \Delta p_2 - [q(\theta_A^{1*} \theta_{KA} - \theta_A^1 \theta_{KA}^*) + r(\theta_S^1 \theta_{KA}^* + \theta_A^{1*} \theta_{SK})$$

$$+ s(\theta_K^{1*} \theta_{SA}) + t(-\theta_A^{1*} \theta_{SA})] \hat{p}_{S1}\}$$

Hence one gets the final result:

$$\frac{\hat{\bar{K}}}{\hat{p}_{S1}} = \frac{1}{Y_{\bar{K}} \Delta_2} \{-u \frac{\hat{p}_{21}}{\hat{p}_{S1}} + r \frac{\hat{p}_{A1}}{\hat{p}_{S1}} + s \frac{\hat{p}_{A1}^*}{\hat{p}_{S1}} + t \frac{\hat{p}_{K1}}{\hat{p}_{S1}} + q\} \qquad (11.1.1)$$

$$= \frac{1}{Y_{\bar{K}} \Delta_2} \{D^* X + DY + dZ\}$$

where D, D^*, d and X, Y, Z are as defined in table 11.3.

All other quantity effects can be attained by the same procedure, where only u,r,s,t,q, have to be redefined accordingly. Equation 11.1.1 will hold in all cases with the respective Y_j ($j=E_1, E_2, Q_1, Q_2$) and the respectively changed q,r,s,t,u.

12. Recycling

In recent years economists showed increasing consciousness and concern for environmental disruption. When they started to thoroughly investigate causes and consequences of pollution its close relationship to the economics of natural resources became evident. In fact, both issues are interdependent in a way that was adequately illustrated by Boulding's well-known paradigm of the earth as a spaceship: Pollution and natural resource depletion are joint plagues which inevitably accelerate each other. Among the various policy proposals for environmental management and basic materials management there is one that promises to fight simultaneously and successfully the battle against both pollution and resource depletion. It is the device of recycling which we broadly conceive of as the recovery and re-use of basic materials from the stream of waste products or secondary materials that is generated in the economic activities of production and consumption[1].

In the context of resource economics recycling has an obvious international dimension for two major reasons. First, the world-wide reserves of many 'virgin' materials are declining rapidly and some may already be exhausted in a few decades from now. Recycling, then, has the effect of economising on the world's global reserves of basic material. Second, these reserves are distributed extremely unevenly between countries, so that for many countries the recycling issue has received great attention as a means of reducing the dependence on (uncertain) foreign supply.

In contrast, the international aspects of recycling within the context of the economics of pollution (environmental economics in the narrow sense) do not appear to be so evident.

There is already a broad body of literature analysing the relevance of recycling for the enforcement of national environmental objectives. Also, various international

---

1) There is considerable semantic confusion about the terms recycling, re-use, reclamation etc.; for some operational definitions see B.T. Bower (1977, p. 1-19).

dimensions of environmental management have already been studied and clarified[1]. But it seems that with the exception of a recent paper of I. Walter (1975) there is no investigation on the conceptual level of the impact of "comparative advantages of recycling" on environmental and basic materials management.

Bower (1977, p. 18 n.) correctly argues that "... policies not specifically directed toward recycling can have important effects on recycling ...". This is true, in particular, for national pre-trade environmental policy. But the allocative effects of trade will in general also have significant impact on the rate of recycling. Therefore, it is the interdependencies between recycling, environmental policy and trade that are the central issues of the subsequent analysis.

Trade may take place in final consumption goods and/or in intermediate products, such as material and secondary material (scrap. etc.), and the trade effects clearly depend on the specific pattern of trade. We know from Yates (1959) that the bulk of trade in the real world is in intermediate products. In addition, Walter (1975) showed convincingly that a non-negligible part of trade consists of waste products or secondary materials which typically are intermediate goods. We therefore take the view that it is not only important to consider trade in final consumption goods but also trade in intermediate products. In regard to the latter the following questions demand some answers: What are the determinants of the pattern of trade in intermediate products? How does trade in secondary materials affect the national and the over-all rates of recycling. What is the relationship between international markets for secondary materials and national environmental management programs?

Sections 12.1 and 12.2 start with describing technologies and production possibilities. Then in section 12.3 we study some properties of price and standard equilibria in the closed economy.

1) All previous parts of this book are devoted to these issues.

This appears both necessary and economically interesting since the waste product will turn out to be a pure intermediate good commanding a positive price if the recycling activity is sufficiently efficient relative to the virgin material production. Section 12.4 proceeds with the comparative statics of the closed economy showing, in particular, price and quantity displacements of changes in factor endowments and environmental quality standards. Finally, section 12.5 serves to draw the conclusions with respect to the interdependencies of environmental policy, recycling, comparative advantage and trade.

12.1 Technologies

We consider an economy that produces two (private) consumption goods with two inputs: labour and basic material. The production technology is such that along with the consumption goods a by-product (secondary material) is generated. This by-product is assumed to be useless for consumption; it may be either discharged into the environment or used as an input in the production of basic material (recycled).

The basic material industry has two options: It may either produce basic material with labour as the only input (virgin material technology) or it may combine labour and secondary material to recover basic material from secondary material (recycling technology). For simplicity we assume that virgin and recycled material are homogeneous goods. It is possible that the basic material industry does not demand all secondary material generated. Then the excess supply of secondary material is released into the environment, thus lowering the environmental quality and affecting the consumers' well-being (preference satisfaction).

Diagram 12.1 illustrates these relationships and interdependencies. It demonstrates that basic material is a pure intermediate good: It is an input as well as an output but no consumption good. The same is true for the secondary material if recycling takes place. However, secondary material need not be completely recycled. Note that in diagram 12.1 some interdependencies are suppressed, in particular additional arrows from boxes 5, 6 and 8 to box 7 and from box 9 to all other boxes. There is, of course, evidence for the relevance of these interdependencies[1)], but they will be ignored here to keep the analysis manageable.

The production technology for the private consumption good i is given by the function $F^i : D_{Fi} \to \mathbb{R}^1_+$, where the domain

---

1) The importance of the arrow from box 5 to box 7 is stressed by D. Pearce (1974, p. 83-105). The arrow from box 8 to box 7 is analysed by K.G. Mäler (1974) and by R. Pethig (1979a); For the arrow from box 9 to box 4 see L.E. Ruff (1972), T.H. Tietenberg (1973b), H. Siebert (1975) and R. Pethig (1977a).

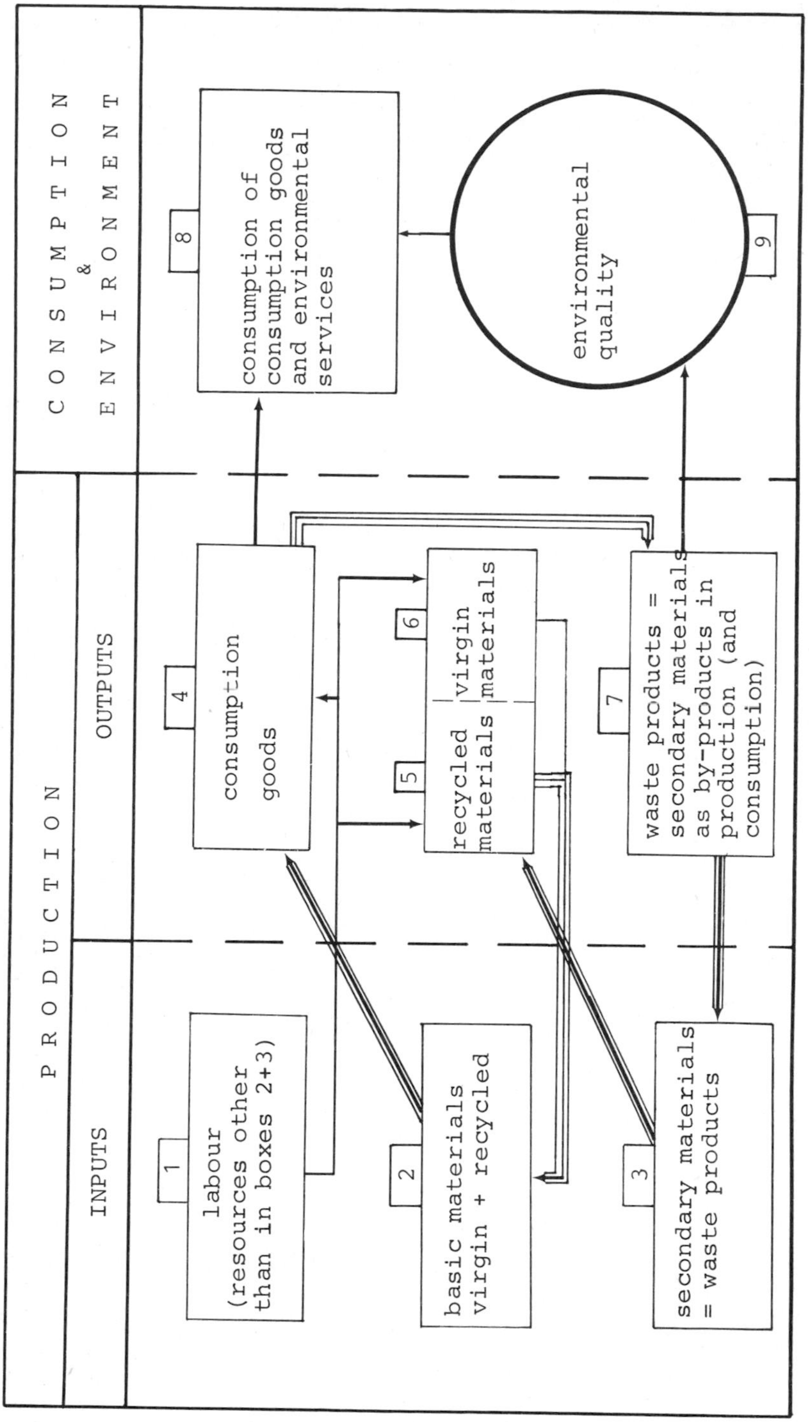
PRODUCTION
CONSUMPTION & ENVIRONMENT
INPUTS
OUTPUTS
1
labour (resources other than in boxes 2+3)
2
basic materials virgin + recycled
3
secondary materials = waste products
4
consumption goods
5
recycled materials
6
virgin materials
7
waste products = secondary materials as by-products in production (and consumption)
8
consumption of consumption goods and environmental services
9
environmental quality

Diagram 12.1

D_{Fi} is defined below and where $Q_i = F^i (A_i, M_i, S_i)$ denotes the quantity of good i that can be produced when the labour input is A_i, the basic material input is M_i and the by-product (secondary material) generated is S_i.

This net production function F^i represents a two-outputs-two-inputs production technology as was applied in Chapter 9 of this book, except that one input is called basic material instead of capital - which is only a matter of interpretation. This similarity suggests that the assumptions on the production technology as introduced in chapter 9 should be adopted in this section, too. It will turn out to be analytically convenient, however, to modify these assumptions in two respects. First, we relax the assumptions from chapter 9 in several points and second, we change the sign convention used so far for S_i. While Q_i, A_i and M_i remain non-negative variables, $|S_i|$ now denotes the quantity of secondary material generated in sector i, if $S_i < 0$, and $|S_i|$ denotes the quantity of secondary material used as input in sector i, if $S_i > 0$. With this purely formal change of notation in mind we now summarize the properties of F^i, the net production function for consumption good i, in the subsequent assumption A 12.1.

A 12.1i. Joint production property:

There is $(A_i, M_i, S_i) \in D_{Fi}$ with $S_i < 0$ such that $F^i_S \Big|_{(A_i, M_i, S_i)} < 0$.

A 12.1ii. No free production:

$(A_i, M_i, S_i) \in D_{Fi}$, $A_i = 0$ and $M_i \geq 0$ implies

$F^i(A_i, M_i, S_i) = 0$ and $S_i = 0$

A 12.1iii. Bounded domain for given labour and material input.

D_{Fi} has the following properties

(a) $(A_i, M_i, S_i) \notin D_{Fi}$, if $A_i < 0$ or $M_i < 0$

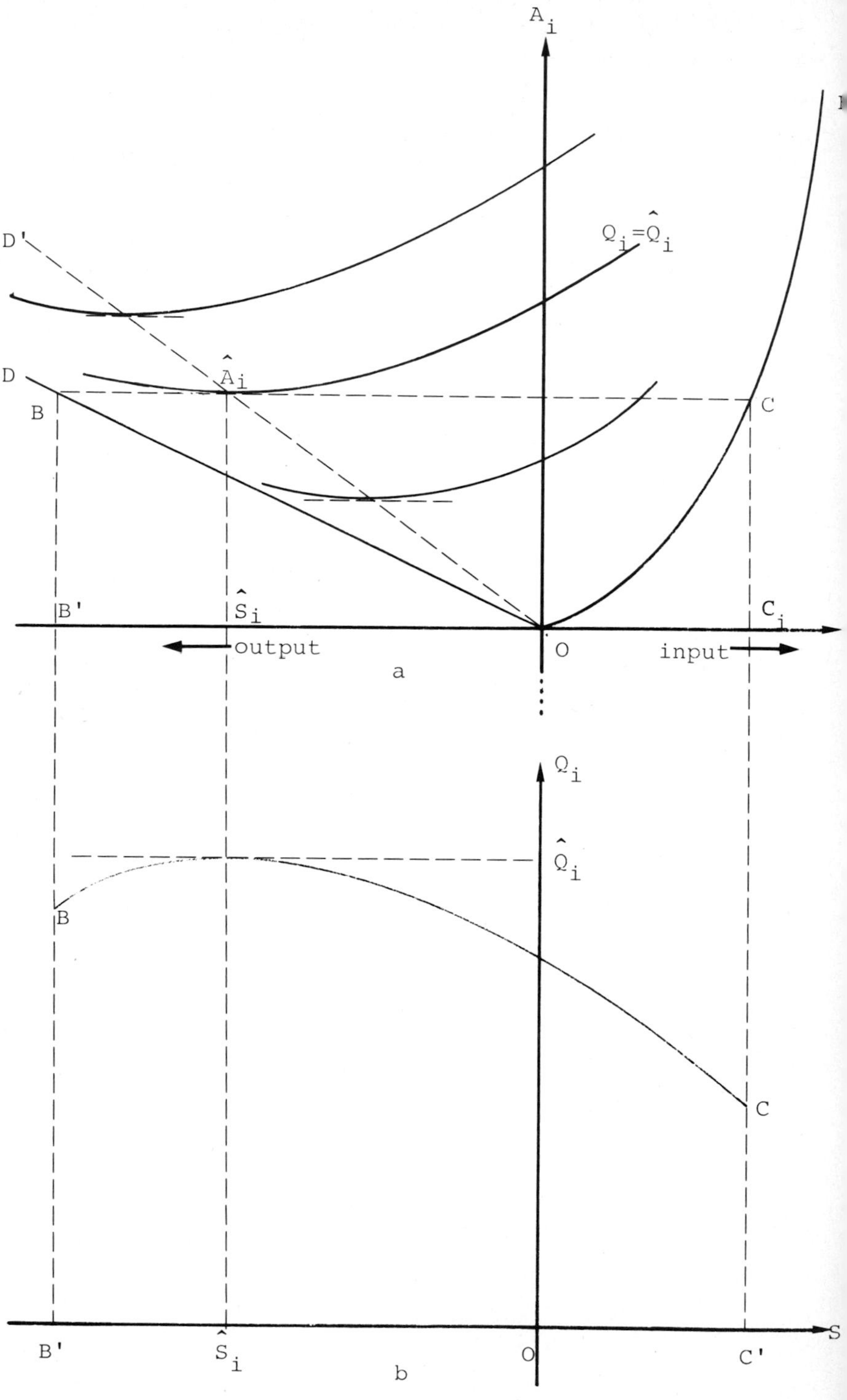

A_i
D'
$Q_i = \hat{Q}_i$
D
$\hat{A}_i$
B
C
B'
$\hat{S}_i$
C_i
output
O
input
a
Q_i
$\hat{Q}_i$
B
C
B'
$\hat{S}_i$
O
C'
S
b

Diagram 12.2

(b) There is a strictly monotone decreasing function
$\varphi^{i-} : \mathbb{R}_+^2 \rightarrow \mathbb{R}_-^1$ with $\varphi^{i-}(A_i, M_i) = 0$ for $A_i = 0$ or
$M_i = 0$, such that
$(A_i, M_i, S_i) \notin D_{Fi}$, if $S_i < \varphi^{i-}(A_i, M_i)$

(c) There is a strictly monotone increasing function
$\varphi^{i+} : \mathbb{R}_+^2 \rightarrow \mathbb{R}_+^1$ with $\varphi^{i+}(A_i, M_i) = 0$ for $A_i = 0$ or
$M_i = 0$, such that $(A_i, M_i, S_i) \notin D_{Fi}$, if $S_i > \varphi^{i+}(A_i, M_i)$.

A 12.1iv. Non-increasing returns to scale:

D_{Fi} is convex and F^i is a concave function.

It is easy to see that except for the different sign convention with respect to S_i, assumption A 12.1 differs from assumption A 2.8 only in that A 12.1 takes into account two inputs instead of one.

Diagram 12.2a illustrates the domain of F^i, projected into the (A_i, S_i)-plane for some given $M_i = \hat{M}_i > 0$. The curve OD [1] is the graph of the function $S_i = \varphi^{i-}(A_i, \hat{M}_i)$ and the curve OE is the graph of the function $S_i = \varphi^{i+}(A_i, \hat{M}_i)$ from assumption A 12.1iii. Diagram 12.2b, shows the graph of the function $Q_i = F^i(\hat{A}_i, \hat{M}_i, S_i)$, that is, all combinations of Q_i and S_i that can be produced with fixed positive inputs $\hat{A}_i$ and $\hat{M}_i$. Observe that the close interrelationship between the diagrams 12.2a and b is exemplified by the coinciding symbols B, B', C, C', $\hat{Q}_i$ and $\hat{S}_i$.

A 12.2. Basic material production technology.

We now turn to the description of the technological aspects of basic material production that consists of virgin material production and of recycling.

By the "production" of virgin material we mean the extraction

1) The line OD in diagram 12.2a could be moved to the right-hand side, such that it coincides, e.g., with OD'.

of natural resources from the environment with the help of labour. Mining and processing of minerals would seem to be a typical example, but renewable resources, like timber, are also conceivable specifications of our basic material variable. The virgin material technology is described by the function $G^V : \mathbb{R}^1_+ \rightarrow \mathbb{R}^1_+$, where $M_V = G^V (A_V)$ is the basic material produced (or extracted) with the help of the labour input A_V.

We require G^V to satisfy

A 12.2i. Virgin material production function:

G^V is strictly concave and satisfies $G^V (0) = 0$.

The graph of G^V, satisfying A 12.2i, is depicted in diagram 12.3.

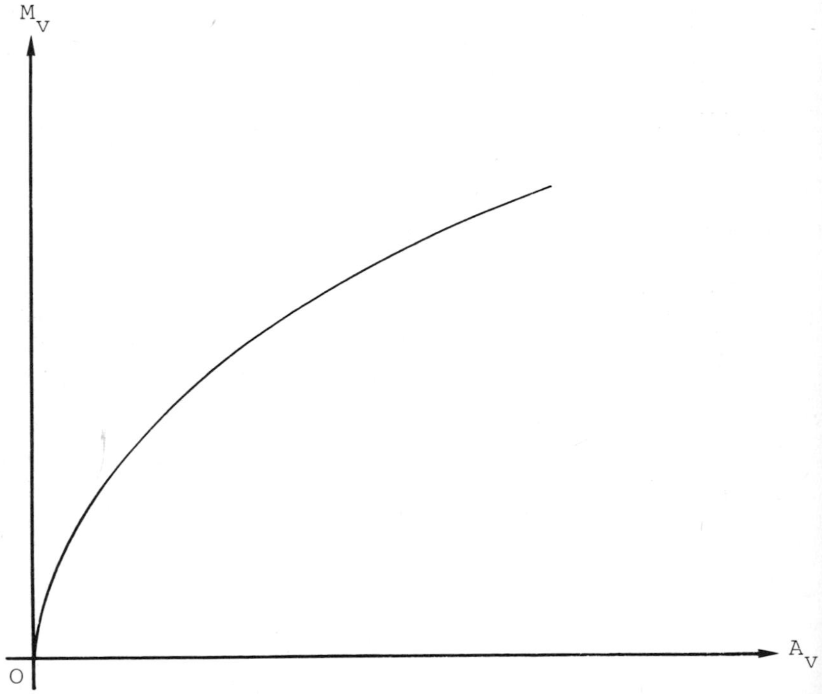

Diagram 12.3

We denote as recycling technology a production process by which basic material is regained from secondary material where this reclamation of basic material requires labour input. More specifically, we introduce the function $G^{\rho} : D_{G\rho} \rightarrow \mathbb{R}_+$, where $D_{G\rho}$ is defined below and where $M_{\rho} = G^{\rho}(A_{\rho}, S_{\rho})$ is the quantity of basic material produced when the labour input is A_{ρ} and the input of secondary material (from which M_{ρ} is reclaimed) is S_{ρ}.

In order to motivate and rationalize the assumptions that will be applied to G^{ρ} below, we first recall the waste abatement technology Y^{β} from section 2.3 that essentially describes a recycling technology, if V_{β} is not interpreted as a useless and harmless secondary waste product but as basic material. Hence recycling and abatement technologies basically have the same technological structure[1]. Yet we want to list the assumptions on G^{ρ} in detail since it appears necessary to introduce a few plausible modifications of G^{ρ} as compared to Y^{β}.

A 12.2ii. No free disposal of secondary material:

$D_{G\rho} := \{(A_{\rho}, S_{\rho}) \in \mathbb{R}^2_+ \mid S_{\rho} \leq \varphi^{\rho}(A_{\rho})\}$, where $\varphi^{\rho} : \mathbb{R}^1_+ \rightarrow \mathbb{R}^1_+$ is a strictly increasing function with $\varphi^{\rho}(0) = 0$.

It is important to emphasize that in spite of its formal similarity to assumption A 12.1iii or A 2.8iii, function φ^{ρ} in A 12.2ii plays a completely different role as the functions φ^{i} or Z^{i} in A 12.1iii and A 2.8iii, respectively. $S_{\rho} = \varphi^{\rho}(A_{\rho})$ is the maximum amount of secondary material that can be transformed into basic material with the help of the labour input A_{ρ}. More secondary material can not be processed with given labour input. Allowing for an unbounded domain of G^{ρ} for given A_{ρ} would then imply the tacit assumption that all secondary material that exceeds $\varphi^{\rho}(A_{\rho})$ is costlessly abated, neutralized or "disposed of". Note also that A 12.2ii rules out the possibility of recycling without labour input.

---

1) An environmentally neutral and useless output in Y^{β} may turn into a detrimental or into a useful output and vice versa, when technologies, tastes or the environmental assimilative capacity changes with time.

Some kind of "local" free disposal of secondary material would still prevail, if $(A_\rho, S_\rho), (\bar{A}_\rho, \bar{S}_\rho) \in D_{G\rho}$, $\bar{S}_\rho > S_\rho$, $\bar{A}_\rho = A_\rho$ and $G^\rho_S\big|_{(A_\rho, S_\rho)} = 0$ implies $G^\rho_S\big|_{(\bar{A}_\rho, \bar{S}_\rho)} = 0$.

So, as environmentally conscious economic theoreticians, we h to exclude even this possibility by assumption.

A 12.2iii. Impossibility of virgin material production:

$$G^\rho\ (A_\rho, S_\rho) = 0, \text{ if } A_\rho \geq 0 \text{ and } S_\rho = 0.$$

A 12.2iii serves to analytically distinguish the pure virgin material production, G^v, from the pure recycling, G^r.

A further implication of this strict separation is

A 12.2iv. Limited basic material content in secondary material.

The basic material reclaimed from one unit of secondary material cannot be arbitrarily increased by increasing the labour input. This follows from mass balance considerations, if secondary material is the only source of basic material (as is assumed in the pure recycling case). The assumption of limited basic material content in secondary material therefore means that there is a maximum ratio between reclaimed basic material and secondary material independent of the scale of production. This evident requirement can be rigorously formulated as follows:

There is $c \in \mathbb{R}^1_{++}$ such that for every

$S_\rho \in \{S_\rho | (A_\rho, S_\rho) \in D_{G\rho}\}$ we have

$$\max_{(A_\rho, S_\rho) \in D_\rho (S_\rho)} \frac{G^\rho\ (A_\rho, S_\rho)}{S_\rho} = c$$

where $D_\rho\ (S_\rho) \equiv \{(A_\rho S'_\rho) \in D_{G\rho} | S'_\rho = S_\rho\}$.

A 12.2v. Non-increasing returns to scale:

$D_{G\rho}$ is convex and G^ρ is a concave function.

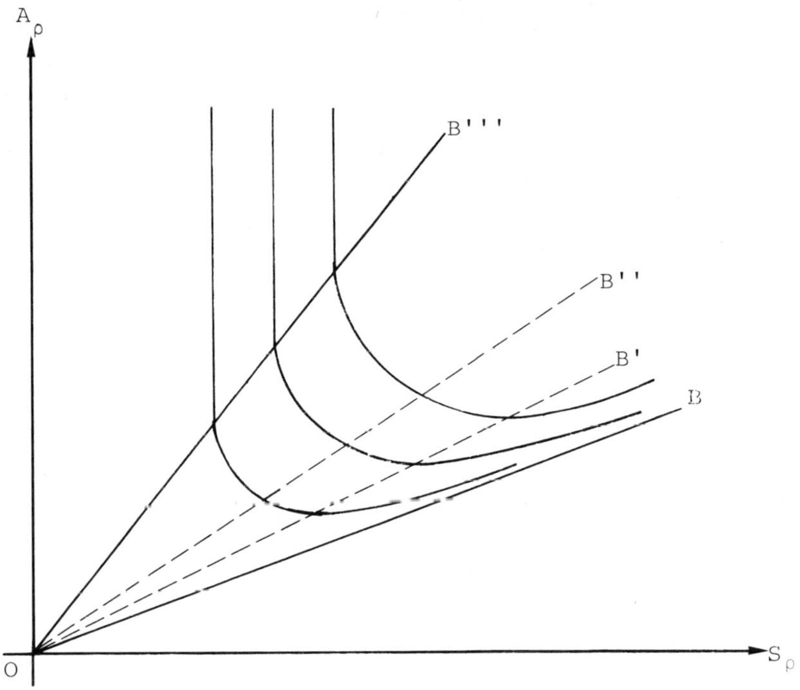

Diagram 12.4

Diagram 12.4 illustrates the pure recycling function G^ρ. The line OB is the graph of φ^ρ from A 10.2ii and the line OB''' consists of all points (A_ρ, S_ρ) that satisfy the maximum condition of assumption A 12.2iv. The basic material isoquants in diagram 12.4 are drawn such that they attain a minimum along the ray OB'. Therefore, for the subset of $D_{G\rho}$ to the left of OB' the production process may be interpreted as a special type of secondary material abatement activity: With given A_ρ it is possible to use increasing amounts of secondary material, but only at the cost of decreasing quantities of basic material output. If in diagram 12.4 the graph of φ^ρ were given by OB' (or OB'' or OB''') instead of OB, we would have examples of recycling technologies without such secondary material abatement.

Suppose that both the virgin material and the recycling production process are active. Then one may wish to know which fraction of the total production of basic material is generated by pure recycling. We therefore define the recycling ratio[1] by the function $\hat{\hat{R}} : \mathbb{R}^3_+ \to \mathbb{R}^1_+$, where

$$r = \hat{\hat{R}}\ (A_V, A_\rho, S_\rho) := \frac{G^\rho\ (A_\rho, S_\rho)}{G^V\ (A_V) + G^\rho\ (A_\rho, S_\rho)} \tag{12.1}$$

For analytical purposes we now combine and integrate the virgin material production function and the recycling technology as follows: We define the (basic) material production $G : D_G \to \mathbb{R}^1_+$ by $D_G = D_{G\rho}$ and by

$$G\ (A_r, S_r) := \max_{A_V \in \alpha(A_r, S_r)} [G^\rho\ (A_r - A_V, S_\rho = S_r) + G^V\ (A_V)] \tag{12.2}$$

where $\alpha\ (A_r, S_r) := \{A | 0 \leq A \leq A_r - \varphi^{\rho(-1)}\ (S_r)\}$

Clearly, since $\alpha(A_r, S_r)$ is a compact set, a solution to the maximization problem in equation 12.2 exists. Since G^V is strictly concave and G^ρ is concave by A 12.2i and A 12.2v, respectively, the solution is unique. We will, however, obtain a corner solution, if for given $(A_r, S_r) \in D_G$ for every $A_V \in \alpha(A_r, S_r)$ either

$$G^V_A\ (A_V) > G^\rho_A\ (A_r - A_V, S_r) \text{ or } G^V_A\ (A_r) < G^\rho_A\ (A_r - A_V, S_R). \tag{12.4}$$

In the first case we say that, at $(A_r, S_r) \in D_G$, the virgin material technology dominates the recycling technology whereas in the second case the converse holds[2].

Associated to the function G and G^ρ there is the recycling ratio

$$r = \hat{R}\ (A_r, S_r) := \frac{G^\rho\ (A^*_\rho, S_r)}{G\ (A_r, S_r)}, \tag{12.3}$$

where $A^*_\rho := A_r - A^*_V$ and, by definition, A^*_V maximizes

---

1) Compare D. Pearce (1974, p. 89). This ratio must be strictly distinguished from the ratio $[- S_\rho/(S_1 + S_2)]$. Both ratios coincide at zero, but not at one. If the latter attains the value one the former may well be less than one.

2) This notion of dominance naturally extends to the technologies on the whole, if equation 12.4 holds for every $(A_r, S_r) \in D_G$.

$G^{\rho}(A_r - A_v, S_r) + G^v(A_v)$ over the interval $\alpha(A_r, S_r)$

Lemma 12.1: Let the assumptions A 12.1 and A 12.2 hold.

(i) G is a concave function.

(ii) Suppose that $G_S^{\rho}(A_{\rho}^*, S_r) > 0$ and that no technology is dominated by the other one in the sense of equation 12.4. Then for every $\bar{M} \in \mathbb{R}_{++}^1$ the implicit (isoquant) function $G(A_r, S_r) - \bar{M} = 0$ is representable by a function $\hat{S} : \mathbb{R}_+^2 \to \mathbb{R}_+^1$ with $A_r = \hat{S}(S_r, \bar{M})$ satisfying $\hat{S}_S(S_r, \bar{M}) < 0$.

(iii) For every $(A_r, S_r) \in D_G$ and for every $\bar{M} \in \mathbb{R}_{++}^1$,

$$\frac{d\hat{R}[\hat{S}(S_r, \bar{M}), S_r]}{dS_r} = \hat{R}_A\hat{S}_S + \hat{R}_S > 0, \text{ if, in addition}$$

to the presuppositions of Lemma 12.1ii, $G_{AS}^{\rho} \geq 0$ and $G_{AA}^{\rho} < 0$ (evaluated at (A_{ρ}^*, S_r)).

Proof: Ad (i): We define $\Gamma_v := \{(M_v, A_v, S_v) \in \mathbb{R}_+^3 | M_v \leq G^v(A_v)$, $S_v = 0\}$ and $\Gamma_{\rho} := \{(M_{\rho}, A_{\rho}, S_{\rho}) \in \mathbb{R}_+^3 | M_{\rho} \leq G^{\rho}(A_{\rho}, S_{\rho})$ and $(A_{\rho}, S_{\rho}) \in D_{G\rho}\}$. By A 12.1iv and A 12.2v Γ_v and Γ_{ρ} are convex sets. Hence $\Gamma := \Gamma_v + \Gamma_{\rho}$ is convex. The "upper boundary" of this set Γ,

$$\Gamma_o := \{(M, A, S) | (M, A, S) \in \Gamma \text{ and } (\bar{M}, A, S) \notin \Gamma, \text{ if } \bar{M} > M\}$$

is the graph of the function G as defined by equation 12.2 [1]. The concavity of G follows from the convexity of Γ.

Ad (ii): From $G(A_r, S_r) = G^{\rho}(A_r - A_v, S_r) + G^v(A_v)$ we obtain for the isoquant condition $dG = 0$ the term

$$dG = G_A^{\rho}(dA_r - dA_v) + G_S^{\rho}dS_r + G_A^v dA_v = 0 \text{ and}$$

$$dG = G_A^{\rho}dA_r + G_S^{\rho}dS_r + (G_A^v - G_A^{\rho})\,dA_v = 0. \text{ Hence}$$

$$\hat{S}_S = \frac{dA_r}{dS_r} = -\frac{G_S^{\rho}}{G_A^{\rho}} + \left(1 - \frac{G_A^v}{G_A^{\rho}}\right)\frac{dA_v}{dS_r}. \qquad (12.5)$$

1) Compare the analogue argument in section 2.3.

Suppose, A_V^* maximizes 12.2 in the interior of α (A_r, S_r). Then $\hat{R}$ $(A_r, S_r) \in (0,1)$ and $G_A^V = G_A^\rho$ as an implication of the maximization problem of equation 12.2. Hence $\hat{S}_S < 0$ for $G_S^\rho > 0$ (and $G_A^\rho > 0$, which follows from assumption A 12.2).

Ad (iii): Lemma 12.1iii is proved, if we can show that along an isoquant of G the labour input A_V decreases with increasing S_r. We therefore differentiate the equation G_A^V (A_V) - - G_A^ρ $(A_r - A_V, S_r) = 0$ (from solving equation 12.2) with respect to S_r to obtain

$$G_{AA}^V \frac{dA_V}{dS_r} - G_{AA}^\rho \left(\hat{S}_S - \frac{dA_V}{dS_r}\right) - G_{AS}^\rho = 0 \text{ and } \frac{dA_V}{dS_r} = \frac{G_{AS}^\rho + G_{AA}^\rho \hat{S}_S}{G_{AA}^V + G_{AA}^\rho}.$$

Lemma 12.1iii follows immediately.

q.e.d.

Diagram 12.5 illustrates how the production isoquants of the function G are constructed from those belonging to G^V and G^ρ. Suppose that the lines ABC and DEF are isoquants associated to G^ρ for $M_\rho = 5$ and $M_\rho = 10$, respectively. Furthermore, we assign $A_V^M = OM$ and $A_V^H = OH$ in diagram 12.5 and assume G^V $(A_V^M) = 5$ and G^V $(A_V^H) = 10$. Obviously, point P in diagram 12.5 corresponds to the operation of the recycling process in B with $M_\rho = 5$ and to the operation of the virgin material production process in M with $M_V = 5$. If A_V^M solves the maximization problem from 12.2 for $S_r = OK$ and $A_r = ON$ then, in fact, P is a point on the isoquant HPEF of the function G for M = 10. If, in addition, A_V^M is an interior solution of 12.2, then we see from equation 12.4 that the slope of the isoquant HPEF in point P is equal to the slope of the isoquant ABC in point B.

In lemma 12.1 we have not considered "corner solutions" in the maximization problem of equation 12.2. We will not here pursue this issue rigorously, but a few remarks and conjectures should be made.

Suppose, that the virgin material production dominates the recycling technology as defined in the context of equation

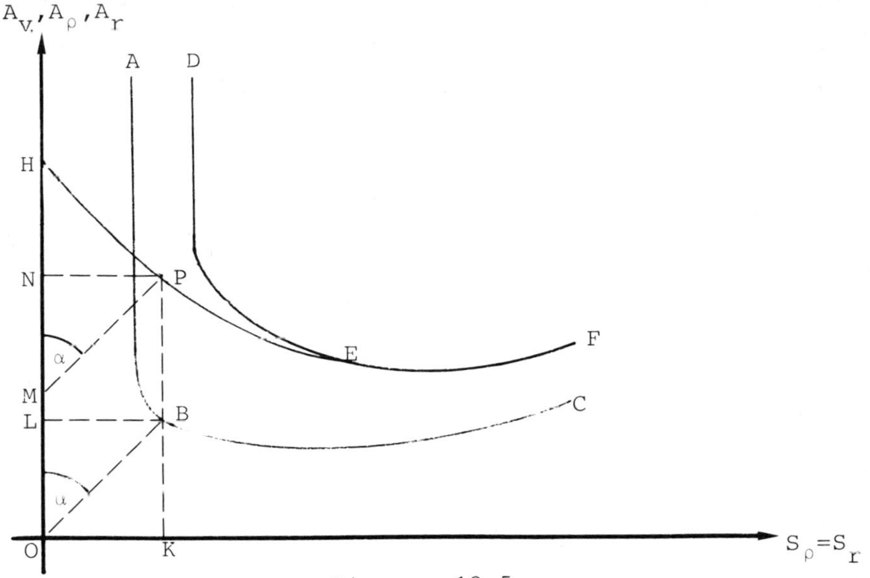

Diagram 12.5

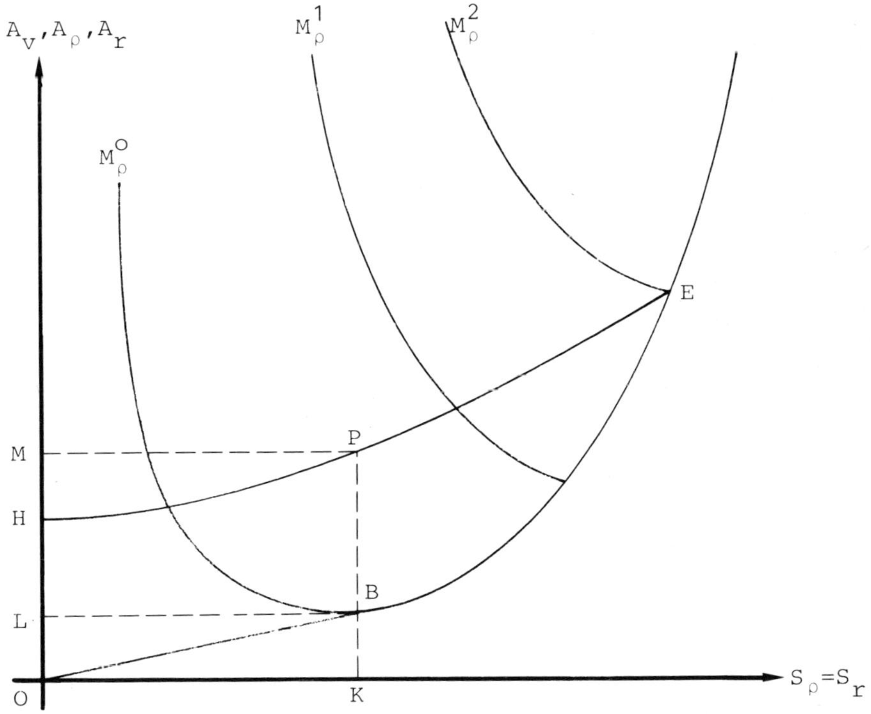

Diagram 12.6

12.2 on page 288, then A_v^*, the solution of equation 12.2 will be the maximum element of α (A_r, S_r) and $A_\rho^* = A_r - A_v^* = \varphi^\rho(S_r)$. It is intuitive, that the isoquant of G will be flatter than in the case of non-dominance. If the virgin material production is sufficiently more efficient than recycling, the isoquants of G will have a positive slope, even in the case that $G_S^\rho > 0$ everywhere on $D_{G\rho}$ [1].

This situation is illustrated in diagram 12.6, where HPE is an isoquant of G. Suppose, for example that $M_\rho^2 = 10$ and G^v $(A_v^H) = 10$ with $A_v^H = OH$. Then in point P, the recycling process is active at $S_r = OK$, $A_\rho = OL$, whereas the virgin material production is G^v $(A_v^M) = 10 - M_\rho^o$ with $A_v^M = LM$. Observe, that the recycling ratio increases continuously along HPE from H to E.

As far as the opposite case is concerned in which the recycling technology dominates the virgin material technology, we should expect that we have negatively sloped and steep isoquants for the function G. Point H in diagram 12.5 moves further up and simultaneously point E moves to the right on the line DF.

12.2 Production Possibilities

We now turn to consider the production possibilities of the economy. For this purpose we introduce:

Assumption A 12.3. Initial factor endowments. The economy's endowments of labour, material and secondary material are given by the non-negative quantities

$A_o > 0$ (labour),
$M_o \geq 0$ (material), and
$S_o \geq 0$ (secondary material).

1) More specifically, this "strong dominance" occurs, if at $(A_r, S_r) \in D_G$ there is $A_v < A_r$, such that G^ρ $(A_r, S_r) = G^v$ (A_v). Since G^v is strictly concave, the virgin material production may (strongly) dominate the recycling technology for low values of material output while the converse holds for high values.

We are again interested in the transformation space T of all triples (Q_1, Q_2, U) that are feasible under the assumptions A 12.1 to A 12.3. More formally, we define

$$T := \{(Q_1, Q_2, U) \in \mathbb{R}^3 \mid (Q_1, Q_2, U) \text{ satisfies the equation system 12.6 below}\},$$

where

$$\left.\begin{aligned}
&Q_i = F^i\ (A_i, M_i, S_i) \text{ with } (A_i, M_i, S_i) \in D_{Fi},\ i = 1,2\\
&M_3 = F^3\ (A_3, S_3) \text{ with } (A_3, S_3) \in D_{F3}\\
&U = G\ (S) \text{ with } S := S_o - S_1 - S_2 - S_3\\
&M_o - M_1 - M_2 + M_3 \geq 0\\
&A_o - A_1 - A_2 - A_3 \geq 0\\
&S_o - S_1 - S_2 - S_3 \geq 0
\end{aligned}\right\}\quad (12.6)$$

As in subsection 2.2.2 we define

$\overline{T} := \{y \mid y \leq \overline{y} \text{ and } \overline{y} \in T\}$ and we establish

<u>Lemma 12.2:</u> Under the assumptions A 12.1, A 12.2, A 12.3 and A 2.5 $\overline{T}$ is convex.

Proof: Let $y, y' \in \overline{T}$ and associate to y and y' the technologically feasible input-output vectors $V := (A_i, M_i, S_i)_{i=1,2,3}$ and $V' := (A_i', M_i', S_i')_{i=2,2,3}$, respectively. $\overline{T}$ is convex, if $y^\lambda := (\lambda y + (1 - \lambda)\ y') \in \overline{T}$ for $\lambda \in [0,1] \subset \mathbb{R}$. The vector $V^\lambda := \lambda V + (1 - \lambda)\ V'$ satisfies the inequalities in the fourth and fifth row of the equation system 12.6. In fact, it fulfills 12.6 completely, since by concavity of F^3 (lemma 12.1i) it follows that $F^3\ (A_3^\lambda, S_3^\lambda) - M_1^\lambda - M_2^\lambda \geq M_3^\lambda - M_1^\lambda - M_2^\lambda \geq 0$. Consequently, $y'' := [F^1\ (A_1^\lambda, M_1^\lambda, S_1^\lambda),\ F^2\ (A_2^\lambda, M_2^\lambda, S_2^\lambda),\ G\ (S^\lambda)] \in T$. By the assumptions A 2.5 and A 12.1iv the functions F^1, F^2 and G are concave. Hence y" is componentwise not less than y^λ. Thus $y^\lambda \in \overline{T}$.

q.e.d.

Lemma 12.2 is clearly the analogue to lemma 2.1 and it is

tempting to conclude that diagram 2.3 will also be the adequate graphical representation of the production possibilities of the economy presently under study. It will be shown in the sequel, however, that the transformation space of the recycling economy is not necessarily shaped as shown in diagram 2.3. In order to simplify the argument we assume that commodity 2 is not produced at all. For this case, production points (Q_1, U) are feasible, if they satisfy

$$Q_1 = F^1 [A_o - A_3, F^3 (A_3, S_3) + M_o, S_o - S_3 - G^{-1} (U)]. \quad (12.7)$$

Total differentiation with respect to U of equation 12.7 yields

$$\frac{dQ_1}{dU} = (F_M^1 F_A^3 - F_A^1) \frac{dA_3}{dU} + (F_M^1 F_S^3 - F_S^1) \frac{dS_3}{dU} - F_S^1 G_U^{-1}. \quad (12.8)$$

Equation 12.8 can be considerably simplified by using additional information about the transformation relationship between Q_1 and U (for Q_2 = O). We obtain this information from maximizing the output Q_1 for given U under the technological constraints F^1 and F^3 and under the resource constraints for material, labour and secondary material. In an interior solution this maximization problem yields

$$F_M^1 F_A^3 - F_A^1 = F_M^1 F_S^3 - F_S^1 = O. \quad (12.9)$$

The first part of equation 12.9 requires that the labour input must be allocated to the two production processes in such a way that withdrawing one unit of labour from sector 1 reduces the production of good 1 by exactly that amount by which the use of this labour unit increases the production of good 1 indirectly via additional production of material. A similar interpretation holds for the second part of equation 12.9.

When 12.9 is considered in equation 12.7, the rate of transformation becomes

$$\frac{dQ_1}{dU} = - F_S^1 G_U^{-1} \quad (12.10)$$

By assumption A 2.5 we have $G_U^{-1} < 0$, so that the sign of equation 12.10 depends on the sign of F_S^1. From A 12.1i we know that $F_S^1 < 0$, if secondary material is a by-product of the consumption good. Hence if $F_S^1 < 0$ and if (A_1, M_1, S_1) is an interior point of D_{F1}, then the rate of transformation is negative. This case is depicted in diagram 2.3. Observe, however, that $F_S^1 > 0$ is not excluded by assumption A 12.1, so that the transformation curve may be positively sloped on the whole domain. A positive rate of transformation is also conceivable if $F_S^1 \leq 0$ everywhere on D_{F1} and if the problem of maximizing Q_1 for given U has a boundary solution in D_{F1}.

From a theoretical point of view the coincidence of maximal environmental quality with maximal (feasible) production of good 1 does not seem at all to be irrelevant or even pathological. It implies that the recycling technology is highly efficient relative to the by-product generation. In this case secondary material is no longer an obnoxious waste product but rather a "regular" productive input. Since it is a produced input that is not used for consumption purposes, it is, in Batra's (1973) terms, a "pure intermediate good".

12.3 Price and Standard Equilibria

The possibility of a positively sloped transformation curve for environmental quality and one consumption good suggests that under certain conditions secondary material may command a positive price whereas under different circumstances with active environmental controls, a negative price (emission tax) will be attached to this commodity. It is the purpose of this subsection to rigorously elaborate these phenomena.

First we complete our three-sector recycling economy by introducing the assumption

A 12.4 Social welfare function.
There is a social welfare function $W : \mathbb{R}_+^3 \longrightarrow \mathbb{R}_+$ that is quasi-concave, strictly monotone increasing in Q_1^d and Q_2^d, and monotone increasing in U[1)].

1) Observe that this social welfare function is far less restrictive than that of assumption A 7.1.

We further assume that in our economy there are perfectly competitive markets for the two (private) consumption goods, for labour, basic material, and - possibly - for the secondary material. The market prices are denoted p_1, p_2, p_A, p_M, and p_S, respectively.

As in chapter 7 we also attach a price p_U to the public good "environmental quality".

All three production sectors maximize profits as price takers, that is, they solve the problems[1].

$$\left.\begin{aligned} &\max_{(Q_i,A_i,M_i,S_i)} \ \min_{(\beta_1^i,\beta_2^i,\beta_3^i)} \ L^i(Q_i,A_i,M_i,S_i,\beta_1^i,\beta_2^i,\beta_3^i) := \\ &:= p_iQ_i - p_AA_i - p_MM_i - p_SS_i + \beta_1^i\,[F^i\,(A_i,M_i,S_i) - \\ &\quad Q_i] + \beta_2^i\,[S_i - \varphi^{i-}\,(A_i,M_i)] + \beta_3^i\,[\varphi^{i+}\,(A_i,M_i) - S_i], \end{aligned}\right\} \quad \begin{aligned}&(12.11)\\&(i=1,2)\end{aligned}$$

$$\left.\begin{aligned} &\max_{(M_3,A_3,S_3)} \ \min_{(\beta_1^3,\beta_2^3)} \ L^3\,(M_3,A_3,S_3,\beta_1^3,\beta_2^3) := \\ &:= p_MM_3 - p_AA_3 - p_SS_3 + \beta_1^3\,[F^3\,(A_3,S_3) - M_3] + \\ &\quad + \beta_2^3\,[A_3 - \varphi^{\rho}(S_3)]. \end{aligned}\right\} \quad (12.12)$$

The consumption sector solves

$$\left.\begin{aligned} &\max_{(Q_1^d,\,Q_2^d)} \ \min_{\alpha_Y} \ L^C\,(Q_1^d,\,Q_2^d,\,\alpha_Y) := \\ &:= W\,(Q_1^d,\,Q_2^d,\,\bar{U}) + \alpha_Y\,(\bar{Y} - p_1Q_1^d - p_2Q_2^d), \end{aligned}\right\} \quad (12.13)$$

where $\bar{U} = G\,(\bar{S})$, $\bar{S} := \mathrm{Max}\,[0,\, S_o - \hat{S}_1 - \hat{S}_2 - \hat{S}_3]$,

$$\bar{Y} := p_AA_o + p_MM_o + p_SS_o + \sum_{i=1,2}(p_i\hat{Q}_i - p_A\hat{A}_i - p_M\hat{M}_i - p_S\hat{S}_i) + (p_M\hat{M}_3 - p_S\hat{S}_3) - p_S\bar{S}$$

and where the "hat" letters are the solution values of the

1) For this way of writing the following nonlinear programming problems see, e.g., P. van Moeseke (1974). The functions φ^{i-}, φ^{i+} and φ^{ρ} used below are defined in the assumptions A 12.1 and A 12.2.

problems 12.11 and 12.12.

According to equation 12.13, the consumers take the "prevailing" level of environmental quality, $U = \bar{U}$, as given. This is a consequence of the assumption that the environmental quality is a pure public consumption good.

With some formal modifications we can now apply the definition D 7.2 of a price and standard equilibrium to the recycling economy. We say that a price system $p := (p_1, p_2, p_A, p_M, p_S, p_u)$ and an allocation $a := [Q_1^d, Q_2^d, U, Q_1, Q_2, (A_i, M_i, S_i)_{i=1,2,3}, S^S]$ constitute a price and standard equilibrium, if the allocation a satisfies the equation system 12.6, if the allocation a is a solution to the problems 12.11, 12.12 and 12.13 relative to p, if $p_u = 0$ and if S maximizes $[p_u G(S') - p_S S']$ on $\mathbb{R}_+$.

Our next step is to derive a theorem on the existence of price and standard equilibria in the recycling economy. For this purpose we make use of the following formal concepts:

First we define the Lagrangean

$$\left.\begin{aligned} L^W(a, \alpha) := {} & W(Q_1^d, Q_2^d, U) + \sum_{i=1,2} \{\alpha^i [F^i(A_i, M_i, S_i) - \\ & - Q_i] + \alpha_1^i [S_i - \varphi^{i-}(A_i, M_i)] + \alpha_2^i [\varphi^{i+}(A_i, M_i) - S_i] + \\ & + \bar{\alpha}^i (Q_i - Q_i^d)\} + \alpha^3 [F^3(A_3, S_3) - M_3] + \alpha_1^3 [A_3 - \varphi^{\rho}(S_3)] + \\ & + \alpha^a (A_o - A_1 - A_2 - A_3) + \bar{\alpha}^3 (M_o - M_1 - M_2 + M_3) + \\ & + \alpha^4 (S_o - S_1 - S_2 - S_3) + \alpha^s (S - S_o + S_1 + S_2 + S_3) + \\ & + \alpha^o (S^S - S) + \alpha^u [G(S) - U] \end{aligned}\right\} \quad (12.14)$$

and introduce the two programming problems

$$\max_{a} \ \min_{\alpha^{(o)}} \ L^W(a, \alpha) \quad \text{and} \qquad (12.15)$$

$$\max_{a^{)u(}} \ \min_{\alpha^{(u)}} \ L^W(a, \alpha), \qquad (12.16)$$

where

$$a := [Q_1^d,\ Q_2^d,\ U,\ Q_1,\ Q_2,\ (A_i,\ M_i,\ S_i)_{i=1,2,3},\ S] \in \mathbb{R}^{15},$$

$$a^{)u(} := [Q_1^d,\ Q_2^d,\ Q_1,\ Q_2,\ (A_i,\ M_i,\ S_i)_{i=1,2,3},\ S] \in \mathbb{R}^{14},$$

$$\alpha := [(\alpha^i,\ \alpha_1^i,\ \alpha_2^i,\ \bar{\alpha}^i)_{i=1,2},\ \alpha^3, \alpha_1^3, \alpha^a, \bar{\alpha}^3,\ \alpha^4, \alpha^s, \alpha^o, \alpha^u] \in \mathbb{R}^{16},$$

$\alpha^{(o)}$ as α except that $\alpha^o = 0$ in $\alpha^{(o)}$,

$\alpha^{(u)}$ as α except that $\alpha^u = 0$ in $\alpha^{(u)}$.

Setting $\alpha^o = 0$ in the vector $\alpha^{(o)}$ means that no emissions standard is enforced. In problem 12.16, on the other hand, an emissions standard is implemented, but the maximization procedure does not refer to the variable U (similar as in problem 12.13). The requirement $\alpha^u = 0$ corresponds to the condition $p_U = 0$ in the definition of a price and standard equilibrium.

Finally, let $(a^+,\ \alpha^+)$ be alternatively defined by the vectors $(a^+,\ \alpha^{(o)+})$ and $(a^{)u(+},\ \alpha^{(u)+})$ that solve the problems 12.15 and 12.16, respectively. By the Kuhn-Tucker theorem[1] these vectors satisfy the conditions

$$\left.\begin{aligned} \left.\frac{\partial L^W}{\partial \xi}\right|_{(a^+,\ \alpha^+)} &\leq 0, & a^+ \left.\frac{\partial L^W}{\partial \xi}\right|_{(a^+,\ \alpha^+)} &= 0 \\ \left.\frac{\partial L^W}{\partial \rho}\right|_{(a^+,\ \alpha^+)} &\geq 0, & \alpha^+ \left.\frac{\partial L^W}{\partial \rho}\right|_{(a^+,\ \alpha^+)} &= 0 \end{aligned}\right\} \qquad (12.17)$$

where ξ is equal to the vector a or $a^{)u(}$ and where ρ represen the vector $\alpha^{(o)}$ or $\alpha^{(u)}$.

---

1) Compare, for example, M.D. Intriligator (1971, p. 44n) and P. van Moeseke (1974). In its standard version the Kuhn-Tucker Theorem requires $a^+ \geq 0$ which in the present case may be violated by S_1, S_2 and U. For these variables there exist lower bounds in the relevant domain (of attainable allocations) such that they could be made nonnegative by a suitable linear transformation. Note further that in contrast to all other components of the vector α^+ its component α^{s+} need not be nonnegative since the associated constraint is identically equal to zero by the definition of S. See P. van Moeseke (1974).

Theorem 12.1: Let the assumptions A 12.1 to A 12.4 hold and consider a vector (a^+, α^+) such that (A_i, M_i, S_i) for i = 1,2 and (A_3, S_3) are interior points of D_{Fi} for i = 1,2,3, respectively.

(i) If (a^+, α^+) is a solution to the problem 12.15 or 12.16 then there exists a price system p with $p_U = 0$, such that a^+ and p constitute a price and standard system satisfying $S^+ \leq S^S$.

(ii) If (a^+, α^+) is a solution to the problem 12.15, then the associated price and standard system is welfare maximal (Pareto-optimal).

(iii) There exists a nonnegative real number $\bar{S}$ with the following property: If in equation 12.14 $S^S > \bar{S}$ is chosen and if (a^+, α^+) is a solution to the problem 12.16, then the associated price and standard equilibrium is a laissez-faire equilibrium.

Proof: Ad (i): Let (a^+, α^+) be a solution to the problem 12.15 or 12.16. The conditions 12.17 when combined with the presupposition of theorem 12.1 imply that (a^+, α^+) satisfies the equations

$$\alpha^{i+}F_M^{i+} - \alpha^{3+} = 0, \qquad i = 1,2,$$

$$\left.\begin{aligned} &\alpha^{i+}F_A^{i+} - \alpha^{a+} = 0, \\ &\alpha^{i+}F_S^{i+} - \alpha^{4+} + \alpha^{s+} = 0, \end{aligned}\right\} \quad i = 1,2,3 \tag{12.18}$$

and

$$Q_i^{d+} - Q_i^+ = 0,$$

$$V_o - \sum_{i=1,2,3} V_i^+ = 0, \qquad V = A,S \tag{12.19}$$

$$M_o - M_1^+ - M_2^+ - M_3^+ = 0.$$

Consider the price vector

$$p := (p_1=\alpha^{1+},\ p_2=\alpha^{2+},\ p_A=\alpha^{a+},\ p_M=\alpha^{3+},\ p_S=\alpha^{4+}-\alpha^{s+},\ p_U=0)$$

and solve the problems 12.11 and 12.12 for p. It follows from A 12.1 and A 12.2 that the corresponding Kuhn-Tucker conditions are necessary and sufficient for a solution. We therefore know that the production plans $(Q_i^+, A_i^+, M_i^+, S_i^+)$ for i = 1,2 and (M_3^+, A_3^+, S_3^+) maximize profits at prices p. Similarly, by assumption A 12.3 the Kuhn-Tucker conditions from solving 12.13 relative to p, to $\overline{U} := G(S^+)$ and relative to

$$\overline{Y} := p_A A_o + p_M M_o + p_S S_o + \sum_{i=1,2} (p_i Q_i^+ - p_A A_i^+ - p_M M_i - p_S S_i^+ + (p_M M_3^+ - p_S S_3^+) - p_S S^+ \quad (12.2$$

are necessary and sufficient for a solution $(\hat{Q}_1^d, \hat{Q}_2^d, \hat{\alpha}_Y)$ of problem 12.13.

Among these conditions are

$$\hat{W}_i - \hat{\alpha}_Y p_i = 0 \quad (i = 1,2). \quad (12.2$$

It follows from the presuppositions of theorem 12.1 that α^{i+} $p_i > 0$. Hence by assumption A 12.3 we have $\hat{\alpha}_Y > 0$ in equation 12.21 and therefore $\overline{Y} = p_1\hat{Q}_1^d + p_2\hat{Q}_2^d$. Then the equations 12.19 and 12.20 imply that the solution $(\hat{Q}_1^d, \hat{Q}_2^d, \hat{\alpha}_Y)$ of 12.13 satisfies $\hat{Q}_i^d = Q_i^{d+}$ for i = 1,2 and $\hat{\alpha}_Y = 1$. This proves that p has the desired properties.

Ad (ii): This part of the theorem is obvious from the proof o theorem 12.1i and from the definition of the problem 12.15

Ad (iii): It can be shown by standard arguments[1] that under the assumptions A 12.1 to A 12.4 the set of attainable allocations is bounded. We define $\overline{S}$ to be a positive real number that is greater than the greatest aggregate amount of secondary material being producible in any attainable allocation. Since a^+ is an attainable allocation, the inequality $S^+ < \overline{S} < S^S$ holds. Hence $\lambda^{o+} = 0$, i.e. the emission standard S^S is not binding.

q.e.d.

Suppose, that under the assumptions of theorem 12.1 a solution (a^+, α^+) of the problem 12.15 or 12.17 satisfies $F_S^{3+} > 0$. In this case the recycling process is active (since, in addition, (A_3^+, S_3^+) is not boundary point of D_{F3}), and one

1) Compare R. Pethig (1979 a, p. 49).

obtains from the equations 12.17 and 12.18 (for i = 1,2)

$$p_S = \alpha^{4+} - \alpha^{s+} = \alpha^{3+}F_S^{3+} = W_i^+F_M^{i+}F_S^{3+} > 0$$

From condition iv of definition D 7.2 and from $p_U = 0$ it follows immediately that $S^+ = 0$. Hence secondary material is a (scarce) pure intermediate good and pollution is not a problem in such an economy[1]. Observe also that in this case every laissez-faire equilibrium is welfare maximal.

In the last paragraph we deduced $p_S > 0$ from $F_S^{3+} > 0$. But from equation 12.18 we also have $p_S = \alpha^{i+}F_S^{i+}$ and hence $F_S^{i+} > 0$ for i = 1,2. This conclusion follows from our presupposition that (A_i^+, M_i^+, S_i^+) is a point of the interior of D_{Fi}. More generally, $p_S > 0$ is also compatible with the assumption that $F_S^i \leq 0$ everywhere on D_{Fi}. If $F_S^{3+} > 0$ and hence $p_S > 0$ in this case, then (A_i^+, M_i^+, S_i^+) would have to satisfy $S_i^+ = \varphi^{i-}(A_i^+, M_i^+)$, and for i = 1,2 the last row of 12.18 has to be substituted by $\alpha^{4+} - \alpha^{s+} > \alpha^{i+}F_S^{i+} \leq 0$.

The two diagrams 12.7a and 12.7b illustrate the case where secondary material is a pure intermediate good commanding a positive price. We assign $\tan\alpha = -p_{SA} < 0$, and the tangency points B and C represent the optimum conditions $F_S^{i+}/F_A^{i+} = F_S^{3+}/F_A^{3+} = p_{SA} > 0$. Suppose now, the graph of the function φ^{i-} in diagram 12.7a is the line OA' instead of OA. Then the point B' illustrates a boundary solution where $F_i^{S+} < 0$ while still $p_{SA} > 0$.

It should be emphasized that due to the by-product property of secondary material assumed in A 12.1, an equilibrium with $p_S > 0$ implies that recycling takes place. Since $p_{SA} > 0$ this is only possible, if the isoquants of F^3 are downward sloping at least on a subset of D_{F3}. Hence secondary material can only be a pure intermediate good, if the basic material production does not strongly dominate the recycling technology.

---

1) In a more realistic setting one should, of course, introduce more than one by-product and different recycling technologies. Then perhaps some by-products will turn out to be pure intermediate goods while others are discharged into the environment at zero or negative prices.

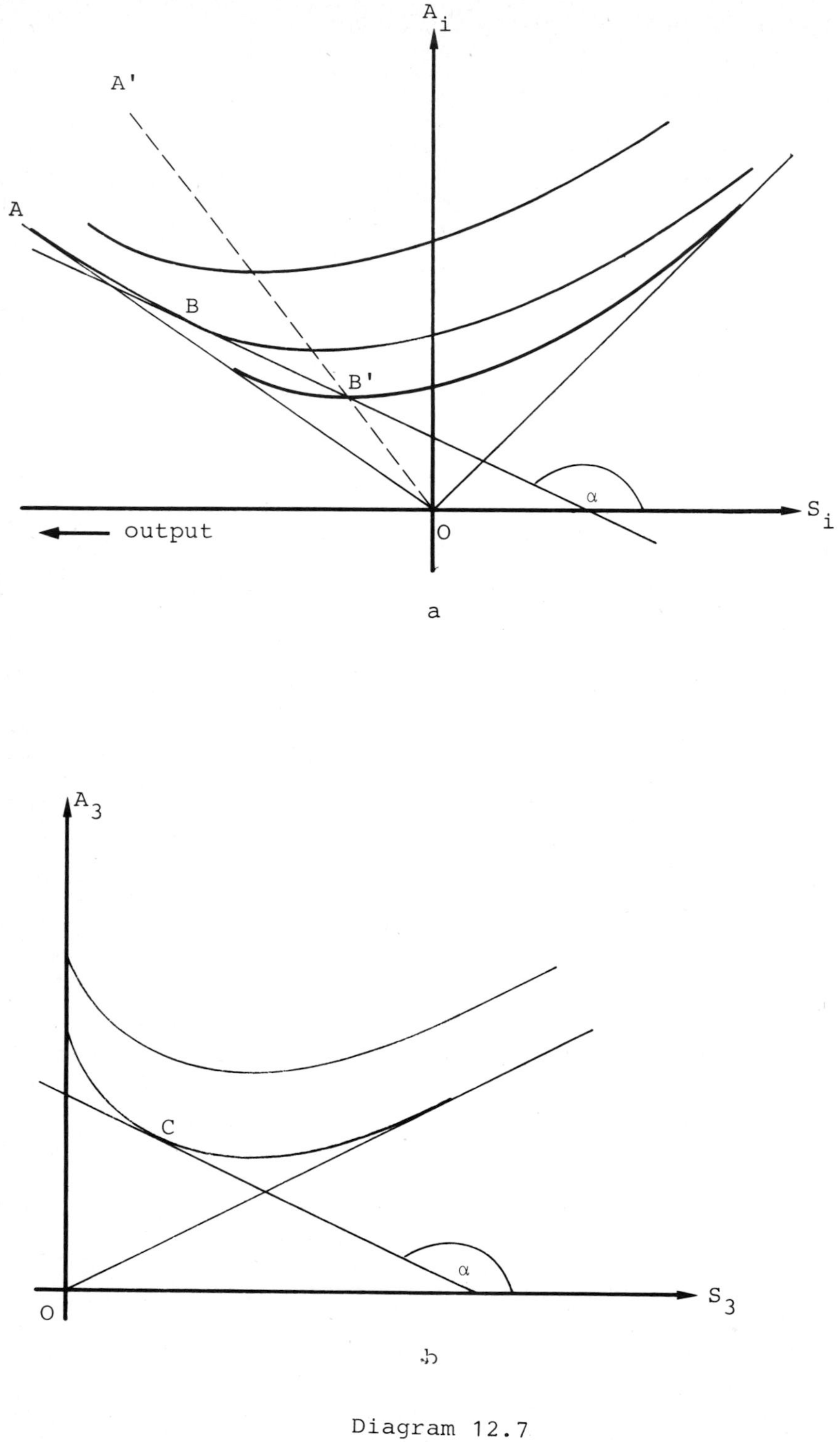

Diagram 12.7

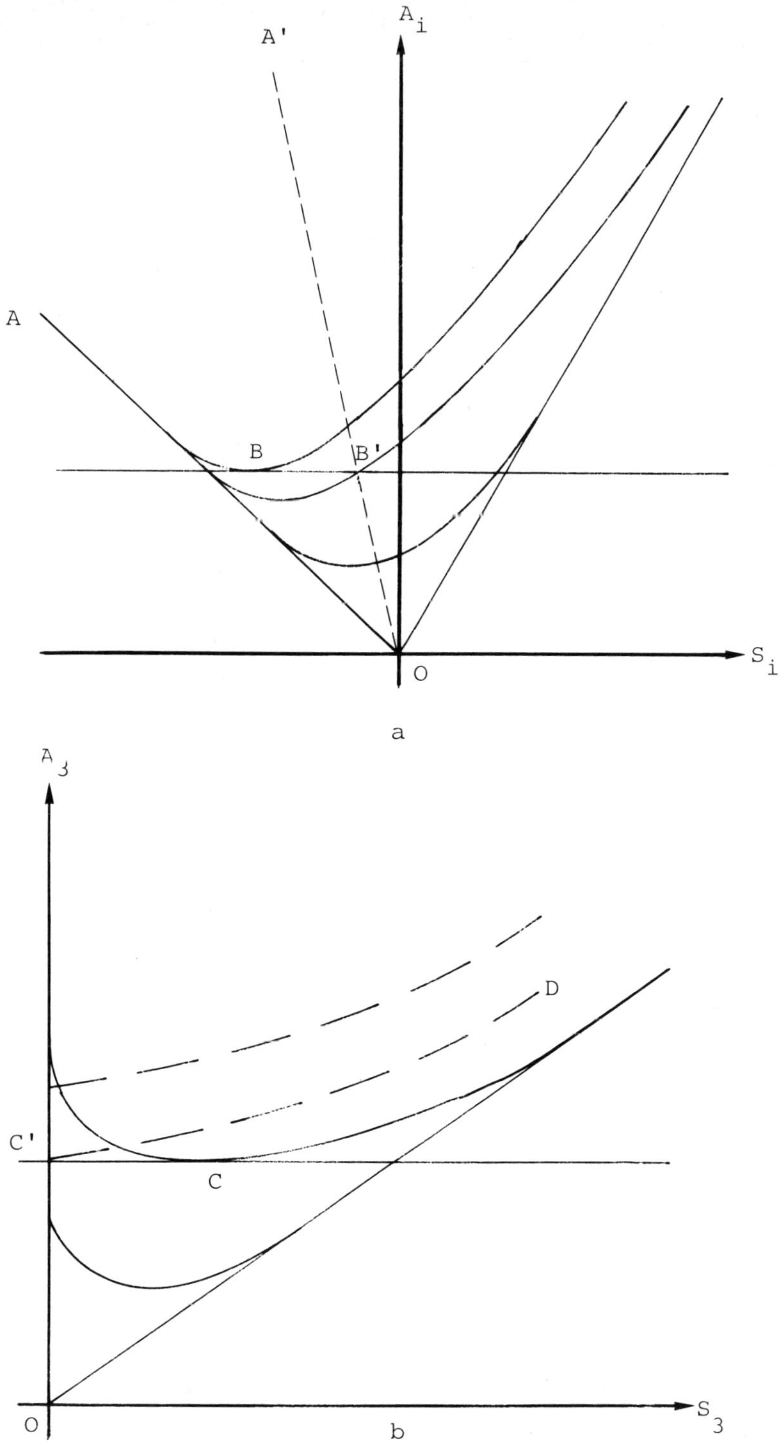

Diagram 12.8

If, on the other hand, there is a solution (a^+, α^+) of 12.16 with $s^+ > 0$, then $\alpha^{4+} = 0$ by 12.17. Now two cases have to be distinguished. Suppose first, that $\alpha^o = 0$, i.e., that the emission standard S^S is not (or only weakly) binding. Then $\alpha^{s+} = \alpha^{o+} = 0$ by 12.17 and hence $p_S = 0$. Hence (a^+, p) is a laissez-faire equilibrium with environmental disruption. This situation is illustrated with the help of the diagrams 12.8a and 12.8b. It is easy to see that recycling takes place in point C in the right part of diagram 12.7b. But this result depends very much on the efficiency of recycling relative to the primary material production. Technically speaking, it presupposes that the isoquants are downward sloping at least on a subset of D_{F3}. If primary material production strongly dominates the recycling technology, then no material is recycled in a laissez-faire equilibrium. This possibility is indicated in diagram 12.8b by the point C' assuming that the dotted line C'D represents an isoquant of F^3.

We now consider the alternative that the constraint $S^S - s^+$ is active in the sense that $\alpha^{o+} > 0$. Then $\alpha^{s+} = \alpha^{o+} > 0$ and $p_S < 0$. The negative price p_S, the emission tax, does not emerge in the unregulated market but must be enforced either as an emission tax or by restricting pollution licenses[1].

We now consider the case that (a^+, α^+) is a solution to the problem 12.15 such that $s^+ > 0$. Again we obtain $\alpha^{4+} = 0$ but now 12.17 yields $\alpha^{s+} = -\alpha^u + G_S^+$, $\alpha^{u+} = W_u^+$ and hence

$$p_S = -\alpha^{s+} = +W_u^+G_S^+ = p_iF_S^{i+} < 0 \quad (i = 1,2,3).$$

$W_u^+G_S^+$ is the (partial) welfare loss resulting from the discharge of an additional unit of secondary material (= waste). If the emission tax is set equal to this welfare loss (evaluated at the allocation a^+!) then the welfare maximum is attained.

A (partial) graphical representation of a price and standard equilibrium with a strictly binding standard is given in

1) See also section 7.1.

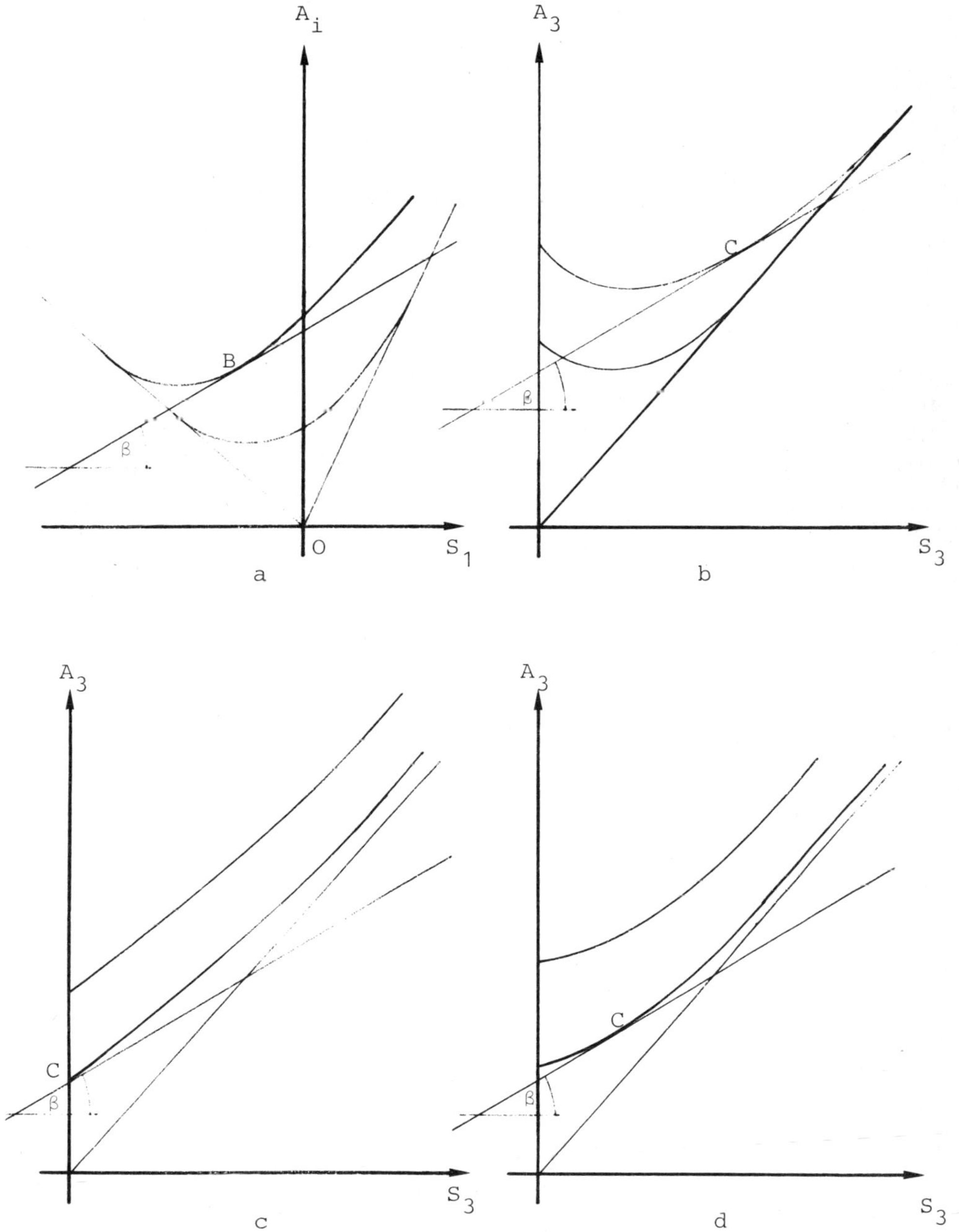

Diagram 12.9

diagram 12.9. Point B in diagram 12.9a shows that in the production process of the consumption good i = 1,2 we have $F_S^{i+} < 0$. Diagrams 12.9b, c and d illustrate alternative constellations of material production, where recycling may or may not occur. Observe, that opposite to the situation in a laissez-faire equilibrium material may (but need not) be reclaimed from secondary material even if the primary material production strongly dominates the recycling technology (diagram 12.9d). This can be the more expected the higher the emission tax in absolute value.

12.4 Comparative Statics of the Closed Economy

12.4.1 Reformulation of the Model

The basis of our comparative static analysis is a price and standard equilibrium of the recycling economy as it is established by theorem 12.1[1]. In order to apply the so-called "hat calculus", we first modify and slightly strengthen the assumptions A 12.1, A 12.2 and A 12.4 as follows:

A 12.5 Linear homogeneity of production functions.
The functions F^i, i = 1,2,3 are linear homogeneous and strictly quasi-concave (and hence concave).

A 12.6 Initial factor endowments.
For analytical convenience we specify the economy's endowments as follows: $A_o > 0$, $M_o = 0$ and $S_o > 0$.

A 12.7 Social welfare function.
The function W is strictly quasi-concave.

Under the assumption A 12.7 there exist demand functions $D^i : \mathbb{R}_+^3 \rightarrow \mathbb{R}_+$, i = 1,2, where $Q_i^d = D^i\,(p_{21}, Y, U)$, i =1,2, is the amount of consumption good i demanded by the consumption sector, when the price ratio is $p_{21} := p_2/p_1$, the income (measured in units of good 1) is $Y := Q_1 + p_{21}Q_2$ and when the environmental quality U prevails.
For analytical convenience we use the demand functions D^i

1) This implies, in particular, that (A_i, M_i, S_i) for i = 1,2 and (A_3, S_3) are interior points of the domains D_{Fi}, i = 1,2,3, respectively.

in the following instead of the welfare function W. This substitution of W by D^i does not change the model discussed so far except that assumption A 12.4 is strengthened by A 12.7.

With these additional assumptions we are able to reformulate and to completely represent the recycling model by the subsequent equations 12.21 to 12.31.

There are three price equations[1]

$$a_{Ai}p_A + a_{Mi}p_M + a_{Si}p_S = p_i, \tag{12.21}$$

$$a_{A3}p_A + a_{S3}p_S = p_M, \tag{12.22}$$

where sectoral input and emission coefficients, respectively, are defined as in the previous chapters by

$$a_{Vi} := \frac{V_i}{Q_i} \text{ for } V = A,M,S \text{ and } a_{V3} := \frac{V_3}{M_3} \text{ for } V = A,S.$$

There are four quantity equations

$$a_{M1}Q_1 + a_{M2}Q_2 = M_3, \tag{12.23}$$

$$a_{A1}Q_1 + a_{A2}Q_2 + a_{A3}M_3 = A_o, \tag{12.24}$$

$$a_{S1}Q_1 + a_{S2}Q_2 + a_{S3}M_3 - S_o - S, \tag{12.25}$$

$$\tilde{S} := S^S - S \geq 0. \tag{12.26}$$

In equation 12.26 we require that the aggregate excess supply of secondary material (bound to be discharged into the environment) must not exceed the exogenously given emission standard S^S. $\tilde{S}$ is a slack variable defined by 12.26.

Under the assumptions A 12.1 to A 12.7 the coefficients a_{Vj} ($V = A,M,S$ and $j = 1,2,3$; $a_{Vj} \neq a_{M3}$) are determined by eight functions A_{Vj} such that

$$a_{Vi} = A_{Vi}\,(p_A,\ p_M,\ p_S) \quad \text{for } V = A,\ M,\ S, \tag{12.27}$$

$$a_{V3} = A_{V3}\,(p_A,\ p_S) \quad \text{for } V = A,S \tag{12.28}$$

---

1) In the following subsections the index i always covers i = 1,2 unless a different rule is explicitly indicated.

are the minimal input requirement or secondary material outputs, respectively, per unit of consumption good or material output. Further we have to require market clearing on the consumption good markets[1),]

$$Q_i = Q_i^d \tag{12.29}$$

as well as the aggregate budget constraint being satisfied as an equality,

$$Y = Q_1^d + p_{21}Q_2^d, \tag{12.30}$$

where[2)] $Y := p_{A1}A_o + p_{S1}(S_o - S)$

Considering, finally, the environmental quality function G from A 2.5 we complete the description of our model by the two equations

$$Q_i^d = D^i\,[p_{21}, Y, G(S)]. \tag{12.31}$$

Thus the equation system 12.21 to 12.31 contains twenty one equations and the twenty one variables p_i, p_V, $a_{Vj} \neq a_{M3}$, Q_i, Q_i^d, M_3, Y, S and $\tilde{S}$ (for V = A, M, S; je = 1, 2, 3; i = 1, 2).

12.4.2 Changes in Relative Prices

We apply the "hat" calculus to the price equations 12.21 and 12.22 and write

$$\rho_{Ai}\hat{p}_A + \rho_{Mi}\hat{p}_M + \rho_{Si}\hat{p}_S = \hat{p}_i - [\rho_{Ai}\hat{a}_{Ai} + \rho_{Mi}\hat{a}_{Mi} + \rho_{Si}\hat{a}_{Si}], \tag{12.32}$$

$$\rho_{A3}\hat{p}_A + \rho_{S3}\hat{p}_S = \hat{p}_M - [\rho_{A3}\hat{a}_{A3} + \rho_{S3}\hat{a}_{S3}], \tag{12.33}$$

where $\rho_{Ai} := \alpha_{Ai}p_{Ai}$, $\rho_{S3} := a_{S3}p_{SM}$ etc.

Cost minimization as a necessary condition of profit maximization implies that the bracketed terms in 12.32 and 12.33

1) The equilibrium conditions for the labour, material and secondary material markets are already incorporated into the equations 12.23, 12.24 and 12.26.
2) Emission tax revenues and profits are redistributed to the households. But note that maximum profits are zero due to assumption A 12.5.

vanish. We solve 12.32 for $\hat{p}_M$, substitute $\hat{p}_M$ in 12.33 and obtain

$$\Theta_{Ai}\hat{p}_A + \Theta_{Si}\hat{p}_S = \hat{p}_i, \tag{12.34}$$

where for V = A, S

$$\Theta_{Vi} := \rho_{V3}\rho_{Mi} + \rho_{Vi} = r_{Vi}p_{Vi} \text{ with } r_{Vi} := a_{V3}a_{Mi} + a_{Vi}.$$

r_{Ai} is the gross labour coefficient in the production of the consumption good i. It has to be strictly distinguished from a_{Ai}, the net labour coefficient. The analogue distinction applies to r_{Si} and a_{Si}, the gross and net secondary material coefficients, respectively. Recalling the sign restrictions for A_i, S_i, Q_i and M_3 it is easy to see that for V = A, S we have $r_{Vi} \geq a_{Vi}$.

We now subtract 12.34 for i = 1 from 12.34 for i = 2 which yields

$$\hat{p}_{21} = |\Theta|\hat{p}_{SA}, \tag{12.35}$$

$$\text{where } |\Theta| := \begin{vmatrix} \Theta_{A1} & \Theta_{S1} \\ \Theta_{A2} & \Theta_{S2} \end{vmatrix} = \Theta_{A1} - \Theta_{A2} = \Theta_{S2} - \Theta_{S1},$$

$$\hat{p}_{21} := \widehat{\left(\frac{p_2}{p_1}\right)} = \hat{p}_2 - \hat{p}_1 \text{ and } \hat{p}_{SA} := \widehat{\left(\frac{p_S}{p_A}\right)} = \hat{p}_S - \hat{p}_A.$$

<u>Lemma 12.3:</u> Let $p_S \neq 0$. Then $p_S\ |\Theta| \gtrless 0$

(i) if and only if $x_g^2 \gtrless x_g^1$,

(ii) if $x_n^2 \gtrless x_n^1$, $x_n^i \leq 0$, and $\dfrac{a_{M2}}{a_{A2}} \begin{Bmatrix} \geq \\ \leq \end{Bmatrix} \dfrac{a_{M1}}{a_{A1}}$,

$$\text{where } x_g^i := \frac{r_{Si}}{r_{Ai}} \text{ and } x_n^i := \frac{a_{Si}}{a_{Ai}}.$$

Proof: Lemma 12.3i follows immediately from

$$|\Theta| = \Theta_{A1}\Theta_{S2} - \Theta_{A2}\Theta_{S1} = \frac{p_A p_S}{p_1 p_2}(r_{A1}r_{S2} - r_{A2}r_{S1}) =$$

$$= \frac{p_A p_S}{p_1 p_2} (X_g^2 - X_g^1) \, r_{A1} r_{A2}.$$

For the proof of lemma 12.3ii we make use of the definitions of r_{Si} and r_{Ai}:

$$(r_{A1} r_{S2} - r_{A2} r_{S1}) = a_{A1} a_{A2} (X_n^2 - X_n^1) + a_{A2} a_{A3} a_{M1} (X_n^2 - \frac{a_{S3}}{a_{A3}}) + a_{A1} a_{A3} a_{M2} (\frac{a_{S3}}{a_{A3}} - X_n^1) = a_{A1} a_{A2} (X_n^2 - X_n^1) + a_{A1} a_{A2} a_{S3} (\frac{a_{M2}}{a_{A2}} - \frac{a_{M1}}{a_{A1}}) + a_{A1} a_{A2} a_{A3} (X_n^2 \frac{a_{M1}}{a_{A1}} - X_n^1 \frac{a_{M2}}{a_{A2}}).$$

The ratios $\frac{a_{Mi}}{a_{Ai}}$ are non-negative. Hence the right-hand side of the above equation is positive under the conditions listed in lemma 12.3ii.

q.e.d

Before we give some economic interpretations to the result of lemma 12.3, let us reconsider the coefficients a_{Si} and r_{Si}. Obviously recycling occurs if and only if $r_{Si} - a_{Si} > 0$. Hence one can look at r_{Si} as the "gross excess demand for secondary material per unit of commodity i produced", where according to the usual sign convention negative values indicate a (proper) excess supply. This excess demand r_{Si} is composed of a_{Si}, sector i's per unit supply of the by-product secondary material, and sector i's per unit demand $a_{S3} a_{Mi}$ which it indirectly exerts via its material demand M_i.

In contrast to one-resource models in earlier chapters there are now two different ways to compare the production sectors' generation of secondary material. One can either compare the gross secondary material intensities X_g^i or the net secondary material intensities X_n^i. We say that the production of good 1 is more gross [net] secondary material intensive, if $X_g^1 < X_g^2$ [$X_n^1 < X_n^2$]. Observe that r_{Si} and hence X_g^i may be positive. In such a case the secondary material intensity is a proper factor intensity and not equivalent to the notion of emission intensity. If, however, $r_{S1} + r_{S2} < 0$, then it follows from $X_g^1 < X_g^2$ that sector 1 is more emission intensive than sector 2.

According to lemma 12.3 the ranking of the gross secondary material intensities of the two sectors uniquely determines the sign of $p_S|\Theta|$, whereas the ranking of the net intensities X_n^1 is neither necessary nor sufficient for the sign of the difference $X_g^1 - X_g^2$. This result can be qualitatively compared to that of Batra and Casas (1973, p. 304), who showed that the rankings of goods according to their gross and net factor intensities do not generally coincide in economies with pure intermediate goods[1].

On the other hand, their results differ from lemma 12.3 in two major aspects: The sufficient conditions given in lemma 12.3ii for identical rankings of gross and net intensities are not equivalent and, furthermore, the sign of $|\Theta|$ does not only depend on the gross intensities ranking in our model, but also on the sign of p_S.

Observe, however, that in spite of (or rather: due to) the sign switching variable p_S the relative price p_{21} is a strictly monotone (and hence invertible) function of p_{SA}, whose elasticity is given by $|\Theta|$ in equation 12.35. In order to show this, suppose that sector 1 is relatively secondary material intensive ($X_g^1 < X_g^2$). Then p_{21} is a strictly monotone increasing function of p_{SA} independent of the sign of p_S, since by lemma 12.3 and by equation 12.35 we have

$$\frac{dp_{21}}{dp_{SA}} = \frac{\hat{p}_{21}}{\hat{p}_{SA}} \frac{p_{SA}}{p_{21}} = \frac{p_S|\Theta|}{p_A p_{21}} > 0.$$

Another interdependency between relative prices follows from

1) The differences between lemma 12.3ii and Batra's and Casas's result can be traced back to the by-product property of secondary material. Note also, that r_{Si} may be non-positive. If $p_S > 0$, at most one of the coefficients r_{Si} is negative. But it will be shown that the sign of r_{Si} has no influence on many results.

solving 12.33 for $\hat{p}_A$ and substituting $\hat{p}_A$ in 12.32. Since the bracketed terms in the equations 12.32 and 12.33 are equal to zero one obtains

$$\frac{\theta_{Ai}}{\rho_{A3}}\hat{p}_M + \frac{(\rho_{A3}\rho_{Si} - \rho_{S3}\rho_{Ai})}{\rho_{A3}}\hat{p}_S = \hat{p}_i. \qquad (12.36)$$

Equations 12.21 and 12.22 yield $\rho_{Ai} + \rho_{Mi} + \rho_{Si} = 1$ as well as $\rho_{A3} + \rho_{S3} = 1$ such that the bracketed term in 12.36 is equal to $(\theta_{Si} - \rho_{S3})$. We introduce this term into equation 12.36, substract 12.36 for i = 2 from 12.36 for i = 1 to end up with

$$\hat{p}_{21} = \frac{|\theta|}{\rho_{A3}}\hat{p}_{SM}, \qquad (12.37)$$

When this result is combined with 12.35 one also obtains

$$\hat{p}_{SA} = \frac{1}{\rho_{A3}}\hat{p}_{SM} \qquad (12.38)$$

Since $\rho_{A3} > 0$, equation 12.38 spells out the significant property that changes in the relative price of secondary material have the same sign independent of choosing labour or material as a numéraire.

12.4.3 Comparative Statics of the Supply Side

We now investigate some implications of the equations 12.23 to 12.28. Solving 12.23 for M_3 and substituting M_3 into 12.24 and 12.25 yields for V = A, S

$$r_{V1}Q_1 + r_{V2}Q_2 = V_\omega \quad \text{and} \qquad (12.39)$$

$$\lambda_{V1}\hat{r}_{V1} + \lambda_{V2}\hat{r}_{Vs} + \lambda_{V1}\hat{Q}_1 + \lambda_{V2}\hat{Q}_2 = \hat{V}_\omega, \qquad (12.40)$$

where $A_\omega := A_o$, $S_\omega := S_o - S$, $\hat{A}_\omega = \hat{A}_o$,

$$\hat{S}_\omega = \frac{S_o}{S_\omega}\hat{S}_o - \frac{S}{S_\omega}\hat{S} \quad \text{and} \quad \lambda_{Vi} := \frac{r_{Vi}Q_i}{V_\omega}.$$

With the help of the equations 12.27 and 12.28 it can be shown similarly as in Batra (1973, p. 199 n) that

$$\left.\begin{aligned}\hat{a}_{Ai} &= (\rho_{Si}\sigma^i_{SA} + \rho_{Mi}\rho_{S3}\sigma^i_{AM})\ \hat{p}_{SA},\\ \hat{a}_{Mi} &= (\rho_{Si}\rho_{A3}\sigma^i_{SM} - \rho_{Ai}\rho_{S3}\sigma^i_{AM})\ \hat{p}_{SA},\\ \hat{a}_{Si} &= -\ (\rho_{Ai}\sigma^i_{SA} + \rho_{Mi}\rho_{A3}\sigma^i_{SM})\ \hat{p}_{SA},\end{aligned}\right\} \tag{12.41}$$

$$\left.\begin{aligned}\hat{a}_{S3} &= -\ \rho_{A3}\sigma_3\hat{p}_{SA},\\ \hat{a}_{A3} &= \rho_{S3}\sigma_3\hat{p}_{SA},\end{aligned}\right\} \tag{12.42}$$

$$\hat{r}_{Ai} = \frac{\alpha_i + \beta_i}{\theta_{Ai}}\ \hat{p}_{SA} \quad \text{and} \quad \hat{r}_{Si} = -\ \frac{\alpha_i + \beta_i}{\theta_{Si}}\ \hat{p}_{SA}, \tag{12.43}$$

where in 12.42 $\sigma^3 := \dfrac{d\left(\dfrac{a_{A3}}{a_{S3}}\right)}{\dfrac{a_{A3}}{a_{S3}}} \cdot \dfrac{dp_{SA}}{p_{SA}}$,

where in 12.43 $\beta_i := \rho_{S3}\rho_{A3}\rho_{Mi}\sigma_3$ and where

$$\alpha_i := \rho_{Si}\rho_{Ai}\sigma^i_{SA} + \rho^2_{A3}\rho_{Si}\rho_{Mi}\sigma^i_{SM} + \rho^2_{S3}\rho_{Ai}\rho_{Mi}\sigma^i_{AM}.$$

σ^3 denotes the elasticity of substitution between labour and secondary material in the recycling sector and σ^i_{AM}, σ^i_{SM}, σ^i_{SA} are partial elasticities of substitution[1] in sector i.

It follows from the equations 12.41 to 12.43 and from 12.38 that

$$\hat{x}^i_g = -\ \frac{\alpha_i + \beta_i}{\rho_{A3}\theta_{Ai}\theta_{Si}}\ \hat{p}_{SM} = -\ \frac{\alpha_i + \beta_i}{\theta_{Ai}\theta_{Si}}\ \hat{p}_{SA} \tag{12.44}$$

$$\hat{x}^i_n = -\ [\ (\rho_{Ai} + \rho_{Si})\ \sigma^i_{SA} + \rho_{Mi}\ (\rho_{A3}\sigma^i_{SM} + \rho_{S3}\sigma^i_{AM})]\ \hat{p}_{SM}, \tag{12.45}$$

$$\hat{x}^3 := \hat{a}_{S3} - \hat{a}_{A3} = -\ \frac{\sigma_3}{\rho_{A3}}\ \hat{p}_{SM}. \tag{12.46}$$

The equations 12.46, 12.44, 12.37 and 12.38 are illustrated by the diagrams 12.10. In both cases we assumed that good 1 is

1) For the definition of these elasticities see Allen (1938, p. 503 n).

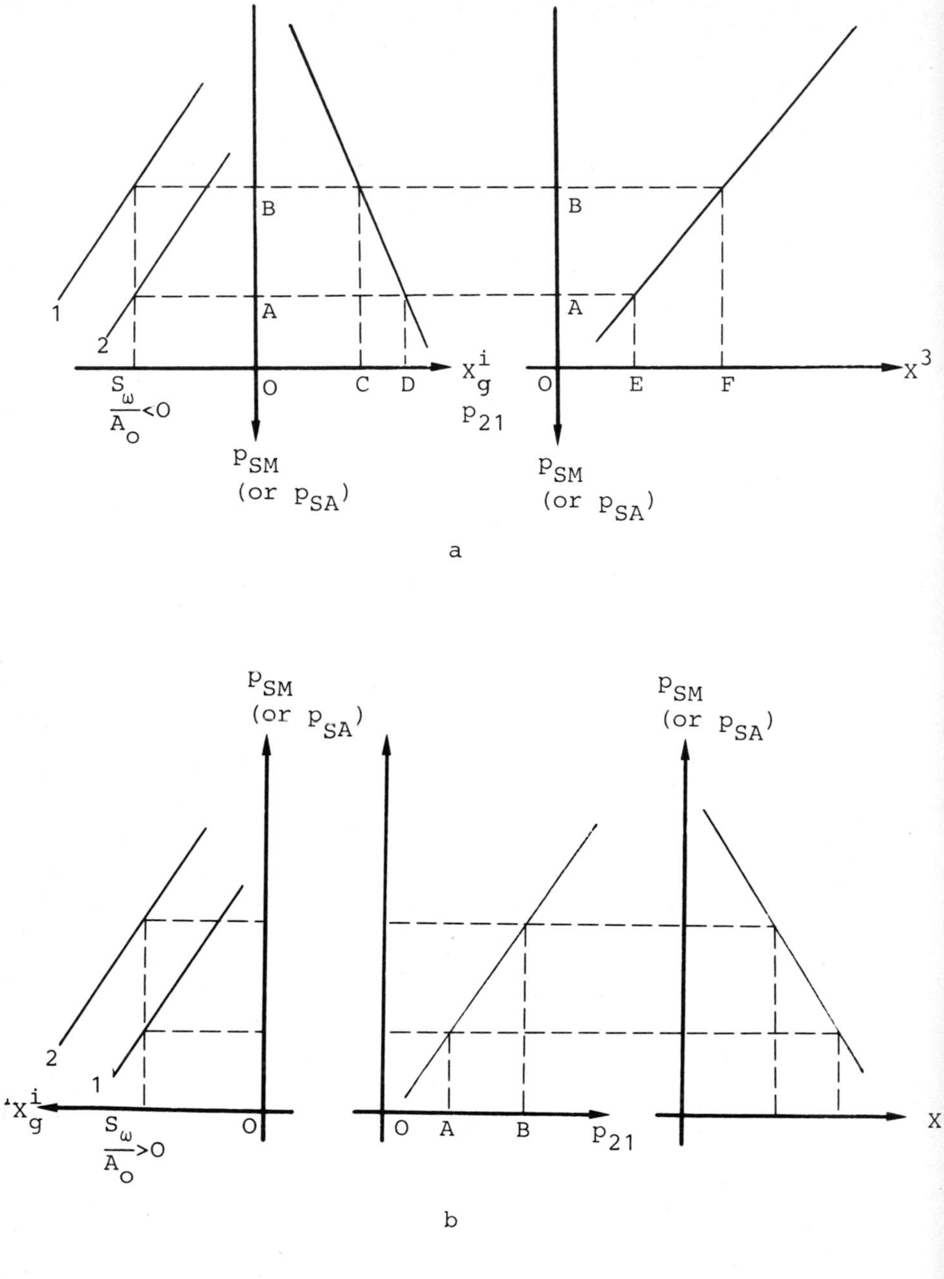

Diagram 12.10

secondary material intensive ($X_g^1 < X_g^2$) and that $p_S r_{Si} > 0$ for $i = 1, 2$.

Diagram 12.10a illustrates the supply side of an economy in which $X_g^i < 0$ for $i = 1, 2$ in the relevant range and where consequently, an emission tax ($p_{SM} < 0$) should be levied. The right-hand part of diagram 12.10a shows how the secondary material intensity $X^3 := a_{S3}/a_{A3}$ in the material production process increases when the emission tax increases in absolute value. In order to determine the slope of this curve, we have to know the sign of σ^3. We show in the proof of lemma 12.4 below that $p_S\sigma_3 > 0$. Hence $\sigma_3 < 0$ and $dX^3/dp_{SM} < 0$, if $p_S < 0$ (as depicted in diagram 12.9a). If in the economy of diagram 12.10a an emission standard $S^S > S_o$ is implemented, then the ratio of "factor endowments", S_ω/A_o is negative (as plotted into diagram 12.10), we know that the equilibrium price ratios p_{SM} and p_{21} can be found in the intervals AB and CD, respectively.

In diagram 12.10b good 3 is implicitly assumed to be a pure intermediate good. This diagram shows a situation where $0 < X_g^1 < X_g^2$, $p_S > 0$ and hence $|\Theta| > 0$ and $\sigma^3 > 0$.

We now continue our analysis by using equations 12.43 in order to write for equations 12.40

$$\gamma_A \hat{p}_{SA} + \lambda_{A1}\hat{Q}_1 + \lambda_{A2}\hat{Q}_2 = \hat{A}_o \quad \text{and} \tag{12.47}$$

$$-\gamma_S \hat{p}_{SA} + \lambda_{S1}\hat{Q}_1 + \lambda_{S2}\hat{Q}_2 = \hat{S}_\omega, \tag{12.48}$$

where for $V = A, S$ $\quad \gamma_V := \Sigma_i \dfrac{\lambda_{Vi}(\alpha_i + \beta_i)}{\theta_{Vi}}$.

<u>Lemma 12.4:</u> $\gamma_A > 0$ and $[p_S S_\omega > 0 \Rightarrow \gamma_S > 0]$

Proof: $\gamma_A > 0$ if $(\alpha_i + \beta_i) > 0$ for $i = 1, 2$. $\alpha_i > 0$ and $\beta_i > 0$ can be proved essentially as in Batra (1973, p. 199 n) taking into account that, in contrast to Batra's case, the signs of the variables ρ_{Sj} for $j = 1, 2, 3$ are unrestricted. $\alpha_i > 0$ follows if in Batra's proof (1973, p. 201) the inequality (written in our present notation)

$$\sigma_{SA}^{i} > \frac{-\rho_{Mi}\sigma_{SM}^{i}\sigma_{AM}^{i}}{\rho_{Si}\sigma_{SM}^{i} + \rho_{Ai}\sigma_{AM}^{i}} \text{ is substituted by}$$

$$\rho_{Si}\sigma_{SA}^{i} > \frac{-\rho_{Si}\rho_{Mi}\sigma_{SM}^{i}\sigma_{AM}^{i}}{\rho_{Si}\sigma_{SM}^{i} + \rho_{Ai}\sigma_{AM}^{i}} .$$

These two inequalities coincide, of course, for $\rho_{Si} > 0$.

$\beta_i > 0$ holds, since $\rho_{A3}\rho_{Mi} > 0$ and $\rho_{S3}\sigma_3 = -\rho_{A3}\sigma^3_{AA} > 0$[1].

From these results the remaining part of lemma 12.4 is straightforward.

q.e.d.

Our next step is to inquire into the change of the ratio of consumption good outputs as a result of changing emission tax, factor endowments or emission standard. We subtract equation 12.47 from equation 12.48 to get

$$\hat{Q}_2 - \hat{Q}_1 = \sigma_S |\Theta| \hat{p}_{SA} + \frac{1}{|\lambda|} (\hat{S}_\omega - \hat{A}_o), \tag{12.49}$$

where $|\lambda| := \begin{vmatrix} \lambda_{A1} & \lambda_{A2} \\ \lambda_{S1} & \lambda_{S2} \end{vmatrix} = \lambda_{S2} - \lambda_{A2} = \lambda_{A1} - \lambda_{S1}$

and where $\sigma_S := \dfrac{\partial (F^2/F^1)}{\partial p_{21}} \dfrac{p_{21}}{Q_2/Q_1} = \dfrac{\hat{Q}_2 - \hat{Q}_1}{\hat{p}_{21}} = \dfrac{\gamma_A + \gamma_S}{|\lambda| \; |\Theta|}$

according to Jones (1965) is called the elasticity of substitution between the goods 1 and 2 on the supply side.

Lemma 12.5: $|\lambda| \; |\Theta| > 0$ if and only if $|\Theta| \neq 0$ and $p_S S_\omega > 0$.

Proof: $|\lambda| = \dfrac{Q_1 Q_2}{A_o S_\omega} (r_{A1} r_{S2} - r_{A2} r_{S1}) = \dfrac{p_1 Q_1 p_2 Q_2}{p_A A_o p_S S_\omega} |\Theta|$.

q.e.d.

1) Compare also equation (A 8.8) in Batra (1973, p. 200). It is important to note that $\rho_{S3}\sigma^3 > 0$ if and only if $p_S \sigma^3 > 0$.

12.4.4 Comparative Statics of the Demand Side

The final step needed to study the full comparative statics of the model is to show the effects of changes in prices and endowments on the demand for consumption goods. From equation 12.31 that represents the demand side of the model we have

$$\hat{Q}_i^d = \eta_{ip}\hat{p}_{21} + \eta_{iY}\hat{Y} + \eta_{iU}\varepsilon_{US}\hat{S} \tag{12.50}$$

where $\eta_{iZ} := \dfrac{\partial D^i}{\partial Z}\dfrac{Z}{Q_i^d}$ for $Z = p\ (= p_{21})$, Y, U and

where $\varepsilon_{US} := \dfrac{dG}{dS}\dfrac{S}{U}$.

Combining the equations 12.31, 12.30 and 12.29 yields

$$\tau_1\eta_{1p} + \tau_2\eta_{2p} = -\tau_2, \tag{12.51}$$

$$\tau_1\eta_{1Y} + \tau_2\eta_{2Y} = 1, \tag{12.52}$$

$$\tau_1\eta_{1U} + \tau_2\eta_{2U} = 0, \tag{12.53}$$

$$\hat{Y} = \tau_1\hat{Q}_1 + \tau_2\hat{Q}_2 + \tau_2\hat{p}_{21}, \tag{12.54}$$

where $\tau_1 := \dfrac{Q_1}{Y}$, $\tau_2 := \dfrac{p_{21}Q_2}{Y}$ and $\tau_1 + \tau_2 = 1$.

We subtract equation 12.50 for i = 1 from equation 12.50 for i = 2 and consider 12.35 to obtain

$$\hat{Q}_2^d - \hat{Q}_1^d = -\sigma_D|\theta|\hat{p}_{SA} + (\eta_{2Y} - \eta_{1Y})\hat{Y} + \\ + (\eta_{2U} - \eta_{1U})\varepsilon_{US}\hat{S}, \tag{12.55}$$

where $\sigma_D := \dfrac{\partial(D^1/D^2)}{\partial p_{21}}\dfrac{p_{21}}{Q_1^d/Q_2^d} = \eta_{1p} - \eta_{2p} > 0$

is called the elasticity of demand substitution by Batra (1973, p. 26). One can also consider the equations 12.35, 12.54 and 12.29 in 12.50, so that

$$d_2\hat{Q}_2^d + d_1\hat{Q}_1^d - dp|\theta|\hat{p}_{SA} = \eta_{2U}\varepsilon_{US}\hat{S}, \tag{12.56}$$

where $d_i := \tau_1\eta_{jY}$ $(i,j = 1,2;\ i \neq j)$ and where $dp := \eta_{2p} + \tau_2\eta_{2Y} < 0$ is the negative pure substitution effect following from Slutsky's rule[1)].

12.4.5 Complete Comparative Statics

In 12.29 we assumed that the markets for the consumption goods have been cleared in the initial state. Since we also require market clearing in the final state we put $\hat{Q}_i^d = \hat{Q}_i$. Furthermore we restrict our analysis to situations where in the initial equilibrium either $p_{SA} > 0$ and hence $S = S^s = 0$ or $p_{SA} < 0$ and hence $S = S^s > 0$. Under these conditions we can substitute $\hat{S}$ in equation 12.56 by $\hat{S}^s$ (which is always zero if $p_{SA} > 0$), so that the equations 12.56, 12.48 and 12.47 completely determine the changes of p_{SA}, Q_1^d and Q_2^d that are caused by (very small) changes in A_o, S_o and S^s.[2)] These three equations are rearranged in equation 12.57

$$\begin{bmatrix} -d_1 & d_2 & -d_p|\theta| \\ \lambda_{S1} & \lambda_{S2} & -\gamma_S \\ \lambda_{A1} & \lambda_{A2} & \gamma_A \end{bmatrix} \begin{bmatrix} \hat{Q}_1^d \\ \hat{Q}_2^d \\ \hat{p}_{SA} \end{bmatrix} = \begin{bmatrix} \eta_{2U}\varepsilon_{US}\hat{S}^s \\ \hat{S}_\omega \\ \hat{A}_o \end{bmatrix} \tag{12.57}$$

The determinant of the matrix in 12.57 is

$$|A| := -(\Delta_A\gamma_S + \Delta_S\gamma_A - dp|\theta||\lambda|), \tag{12.58}$$

where $\Delta_v := d_1\lambda_{v2} + d_2\lambda_{v1}$ for $v = A, S$.
Applying Cramer's rule we obtain from 12.57

$$\hat{p}_{SA} = -\frac{1}{|A|}\left[\Delta_S\hat{A}_o - \frac{\Delta_A S_o}{S_\omega}\hat{S}_o + \left(\frac{\Delta_A S^s}{S_\omega} + |\lambda|\eta_{2U}\varepsilon_{US}\right)\hat{S}^s\right] \tag{12.59}$$

---

1) Compare section 3.3.
2) If $p_{SA} < 0$, then we take the changes in emission standard, $\hat{S}^s$, as the (exogenous) environmental policy variable while $\hat{p}_{SA}$ is treated as an endogenous variable. However, one could also interchange the rôle of the variables $\hat{p}_{SA}$ and $\hat{S}^s$, as is done in part 2 and in chapter 11 of this book.

$$\hat{Q}_1^d = -\frac{1}{|A|}\{-[\eta_{2U}\varepsilon_{US}(\lambda_{S2}\gamma_A + \lambda_{A2}\gamma_S) + \frac{S^s}{S_\omega}(\lambda_{A2}d_p|\theta| + \gamma_A d_2)]\hat{S}^s$$

$$- (\lambda_{S2}d_p|\theta| - \gamma_S d_2)\hat{A}_o + [\frac{S_o}{S_\omega}(\lambda_{A2}d_p|\theta| + \gamma_A d_2]\hat{S}_o\} \quad (12.60)$$

$$\hat{Q}_2^d = -\frac{1}{|A|}\{[\eta_{2U}\varepsilon_{US}(\lambda_{A1}\gamma_S + \lambda_{S1}\gamma_A) - \frac{S^s}{S_\omega}(d_1\gamma_A - \lambda_{A1}d_p|\theta|)]\hat{S}^s +$$

$$+ (\lambda_{S1}d_p|\theta| + \gamma_S d_1)\hat{A}_o + [\frac{S_o}{S_\omega}(d_1\gamma_A - \lambda_{A1}d_p|\theta|)]\hat{S}_o\} \quad (12.61)$$

We are now in the position to state several interesting results in

Theorem 12.2: Let the assumptions A 12.1 to A 12.8 hold and let the initial price and standard equilibrium (a,p) satisfy

C 1: (A_i, M_i, S_i) for i = 1,2 and (A_3, S_3) are interior points of D_{Fi} for i = 1,2,3, respectively;

C 2: $p_S S_\omega > 0$, $r_{Si}S_\omega \geq 0$ and $X_g^1 \neq X_g^2$

C 3: $\eta_{iY} \geq 0$.

(i) [Strictly binding emission standard]. Then for $p_S < 0$ and i,j = 1,2 (i ≠ j) we have

$$\frac{\hat{p}_{SA}}{\hat{S}^s} < 0 \text{ and } \frac{\hat{p}_{ij}}{\hat{S}^s} < 0, \text{ if } X_g^i < X_g^j \text{ and } \eta_{iU} \geq 0$$

$$\frac{\hat{Q}_i^d}{\hat{S}^s} > 0 \text{ and sign } \frac{\hat{Q}_j^d}{\hat{S}^s} \text{ undetermined,}$$

$$\text{if } X_g^i < X_g^j \text{ and } \eta_{iU} \leq 0$$

$$\frac{\hat{p}_{SA}}{\hat{A}_o}, \frac{\hat{p}_{SA}}{\hat{S}_o} > 0$$

(ii) [No environmental disruption]. Then for $p_S > 0$

$$\frac{\hat{p}_{SA}}{\hat{A}_o} > 0 \text{ and } \frac{\hat{p}_{SA}}{\hat{S}_o} < 0$$

$$\frac{\hat{p}_{SA}}{\hat{\delta}} \gtrless 0, \text{ if } X_g^1 \lesseqgtr X_g^2 \quad \text{for } \hat{\delta} := \hat{A}_o = \hat{S}_o;$$

$$\frac{\hat{p}_{21}}{\hat{\delta}} > 0;$$

$$\left.\begin{array}{l} \dfrac{\hat{Q}_i^d}{\hat{A}_o} > 0, \text{ if } X_g^i < X_g^j \\[2em] \dfrac{\hat{Q}_i^d}{\hat{S}_o} > 0, \text{ if } X_g^i > X_g^j \end{array}\right\} \quad (i,j = 1,2;\ i \neq j)$$

Proof: Conditions C 1, C 2 and C 3 are sufficient for $|A| < 0$. Then the theorem follows from equations 12.59 to 12.61 considering in particular the lemmata 12.3, 12.4 and 12.5.

q.e.d.

Conditions C 1, C 2 and C 3 do not appear to be very restrictive. C 1 is already used throughout this chapter, mainly for analytical convenience. It implies that the rate of recycling is greater than zero in the initial equilibrium. $p_S S_\omega > 0$ from C 1 covers the most interesting cases, namely, that $S_\omega = S_o > 0$ for $p_S > 0$ and $S_\omega = - S^s < 0$ for $p_S < 0$. In contrast, the condition $r_{Si} S_\omega \geq 0$ appears to exclude some non-pathological constellations. It is not only conceivable that $p_S < 0$ and $S_\omega < 0$ coincides with $r_{S1} > 0$ or $r_{S2} > 0$ but also that $p_S > 0$, $S_\omega > 0$ and $r_{S1} < 0$ occur simultaneously. The requirement of non-inferior consumption goods (C 3) shoul be acceptable; it already played an important rôle in part 2 of this book.

In theorem 12.2 we focussed our attention on some specific properties of the model. In particular, we left out those comparative-static results that are not determinate in sign under some economically interesting conditions. $(\hat{p}_{SA}/\hat{S}^s) < 0$

means that the emission tax has to be raised (in absolute value) if a more restrictive emission standard is to be implemented. One would consider this as the typical or normal reaction that is in agreement with intuition being trained in partial equilibrium analysis. As a sufficient condition for such a normal reaction it is required that the "environmental quality elasticity" of the demand for the emission intensive good must be non-positive: If the emission standard is strengthened (and hence the environmental quality raised) the consumption demand must not shift in favour of that good which is less emission intensive in its production. It is easy to see that such a demand shift would per se tend to reduce the aggregate emission such that with a sufficiently strong structural change of this kind it may well occur that an (exogenous) emission standard reduction requires to also reduce the emission tax (in absolute value). It is possible to give sufficient conditions for an anomalous reaction $(\hat{p}_{SA}/\hat{S}^s) > 0$ from equation 12.59, but we postpone this issue for the next theorem which will be slightly more restrictive in its presuppositions.

The result $(\hat{p}_{ij}/\hat{S}_s) < 0$ can be viewed as the normal reaction of relative commodity prices to an emission standard variation: The relative price of the emission intensive good increases if the demand does not shift away from that good as a consequence of a raise in environmental quality. Observe, however, that the quantity supplied and demanded of the emission intensive good may well increase if its relative price increases due to $\hat{S}^s < 0$. In various sections of this book the assumptions on the social welfare function have been more restrictive than the assumptions A 12.4 and A 12.7. In particular, it is standard and convenient from the technical point of view in pure trade theory to require the homotheticity property. This implies in turn that the condition

C 4: $\eta_{1Y} = \eta_{2Y} = 1$

holds. Consideration of this condition yields[1]:

1) Compare also R. Pethig (1979b, p. 133 n).

<u>Theorem 12.3:</u> Let C 4 in addition to the presuppositions of theorem 12.2 hold.

(i) [Strictly binding emission standard]. Then for $p_S < 0$, $S_o = 0$ and $i,j = 1,2$ $(i \neq j)$ we obtain

$$\frac{\hat{p}_{SA}}{\hat{A}_\omega}, \frac{\hat{p}_{S3}}{\hat{A}_\omega} > 0;$$

$$\frac{\hat{X}_g^i}{\hat{A}_\omega} \lesseqgtr 0, \text{ if and only if } r_{Si} \lesseqgtr 0;$$

$$\frac{\hat{Q}_2^d - \hat{Q}_1^d}{\hat{A}_\omega} \gtrless 0, \text{ if and only if } \begin{cases} X_g^2 \gtreqless X_g^1 \text{ and } \sigma_S \lesseqgtr \dfrac{1}{|\theta||\lambda|} \\ X_g^2 \gtreqless X_g^1 \text{ and } \sigma_S \gtreqless \dfrac{1}{|\theta||\lambda|} \end{cases}$$

$$\frac{\hat{p}_{21}}{\hat{A}_\omega} \gtreqless 0, \text{ if and only if } X_g^2 \lesseqgtr X_g^1;$$

$$\left.\begin{aligned} &\frac{\hat{p}_{SA}}{\hat{S}^s} < 0, \text{ if and only if} \\ &\frac{\hat{p}_{S3}}{\hat{S}^s} < 0, \text{ if} \end{aligned}\right\} [\varphi_1 \text{ or } \varphi_2];$$

$$\frac{\hat{X}_g^i}{\hat{S}^s} \gtreqless 0, \text{ if } [\varphi_1 \text{ or } \varphi_2] \text{ and } r_{Si} \gtreqless 0;$$

$$\frac{\hat{p}_{21}}{\hat{S}^s} \gtreqless 0, \text{ if } \begin{cases} \varphi_1 \\ \varphi_2 \end{cases};$$

$$\frac{\hat{Q}_2^d - \hat{Q}_1^d}{\hat{S}^s} < 0, \text{ if } [X_g^1 < X_g^2 \text{ and } \eta_{1U} > -\frac{\tau_2}{\varepsilon_{US}} < 0]$$

$$\text{or if } [X_g^2 < X_g^1 \text{ and } \eta_{2U} > \frac{\tau_1}{\varepsilon_{US}} < 0];$$

where φ_1 reads: "$X_g^1 < X_g^2$ and $\eta_{1U} > + \frac{\tau_2}{\varepsilon_{US}|\lambda|} > 0$" and

where φ_2 reads: "$X_g^2 < X_g^1$ and $\eta_{2U} > - \frac{\tau_1}{\varepsilon_{US}|\lambda|} > 0$".

(ii) [No environmental disruption]. Then for $p_S > 0$, $S_o > 0$ and $\hat{V} = S_o\hat{A}_o - \hat{S}_o, \hat{A}_o, - \hat{S}_o$ we have

$$\frac{\hat{p}_{SA}}{\hat{V}}, \frac{\hat{p}_{SA}}{\hat{V}} > 0;$$

$$\frac{\hat{X}_g^i}{\hat{V}} \lesseqgtr 0, \text{ if and only if } r_{Si} \gtreqless 0;$$

$$\frac{\hat{Q}_2^d - \hat{Q}_1^d}{\hat{V}} \gtreqless 0, \text{ if and only if } \begin{cases} X_g^2 \gtrless X_g^1 \text{ and } \sigma_S \gtrless \frac{1}{|\theta||\lambda|} \\ X_g^2 \gtrless X_g^1 \text{ and } \sigma_S \lessgtr \frac{1}{|\theta||\lambda|} \end{cases}$$

$$\frac{\hat{p}_{21}}{\hat{V}} \gtrless 0, \text{ if and only if } X_g^2 \gtrless X_g^1.$$

Proof: The condition for a new equilibrium after small exogenous changes of A_o or S^s is $\hat{Q}_2^d - \hat{Q}_1^d = \hat{Q}_2 - \hat{Q}_1$. Hence the right-hand sides of the equations 12.55 and 12.49 are equal. If, in addition, the assumption C 4 is considered, as well as $\hat{S}_\omega = - \hat{S}^s$ (for $S_o = 0$), we obtain

$$\hat{p}_{SA} = \frac{[|\lambda|(\eta_{2U} - \eta_{1U})\varepsilon_{US} + 1]\hat{S}^s + \hat{A}_o}{(\sigma_S + \sigma_D)|\theta||\lambda|} \qquad (12.58)$$

Under the assumptions of theorem 12.3i the denominator of the right-hand side of 12.58 is negative. Hence theorem 12.3i follows from 12.58 in combination with the equations 12.35, 12.38, 12.44, 12.53 and 12.55. On the other hand, the denominator of the right-hand side of 12.58 is positive under the presuppositions of theorem 12.3ii. Together with equations 12.35, 12.38, 12.44 and 12.49 theorem 12.3ii follows immediately.

q.e.d.

Our comment on theorem 12.3 will be concentrated on four aspects.

(1) Theorem 12.3i contains a far stronger statement about the relationship between p_{SA} and alternative emission standards than theorem 12.2. Given the other assumptions of theorem 12.3i, the conditions φ_1 or φ_2 are necessary and sufficient for the "normal reaction" of the relative emission tax p_{SA} with respect to changes in emission standards. Hence an atypical reaction occurs, whenever φ_1, φ_2 or both conditions are not satisfied. In other words, an atypical reaction follows, if a sufficiently strong shift of demand in favour of the less emission intensive good results from strengthening the emission standard.

(2) The observation on the sign of $(\hat{Q}_2^d - \hat{Q}_1^d)/\hat{V}$ in theorem 12.3ii is mainly derived from equation 12.55, whereas the sign of $(\hat{Q}_2^d - \hat{Q}_1^d)/\hat{S}^s$ in theorem 12.3i could be specified with the help of equation 12.49. The first condition for $[(\hat{Q}_2^d - \hat{Q}_1^d)/\hat{S}^s] < 0$ (in theorem 12.3i) differs only slightly from φ_2, which is sufficient for a "normal reaction" of $\hat{p}_{SA}$ on $\hat{S}^s \neq 0$. We consider this structural change as a typical reaction, since the production of the relative emission intensive sector diminishes in favour of the production of the other good when the emission standard becomes more restrictive (or when the emission tax is raised). But the opposite and atypical reaction is not excluded, in general: The less emission intensive sector may reduce its production following $\hat{S}^s < 0$, if (in theorem 12.3i) the value of η_{2U} is sufficiently small.

(3) The conclusions of theorem 12.3ii are relevant in the context of environmental economics even though no pollution occurs. It appears to be intuitively acceptable that according to theorem 12.3ii labour becomes cheaper relative to the pure intermediate product "secondary material", if A_o grows faster than S_o. But there are no evident economic reasons why $\hat{p}_{S3}/\hat{A}_o > 0$ in this situation. An important implication of this result is that a completely recycled secondary material never turns into a polluting waste product in a growing economy ($\hat{A}_o > 0$) without technical change.

(4) Theorems 12.3 and 12.2 contain various implications concerning the change of the recycling ratio as defined by equation 12.3. Recalling lemma 12.1iii and several applications and illustrations in section 12.4 we know that changes in the recycling ratio are closely linked to changes in the slope of the isoquant of the material production function (comparing the material production in the old and in the new equilibrium). In the case of strictly binding emission standards the recycling ratio always increases when the emission standard is strengthened, unless this ratio takes the value zero or one in the initial price and standard equilibrium.[1)]

12.5 Trade Implications

So far we investigated in chapter 12 the properties of a simple economy with material recycling. In its structure and results this model is much more complex than, for example, the basic model of chapters 7 and 8. We want to indicate, however, that trade implications in a world with recycling are, in principle, similar to those of chapter 8. To show this we first analyze the direction of trade flows between two recycling economies for the case that both countries implement price and standard systems with the help of theorem 12.3i and then compare our findings to theorem 8.3. For the sake of easy understanding we do not formally refer to the presuppositions of theorem 12.3 and leave off minor qualifications. Thus we obtain the following two statements on comparative advantage of trade in consumption goods:

(1) Suppose that both countries are identical except that the home country has a greater labour endowment. Then the foreign country exports and specializes on the production of the relatively emission-intensive good.

In order to see the close relationship between this proposition and theorem 8.3 we first observe that the statement (1) above is based on the condition $S^s/A_o < S^{s*}/A_o^*$, since $S^s = S^{s*}$ and $A_o > A_o^*$ is assumed. Moreover, if we take into account the (diverging) sign conventions for p_S as well as

1) Compare also the diagrams 12.9a - d and the remarks in connection with these diagrams.

$\hat{p}_{SA}/\hat{A}_{\omega} > 0$ from theorem 12.3 we conclude that statement (1) presupposes the inequality $|p_{SA}| > |p^*_{SA}|$ for relative emissio taxes in autarky. Therefore the proposition (1) implies that the price and standard system is more restrictive in the home country than in the foreign country according to the criteric of relative emission standards as well as to the criterion of relative emission taxes (definition D 8.1). For such a situation of "factor abundance" theorem 8.3 predicts that the hom country exports and specializes on the production of the less emission-intensive good. In this sense statement (1) is compatible with theorem 8.3.

(2) Suppose that both countries are identical except that the emission standard in the home country is less restrictive than in the foreign country ($S^s > S^{s*}$). Then the home country exports and specializes on the production of the relatively emission-intensive good.

This observation is again compatible with theorem 8.3. But note, that in theorem 12.3 only sufficient conditions for the "normal reaction" of commodity prices on changes of emission standards are given. One can find, therefore, parameter constellations in which the statement (2) does not hold.

In order to avoid excessive repetitiveness we contend ourselves with these remarks on comparative advantages. For the same reason we do not elaborate here on the analysis of allocative displacements of trading equilibria being caused by exogenous changes in endowments or emission standards. Such an analysis that has been carried through in previous chapter for different models is of particular relevance if one is interested in the impact of environmental management on the national and overall ratios of recycling in a trading world.

The model of chapter 12 is not only suitable to study trade in consumption goods but also trade in basic and secondary material[1]. Trade in these latter two products is of great empirical relevance, if the secondary material is a pure intermediate good commanding a positive price. Less obvious but conceptually interesting is the possibility of trading

1) This issue is discussed in detail by R. Pethig (1977b, p. 191 - 206).

negatively priced secondary material "against" positively priced basic material according to the rule of comparative advantage. In this case there turn out to be two unidirectional trade flows, i.e. one country exports detrimental secondary material and pays for this export by also exporting basic material. It is easy to show that such unusual trading activity is guided by mutual gains from trade.

Bibliography

Allen, R.G.D. (1938), Mathematical Analysis for Economists, New York

D'Arge, R.C. and A.V. Kneese (1972), Environmental Quality and International Trade, in: Kay, D.E. and E.B. Skolnikoff (eds.) (1972), World Eco Crisis 26, 419 - 465

Arrow, K.J. (1951), Social Choice and Individual Values, New York

Batra, R.N. (1973), Studies in the Pure Theory of International Trade, London

Batra, R.N. and F.R. Casas (1973), Intermediate Products and the Pure Theory of International Trade: A Neo-Heckscher-Ohlin Framework, in: American Economic Review 63, 297 - 311

Batra, R.N. and F.R. Casas (1976), A Synthesis of the Heckscher-Ohlin and the Neoclassical Models of International Trade, in: Journal of International Economics, 21 - 38

Baumol, W.J. (1971), Environmental Protection, International Spillovers and Trade, Stockholm

Baumol, W.J. (1972), On Taxation and the Control of Externalities, in: American Economic Review 62, 307 - 322

Baumol, W.J. and W.E. Oates (1971), The Use of Standards and Prices for the Protection of the Environment, in: Swedish Journal of Economics 73, 42 - 54

Baumol, W.J. and W.E. Oates (1975), The Theory of Environmental Policy, Englewood Cliffs, N. J.

Bower, B.T. (1977), Economic Dimensions of Waste Recycling and Re-use: Some Definitions, Facts and Issues, in: D.W. Pearce and I. Walter (eds.) (1977), Resource Conservation, Social and Economic Dimensions of Recycling, New York, 1 - 19

Casas, F.R. (1972), The Theory of Intermediate Products, Technical Change, and Growth, in: Journal of International Economics 2, 189 - 200

Caves, R.E. and R.W. Jones (1973), World Trade and Payments, An Introduction, Boston

Chipman, J.S. (1966), A Survey of the Theory of Internationa[l] Trade: Part III, The Modern Theory, in: Econometrica 34, 18 - 76

Chipman, J.S. (1971), International Trade with Capital Mobility: A Substitution Theorem, in: Bhagwati, J.N., R.W. Jones, R.W. Mundell, J. Vanek (eds.) (1971), Trade, Balance of Payments, and Growth, Amsterdam, London, 201 - 2[...]

Coase, R.H. (1960), The Problem of Social Cost, in: Journal of Law and Economics 3, 1 - 44

Dales, J.H. (1968), Pollution, Property and Prices, Toronto

Dorfman, R., P.A. Samuelson, and R. Solow (1958), Linear Programming and Economic Analysis, New York

Eichberger, J. (1978), Patterns of International Production with Capital Mobility, Beiträge zur angewandten Wirtschaftsforschung, Discussion Paper 108/78, Universität Mannheim

Fischer, G. (1975), Lineare Algebra, Reinbeck

Gandolfo, G. (1972), Mathematical Methods and Models in Economic Dynamics, Amsterdam, London, New York, 2nd printing

General Agreement on Tariffs and Trade (1971), Inustrial Pollution Control and International Trade, GATT Studies in International Trade 1, Genf

Gronych, R. (1980), Allokationseffekte und Außenhandelswirkungen der Umweltpolitik, forthcoming

Grubel, H.G. (1976), Some Effects of Environmental Controls on International Trade: The Heckscher-Ohlin Model, in: I. Walter (ed.) (1976)

Gutenberg, E. (1972), Grundlagen der Betriebswirtschaftslehre Band 1: Die Produktion, 19. Aufl., Berlin, Heidelberg, New York

Herberg, H. (1969), On the Shape of the Transformation Curve in the Case of Homogeneous Production Functions, in: Zeitschrift für die gesamte Staatswissenschaft 125, 202 - 210

Hildenbrand, W. (1966), Mathematische Grundlagen zur nichtlinearen Aktivitätsanalyse, in: Unternehmensforschung 10, 65 - 80

Intriligator, M.D., (1971), Mathematical Optimization and Economic Theory, Englewood Cliffs

Johnson, H.G. (1958), International Trade and Economic Growth, Studies in Pure Theory, London

Jones, R.W. (1965), The Structure of Simple General Equilibrium Models, in: Journal of Political Economy 73, 557 - 572

Jones, R.W. (1971), A Three-Factor Model in Theory, Trade, and History, in: J.N. Bhagwati, R.W.Jones, R.W. Mundell and J. Vanek (eds) (1971), Trade, Balance of Payments and Growth, Amsterdam, London, 3 - 21

Jones, R.W. and J.A. Scheinkman (1977), The Relevance of the Two-Sector-Production Model in Trade Theory, in: Journal of Political Economy 85, 909 - 935

Kapp, K.W. (1958), Volkswirtschaftliche Kosten der Privatwirtschaft, Tübingen

Kemp, M.C. (1969), The Pure Theory of International Investment and Trade, Englewood Cliffs

Klevorick, A.K. and G.H. Kramer (1973), Social Choice on Pollution Management: The Genossenschaften, in: Journal of Political Economy 2, 101 - 146

Kneese, A.V. (1964), The Economics of Regional Water Quality Management, Baltimore

Kneese, A.V. (1971), The Economics of Environmental Management in the United States, in: Kneese, A.V., S.E. Rolfe and J.W. Harned (eds.) (1971), Managing the Environment. International Economic Cooperation for Pollution Control, New York, 3 - 52

Kneese, A.V., R.U.Ayres and R.C. d'Arge (1970), Economics and the Environment: A Materials Balance Approach, Baltimore

Kneese, A.V. and B.T. Bower (1972), Die Wassergüterwirtschaft Wirtschaftstheoretische Grundlagen, Technologien, Institutionen, München

Koo, A.Y.C. (1974), Environmental Repercussions and Trade Theory, in: Review of Economics and Statistics 56, 235 - 2

Leontief, W. (1973), National Income, Economic Structure and Environmental Externalties, in: Moss, M. (ed.) (1973), The Measurement of Economic and Social Performance, National Bureau of Economic Research, New York, 565 - 579

Mäler, K.G. (1974), Environmental Economics: A Theoretical Inquiry, Baltimore

Magee, S.P. and W.F. Ford (1972), Environmental Pollution, the Terms of Trade and the Balance of Payments, in: Kyklos 25, 101 - 118

Majocchi, A. (1972), The Impact of Environmental Measures on International Trade, Rivista Internazionale di Scienze Economiche e Commerciali 19, 458 - 479

Meade, J.E. (1952), A Geometry of International Trade, London

Mishan, E.J. (1971), The Post-War Literature on Extrenalties: An Interpretative Essay, in: Journal of Economic Literature 9, 1 - 28

Van Moeseke, P. (1974), Constraint Maximization and Efficient Allocation, in: van Moeseke, P. (ed) (1974), Mathematical Programs for Activity Analysis, Amsterdam

Mutti, J.H. and J.D. Richardson (1976), Industrial Displacement Through Environmental Controls: The International Competitive Aspects, in: I. Walter, (ed.)(1976), 57 - 102

OECD (1972), Problems of Environmental Economics, Paris

Pearce, D.W. (1974), Fiscal Incentives and the Economics of Waste Recycling: Problems and Limitations, in: Institute for Fiscal Studies Conference on Fiscal Policy, IFS, London, 83 - 105

Pethig, R. (1975), Umweltverschmutzung, Wohlfahrt und Umweltpolitik in einem Zwei-Sektoren-Gleichgewichtsmodell, in: Zeitschrift für Nationalökonomie 35, 99 - 124

Pethig, R. (1976), Pollution, Welfare, and Environmental Policy in the Theory of Comparative Advantage, in: Journal of Environmental Economics and Management 2, 160 - 169

Pethig, R. (1977a), Die gesamtwirtschaftlichen Kosten der Umweltpolitik, in: Zeitschrift für die gesamte Staatswissenschaft 133, 322 - 342

Pethig, R. (1977b), International Markets for Secondary Materials, in: D.W. Pearce and I. Walter (eds.) (1977), Resource Conservation. Social and Economic Dimensions of Recycling, New York, 191 - 206

Pethig, R. (1978), Das Freifahrerproblem in der Theorie der öffentlichen Güter, in: Helmstädter, E. (ed.) (1978), Neuere Entwicklung in den Wirtschaftswissenschaften, Berlin, 75 - 100

Pethig, R. (1979a), Environmental Management in General Equilibrium: A New Incentive Compatible Approach, in: International Economic Review (forthcoming).

Pethig, R. (1979b), Umweltökonomische Allokation mit Emissionssteuern, Tübingen

Pigou, A.C. (1920), The Economics of Welfare, First Printing, London

Ricardo, D. (1817), On the Principles of Political Economy and Taxation, Hildesheim, New York 1977, Reproduction of the issue London 1817

Ruff, L.E. (1972), A Note on Pollution Prices in a General Equilibrium Model, American Economic Review 62, 186 - 192

Rybczyński, T.M. (1955), Factor Endowment and Relative Commodity Prices, Economica, N.S. 22, 336 - 341

Samuelson, P.A. (1947), Foundations of Economic Analysis, Cambridge

Samuelson, P.A. (1953), Prices of Factors and Goods in General Equilibrium, in: Review of Economic Studies 21, 1 - 20

Schittko, U. (1976), Lehrbuch der Außenwirtschaftstheorie, Stuttgart

Shoup, C.S. (1965), Public Goods and Joint Production, in: Rivista Internazionale di Scienze Economiche e Commerciali 12, 254 - 264

Siebert, H. (1974a), Comparative Advantage and Environmental Policy: A Note, in: Zeitschrift für Nationalökonomie 34, 397 - 402

Siebert, H. (1974b), Environmental Protection and International Specialization, in: Weltwirtschaftliches Archiv 110, 494 - 508

Siebert, H. (1974c), Trade and Environment, Comment, in: Giersch, H. (ed.) (1974), The International Division of Labour Problems and Perspectives, Tübingen, 108 - 121

Siebert, H. (1975), Externalties, Environmental Quality, and Allocation, in: Zeitschrift für Wirtschafts- und Sozialwissenschaften 2, 17 - 32

Siebert, H. (1976), Emissionssteuern im Monopol. Eine Anmerkung, in: Zeitschrift für die gesamte Staatswissenschaft 132, 679 - 682

Siebert, H. (1978a), Ökonomische Theorie der Umwelt, Tübingen

Siebert, H. (1978b), Voerde und eine neue Umweltpolitik, in: Wirtschaftsdienst 85, 36 - 40

Siebert, H. (1979), Environmental Policy in the Two-Country-Case, in: Zeitschrift für Nationalökonomie, forthcoming

Sontheimer, K. (1975), Technical Change and the Choice Between Standards and Charges for Environmental Control, Paper presented at the Third Reisenburg Symposium: On the Stability of Contemporary Economic Systems, (mimeographed)

Takayama, A. (1972), International Trade. An Approach to the Theory, New York

Tietenberg, T.H. (1973a), Controlling Pollution by Price and Standard Systems: A General Equilibrium Analysis, in: Swedish Journal of Economics 75, 193 - 203

Tietenberg, T.H. (1973b), Specific Taxes and the Control of Pollution: A General Equilibrium Analysis, in: Quaterly Journal of Economics 87, 503 - 522

Walter, I. (1973), The Pollution Content of American Trade, in: Western Economic Journal 11, 61 - 70

Walter, I. (1974a), International Trade and Resource Diversion: The Case of Environmental Management, in: Weltwirschaftliches Archiv 110, 482 - 493

Walter, I. (1974b), Pollution and Protection: U.S. Environmental Controls as Competitive Distortions, in: Weltwirtschaftliches Archiv 110, 104 - 113

Walter, I. (1975), International Economics of Pollution, London

Walter, I. (ed.) (1976), Studies in International Environmental Economics, New York

Whitcomb, D.K. (1972), Externalities and Welfare, New York, London

Yates, P.L. (1959), Forty Years of Foreign Trade, London

Author Index*

*The author and subject indices were prepared by H. Gebauer.

Subject Index*

*The author and subject indices were prepared by H. Gebauer.